Lecture Notes in Artificial Intelligence 11659

Subseries of Lecture Notes in Computer Science

More information about this series at http://www.springer.com/series/1244

Andrey Ronzhin · Gerhard Rigoll ·
Roman Meshcheryakov (Eds.)

Interactive
Collaborative Robotics

4th International Conference, ICR 2019
Istanbul, Turkey, August 20–25, 2019
Proceedings

Editors
Andrey Ronzhin (iD)
Russian Academy of Sciences
St. Petersburg, Russia

Gerhard Rigoll (iD)
Technical University of Munich
Munich, Germany

Roman Meshcheryakov (iD)
Russian Academy of Sciences
Moscow, Russia

ISSN 0302-9743   ISSN 1611-3349 (electronic)
Lecture Notes in Artificial Intelligence
ISBN 978-3-030-26117-7   ISBN 978-3-030-26118-4 (eBook)
https://doi.org/10.1007/978-3-030-26118-4

LNCS Sublibrary: SL7 – Artificial Intelligence

This Springer imprint is published by the registered company Springer Nature Switzerland AG
The registered company address is: Gewerbestrasse 11, 6330 Cham, Switzerland

ICR 2019 Preface

The 4th International Conference on Interactive Collaborative Robotics (ICR) was organized as a satellite event of the 21st International Conference on Speech and Computer (SPECOM) by St. Petersburg Institute for Informatics and Automation of the Russian Academy of Sciences (SPIIRAS, St. Petersburg, Russia) and Technical University of Munich (TUM, Munich, Germany).

Challenges of human–robot interaction, robot control and behavior in social robotics and collaborative robotics, as well as applied robotic and cyber-physical systems are mainly discussed during the conference.

ICR 2019 was hosted by the Boğaziçi University in cooperation with SPIIRAS and TUM. The conference was held during August 20–25, 2019 at Boğaziçi University, Istanbul, one of the top research universities in Turkey, established in 1863.

During the conference an invited talk, "Animating Industrial Robots for Human-Robot Interaction," was given by Prof. Erol Sahin (KOVAN Research Lab, Computer Engineering Department, Middle East Technical University, Ankara, Turkey).

This volume contains a collection of submitted papers presented at the conference, which were thoroughly reviewed by members of the Program Committee consisting of more than 20 top specialists in the conference topic areas. Theoretical and more general contributions were presented in common (plenary) sessions. Problem-oriented sessions as well as panel discussions then brought together specialists in limited problem areas with the aim of exchanging knowledge and skills resulting from research projects of all kinds.

Last but not least, we would like to express our gratitude to the authors for providing their papers on time, to the members of the conference reviewing team and Program Committee for their careful reviews and paper selection, and to the editors for their hard work preparing this volume. Special thanks are due to the members of the local Organizing Committee for their tireless effort and enthusiasm during the conference organization. We hope that you will benefit from these proceedings.

August 2019

Andrey Ronzhin
Gerhard Rigoll
Roman Meshcheryakov

Organization

The conference ICR 2019 was organized by the Boğaziçi University (BU, Istanbul, Turkey) in cooperation with St. Petersburg Institute for Informatics and Automation of the Russian Academy of Sciences (SPIIRAS, St. Petersburg, Russia) and the Technical University of Munich (TUM, Munich, Germany). The conference website is located at: http://www.specom.nw.ru/icr2019/.

Program Committee

Roman Meshcheryakov (Co-chair), Russia
Gerhard Rigoll (Co-chair), Germany
Andrey Ronzhin (Co-chair), Russia
Christos Antonopoulos, Greece
Branislav Borovac, Serbia
Sara Chaychian, UK
Ivan Ermolov, Russia
Oliver Jokisch, Germany
Dimitrios Kalles, Greece
Igor Kalyaev, Russia
Alexey Kashevnik, Russia
Gerhard Kraetzschmar, Germany

Dongheui Lee, Germany
Iosif Mporas, UK
Vladmir Pavlovkiy, Russia
Viacheslav Pshikhopov, Russia
Mirko Rakovic, Serbia
Yulia Sandamirskaya, Switzerland
Jesus Savage, Mexico
Hooman Samani, Taiwan
Evgeny Shandarov, Russia
Lev Stankevich, Russia
Tilo Strutz, Germany
Sergey Yatsun, Russia
Zeynep Yucel, Japan

Organizing Committee

Andrey Ronzhin (Chair)
Alexander Denisov
Anton Saveliev
Dmitry Ryumin

Ekaterina Miroshnikova
Natalia Dormidontova
Natalia Kashina

Contents

Contents

Close-Loop Control of Microrobot Within a Constrained Environment Using Electromagnet Pairs

Nail Akçura[1] , Aytaç Kahveci[2], Levent Çetin[3(✉)] ,
Abdulkareem Alasli[3], Fatih Cemal Can[3] , Erkin Gezgin[3] ,
and Özgür Tamer[1]

[1] Dokuz Eylül University, Tınaztepe Campus, İzmir, Turkey
{nail.akcura, ozgur.tamer}@deu.edu.tr
[2] İzmir Katip Çelebi University, Çiğli Campus, İzmir, Turkey
aytackahveci93@gmail.com
[3] Nagoya University, Furo, Chikusa, Nagoya 464-8603, Japan
{levent.cetin, fatihcemal.can,
erkin.gezgin}@ikc.edu.tr,
al.asli.abdulkareem@f.mbox.nagoya-u.ac.jp

Abstract. This paper describes a macro/micro robot manipulation system consisting of an electromagnet couple and an industrial manipulator. The system has capability of motion 6 Degrees of Freedom (6 DOF) providing the same amount of DOFs to the manipulation of the microrobot. A custom-design mechanism which is attached onto the tip of the industrial manipulator provides the required magnetic field profiles for force and torque generation using coil couple and their ability sliding motion in linear directions. This combination provides reprogrammable working space for the microrobot manipulation. Robot Operating System (ROS) based programming integrates all the subsystem software. Visual feedback assures the real-time microrobot position and orientation data. Close-loop motion control of the microrobot was tested using custom designed constrained paths take part in a plane. Experiment were presented for specific motions of the microrobot to show the microrobot motion abilities. The results are promising which may orient to the applications like micro assembly and micromanipulation.

Keywords: Microrobot · Electromagnet · Actuation

1 Introduction

In the future, microrobot application areas are expected to be vary from special cases in biomedical and military to daily routines. Many researchers contributed in magnetically driven microrobots field, especially using magnetic fields in DC, rotating and oscillating forms in order to further the advantages. These variances also bring up different microrobot swimming methodologies.

In biomedical applications including manipulation, transportation, minimally invasive surgery and drug delivery, it requires high precision both in-vivo and in-vitro. Some

A. Ronzhin et al. (Eds.): ICR 2019, LNAI 11659, pp. 1–9, 2019.
https://doi.org/10.1007/978-3-030-26118-4_1

magnetic actuator systems proved themselves to be standard actuators in this field. There are so many researches using Helmholtz coil pairs that has limited working space and magnetic field strength [1–7]. Then, Nelson and his friends came up with OctoMag [8] and MiniMag [9] providing 5 DOF motion for microrobots. Sitti et al. constructed a system which provides 6 DOF [10, 11]. These researches made so much progress in microrobot structures with various kinds using magnetic gradient or rotating magnetic field.

Using an industrial manipulator for conveying the actuator mechanism to desired locations provides reconfigurable space. Mahoney et al. developed systems using permanent magnet attached to the tip of the industrial manipulator, providing magnetic field source for the motion [12, 13], followed by their recent prototype [14]. These systems can provide the magnetic field in DC form and rotating form to macro-scaled capsules for locomotion. Some of the systems are already used for biomedical applications on living creatures, using open-loop endoscopy camera steering control [15, 16]. Amokrane et al. developed a system using permanent magnet pairs for microrobot locomotion performed in ear drum model [17].

In this paper, a close-loop control methodology is presented where a mechanism with a pair of coils is attached to a serial industrial manipulator. The control strategy consists of intermediate target points synchronously given by the operator using a Human Machine Interface (HMI) or the trajectory planner program. As the magnetic torque is applied by symmetric coil pairs with the orientation ability of industrial manipulator, the magnetic force is generated by changing linear position of one of the electromagnets where an asymmetry occurs. This way, the complexity of the system is reduced by lowering the number of electromagnets while 6 Degrees of Freedom (DOF) can be provided. The methodology is tested using two constrained paths and the results are presented.

2   System Configuration

The mechanical system consists of actuation and motion groups. The actuation group consists of two electromagnets facing to each other along the same axis. The motion group includes a custom-designed actuator mechanism and an industrial manipulator. The software system is formed of subcategories, including electromagnet current drivers, industrial manipulator controller, visual feedback controllers, actuator mechanism controller, motion controller and HMI, integrated with Robot Operating System (ROS). The mechanical system is given in Fig. 1.

2.1   Electromagnet Based Manipulation

Magnetic force affecting onto a particle with magnetization vector $\vec{M}$, depends on the gradient of the external magnetic field $\vec{B}$, which is $\nabla \vec{B}$. The magnetic field vector also generates a magnetic torque $\vec{\tau}$ which may provide rotation motions. The related equations are given in (1) and (2), respectively.

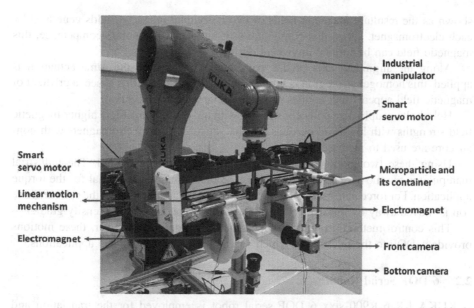

Fig. 1. Mechanical system and system configuration.

$$\vec{F} = v(\vec{M} \cdot \nabla)\vec{B} \tag{1}$$

$$\vec{\tau} = v(\vec{M} \times \vec{B}) \tag{2}$$

Here, v stands for volume of the particle. The force and torque directions and strengths are directly dependent to the externally applied magnetic field properties. Also, a visualization for motions generated magnetic force and torque acting onto a magnetic particle due to the magnetic field are given in Fig. 2.

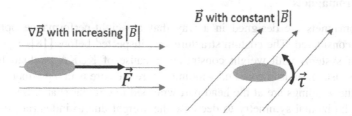

Fig. 2. Fundamental magnetic force and torque generation onto a magnetic particle dependent to $\vec{B}$.

The most popular method for homogenous magnetic field generation depends on a system configuration consisting of two identical electromagnets facing each other with the same amount of current flowing through and in the middle of their distances a homogenous magnetic field occurs within a limited space. This can be mathematically shown as the resultant magnetic fields of two individual magnetic fields generated by each electromagnet. When this configuration is situated with mobile competence, this magnetic field can be formed anywhere desired.

Along the alignment axis of this coil couple, meanwhile the same actuation is applied, this homogenous region is limited and at the outside of this space, a gradient of magnetic field appears that applies force in gradient vector direction.

Helmholtz couples use coils constructed with air-core that restricts higher magnetic field strengths with low-level currents. So that, custom-built electromagnets with non-air core are used to increase the intensity.

Using these two motion methodologies, a system is constructed. The industrial manipulator can move and orient the system as desired and an essential for the torque application. For force generation, the microrobot is kept at the center of the coils and one coil is moved away by linear mechanisms to expose magnetic flux intensity gradient.

This control method provides a wide space for motion. Moreover, these motions provide 6 DOF to the microrobot which can be handy in most of the applications.

2.2   6 DOF Serial Robot

A KUKA KR 6 R900 sixx 6 DOF serial robot is employed for the translation and rotation motions of the actuator mechanism that is assembled onto the tip of the industrial manipulator. 6 kg payload and ±0,02 mm repeatability capability values are provided with the robot supplier. The industrial manipulator provides a wide range of working space area with high precision, also supplying real-time data for control feedback. The communication with the robot system is constructed on TCP/IP protocol. For this application, the Region-of-Interest (ROI) of the microrobot motion may be very tiny comparing to the working space volume of the industrial manipulator, but in big picture of the system future, this industrial robot can provide a large application freedom where the microrobot ROI drifts by large distance scales, e.g. motion in large human body parts, thus the industrial manipulator should comprises a large working space.

2.3   Electromagnets

The electromagnets are designed in a way that a weight-performance optimization problem is considered. The custom structure was inspected before [18], especially for this kind of systems with weight constraints because of KUKA payload limit. The structure consists of an iron core and winding where the core is in a prismatic rectangle shape and the windings are at the head part wrapped in circular shape. Some parts are trimmed in horizontal symmetry to decrease the weight due to industrial manipulator load limits.

2.4   Electromagnetic Actuator (EMA) Mechanism

On the tip of the industrial robot, the mechanism holds the electromagnets their common axis aligned. Also, a sliding mechanism actuated by a smart servo motor (Dynamixel) using timing belts provides the configurable linear position control. Thus, the resultant of magnetic field strength and region can be controlled.

2.5   Other System Components

ROS is an open source robotics middleware which is widely used among the researchers. This structure uses cluster computing, providing running multiple individual programs (called 'nodes') for individual purposes, and communication between nodes using services and other properties. In this system, ROS integrates all the nodes for industrial manipulator control, electromagnet driver control, mechanism control, motion control and visual feedback using OpenCV libraries, and logging all the data, providing a user interface for visual feedback and motion controls.

The visual feedback for the system is provided by cameras, one at the bottom facing to the bottom of the container and the other one is attached to mechanism facing to the front of the container, providing x, y and z axes coordinates. The bottom camera is stationary, and the front camera is aligned to the center point where the microrobot should be during the motions. Basic transformations are applied for determining the cartesian coordinates from pixels.

3   Micromanipulation Strategy

3.1   Constrained Motion Parameters

The microrobot is a basic cylindrical magnet with the dimensions of 1 mm height and 1 mm diameter, made of N42 class neodymium material. A brake oil with viscosity of 169 mPa.s at room temperature is used as the environment fluid. The environment fluid shows Newtonian characteristics and its Reynolds number is below 1. The electromagnet currents are set to 2 A. In torque configuration, the electromagnets are held in 6 cm distance from the center providing 5,7 mT magnetic flux intensity along the ROI. In force configuration, one of the electromagnets gets 10 mm farther to the center point, providing 24, 28 mT/mm magnetic field gradient to the microrobot. These values were the measurement results using gaussmeter.

Open-loop tests were already studied in previous works [18]. In those tests, with open-loop control, the desired paths can be easily achieved in a container filled with fluid. This work is focusing more on testing its close-loop functionality. So that, two custom paths with simulation path constraint manners were developed. Moreover, the motion capabilities of the industrial manipulator are tested in a way.

3.2   Motion Planning

The control mechanism is linked to the user/motion planner inputs. For human users, a GUI is developed as the input goal coordinates are commanded by clicking on the image obtained from camera video stream. These goal coordinates are given as reference coordinates to the motion controller node.

This should be informed that the obstacles and constrained walls are not detected. Thus, to obtain a motion where obstacles exist between the starting and finishing positions, the reference points are given sequentially during the motions as intermediate points by user as inputs.

To briefly describe the motion controller clearly, the control algorithm pseudocode is given in Fig. 3.

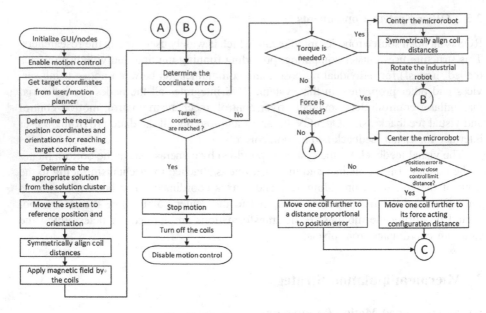

Fig. 3. Motion control flowchart.

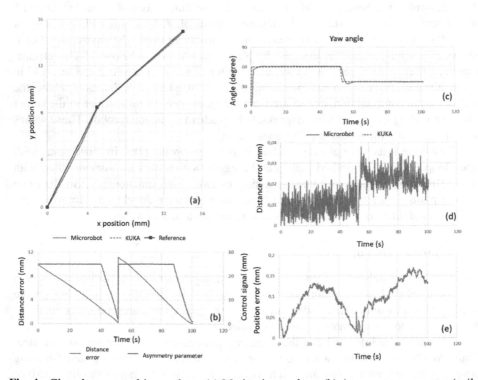

Fig. 4. Close-loop control in xy plane: (a) Motion in xy plane. (b) Asymmetry parameter (coil distance) control related to the point-to-point distance error of microrobot. (c) Yaw angle change. (d) Instant distance error between microrobot and KUKA positions. (e) Position error between reference and microrobot positions.

For close-loop experimental testing, a microrobot is manipulated on xy plane travelling along two target points sequentially in a liquid filled container. The results are given in Fig. 4.

4   Experiments and Results

For this experiment, two kinds of constrained paths were designed and printed by 3D printer. The designs were considered to force the limits of the motion capabilities. Two canals were manufactured, one is in S-shape, the other one has circular shapes. The paths are positioned in a way that the bottom camera system can easily detect.

At the beginning, the container is filled with the liquid and microrobot is positioned inside the canal. Some air blobs might be observed, but during the experiments it is seen that its disturbance is not so effective.

During the motion, the intermediate points throughout the path are clicked sequentially by the operator till the motion is completed. The algorithms mentioned in the previous chapters are performed in the motion. A close-loop control is applied here. The interface program for this motion control and its modules are given in Fig. 5. The motion screenshots are given in Fig. 6. The circular path consists of an inner and outer circle. As the S-shaped path motion intends to locomote from one side to the other, the circular path motion aims to cover all the motions in inner and outer circle.

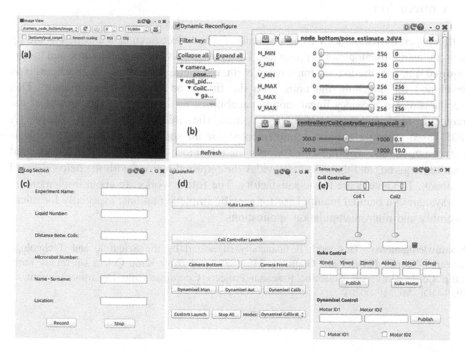

Fig. 5. Interface program modules: (a) Imaging module interface, (b) Dynamic reconfiguration interface, (c) Logging interface, (d) Working mode interface, (e) Command interface.

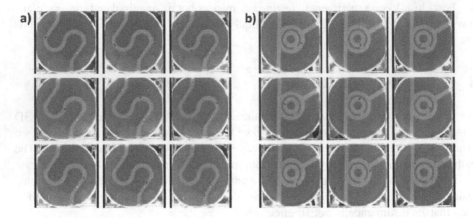

Fig. 6. Motion experiments with constrained path with time lapse: (a) Motion in one half along S-shaped path, (b) A random motion in circular constrained path.

The experiment results show good results where the motion capabilities in xy plane show promising results for applicable abilities. Force and torque generations are successfully applied synchronically with the system.

5   Conclusion

In this paper, a methodology using coaxially aligned electromagnets attached to the tip of an industrial manipulator is presented. These coils provide magnetic force and torque required for the motion of microrobot with magnetic properties. A mechanism is developed for attaching the coils onto the tip of an industrial manipulator. This mechanism also provides linear motion capabilities to the coils for the control of the magnetic field in Region-of-Interest where the microrobot motion occurs. A ROS-based software control is implemented for all software and hardware controls and computations. The presented works include close-loop control that the desired position is given, and the system provides the required actions with the help of visual feedback. The results are found satisfactory. The future works are about implementing this system to a parallel manipulator for specific implementations, especially for micro assembly and micromanipulation applications.

Acknowledgements. This work is financially supported by the Scientific and Technology Research Council (TUBITAK, Grant no. 215M879) and Izmir Katip Çelebi University Izmir Katip Çelebi University Scientific Research Projects Coordinatorship Department (grant no 2018-ÖDL-MÜMF-0020).

References

1. Zhang, L., Peyer, K.E., Nelson, B.J.: Artificial bacterial flagella for micromanipulation. Lab Chip **10**(17), 2203–2215 (2010)
2. Mahoney, A.W., Sarrazin, J.C., Bamberg, E., Abbott, J.J.: Velocity control with gravity compensation for magnetic helical microswimmers. Adv. Robot. **25**(8), 1007–1028 (2011)
3. Sendoh, M., Yamazaki, A., Chiba, A., Soma, M., Ishiyama, K., Arai, K.I.I.: Spiral type magnetic micro actuators for medical applications. In: Micro-Nanomechatronics and Human Science, 2004 and The Fourth Symposium Micro-Nanomechatronics for Information-Based Society 2004, vol. 1, pp. 1–6 (2004)
4. Xu, T., Hwang, G., Andreff, N., Regnier, S.: Characterization of three-dimensional steering for helical swimmers. In: Proceedings of the IEEE International Conference on Robotics Automation, pp. 4686–4691 (2014)
5. Ko, Y., et al.: A jellyfish-like swimming mini-robot actuated by an electromagnetic actuation system. Smart Mater. Struct. **21**(5), 57001 (2012)
6. Gao, W., Sattayasamitsathit, S., Manesh, K.M., Weihs, D., Wang, J.: Magnetically powered flexible metal nanowire motors. J. Am. Chem. Soc. **132**(41), 14403–14405 (2010)
7. Go, G., et al.: Electromagnetic navigation system using simple coil structure (4 coils) for 3-D locomotive microrobot. IEEE Trans. Magn. **51**(4), 1–7 (2015)
8. Kummer, M.P., Abbott, J.J., Kratochvil, B.E., Borer, R., Sengul, A., Nelson, B.J.: Octomag: an electromagnetic system for 5-DOF wireless micromanipulation. IEEE Trans. Robot. **26**(6), 1006–1017 (2010)
9. Schuerle, S., Erni, S., Flink, M., Kratochvil, B.E., Nelson, B.J.: Three-dimensional magnetic manipulation of micro- and nanostructures for applications in life sciences. IEEE Trans. Magn. **49**(1), 321–330 (2013)
10. Pawashe, C., Floyd, S., Sitti, M.: Modeling and experimental characterization of an untethered magnetic micro-robot. Int. J. Rob. Res. **28**(8), 1077–1094 (2009)
11. Diller, E., Giltinan, J., Sitti, M.: Independent control of multiple magnetic microrobots in three dimensions. Int. J. Rob. Res. **32**(5), 614–631 (2013)
12. Mahoney, A.W., Abbott, J.J.: Five-degree-of-freedom manipulation of an untethered magnetic device in fluid using a single permanent magnet with application in stomach capsule endoscopy. Int. J. Rob. Res. **35**(1–3), 129–147 (2016)
13. Mahoney, A.W., Abbott, J.J.: Control of untethered magnetically actuated tools with localization uncertainty using a rotating permanent magnet. In: Proceedings of the IEEE RAS EMBS International Conference Biomedical Robotics and Biomechatronics, pp. 1632–1637 (2012)
14. Wright, S.E., Mahoney, A.W., Popek, K.M., Abbott, J.J.: The spherical-actuator-magnet manipulator: a permanent-magnet robotic end-effector. IEEE Trans. Robot. **33**(5), 1013–1024 (2017)
15. Duan, X., Xiao, G., Wang, X.: Apparatus and method for controlling movement of a capsule endoscope in digestive tract of a human body. US patents, US20150018615A1 (2015)
16. Ciuti, G., et al.: Robotic versus manual control in magnetic steering of an endoscopic capsule. Endoscopy **42**(2), 148–152 (2010)
17. Amokrane, W., Belharet, K., Souissi, M., Grayeli, A.B., Ferreira, A.: Macro–micromanipulation platform for inner ear drug delivery. Rob. Auton. Syst. **107**, 10–19 (2018)
18. Alasli, A., Çetin, L., Akçura, N., Kahveci, A., Can, F.C., Tamer, Ö.: Electromagnet design for untethered actuation system mounted on robotic manipulator. Sens. Actuators, A Phys. **285**, 550–565 (2019)

Architecture of Proactive Localization Service for Cyber-Physical System's Users

Dmitrii Malov$^{(\boxtimes)}$ (ID), Alexander Edemskii (ID), and Anton Saveliev (ID)

SPIIRAS, 14-th Line of V.O, Saint-Petersburg 199178, Russia
dmalov@iias.spb.su

Abstract. In this article, a microservice architecture of cyber-physical space was considered and in particular localization service was implemented. We propose an architecture of proactive localization service, which allows predicting the activity of the tracked object in cyber-physical space. To solve the position prediction problem, we tested machine learning methods and contrasted the results of the trained models. Three machine learning algorithms were tested (artificial neural network, random forest, and decision tree) with two different datasets. The reason of high/low prediction accuracy were identified. As a result of testing, the best result has neural network. In this case mean absolute error is 8.2 and 11.7 m respectively for dataset №1 and №2, while random forest has 13 and 14 m error. The architecture of the service was developed using containerization technologies and special tools for their deployment and management.

Keywords: Proactive localization · Cyber-physical systems · Machine learning · Microservices

1 Introduction

1.1 Microservice Architecture

Currently many experts from various domains are pay close attention to the emergent new engineering system, namely cyber-physical systems. Cyber-physical systems are cross-cutting solutions, ensuring feedback control on massively distributed embedded computing systems, combining computation, communication and control technologies. They have a wide range of applications, such as digital medical instruments and systems adopting automatic acquisition and control technology, distributed energy systems, aerospace and aircraft control, industrial control and so on [1].

For a software implementation of a cyber-physical system, it is convenient to use a microservice architecture – a kind of a service-oriented software architecture designed to develop as small as possible, decoupled (or loosely coupled) and easily modifiable independent modules – microservices [2]. In terms of a cyber-physical system, each service available to users (proactive localization and navigation system, CorporateTV television service, videoconferencing system [3], face recognition system [4] etc.) or any functional unit, being not a full-fledged service on its own, but enabling correct

A. Ronzhin et al. (Eds.): ICR 2019, LNAI 11659, pp. 10–18, 2019.
https://doi.org/10.1007/978-3-030-26118-4_2

functioning of the cyber-physical space in general (face, gestures, speech, etc. recognition systems), is meant to be an independent service [5–7].

To implement a cyber-physical system with such set of services, it is practical to use the open source orchestration tool Kubernetes, designed to deploy and manage Linux containers as a single system. Kubernetes manages and launches Docker containers on a cluster with a large number of nodes [5].

1.2   Docker Containers

In general, containerized applications are more efficient in deploying applications complete with all the necessary environments compared to e.g., virtual machines. Instead of running processes in disparate operating systems, containers run processes in the operating system of the host node. However, every process in the container is still isolated from other processes (by means of Linux namespaces or Linux control groups). Additionally, containers are much more lightweight, so one can run more separate nodes on the shared hardware, as opposed to virtual machine approach.

For example, if you run three virtual machines on a host, you have three completely separate operating systems running unit and sharing the same bare-metal hardware. Containers, on the other hand, all perform system calls on the exact same kernel running in the host OS. This single kernel is the only one performing instructions on the host's CPU. These two cases are shown on Fig. 1.

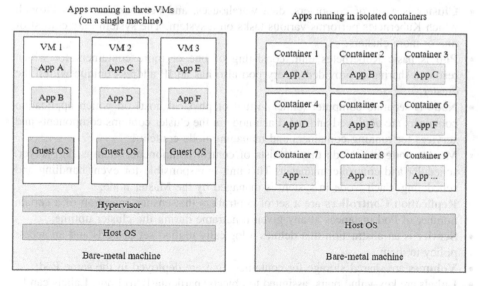

Fig. 1.   Isolating applications using virtual machines vs containers.

There are several platforms, allowing to build and run containers. The most popular one we are working with is called Docker [8]. Docker allows you to pack your application with all the necessary environment into a Docker image. You can run that image on your computer or push it to remote repository to expose it for future download from any remote node with Docker installed on it. Eventually from this image you can deploy a container which is essentially an isolated process running on the host with Docker.

1.3 Kubernetes

Kubernetes is a platform, containing a large number of services and functions. Its main purpose can be described as ensuring orchestration of the deployment and scaling of container applications and managing such applications. The main function of Kubernetes is to assist you in planning container workloads within your infrastructure. Further are listed some additional features of Kubernetes:

- storage monitoring;
- application health check;
- replication of nodes with applications;
- horizontal autoscaling of pods;
- load balancing;
- resource monitoring.

This functionality ensures, that the combination of Docker and Kubernetes becomes a perfect tool for building a system, containing several connected microservices.

To fully understand Kubernetes, it is necessary to explain some basic concepts of this platform:

- **Cluster** is a set of computers, data warehouses, and network resources through which Kubernetes performs various tasks on a system. The system may consist of one or more clusters;
- **Pod** is basic Kubernetes unit, consisting of one or more containers for which resource sharing is provided. Every pod also has an IP address unique within the cluster;
- **Node** is separate computer (either virtual or physical host) on which application containers are deployed and run. Each node in the cluster contains components and services for running containers and managing node content;
- **Master node** is a Node that consists of control components such as API-server, scheduler and controller manager. This unit is responsible for event handling and scheduling. Each Node in system is managed by the Master node;
- **Replication Controllers** are a set of controllers that ensure operation of a certain number of Pod instances at any given timeframe during the cluster uptime;
- **Service** is an abstraction that defines a logically unified set of Pods and an access policy to them;
- **Volumes** are shared storage for containers that are deployed in the same Pod;
- **Labels** are key-value pairs, assigned to objects, particularly to Pods. Labels can be used to create and select a collection of objects;
- **Kubectl** is a command line interface for managing Kubernetes.

2 Proactive Localization System

2.1 Kubernetes Architecture

Figure 2 shows the architecture that can be used in the development of a cyber-physical system consisting of several independent modules. Each node contains several Pods in which there are one or several containers representing one microservice. Since each Pod provides a unique IP address and shared resources to the containers that are running inside it, microservices remain as independent as possible and can be easily scaled. For communication between the Master node and every Slave node kubelet module is used. It runs on every node and manages the Pods and the containers running on a machine.

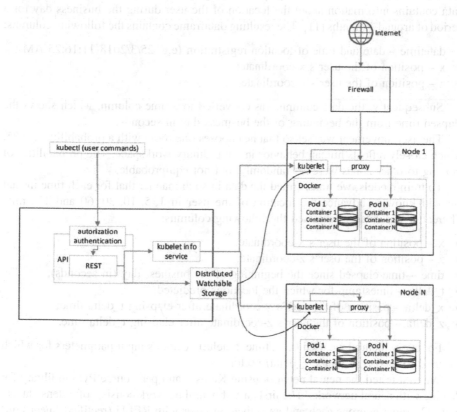

Fig. 2. Kubernetes architecture for cyber-physical system.

Every pod in this architecture represents a single microservice from our cyber-physical system. Here are some examples of these microservices:

• proactive localization system;
• navigation system;
• corporate television service;

- video conferencing system;
- face recognition service;
- passport recognition system (Russian Federation format).

In this paper, we take a closer look at the development of the proactive localization service.

2.2 Proactive Localization System

Proactive localization system is conceptually intended not only to get user position in cyber-physical space but predict his upcoming position as well [9, 10]. To do that we tested several machine learning algorithms and models. To train machine learning model, we used a dataset, collected by simulating the user movement in Unity3D. This data contains information about the location of the user during the business day for a period of around 2 months [11]. The resulting dataframe contains the following columns:

- datetime – date and time of location registration (e.g. 25/3/2018 11:16:25 AM);
- x – position of the user's x-coordinate;
- z – position of the user's z-coordinate.

Subsequently, the date column was converted to a time column, which shows the elapsed time from the beginning of the business day in seconds.

The user movement was set so that he chooses one room with a probability of 0.85, which closely reflects human behavior in the ordinary workspace. The probabilities of moving to other zones were set randomly, but not equiprobable.

To train models, we transformed the data in such manner that for each time instant we will know in advance the location of the user in 1, 5, 10, 30, 60 and 120 min. Thereafter our dataset contained the following columns:

- x – position of the user's x-coordinate;
- z – position of the user's z-coordinate;
- time – time elapsed since the beginning of the business day (in seconds);
- t_delta – timestamp for which the locations predicted;
- x_delta – position of the user's x-coordinate after elapsing t_delta time;
- z_delta – position of the user's z-coordinate after elapsing t_delta time.

For every method we used (x, z, time, t_delta) vector as input parameters for which we tried to predict (x_delta, z_delta) vector.

We first tested the neural network using Keras – an open source Python library for dealing with neural networks. The first part of neural network consists of 4 dense layers with 32 output neurons each and an activation layer with RELU (rectified linear unit) function. After that output of Activation layer is merged with the second output of neural network – timestamp vector. This vector represents our timestamps for which we want to predict user location in categorical format. So, we have 6 timestamps, and the dimension of this vector is also 6. Each vector represents a single timestamp by setting the value of the vector element corresponding to the index of the timestamp in array equal to 1 and 0 for other elements. For example, vector (1,0,0,0,0,0) corresponds to 1-min timestamp, vector (0,1,0,0,0,0) – to 5 min timestamp and so on. The last layer of the neural network is a Dense layer with 2 outputs, which corresponds to x_delta and z_delta coordinates.

Consequently, we had a mean error of 8.2 m and median error of 0.43, when predicting user location. Looking at Fig. 3, which show the distribution of actual and predicted values, we can see, why such a large error occurs. Neural network makes predictions only for this small area in which the user was located most of the time and ignores other zones.

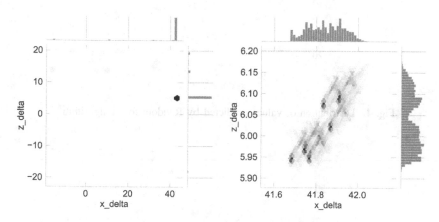

Fig. 3. Distribution of the true values (left) and values predicted by neural network (right).

Alternatively, random forest and decision tree algorithms were tested. The output of a random forest algorithm is shaped like a log-normal distribution with peak values in the zone, where the user was located most often (Fig. 4). It might seem well at first, but in this case mean error of location prediction is 13 m and median are 6.8 m which is even worse than the neural network result.

The distribution of decision tree predictions looks almost the same as the distribution of actual values (Fig. 5). In this case mean error of location prediction is 11 m and median error is 0 m. Based on this, we can conclude that at least half of the predictions have a zero error.

Afterwards, these methods were tested on another dataset. The new data, the probability of moving to the most popular room was reduced from 0.85 to 0.5, so that the distribution had not shown a clear peak in any single zone.

The results of testing on both datasets (№1 with 0.85 probability of choosing most popular location and №2 with 0.5 probability) are given in Table 1.

As we can see, the quality of the models depends on the uniformity of the movement data–the greater is the peak in the data distribution, the higher is the prediction accuracy [12].

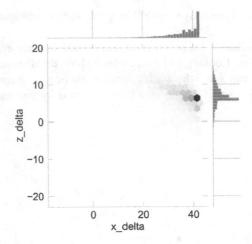

Fig. 4. Distribution of values predicted by Random forest algorithm.

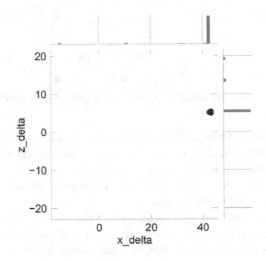

Fig. 5. Distribution of values predicted by Decision tree algorithm.

Table 1. Results of training.

Method	№ of dataset	Mean absolute error (meters)	Median error (meters)
Neural network	1	8.2	0.43
	2	11.7	11.9
Random forest	1	13.0	6.8
	2	14.0	12.6
Decision tree	1	11.0	0
	2	13.0	11.5

2.3   Service Deployment

Our proactive localization service itself is a server, written using Flask framework in Python. At startup, the server loads the trained models from remote storage and waits for requests. In order to get prediction for next user location, the server must receive a GET request with the following parameters:

- x – last recorder position of the user's x-coordinate;
- z – last recorded position of the user's z-coordinate;
- time – time elapsed since the beginning of the business day (in seconds);
- t_delta – timestamp for which we predict the location;
- user_id – user id; the server decides upon it, which model to use.

After receiving a request with such parameters, the server takes the necessary model using the user_id parameter, and passes it the (x, z, time) parameters vector. The result of the model execution, which contains the predicted coordinates, will be sent from the server as a response in JSON format.

Because the service is deployed using Docker, we had to "package" the server into a docker-container together with all the necessary environment. The official Ubuntu 16.04 image was downloaded and used as the basic environment. Having installed all the required Python libraries for this service (python, numpy, keras, tensorflow, etc.) this custom image was pushed to Docker Hub, to make it available for download from any machine, equipped with Docker. Then a new image was built, containing the server files in the required environment. When you run this image, a docker-container is created that runs the proactive localization service server decoupled from the machine you are using. Since this image was also loaded into Docker Hub, such a container can be easily deployed to any machine on which Docker is installed.

3   Conclusion

We presented the architecture of the proactive localization system as a service of a smart cyber-physical space, based on collaboration of Docker and Kubernetes tools. Also, the results of testing machine learning algorithms for multidimensional time series prediction are presented and its implementation within the Docker container.

Acknowledgement. The present research was partially supported by project No. MK-383.2018.9.

References

1. Liu, Y., Peng, Y., et al.: Review on cyber-physical systems. IEEE/CAA J. Automatica Sinica **4**(1), 27–40 (2017)
2. Dragoni, N., Lanese, I., Larsen, S.T., Mazzara, M., Mustafin, R., Safina, L.: Microservices: how to make your application scale. In: Petrenko, Alexander K., Voronkov, A. (eds.) PSI 2017. LNCS, vol. 10742, pp. 95–104. Springer, Cham (2018). https://doi.org/10.1007/978-3-319-74313-4_8

3. Karasev, E.Yu., Vatamaniuk, I.V., Saveliev, A.I., Ronzhin, A.L.: Architectural solutions for integrating a video conferencing module into cyberphysical intelligent space. Informatsionno-upravliaiushchie sistemy [Inf. Control Syst.] **1**, 2–10 (2018)
4. Malov, D., Letenkov, M.: Method of synthetic data generation and architecture of face recognition system for interaction with robots in cyberphysical space. Robot. Tech. Cybern. **7**(2), 100–108 (2019). https://doi.org/10.31776/RTCJ.7203
5. Malov, D.A., Edemskii, A.Yu., Saveliev, A.I.: Development of a system of proactive localization of the cyber-physical space based on machine learning methods. Informacionnye tekhnologii I vichslitel'nyesistemy [J. Inf. Technol. Comput. Syst.] **4**, 72–83 (2018)
6. Levonevskiy, D., Vatamaniuk, I., Malov D.A.: Obespechenie dostupnosti servisov korporativnogo intellektual'nogo prostranstva posredstvom upravleniya potokom vhodnyh dannyh [Ensuring the availability of corporate intellectual space services by managing the flow of input data]. Programmnaya inzheneriya [Softw. Eng.] **10**(1), 20–29 (2019). (in Russian)
7. Levonevskiy, D., Vatamaniuk, I., Saveliev, A.I.: MINOS multimodal information and navigation cloud system for the corporate cyber-physical smart space. Programmnaya inzheneriya [Softw. Eng.] **8**, 120–128 (2017)
8. Bashari Rad, B., Bhatti, H., Mohammad, A.: An introduction to docker and analysis of its performance. IJCSNS Int. J. Comput. Sci. Netw. Secur. **173**(8), 228–236 (2017)
9. Lavrenov, R.O., Magid, E.A., Matsuno, F., Svinin, M.M., Suthakorn, J.: Development and implementation of spline-based path planning algorithm in ROS/Gazebo environment. SPIIRAS Proc. **18**(1), 57–84 (2019)
10. Negrete, M., Savage, J., Contreras, L.: A motion-planning system for a domestic service robot. SPIIRAS Proc. **5**(60), 5–38 (2018)
11. Saveliev, A., Malov, D., Edemskii, A., Pavliuk, N.: Proactive localization system concept for users of cyber-physical space. In: Ronzhin, A., Rigoll, G., Meshcheryakov, R. (eds.) ICR 2018. LNCS (LNAI), vol. 11097, pp. 233–238. Springer, Cham (2018). https://doi.org/10.1007/978-3-319-99582-3_24
12. Teilans, A.A., Romanovs, A.V., Merkuryev, Yu.A., Dorogovs, P.P., Kleins, A.Ya., Potryasaev, S.A: assessment of cyber physical system risks with domain specific modelling and simulation. SPIIRAS Proc. **4**(59), 115–139 (2018)

Implementation of Control System and Tracking Objects in a Quadcopter System

Siva Ariram[1]($\boxtimes$), Juha Röning[1], and Zdzisław Kowalczuk[2]

[1] Biomimetics and Intelligent Systems Group (BISG),
University of Oulu, Oulu, Finland
siva.ariram@oulu.fi
[2] Gdansk University of Technology, Gdansk, Poland

Abstract. In this paper, we implement a quadcopter assembly with control and navigation module. The project also includes the design of the control panel for the operator which consists of a set of the microcontroller and the glove equipped with sensors and buttons. The panel has a touch screen which displays current parameters such as vehicle status, including information about orientation and geographical coordinates. The concept of quadcopter control is based on the movement of the operator hand. In addition, we have included the object detection for detecting the objects from the quadcopter view of point. To detect an object, we need to have some idea of where the object may be and how the image is divided into segments. It creates a kind of chicken and egg problem, where we must recognize the shape (and class) of the object knowing its location and recognize the location of the object knowing its shape. Some visual characteristics such as clothing and the human face, they can be part of the same subject, but it is difficult to recognize this without recognizing the object first.

Keywords: Drone · Quadcopter · Kalman filter · GPS · IMU

1 Introduction

The widespread use of drones in the present times and the desire to use the current knowledge acquired by students during their studies inspired the team of authors to create their own flying vehicle and supply it with an appropriate control program. Starting from defining the concept of drone systems and qualifying them in accordance with the applied construction, the principles of quadcopter operation and maneuvering are presented. Next, we describe examples of realizations available on the market, including their goals, as well as the scope of this work.

One of the most important issues in automation (control) is to estimate the pose (posture) of the quadcopter, which includes the inclination, tilt and rotation angles, called roll, pitch and yaw. The estimation of the pitch and roll angles is obtained by means of the operation of two independent Kalman filters, and the yaw angle is obtained thanks to the gyroscope data integration operation. On the basis of the current measurements and set value, an error is calculated, which is given to the input of the proportional-integral-derivative (PID) regulator [1]. The controller generates the control signal in the PWM form, which is then sent to the motorized actuators.

© Springer Nature Switzerland AG 2019
A. Ronzhin et al. (Eds.): ICR 2019, LNAI 11659, pp. 19–29, 2019.
https://doi.org/10.1007/978-3-030-26118-4_3

Computer simulation simulating the operation of designed complementary filters using gyroscope and accelerometer readings was carried out. Due to the fact that the results obtained from the supplementary filters were not satisfactory, we decided to implement the Kalman filter, which improved the efficiency of the system and gave us satisfactory results. That is why we have implemented this KF solution in the reported project. Finally, several tests were carried out to stabilize and control the system of the flying vehicle, allowing controlled rotation in 3 axis.

1.1 System Description

The operation of the developed system is based on communication between quadcopter control modules. The operator panel is a module with diagnostic and control functions. The module consists of an electronic system equipped with a touch screen displaying parameters such as the current quadcopter states (modes) and geographical coordinates. This operator's kit will also be equipped with a button responsible for activating the engines, changing the speed of the engines and activating certain control modes. The device will be powered by a lithium-polymer battery. The principle of system operation is presented in Fig. 1.

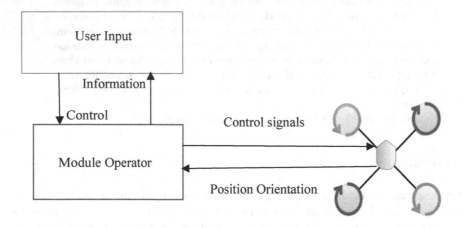

Fig. 1. Basic Quadcopter architecture

A part of the quadcopter and the operator's panel has been found on the market. The project uses: lithium-polymer batteries, RC apparatus, 4x motors, 4x ESC regulators, propellers, voltage converters, IMU sensors, microcontrollers, radio systems and a GPS pick box. Using the above-mentioned parts, a new quadcopter and the operator panel were assembled.

The assembly process of the vehicle has been divided into two parts. In the first part, a subset of the frame was considered. The ESC regulators were then attached to the arms with clamps and the motors were fastened with screws. In the lower part of the central lobe using a Velcro, a battery was attached, while the upper part contained a microcontroller, a GPS receiver, a radio system, an RC apparatus receiver and an IMU system.

2 System Implementation

One of the main problems in the implementation of the project is to determine the current orientation of the copter. The estimation of the vehicle pose consists in determining the values of the angle of inclination, deflection and rotation (roll, pitch, and yaw). For this purpose, a gyroscope and accelerometer were used. To eliminate the disadvantages associated with such sensors, special filters have been implemented that combine (fuse) measurements.

This section shows the results of estimating only the value of the deviation angle, while the designed system uses orientation estimates in all axis.

2.1 Gyroscope

A sensor was used to read the data, which was placed on a quadcopter that was initially immobilized and stood on a flat surface. A graph of the angular velocity measurement measured with a Y-axis gyroscope is shown in Fig. 2.

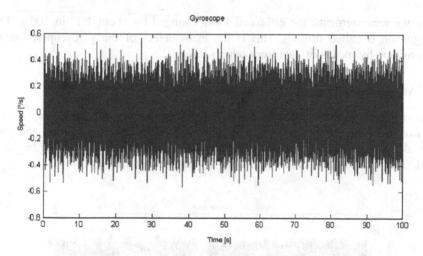

Fig. 2. A graph showing the angular velocity in the Y axis read using the gyroscope.

In Fig. 2, it is confirmed that the rate measured with a gyroscope is noisy, with noise reaching values from $-0.5°/s$ to $0.5°/s$. Having gyroscopic angle data, it is possible to obtain information on Roll, Pitch and Yaw angles (φ, θ, ψ) through integration. The total angular velocity shown in Fig. 2 leads to the Pitch value (θ). The integration result is shown in Fig. 3.

The results obtained after integration are clearly characterized by lower noise levels. It can be seen from Fig. 3 that despite the fact that the vehicle was stationary

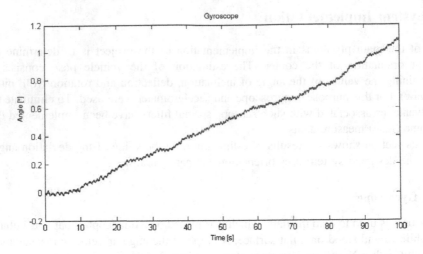

Fig. 3. A graph showing the angle θ after the angular rate integration.

during the measurements, the estimated value changed by about 1.1° in 100 s. This phenomenon is called drifting. This is the main defect of the gyroscopes, forcing compensation by means of data from other sensors.

2.2   Accelerometer

The acceleration sensor returns the acceleration values along the 3 axis (a_x, a_y, a_z). Based on this data and the appropriate trigonometric operations [2], the roll and pitch angles defining the rotation of the quadcopter along the X and Y axis can be determined. The obtained acceleration rates (a_y, a_z) are shown in Fig. 4.

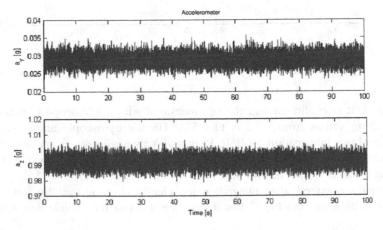

Fig. 4. A graph showing the values of accelerations (a_y, a_z) read from the accelerometer.

Also to determine the pitch value (θ), acceleration measurements from the 3-axis accelerometer were used. Considering quadcopter measurements (as in the case of flat accelerations), because the accelerations had no other components besides gravitational acceleration, the total sum of accelerations (a_x, a_y, a_z) is 1 g. The angle of the pitch was determined based on the data shown in Fig. 3, and the results are shown in Fig. 5.

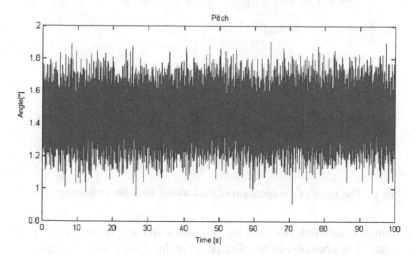

Fig. 5. The value of θ is calculated by means of trigonometric transitions.

By performing the appropriate trigonometric transformations, the Pitch value was obtained. Let us consider that the calculated angle is not affected by drift, which occurs in the case of gyroscopic measurements, but is generally characterized by higher noise. The obtained non-zero angle results from the non-ideal alignment of the sensor during measurements.

2.3   Kalman Filter

The Kalman filter is a linear estimate of the state model [2] and is modeled by means of state:

$$X_{k+1} = Ax_k + Bu_k + W_k \tag{3}$$

$$Y_k = Hx_k + Z_k \tag{4}$$

Where A, B, H denote the state, input and output matrices respectively, X is the state vector, **u** is the input, Y is the measured value, W is the process noise and Z is the measurement noise. The Kalman filter assumes that the measurement and process noise are not correlated with each other and their average values are zero.

The Kalman filter procedure is divided into two stages. The first stage is called the time update. The second stage of the Kalman algorithm is the update of measurements [2]. Figure 6 represents a graph showing the operation of the Kalman filter for a stationary angle.

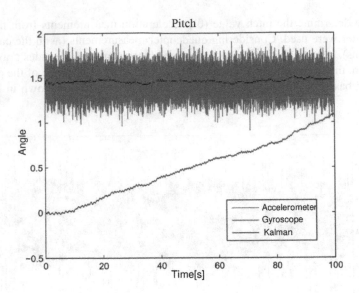

Fig. 6. The result of the operation of the Kalman filter for a stationary case.

The Kalman filter eliminates the initial gyro error and suppresses the noise from the accelerometer. The operation of the Kalman filter for a stationary case gives similar results to the complementary filter. The Kalman filter result for the rapidly changing angle is shown in Fig. 7.

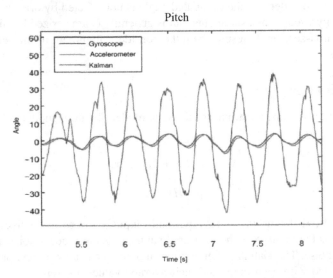

Fig. 7. The result of the Kalman filter operation for rapid angle changes.

Based on Fig. 7, it can be seen that the results obtained using the Kalman filter have a much lower delay (in phase) and show less impact of the accelerometer noise than the one obtained using the accelerator. Finally, a measurement test was carried out to compare the performance of the complementary filter and the Kalman filter when the quadcopter is rotated at different angles. A fragment of the obtained series of measurements is shown in Fig. 8.

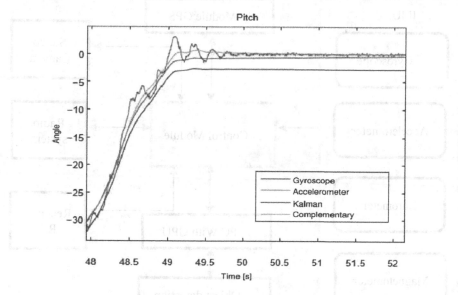

Fig. 8. A graph showing the operation of the Kalman filter.

In conclusion, both filters are suitable for use in systems where the angle changes at low frequencies, while in systems with rapid changes it is recommended to use the quadcopter system based on the Kalman filter. In this project, two separate Kalman filters were used to determine the pitch and roll angles, and gyroscope measurements were used to estimate the yaw angle. Orientation estimation has been implemented both in the quadcopter and in the operator's module.

2.4 Control Module

The quadcopter control module consists of a microcontroller to which external circuits are connected. The diagram of these connections is shown in Fig. 9.

The microcontroller memory has implemented control algorithms and functions that communicate with various systems, such as an IMU sensor, a GPS receiver, a radio system, an RC receiver, a PC computer and engine controllers. By transforming the information coming from the IMU sensor, the microcontroller determines the current orientation of the quadcopter. On the basis of the vehicle configuration and the parameter set coming from the operator module, a corresponding control command is calculated, which is given to the engine controllers in the form of PWM signals (with appropriate filling) [3]. The control signals are only calculated if the user triggers a corresponding signal to activate the motors by means of a brake. Based on the data from the GPS receiver system, the control module determines the GPS coordinates. Communication with a PC allows you to read the data needed to simulate the operation of algorithms on real sensor readings [8].

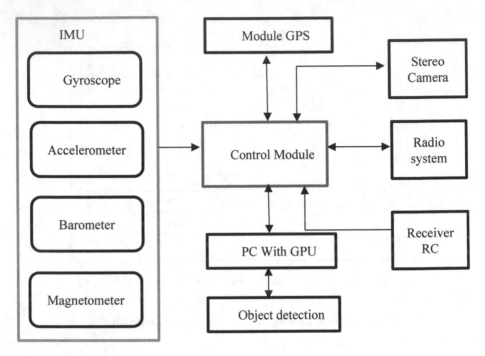

Fig. 9. Diagram of connections of the control module with external circuits.

2.5   UAV Communication

The Ground station and UAV had bi-directional communication between them. The ground station plans the aerial path of the UAV vehicle and keeps the UAV updated. The communication was carried out with the help of a UART serial port. The implemented communication allows for transferring data from the quadcopter sensors to the computer system, concerning cameras, angular speeds, linear accelerations, and coordinate positions and others calculated for systemic purposes [10].

3   Experimental Results

3.1   Stability Testing

At the very beginning it was checked how the quadcopter stabilizes in one axis. For this purpose, the set point value of the considered angle was fixed to 0. The vehicle was prepared for testing by pulling a string through the center of the frame and attaching one end to its railing, while the other end was held by the operator. Initial tests were performed using a standard RC apparatus. The completed aerial vehicle is shown in Fig. 10.

Fig. 10. Testing Stabilization with quad-copter.

The purpose of the test was to check the correctness of the implementation of control algorithms and orientation estimation. After selecting the appropriate PID controller settings, stabilization of the quadcopter was observed. In this way, the test was completed successfully. The next test was an attempt to stabilize the quadcopter in two axis by selecting the appropriate parameters of the PID controllers. In this case, it was possible to move the platform into a specific position. Initial values of integrating and switching elements were set to 0 [4].

The experimental results confirmed the known PID theory. Initially, only the proportional gain was tuned. In the cases when the gain was too small, the quadcopter slowly returned to the steady state, but it was unable to reach it (which caused the regulation to fail). Gradually, with the increase in the factor P, it was noticed that the position of the quadcopter began to stabilize. In the case of excessive gain, oscillations around the steady state were were generated [5, 7]. After determining the proportional gain value, the values of differential and integrating factors were tuned. The differentiating part affected the speed of the quadcopter reaction, while the integrating element reduced the error of the steady state.

3.2   Controllability Testing

The final phase of the tests consisted of controlling the quadcopter with the help of a glove. For this purpose, the vehicle is placed on the platform. During the tests, the operator checked if the quadcopter reacts to the control signals coming from the squeeze. At the beginning, the operation of 4 buttons was checked. According to the assumptions, the vehicle respectively: activated the engines, changed the speed of rotation of the engines and activated the manual control mode. Next, the operator, holding the pressed control button, turned the palm. Quadcopter at that time replicated the operator's movements.

3.3   Object Detection

When it comes to precision, the results are promising. We have shown how to train the system, and that images obtained through the data acquisition system can be used to detect objects as part of motion detection, also showing the effectiveness of the adopted methods [6]. In a few cases, the system detected more objects than those associated with annotators embedded in the original data. However, they have been marked as false positives (false alarms), with a clear classification to the appropriate class of objects using visual inspection. The object detection from the view of quadcopter is shown in Fig. 11.

Fig. 11. Detection from the view of quadcopter.

The proposed detection system was taught according to VOC and COCO data sets for five classes of possible objects on the road (pedestrians, cars, buses, bicycles and motorcycles) instead of using 20 classes characteristic of the VOC data set. In detecting/assessing the vehicle, our detector only generates car detection data (evidence) without taking into account the bus detection data, because buses are assigned to the MISC or trucks in the KITTI data set. When vehicles are detected within five classes, objects with a similar appearance, such as an airplane or a boat, are treated as a background. This increases the effectiveness of the SoftMax classification, which may slightly improve the performance of this system. Pedestrians had also slightly improved detection efficiency, with the exclusion of animal classes (such as cat, cow and horse). We also evaluated the effectiveness of the detection methods, including the background class. Our experimental results have shown that the six-class method, with the background class, surpasses the five-class method [9].

4 Conclusion

In summary, the project concerns the construction of a quadcopter system and equipping it with a navigation module and a control module. The designed quadcopter is able to perform basic maneuvers such as elevation, descent, forward tilt, lateral deviation and rotation around the central vertical axis.

An important issue considered in this project and significant during the control was the estimation of the quadcopter's state and its pose (orientation), which consisted in determining the slope, deviation and rotation angles (referred to as roll, pitch and yaw). A number of tests were also carried out to verify the accuracy of the implemented system, including its algorithms and methods.

References

1. Pedley, M.: Tilt sensing using a three-axis accelerometer. Free. Semicond. Appl. Note 1, 2012–2013 (2013)
2. Romaniuk, S., Gosiewski, Z.: Kalman filter realization for orientation and position estimation on dedicated processor. Acta Mechanica et Aautomatica 8(2), 88–94 (2014)
3. McCarron, B.: Low-Cost IMU Implementation via Sensor Fusion Algorithms in the Arduino Environment. California Polytechnic State University, San Luis Obispo (2013)
4. Ylimäki, M., et al.: Fast and accurate multi-view reconstruction by multi-stage prioritised matching. IET Comput. Vision 9(4), 576–587 (2015)
5. Shah, M.K.N., Dutt, M.B.J., Modh, H.: Quadrotor–an unmanned aerial vehicle. Int. J. Eng. Dev. Res. 2(1), 1299–1303 (2014)
6. Kang, M.S., Lim, Y.C.: High performance and fast object detection in road environments. In: 2017 Seventh International Conference on Image Processing Theory, Tools and Applications (IPTA), pp. 1–6. IEEE (2017)
7. Hentati, A.I., Krichen, L., Fourati, M., Fourati, L.C.: Simulation tools, environments and frameworks for UAV systems performance analysis. In: 2018 14th International Wireless Communications & Mobile Computing Conference (IWCMC), pp. 1495–1500. IEEE (2018)
8. Sagitov, A., Gerasimov, Y.: Towards DJI phantom 4 realistic simulation with gimbal and RC controller in ROS/Gazebo environment. In: 2017 10th International Conference on Developments in eSystems Engineering (DeSE), pp. 262–266. IEEE (2017)
9. Al-Kaff, A., et al.: VBII-UAV: vision-based infrastructure inspection-UAV. In: Rocha, Á., Correia, A.M., Adeli, H., Reis, L.P., Costanzo, S. (eds.) WorldCIST 2017. AISC, vol. 570, pp. 221–231. Springer, Cham (2017). https://doi.org/10.1007/978-3-319-56538-5_24
10. Gasior, P., et al.: Thrust estimation by fuzzy modeling of coaxial propulsion unit for multirotor UAVs. In: 2016 IEEE International Conference on Multisensor Fusion and Integration for Intelligent Systems (MFI), pp. 418–423. IEEE (2016)

Trajectory Planning of a PRR Redundant Serial Manipulator for Surface Finishing Operations on Plane

Duygu Atcı[1], Efecan Akdal[2(✉)], Fatih Cemal Can[1], and Erkin Gezgin[1]

[1] Department of Mechatronics Engineering, Izmir Katip Celebi University, Izmir, Turkey
[2] Department of Mechanical Engineering, Izmir Katip Celebi University, Izmir, Turkey
efecanakdal.akdal@gmail.com

Abstract. Technological advances in recent history allow usage of robot manipulators in every aspects of manufacturing. Integration of robot manipulators into the machining operations not only increases the quality of the end products but also decreases the time required for their machining operations. In terms of delicacy in these operations, robotic grinding can be given as one of the most important applications of the field. Thus this study focuses on the trajectory planning problem of a PRR planar serial redundant manipulator that is proposed to be utilized for surface finishing. Throughout the study kinematic representation of PRR manipulator was given in detail and its kinematic analysis was carried out along with the direct and inverse tasks. After the kinematic equations were obtained, a desired end effector trajectory was given in order to simulate real surface finishing application on a plane. Required joint position functions were taken as polynomial functions. In the light of this, coefficients of the polynomials were solved to approximate the desired trajectory. At the end of the study comparisons between the desired and generated trajectories were plotted graphically.

Keywords: Trajectory planning · Redundant DoF · Robotic surface finishing · Robot manipulators

1 Introduction

Robot manipulators can be defined as several rigid links connected by kinematic pairs which generate desired motion of special designed end effector. Recent mass manufacturing technology has been developed by using robot manipulators since usage of word robot in 1920. Robot manipulators have been used for industrial tasks such as painting, welding, assembling, additive manufacturing and grinding. Therefore, spatial, spherical and, planar motions of the end effector are obtained from kinematic chains of robot manipulators.

In manufacturing of products, robotic grinding process has been used by serial and parallel robot manipulators to get better surface quality of final product. A five bar

© Springer Nature Switzerland AG 2019
A. Ronzhin et al. (Eds.): ICR 2019, LNAI 11659, pp. 30–39, 2019.
https://doi.org/10.1007/978-3-030-26118-4_4

grinding robot manipulator with a spring balancer was designed by Nahavandi et al. [1]. An algorithm of hybrid position/force control scheme was proposed to obtain low-powered manipulator for grinding tasks. Dynamical simulations and experimental results were presented to show effectiveness of the designed manipulator. In this research, grinding tool was attached to end effector of the five bar robot manipulator.

Li et al. [2] presented a hand-eye calibration procedure of visually-guided grinding robot manipulator. A 6-DoF serial robot manipulator was used to make grinding tasks of nuclear turbine's blades. In grinding process, these blades were attached to end effector of serial robot manipulator in this study.

Simulation of robotic belt grinding was presented by Ren et al. [3]. This simulation could help the programmer of grinding task to improve efficiency by predicting results. Surface quality of final part can be predicted before grinding.

Robotic cup grinding was proposed by Persoons and Vanherck [4]. Experimental work of the set-up was presented to determine the relationship between the workpiece material removal rate and the axial grinding force and the grinding angle.

New algorithm for automatic path planning of robotic belt surface grinding was presented by Wang and Yun [5]. Optimization of path planning was realized in this study. Optimized and not optimized experimental grinding results were compared to show efficiency of the proposed method.

Huang et al. [6] reported a robotic grinding and polishing system for automatic grinding of turbine-vane overhaul. Passive compliance tools (PCTs), adaptive path planning and tool path optimization of robotic grinding were presented in the paper.

Force controlled robotic abrasive belt grinding process were proposed by Yan et al. [7]. Force model of grinding process, specific grinding energy for the reasonable grinding parameters, the effects of cutting force components on cut-in, normal and cut-off paths were explained along with experimental analysis.

Path generation for precision machining such as grinding, milling and turning were presented by Wang and Yang [8]. They were able to generate a composite quantic spline based on the basis of a cubic spline with nearly arc-length parameterization, 2nd-order continuity and almost no wanted higher-order oscillations. This toolpath generation method was applied to 5-DoF parallel manipulator by Shen et al. [9]. The machining simulation for parallel manipulator was carried out by using S-shape part.

In the present study, trajectory planning of a PRR redundant serial manipulator is given. Serial manipulator is considered to be used in robotic surface finishing operations with a tool attached to its end effector. Trajectory design of the end effector is performed by introducing time-variable functions for the revolute joint positions. These functions are solved simultaneously by considering the continuity equations of via points on the designed trajectory. After obtaining the relative trajectory of the RR portion of the manipulator, positions of the prismatic joint is given to compensate the horizontal displacement of the end effector. Additionally, continuity of the motion is achieved by dividing the workspace into segments and returning the RR portion of the manipulator back into its starting position. An example for the designed trajectory is given and the resultant trajectory with the comparison to the desired trajectory are plotted in graphs.

2   Kinematics of PRR Serial Manipulator

In order to carry out planar positioning for the tool during finishing operation, three degrees of freedom PRR redundant serial planar manipulator was decided to be utilized. Although the system has sufficient degrees of freedom for the end effector (P) motion on plane (two independent translations and an independent rotation), selected configuration was considered redundant, as the orientation of the end effector will not be required for trajectory planning tasks throughout the study. It should be noted that this study will only cover the generation of desired end effector trajectory on plane. Translational tip motion on plane normal that is required for three dimensional part finishing will be generated by a single degree of freedom tool carried by the end effector of the actual system, yet its design and related calculations will not be mentioned in this study.

Kinematic representation of the selected manipulator is shown in Fig. 1 and it was labeled with respect to the distal Denavit–Hartenberg convention to reveal link and joint parameters.

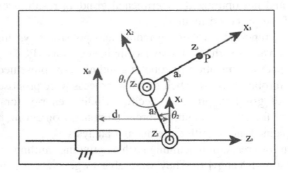

Fig. 1. Kinematic representation of PRR serial planar manipulator.

These parameters are also tabulated in Table 1 for the related kinematic structure to proceed into the direct and inverse task of the manipulator.

Table 1. Denavit–Hartenberg parameters of the PRR serial manipulator.

Joint i	α_i	a_i	d_i	θ_i
1	$-\pi/2$	0	d_1	0
2	0	a_2	0	θ_2
3	0	a_3	0	θ_3

Using four basic transformations related with distal Denavit–Hartenberg convention, transformation matrix between ith and (i−1)th coordinate systems can be obtained as,

$$^{i-1}T_i = T(z_{i-1}, d_i)T(z_{i-1}, \theta_i)T(x_i, a_i)T(x_i, \alpha_i) = \begin{bmatrix} C_i & -C\alpha_i S_i & S\alpha_i S_i & a_i C_i \\ S_i & C\alpha_i C_i & -S\alpha_i C_i & a_i S_i \\ 0 & S\alpha_i & C\alpha_i & d_i \\ 0 & 0 & 0 & 1 \end{bmatrix},$$

$$(1)$$

where, $C_i = \cos\theta_i$, $S_i = \sin\theta_i$, $C\alpha_i = \cos\alpha_i$, and $S\alpha_i = \sin\alpha_i$.

Final transformation matrix $^0T_3$ between the end effector and the base frame can be calculated after the related parameters shown in Table 1 was inserted to the Eq. (1) as,

$$^0T_3 = {}^0T_1\,{}^1T_2\,{}^2T_3 = \begin{bmatrix} u_x & v_x & w_x & p_x \\ u_y & v_y & w_y & p_y \\ u_z & v_z & w_z & p_z \\ 0 & 0 & 0 & 1 \end{bmatrix},$$

$$(2)$$

where, $u_x = C_{23}$, $u_y = 0$, $u_z = -S_{23}$, $v_x = -S_{23}$, $v_y = 0$, $v_z = -C_{23}$, $w_x = 0$, $w_y = 1$, $w_z = 0$, $p_x = a_2C_2 + a_3C_{23}$, $p_y = 0$, $p_z = d_1 - a_2S_2 - a_3S_{23}$, $C_{ij} = \cos(\theta_i + \theta_j)$, and $S_{ij} = \sin(\theta_i + \theta_j)$.

2.1 Direct Kinematics

The main objective of the direct kinematics is the calculation of end effector position and orientation with respect to the base frame by using given input variables of the manipulator, d_1, θ_2, and θ_3. Once the transformation matrix $^0T_3$ (Eq. 2) is formed, it can be used to express any position vector defined in the end effector frame $^3q = [^3q_x, {}^3q_y, {}^3q_z, 1]^T$, with respect to the base frame $^0q = [^0q_x, {}^0q_y, {}^0q_z, 1]^T$ as,

$$^0q = {}^0T_6\,{}^6q.$$

$$(3)$$

Due to the fact that tool attachment point at the end effector of the manipulator located at the origin of the last coordinate frame, $^3P = [0, 0, 0]^T$, position of the end effector with respect to the base frame will be the last column of the transformation matrix $^0T_3, {}^0P = [p_x, p_y, p_z]^T$. Although the orientation of the end effector is not a concern for this study, it can be revealed by forming rotation matrix $^0R_3$ with the unit vectors (u_x, u_y, u_z), (v_x, v_y, v_z) and (w_x, w_y, w_z) as,

$$^0R_3 = \begin{bmatrix} u_x & v_x & w_x \\ u_y & v_y & w_y \\ u_z & v_z & w_z \end{bmatrix}.$$

$$(4)$$

2.2 Inverse Kinematics

Inverse kinematics allows the calculation of required input variables for a given end effector position and orientation. On the other hand, as the orientation information will not be needed during trajectory planning tasks on the scope of this study, it is needed to compute necessary input variables d_1, θ_2, and θ_3 by utilizing only the end effector position information. Thus this fact renders the system to become redundant. As one of the position components is always zero ($p_y = 0$), two equations will be left to calculate three unknown input variables as,

$$p_x = a_2 C_2 + a_3 C_{23}, \quad p_z = d_1 - a_2 S_2 - a_3 S_{23}. \tag{5}$$

It is clear that Eq. (5) have infinite solution sets for the input variables, so a methodology should be followed in order to carry out the inverse task of the given manipulator. In the light of this it is decided to utilize prismatic joint in the system as a compensation actuator for refining the end effector trajectory with respect to the desired trajectory without including it in the inverse task. Following this methodology, by taking $d_1 = 0$ Eq. (5) will be simplified into,

$$p_x = a_2 C_2 + a_3 C_{23}, \quad p_z = -a_2 S_2 - a_3 S_{23}. \tag{6}$$

Taking the squares of each sides of this equation set (Eq. 6) and adding the results together will reveal θ_3 as,

$$\theta_3 = \cos^{-1} \frac{p_x^2 + p_z^2 - a_2^2 - a_3^2}{2a_2 a_3}. \tag{7}$$

In order to calculate θ_2 Eq. (6) can be rearranged with respect to the known and unknown parameters,

$$p_x = k_1 C_2 - k_2 S_2, \quad p_z = -k_1 S_2 - k_2 C_2, \quad k_1 = a_2 + a_3 C_3, \quad k_2 = a_3 S_3. \tag{8}$$

Using Eq. (8), θ_2 can be calculated after simple mathematical operations as,

$$\theta_2 = \text{Atan2}(-p_z, p_x) - \text{Atan2}(k_2, k_1). \tag{9}$$

Note that Eq. (7) will result in dual solutions for θ_3 and for each individual θ_3 values Eq. (9) will result in a single value.

3 Trajectory Planning

Designed PRR serial manipulator is planned to be used in robotics machining operations, particularly for surface finishing and grinding. Planning of the trajectory of the machine tool become a significant task in these high-sensitive operations. In the present study, as machine tool is design to be attached to the end effector of serial PRR mechanism, only the desired trajectory of the end effector will be considered.

It is clear that, in order to achieve continuous finishing operation in large work pieces, actual finishing workspace should be divided into multiple equal segments and RR portion of the proposed mechanism should return to its starting location at the end of each segment during the operation. In this methodology, to provide transition between segments and refine the actual trajectory in horizontal direction, prismatic joint in the system will provide trajectory compensation. In the light of this, an example of trajectory planning case will be described in order to clarify the idea.

Let's assume that a desired continuous tool trajectory of the manipulator is given as shown in Fig. 2a, where solid lines shows the first main segment to be followed afterwards with the dashed lines. During this operation relative desired trajectory of the RR portion of the mechanism was planned as shown in Fig. 2b, in order to start from and reach to the same position at the end of each main segment.

As seen in Fig. 2a desired trajectory is divided into subsections which are located in the figure. Each subsection is labeled by a number. Trajectory variables of each subsection is prearranged as stated in the figure and t_i, $(i = 2, 3, .., 15)$ are the times at via points t_i.

In accordance with the given desired trajectory, the general form of the joint positions of first and second revolute joints are proposed as functions of time:

$$\theta_{k,i}(t) = a_{k,i}t^3 + b_{k,i}t^2 + c_{k,i}t + d_{k,i} \quad k = 2, 3. \quad i = 1, 2, \ldots 14.$$

$$\theta_{k,15}(t) = a_{k,15}t^4 + b_{k,15}t^3 + c_{k,15}t^2 + d_{k,15}t + e_{k,15}, \tag{10}$$

where the coefficients $a_{k,i}$, $b_{k,i}$, $c_{k,i}$, $d_{k,i}$ and $a_{k,15}$, $b_{k,15}$, $c_{k,15}$, $d_{k,15}$, $e_{k,15}$ are unknowns. The first subscript of the functions in Eq. (10) denotes the number of the revolute joint $(k = 2, 3)$ and the second denotes the number of subsection.

There are 61 unknown coefficients to be solved for each two revolute joint. The initial conditions of the trajectory are taken as follows:

$$\theta_{k,1}(t_1) = \theta_{k,1}(0) \quad \dot{\theta}_{k,1}(t_1) = 0 \quad k = 2, 3. \tag{11}$$

The second order continuity equations on the via points are given as below

$$\theta_{k,i}(t_i) = \theta_{k,(i+1)}(t_i)$$
$$\dot{\theta}_{k,i}(t_i) = \dot{\theta}_{k,(i+1)}(t_i) \tag{12}$$
$$\ddot{\theta}_{k,i}(t_i) = \ddot{\theta}_{k,(i+1)}(t_i) \quad i = 2, \ldots, 14. \quad k = 2, 3.$$

Note that joint positions, $\theta_{k,i}(t_i)$, in Eq. (12) are calculated by using the inverse kinematic task relations given in Eqs. (7) and (9) by taking link lengths of the RR portion of the system as 105 mm. Also, in order to provide continuous transition between the main segments, the final continuity equations will be:

$$\theta_{k,15}(t_{15}) = \theta_{k,2}(t_2)$$
$$\dot{\theta}_{k,15}(t_{15}) = \dot{\theta}_{k,2}(t_2) \tag{13}$$
$$\ddot{\theta}_{k,15}(t_{15}) = \ddot{\theta}_{k,2}(t_2) \quad k = 2, 3.$$

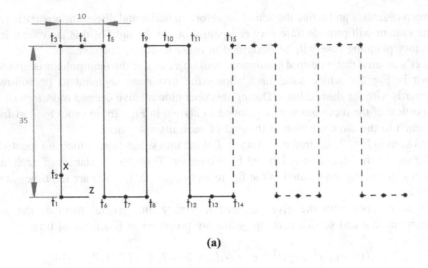

(a)

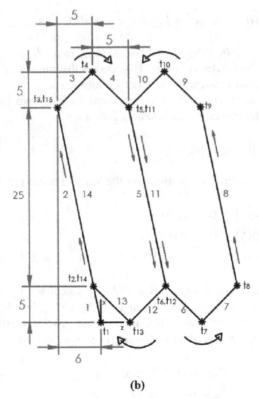

(b)

Fig. 2. Planned tool trajectory of the end effector. (a) Desired trajectory (b) Relative desired trajectory of RR portion.

Taking the time intervals as $t_2 - t_1 = 1$ and $t_{i+1} - t_i = 5$, $i = 2, .., 14.$, unknown coefficients of Eq. (10) are calculated by using the Eqs. (11–13). After obtaining the revolute joint positions as functions of time, actual relative trajectory of the end effector can be plotted as shown in Fig. 3:

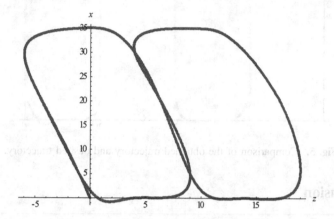

Fig. 3. Relative trajectory of the RR portion of the manipulator.

In order to compensate the actual relative trajectory of RR portion of the mechanism given in Fig. 3, prismatic joint of the system will be used. The final resultant trajectory can be seen in Fig. 4, along with its comparison with the desired trajectory in Fig. 5.

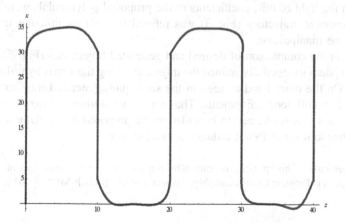

Fig. 4. Resultant trajectory of PRR manipulator.

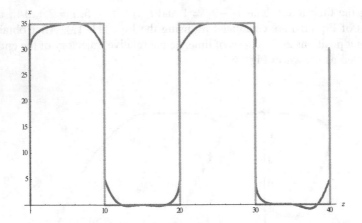

Fig. 5. Comparison of the obtained trajectory and desired trajectory.

4   Conclusion

Throughout the study three degrees of freedom PRR serial redundant manipulator was proposed for robotic grinding and surface finishing operations on plane. In order to simplify trajectory planning, proposed redundant mechanism was separated into two sections as RR and P that are responsible for the end coarse effector trajectory formation and trajectory refinement respectively. After the kinematic analysis procedures were carried out, joint position functions for RR section of the manipulator was proposed as time dependent cubic and quartic polynomial functions. Coarse end effector trajectory (Fig. 2b) was defined with respect to the segmented desired trajectory (Fig. 2a). In the light of this, coefficients of the proposed polynomials were calculated and final generated trajectory (Fig. 3) was refined (Fig. 4) by utilizing translational (P) joint of the manipulator.

As seen in the comparison of desired and generated trajectories (Fig. 5), prismatic joint of the system successfully refined the trajectory along the x axis by utilizing z axis translation. On the other hand as seen in the same plot, generated trajectory portions along the z axis still need refinements. Thus for future studies additional translational redundancy on x axis is planned to be added to the proposed manipulator to form four degrees of freedom serial PPRR redundant manipulator.

Acknowledgements. This project is currently funded by Izmir Katip Celebi University, Scientific Research Projects Coordinatorship. Project No: 2018-GAP-MÜMF-0010.

References

1. Nahavandi, S., et al.: Automated robotic grinding by low-powered manipulator. Robot. Comput. Integr. Manuf. **23**(5), 589–598 (2007)

2. Li, W., Xie, H., Zhang, G., Yan, S., Yin, Z.: Hand–eye calibration in visually-guided robot grinding. IEEE Trans. Cybern. **46**(11), 2634–2642 (2016)
3. Ren, X., Cabaravdic, M., Zhang, X., Kuhlenkötter, B.: A local process model for simulation of robotic belt grinding. Int. J. Mach. Tools Manuf. **47**(6), 962–970 (2007)
4. Persoons, W., Vanherck, P.: A process model for robotic cup grinding. CIRP Ann. **45**(1), 319–325 (1996)
5. Wang, W., Yun, C.: A path planning method for robotic belt surface grinding. Chin. J. Aeronaut. **24**(4), 520–526 (2011)
6. Huang, H., Gong, Z.M., Chen, X.Q., Zhou, L.: Robotic grinding and polishing for turbine-vane overhaul. J. Mater. Process. Technol. **127**(2), 140–145 (2002)
7. Yan, S., Xu, X., Yang, Z., Zhu, D., Ding, H.: An improved robotic abrasive belt grinding force model considering the effects of cut-in and cut-off. J. Manuf. Processes **37**, 496–508 (2019)
8. Wang, F.-C., Yang, D.C.H.: Nearly arc-length parameterized quintic-spline interpolation for precision machining. Comput. Aided Des. **25**(5), 281–288 (1993)
9. Shen, X., et al.: A smooth and undistorted toolpath interpolation method for 5-DoF parallel kinematic machines. Robot. Comput. Integr. Manuf. **57**, 347–356 (2019)

Multi-agent Control System of a Robot Group: Virtual and Physical Experiments

Igor Kozhemyakin, Nickolay Semenov, Vladimir Ryzhov,
and Mikhail Chemodanov(✉)

Saint-Petersburg Marine Technical University, Saint-Petersburg, Russia
chemodanov@smtu.ru

Abstract. The paper describes the modeling, development and testing results of a multi-agent control system for a group of ground-based robots. The developed model of collective behavior was verified in the Matlab system, then transferred to the ROS framework and tested in the virtual Gazebo environment. Such a development path allowed us to obtain a workable code at the computer simulation stage and then use it to ensure the functioning of a group of autonomous ground-based robots in natural conditions. The paper describes all the main stages of the project: development of a mathematical model of the multi-agent control system, implementation in ROS system using Python language and verification by control of real robot group (group of eduMIP robots). Comparison of the results of computer simulation and the physical experiments made it possible to conclude that they are sufficiently consistent, which in turn confirms the correctness of the constructed group control model. Thus, within the framework of the SMTU project, the task of developing models and group control algorithms for a simple multi-agent system has been solved. The purpose of the next stage of work is the adaptation and development of proven models and algorithms for the control system of a group of underwater robots.

Keywords: Group robotics · Multiagent systems · Simulation model · Gazebo

1 Introduction

The model that underlies the robots group control is that to solve any common task assigned to a group of autonomous robots, it needs to be broken into specific subtasks and distributed among individual robots so that the process of solving a common task by the group would be implemented as efficiently as possible. At the same time, efficiency is understood as either the minimum time to complete a task or the minimum necessary resources.

There are some international projects in which researchers developed their own multi-agent control implementations for their own designed robots, for example, Robotarium [1], CoCoRo [2], mROBerto [3], SWARMIX [4], Droplets [5].

© Springer Nature Switzerland AG 2019
A. Ronzhin et al. (Eds.): ICR 2019, LNAI 11659, pp. 40–52, 2019.
https://doi.org/10.1007/978-3-030-26118-4_5

All of the above projects were developed to solve educational and highly specialized tasks implemented by specific robots and their control systems, but such systems turned out to be unsuitable for SMTU devices and for the tasks they implement.

Therefore, the aim of the project presented in this article is the development of a multi-agent control system for a group of robots (for example, underwater robot Akara) developed by SPbSMTU [7] (Fig. 1).

Fig. 1. Robots developed by SPbSMTU.

As the first stage of the project implementation, the simpler task of building a multi-agent control system for a group of ground (surface) robots was considered. This group of robots within the framework of joint participation in a real mission should be able to perform a minimal set of elementary tasks, which includes:

1. following the leader (arrange robots in a compact mobile group). This task is very important for any movement of a group of robots from one place to another - if each robot moves independently, collisions will inevitably arise, which are quite difficult to avoid. By forming a group of robots and using a model "following the leader", such problems disappear - it is enough for robots to maintain a given distance to their neighbors, and for the head to set the direction and speed of movement to the target.

2. obstacle avoidance (moving a group along a difficult trajectory with obstacles). This task arises when a compact group follows the leader, when an obstacle arises in the path of one of the robots - it is required to bypass the obstacle and restore the broken system with minimal time and resources of all robots.

3. inspection of the territory (time-efficient interaction algorithm for finding objects in a complex and previously unknown (almost unknown) territory). This task involves the partial implementation of the final task for the entire group and may include both a search for objects in a given territory, tracking, escorting, and control of the territory.

This paper is devoted to the methods of theoretical and practical solution of these problems within the framework of the project being implemented at SMTU.

2   Group Control Model

If we consider the general task of controlling a group of N robots $R_i(i = 1..N)$, we can describe the state of each robot $S_i(t)$, the state of the environment $E_i(t)$, the set of actions of each robot Ai with which it can change both the state of the environment and the state of other robots. Then we can write [6]:

$$S_i = F_i(S_1, A_1, .., S_N, A_N, E), i = 1..N, \tag{1}$$

$$E = F(S_1, A_1, .., S_N, A_N, E), i = 1..N, \tag{2}$$

The new state of each robot S_i is the function F_i of the states $S_j(j = 1..n)$ of the other robots in the group, their actions A_j and the state of the environment E. The new state of the environment E is a separate function F from the same arguments.

In reality, the actions of robots, as well as the state of robots and the environment, are subject to physical limitations, which can be written in the form of inequalities:

$$G(S_1, ..., S_N, E) \leq 0 \tag{3}$$

$$D(S_1, A_1, ..., S_N, A_N, E) \leq 0 \tag{4}$$

where G is a function of technical limitations of the state of robots and the environment, D is a function of technical limitations on the actions of robots.

The main aim of robots' group is thus transformation of initial E environment to the target one in an optimal way (e.g. spending less time or using less resources).

Since the number of robots in a group is more than 1, a number of subtasks appear, such as determining the composition of a group, the distribution of functions between robots, the implementation of functions by individual robots to accomplish several aims.

In order to find out the composition of the group and the distribution of functions between robots multiagent management system is used, that considers implementation of several simple rules:

1. every robot can settle his task irrespective of the other robots' tasks (autonomy);
2. the distribution of functions between robots is performed during their interaction (cooperation);
3. group's efficiency can not be less than the separate one's, especially in conditions of constantly changing environment (flexibility).

Let us consider every robot's required functionality and their communication protocols when solving supplied problems - following the leader, bypassing obstacles and inspecting the environment.

Effective group functioning is impossible without a communication system and positioning between it's members, which allows to find out every robot's location and task, moreover it is necessary to provide an efficient protocol for the information exchange between group members.

The sequence of every task's implementation comprises of revealing group's composition, tasks distribution between group members and execution of single tasks.

While settling the task of following the leader the communication protocols contains following messages:

1. message about task change (the information about group construction and movement direction);
2. message about the best candidate for leader role (e.g. the closest to the position data). All the robots in a group exchange such kind of messages and the robot, that is nearer to the target data and has enough resources to achieve it becomes a leader. In case of leader's breakdown and lack of resources, a new vote is performed and a new leader is chosen;
3. message about every robot's place and task in group's interaction, with indication of time and resources required to change two robot's tasks (choosing second level leader to follow the first one, third level - to follow the second one etc.) According to this information a local voting for the right to occupy a certain place is performed. When the group composition changes, voting is repeated. The settlement of an optimal decision may be written like: $A_i = argmin\{\Sigma Z(A_i)\}$, where $Z(A_i)$ is function of action resources A_i;

Any situation where a very large number of robots performs a single task can be broken down into subtasks, and robots can be divided into groups to perform these subtasks. Therefore, the problem of communication "every to each other" for a large number of participants is not relevant.

An example of communication in 3 robots group is shown in Fig. 2. Initially, robots are in a state of "idle", but then one of them receives from the control center command with a "task". This robot informs all other robots in the group about "task" and their state became "task". Next, the robots select the leader by voting and calculating the distance to the target, and the remaining robots are ranked in accordance with their initial position. The main state of the robots is "Do". In this state, they perform the main work and monitor the state of neighboring robots. In the case of the failure of one of the robots ("error" state), the process of rank forming is repeated.

In order to settle the task of bypassing the obstacle (robots' rebuilding) the protocol should be modified:

4. message about an obstacle that we need to bypass with indication of it's coordinates. Robot having an obstacle on his way informs neighbours about changing trajectory (a probable new obstacle) and suggests new own trajectories. Other robots, whose way crosses the first robot's trajectory offer their new ways, as a result a set of mutual rebuildings appears with an indication of their "cost", that is, the expenditure of time and energy resources.

Wins the option in which the total cost of time and energy is minimal, that is, the objective function can be expressed as:

$$A_i = argmin\{\Sigma Z(A_i E_k)\}, i = 1..N \qquad (5)$$

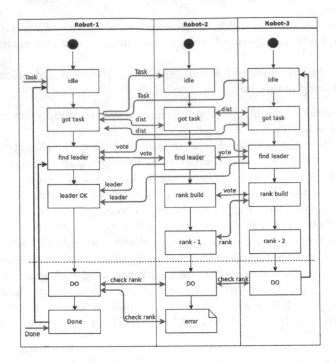

Fig. 2. Communication example.

where E_k is the variant of group rebuilding, $Z(A_i, E_k)$ is the cost function for action A_i under the variant of rebuilding the group E_k.

The set of restrictions for solving the optimization problem is similar to that considered in the algorithm for following the leader.

For settling the task of exploration of a certain territory every robot's trajectories should be prevented from crossing, otherwise the territories already surveyed would be re-examined and the efficacy of the whole group would be reduced.

For this, the concept of "application" for a survey is introduced [7], that is, the entire survey area is divided into segments, the processing time of which is approximately known. The "cost" of the survey of each segment is selected so that the end of the survey occurs near the "finish". The task of each robot is to form such a trajectory in which it will collect the maximum number of applications ("money") with the minimum expenditure of energy and time of the whole group, provided that the whole group will also examine other applications.

Thus, the exchange protocol must contain another type of message - the trajectory proposal. If the other robot has calculated that its trajectory in some areas is more efficient, a conflict arises, which is solved by choosing such a set of trajectories in which the group's total "profit" is maximum (collecting all segments (maximum income) in minimum time and with minimum energy resources (minimum)).

The objective function for the optimization problem can be expressed as:

$$A_i = argmax\{\Sigma Q_i(A_1..A_N)\}, i = 1..N \tag{6}$$

where A_i is the action of the robot "i", Q_j is the profit function of the whole group of robots $A_1..A_N$ at step j (taking into account the expenditure of energy and time resources). Thus, the objective function maximizes the profit of the whole group in the minimum amount of time and energy.

The set of restrictions for solving the optimization problem is similar to that considered in the algorithm of following the leader, but it is supplemented with a restriction on the communication speed and delays in transferring information between the robots in the group.

To verify the correctness of the exchange protocol described above, taking into account technical limitations on the speed of robots, maneuvering features and connection speeds, it is necessary to carry out computer simulation of the interaction of a group of robots.

After obtaining adequate simulation results, we should check the correctness of the model on real robots.

3   Computer Simulations

The task of computer simulation of group of robots is very relevant, since natural testing often involves high labor intensity and lacks such opportunities as pausing, easy repetition of specific situations, cheap changes in the design of robots or in an environment in which robots interact.

Analysis of papers on multi-agent systems of underwater vehicles [1–5,9] shows that most of the work is focused on the study of swarm intelligence, which, in general, implies less complexity of tasks performed by an individual robot and more emphasis on solving a task by a group of a large number of robots (tens and hundreds). Thus, 2d-modeling tools that are less demanding of computational resources, with less attention to modeling the physical environment, are more suitable for testing the algorithms of swarm intelligence. An example is the implementation of simulators based on Matlab and Python [1].

An alternative approach is to select an already existing simulator, such as Webots [10], USARSim [11] Gazebo [12], MuRoSimF [13], refine it or create your own simulator [14].

In this paper, we propose further transfer of the developed and modeled algorithms to underwater robots operating in a complex three-dimensional environment, thus 2d simulators are not very promising.

Due to the fact that the resources of the development team are limited, the development of your own full-fledged simulator was recognized as impossible, and it was decided to use the Gazebo simulator, which favorably differs from the others by the following criteria: a large community of developers and users, and therefore the availability of available training materials, good compatibility with ROS, which is a platform for the majority of robots developed at SMTU [7]. An example of a group interaction of ground robots in Gazebo implemented in SMTU is shown in Fig. 3. In addition, ROS allows the use of a primitive 2d simulator TurtleSim Fig. 3 that allows experiments with a smaller load on the central processor.

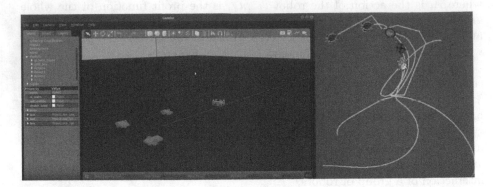

Fig. 3. An example of the operation of the simulator Gazebo (left) and TurtleSim (right).

Thus, Gazebo was chosen as a physical simulator for the task being realized.

Another important task in the development of multi-agent systems of underwater vehicles is to address the issue of data transfer. The fact is that underwater communication has a limited transmission distance, limitations on the speed of sound, channel width, the possibility of bit errors in messages, depending on the transmission distance and noise level. At the same time, it is necessary to take into account the directivity characteristics of antennas, zones of sound shading, vertical distribution of the speed of sound, etc. To simulate these features, it is necessary to introduce a communication channel simulation module into a mathematical and computer model.

The exchange of information on the hydroacoustic channel is implemented in the developed model in a simplified version, with the only restriction on the probability of message delivery, which is determined as follows:

$$P = \begin{cases} 1 & r < r_{min} \\ 1 - (\frac{r - r_{min}}{r_{max} - r_{min}})^2 & r_{min} \leq r \leq r_{max} \\ 0 & r > r_{max} \end{cases} \tag{7}$$

where r is the distance between the signal source and the receiver, r_{min} is the distance at which the message is guaranteed to be delivered, r_{max} is the distance at which the message is not guaranteed to be delivered.

4 Environment for Field Testing of Robot Group

With all the advantages of working with a simulator, field testing can reveal some features of the interaction of robots, for whatever reason, not manifested in the simulator.

The principal difference of the field testing system from the simulation is as follows:

1. availability of self-propelled robotic agents;
2. availability of a server communication system with robotic agents;
3. availability of a positioning system for robotic agents.

Requirements for launching software based on ROS were put forward for robotic objects, which led to the choice of a Linux-based computer. The cheapest and satisfying this requirement robot is the eduMIP platform [16] (see Fig. 4), which was used in the project based on the Beaglebone Blue (BBBl) single-board computer. In this case, one of the standard BBBl communication channels - WiFi was used.

Fig. 4. eduMIP platform.

The following systems were tested as indoor positioning systems:

1. autonomous navigation system (encoders, IMU);
2. Marvelmind ultrasonic positioning system [17];
3. positioning systems using markers and video cameras.

Autonomous methods are distinguished by the accumulation of error with time, however, in the case of developing systems that are further oriented for use in underwater robotics, that is, operating mainly with autonomous positioning, the use of such methods is justified. In addition, this method is used for positioning in the moments when it is impossible to work with external positioning.

The Marvelmind ultrasonic positioning system has proven itself not to the best for the following reasons:

1. additional costs are required (purchase of the Marvelmind module) for each agent;
2. the frequency of obtaining coordinates with an increase in the number of agents falls.

At the same time, the positioning system by markers with Aruco-codes [18–20] (see Fig. 5) is simple, reliable and cheap (this system was assembled from a USB camera and a BananaPi single-board computer). Increasing the number of robots involved in the system only requires printing an additional Aruco-code, reconfiguring the software and manufacturing the code holder on a 3d printer.

Thus, a positioning system using markers with Aruco codes and a USB video camera was chosen as an indoor positioning system.

5   Verification of Computer Simulation Results

In order to assess the correctness of the simulation results of the machine control system in the Matlab environment and the software models in the Gazebo simulator, field experiments were conducted on a group of ground robots and compared the results. As one of the model tasks for which verification was carried out, the task "follow the leader" was chosen. Three agents must follow the leader (lead), and the leader must move according to the trajectory shown in Fig. 6 (upper left). The simulation results in the Matlab system are shown in Fig. 6 (upper right). The simulation results in the Gazebo system are shown in Fig. 6 (down left). The processed video of the field experiment is shown in Fig. 6 (down right).

Verification error was defined as the standard deviation of the coordinates of agents in the computer model of the Matlab environment and the Gazebo simulator from the same coordinates of the field experiment at times with a step of 5 s:

$$error = \sqrt{\frac{1}{3n} \sum_{j=1}^{3} \sum_{i=1}^{n} (x_{i,j}^v - x_{i,j}^{matlab})^2} \tag{8}$$

where n is the number of segments that are multiples of 5 s in the experiment, $x_{i,j}^v$ is the vector of agent coordinates j in the model being verified at time i, $x_{i,j}$ matlab is the vector of agent coordinates j of the model in Matlab at time i.

As a result, the following standard deviations were obtained:

1. for the Gazebo model: 102.4 mm (3.2% of the distance covered);
2. for full-scale model: 96 mm (8.9% of the distance covered).

At the same time, it was not possible to conduct the whole experiment in full-scale modeling due to lack of space and the comparison was made only in part of the trajectory. Error calculation was also carried out only for part of the trajectory.

These deviations can be considered acceptable for the quality of the computer and full-scale model. Deviations themselves may be due to the following reasons:

1. A deeper physical simulation model in Gazebo determines a more accurate description of physical parameters and constraints than a purely mathematical model in Matlab;

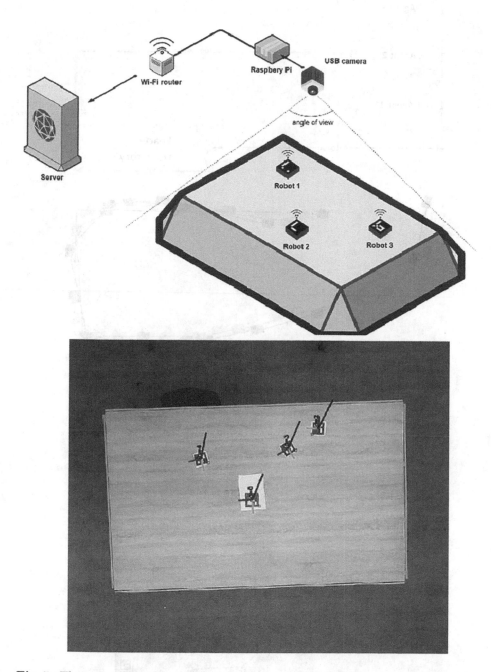

Fig. 5. The structure of the full-scale layout and one frame from the camera after detecting markers.

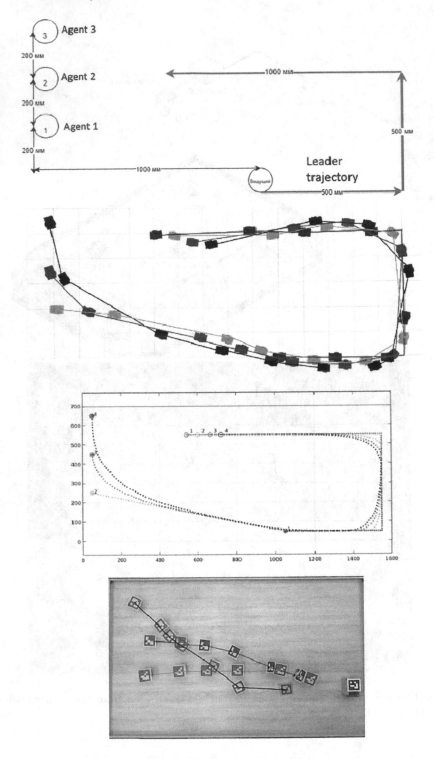

Fig. 6. Verification of model.

2. The motion of the eduMIP platform in the balance mode (inverted pendulum) leads to a number of problems:
   (a) when colliding with obstacles or between each other, the robots cannot move;
   (b) rocking robots in rare cases leads to a loss of detection of the Aruco marker by the camera;
   (c) movement in the balancing mode leads to an unsteady starting imitation picture.

6   Conclusion

As a result of the work, a comparative analysis was performed of the results of modeling simple tasks of the movement of a group of interacting robots in a mathematical model in a matlab, in a Gazebo simulator, and according to physical experiment data.

For physical experiment was developed stand consisting of a positioning system based on a video camera and Aruco-codes. The eduMIP modules running under ROS were selected as mobile agents. This virtual system (in the case of the Gazebo simulator) and field testing showed itself well in tests of the movement of robots behind the leader, but revealed a number of shortcomings inherent in the eduMIP platform.

The results of the project suggest that the developed system is an effective platform for further research on the group interaction of robots, it has a low cost, the ability to scale and extensive use of OpenSource technology.

In addition to the use of agents based on the eduMIP platform in the ongoing research, the company is currently in the process of creating its own mobile agent with lower cost, smaller overall dimensions and a number of additional features, such as using sensors to detect obstacles, exchange data in the near radius via the infrared port and focus on driving mode without balancing. All technical materials on the developed system (software, electronic boards, design drawings) will be placed in the public domain.

References

1. Pickem, D., et al.: The robotarium: a remotely accessible swarm robotics re-search testbed. In: IEEE International Conference on Robotics and Automation (ICRA) 2017, pp. 1699–1706. IEEE (2017)
2. Collective Cognitive Robots, sssa.bioroboticsinstitute.it/projects/CoCoRo. Accessed 26 Feb 2019
3. Kim, J., Colaco, T., Kashino, Z., Nejat, G., Benhabib, B.: mROBerTO: a modular millirobot for swarm-behavior studies. In: IEEE/RSJ International Conference on Intelligent Robots and Systems, IROS 2016, pp. 2109–2114. Daejeon, Korea (2016)
4. Flushing, E.F., Gambardella, L., Di Caro, G.A.: Search and rescue using mixed swarms of heterogeneous agents: modeling, simulation, and planning. In: Technical Report IDSIA-05-12, IDSIA, Lugano, Switzerland, April 2012

5. Droplets: a low-cost swarm robotics platform for teaching and experimentation. https://robohub.org/droplets-a-low-cost-swarm-robotics-platform-for-teaching-and-experimentation/. Accessed 26 Feb 2019
6. Radchenko, I.A.: Intelligent multi-agent systems. Tutorial, p. 88. BSTU, SPb (2006)
7. Kozhemyakin, I., Ryzhov, V., Semenov, N., Chemodanov, M.: Investigation of influence of connection speed and distance between elements of the multiagent network of underwater robots on its sustainability to the change of working conditions. Izvestiya YuFU. Tekhnicheskie nauki [Izvestiya SFedU. Eng. Sci.] 1(195), 227–241 (2018)
8. Kanakia, A., Touri, B., Correll, N.: Modeling multi-robot task allocation with limited information as global game. Swarm Intell. 10(2), 147–160 (2016)
9. Caprari, G., Balmer, P., Piguet, R., Siegwart, R.: The autonomous micro robot "alice": a platform for scientific and commercial applications. In: Proceedings of the 1998 international symposium on paper presented at the micromechatronics and human science. MHS 1998 (1998)
10. Michel, O.: Webots: professional mobile robot simulation. Int. J. Adv. Robot. Syst. 1(1), 39–42 (2004)
11. Carpin, S., Lewis, M., Wang, J., Balakirsky, S., Scrapper, C.: USARSim: a robot simulator for research and education. In: Proceedings of the IEEE Conference on Robotics and Automation (ICRA), pp. 1400–1405. IEEE Press, Piscataway (2007)
12. Koenig, N., Howard, A.: Design and use paradigms for Gazebo, an open-source multi-robot simulator. In: Proceedings of the IEEE/RSJ International Conference on Intelligent Robots and Systems (IROS), pp. 2149–2154. IEEE Press, Piscataway (2004)
13. Friedman, M.: Simulation of autonomous robot teams with adaptable levels of abstraction. Ph.D. dissertation, Technische Universitat, Darmstadt (2010)
14. Pinciroli, C., et al.: ARGoS: a modular, multi-engine simulator for heteroge-neous swarm robotics. In: IROS, pp. 5027–5034 (2011)
15. Arvin, F., Samsudin, K., Ramli, A.R.: Development of a miniature robot for swarm robotic application. Int. J. Comput. Electr. Eng. 1(4), 422–436 (2009)
16. Bewley, T.R., Strawson, J., Briggs, H.C.: Leveraging open standards and credit-card-sized Linux computers in embedded control and robotics education. In: AIAA, pp. 2015–0801. SciTech, Kissimmee (2015)
17. Marvelmind Robotics. Precise (±2 cm) Indoor GPS: For Autonomous Robots, Copters and VR. https://marvelmind.com/. Accessed 26 Feb 2019
18. Romero-Ramirez, F.J., Muñoz-Salinas, R., Medina-Carnicer, R.: Speeded up detection of squared fiducial markers. Image Vis. Comput. 76, 38–47 (2018)
19. Garrido-Jurado, S., Muñoz Salinas, R., Madrid-Cuevas, F.J., Medina-Carnicer, R.: Generation of fiducial marker dictionaries using mixed integer linear programming. Pattern Recognit. 51, 481–491 (2016)
20. Drawing maps with robots, OpenCV, and Raspberry Pi. https://medium.com/@cadanderson/drawing-maps-with-robots-opencv-and-raspberry-pi-3389fa05b90f. Accessed 26 Feb 2019

Mathematical and Algorithmic Model for Local Navigation of Mobile Platform and UAV Using Radio Beacons

Alexander Denisov$^{(\boxtimes)}$ (ID), Roman Iakovlev (ID), and Igor Lebedev (ID)

St. Petersburg Institute for Informatics and Automation of the Russian Academy of Sciences (SPIIRAS), 14th Line, 39, 199178 St. Petersburg, Russia
sdenisov93@mail.ru

Abstract. Robots are used to solve routine, monotonous, difficult and dangerous tasks; therefore, agriculture is one of the largest spheres for using robotic systems. One of the main problems faced by developers of autonomous robotic systems is the navigation of the robot in space. This paper presents a solution to the problem of navigation, based on the maintenance of a constant radio signal between the UAV or mobile platform and control system. Radio communication is maintained by building a mesh network based on LoRa data transmission technology modules throughout the entire path of the robot. Navigation system is a mesh network based on the radio beacon. Three methods for determining the coordinates of additional module location were considered. These methods are intended for organizing mush network from modules that are not connected to each other. Analysis of considered methods was presented. Methods are not designed for arbitrary movement of robotic systems. Each of the presented methods has its advantages and disadvantages, the first two methods have the main advantage being the smallest number of modules used to connect all radio modules to the network, but with a decrease in the number of modules there is a problem of reducing system reliability. The third method solves this problem by clustering and can withstand the failure of a large number of additional modules, and the system itself becomes more like a mesh network.

Keywords: Robot navigation · LoRa · Radio communication · Mesh network

1 Introduction

Robotic systems are actively integrated in agriculture domain. Farmlands occupy dozens of hectares; such large areas are difficult to navigate and maintain communication with the robots across the fields [1–3]. As a universal solution of these problems, it is proposed to use wireless data transmission technologies and combine radio modules into a mesh network, since this network topology enables communication between wireless data transmission modules over long distances and is secured from communication outages when network elements fail. LoRa was chosen as a data transmission technology due to the large range, wide bandwidth, security of the data transfer protocol and low cost of radio modules. Analysis of scientific papers regarding beacon-based robotic systems navigation was carried out.

© Springer Nature Switzerland AG 2019
A. Ronzhin et al. (Eds.): ICR 2019, LNAI 11659, pp. 53–62, 2019.
https://doi.org/10.1007/978-3-030-26118-4_6

High-precision and low-power systems that combine LoRa and RTK DGNSS are presented in [4]. The authors of the aforementioned work have designed their own mobile node, fully powered by solar energy. The paper presents the experimental results, showing the practical benefits of LoRa with RTK for data exchange between the base station and the rover to improve accuracy to the centimeter range.

In [5], a system is presented, which uses a three-dimensional cloud of points for the reconstruction of environment as a triangular grid in real time mode. Then this navigation grid is analyzed for irregularity and terrain and is used for online path planning. The authors tested this approach on the VolksBot XT robotic platform in a real environment.

In [6], a navigation system for autonomous indoor robots was developed. Robotic systems employ custom programmable radio beacons (programmable RadioFrequency beacons). Radio beacons are mutually interconnected into a mesh network, through which the movement and location of the robotic system is tracked. The authors of the paper demonstrated a use case an of an applied scenario of the developed navigation system and the results of testing the system on a robot. The experimental results presented in the paper showed short response time when tracking the correct path from the source node to the destination node and sending it back to the source node to initiate the navigation process. These outcomes confirm the efficiency of the system and its fitness for real time operation.

The paper [7] provides an overview of a wireless navigation system without using any external positioning systems, particularly GPS. The proposed navigation system builds on Bluetooth-like technologies and MANET protocols optimization. The developed system is aimed to provide navigation capabilities for unmanned robots (vehicles) in dangerous conditions, when external positioning resources become completely unavailable. The proposed system is difficult to scale, but features an extensive application range, such as search and rescue, surveillance, etc.

The work [8] describes the development and fabrication of an autonomous mobile robot that uses an RFID system to ensure the movement of the vehicle under known conditions along a predefined route. For this purpose, special software was developed and tested, which allows controlling the robot and efficient interaction with computer and, possibly, other robots.

The works considered above, as well as [9–15], detail algorithms and methods for robot navigation and spatial organization of mesh networks with full radio communication. But the above works do not consider the options for building a network of wireless data transmission modules located too far from each other to maintain two-way radio communication. This paper discusses methods for connecting additional radio modules and building a mesh network of arbitrarily located LoRa radio modules for organizing communication and navigation of a mobile platform and a UAV in agriculture.

2 Calculation of the Radio Signal Range

According to ITU-R P.341-5 (10/99) «The concept of transmission loss for radio links» and ITU-R P.372-9 (08/07) «Radio interference (recommendations of the ITU-R P series - Radio wave propagation», there are many factors to consider, and the figure illustrates only a small part of them. The radio signal weakening can occur not only because of interference from other radio devices or losses in empty space, but also due to increased humidity, vegetation, solar and even stellar activity, etc. Consequently, the solution of specific applied problems of radio wave propagation in real world is an extremely complex, multifaceted problem, strict representation of which is possible only in a very limited number of cases. Therefore, to build a navigation mesh network model, we decided to use ready mathematical solutions to calculate the propagation of radio waves.

The mathematical formulas, describing the propagation of radio waves were taken using the Friis equation [16] (1) and distance equation [17] (2)

$$\frac{P_R}{P_T} = \frac{G_T G_R \lambda^2}{(4\pi R)^2}, \tag{1}$$

$$R = \frac{3 \cdot 10^8}{4\pi F} \cdot 10^{\frac{P_T + G_T + L_T + G_R + L_R + |V|\, dB - P_R}{20}}, \tag{2}$$

where R is the target communication range in meters; F is the frequency in Hz; PT is the transmitter power in dBm; GT is the transmitter antenna gain in dB; LT is the cable loss to the transmitter antenna in dB; GR is the receiver antenna gain in dB; LR is the cable loss to the receiver antenna in dB; PR is the sensitivity of the radio receiver in dBm; | V | dB - attenuation factor, taking into account additional losses due to the influence of the Earth's surface, vegetation, atmosphere and other factors in dB.

Since these equations give an approximate value of the radio signal range, a comparison was made between the results obtained from the selected equations and the experimental results, obtained with ESP-32 LoRa modules. The experiment consisted of measuring the receiver sensitivity using the software supplied with the ESP-32 LoRa in urban conditions on a high traffic road at distances of 50, 100, 300, 500 and 600 m. As stated by Heltec, the SX125x LoRa chip used on the ESP-32 LoRa module, in direct view, provides communication at a distance of up to 3 km [18], but during tests in urban conditions, due to high noise, only data at a distance of 600 m was obtained. In this case, the receiver and transmitter were located at the same height of 2 m and were in direct line of sight relative to each other. Characteristics of the ESP-32 LoRa module are presented in Table 1.

The Fig. 1 shows the results of the calculation and measurement of the ratio of the receiver sensitivity to the distance between the modules.

In the figure, the experimental data are indicated by a line labeled Test dist., the results of the Friis equation are labeled 1 eq dist., the results of equation [17] are labeled 2 eq dist.

Table 1. Characteristics of the ESP-32 LoRa module.

The name of the characteristic	Characteristic value	
Frequency, F	433 MHz	
Transmitter Power, P_T	13 dBm	
	Speed	Sensitivity
	1.2 kbps	-121 dBm
Receiver sensitivity, P_R	4.8 kbps	-117 dBm
	38.4 kbps	-108 dBm
	250 kbps	-95 dBm
Transmitter antenna gain, G_T	2.2 dB	
Receiver Antenna Gain, G_R	2.2 dB	
Cable loss in transmitter, L_T	2.2 dB	
Loss in receiver cable, L_R	2.2 dB	

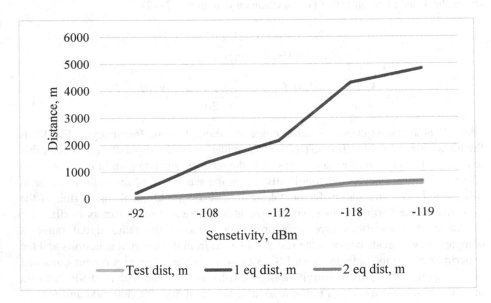

Fig. 1. The ratio of receiver sensitivity to distance.

It is clear from the figure that Eq. 2 most precisely approximates actual data, since the variable uses the "attenuation multiplier" variable | V | dB, which takes into account additional losses due to the influence of the Earth's surface, vegetation, atmosphere and other factors. Therefore, it is practical to use this formula for building a model of the navigation mesh network.

3   Network Mesh Algorithms

In this paper, we consider the task of mesh network establishment, based on the radio beacons, enabling robotic system navigation. Consider organizing a mesh network of radio modules that are not connected to each other because of large initial distance between them. To solve this problem, some methods were developed to determine the location coordinates of additional modules, repeating instructions for connecting disparate modules into a single network.

The first method is based on the creation of a common central line of modules for transmitting data from the periphery to the gateway. The method is presented in Fig. 2.

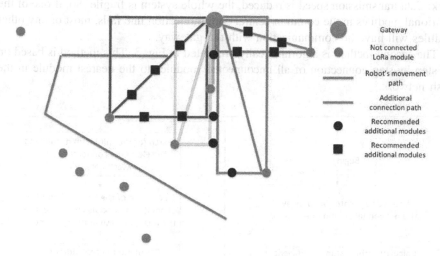

Fig. 2. Method 1 "Central Communication Line".

Figure 2 shows the connection of only 5 modules to the gateway; so we avoid cluttering and keep the diagram clear. So as not to clutter up the drawing. The method consists in building additional communication lines through two right triangles, whereas the hypotenuse of each of them illustrates a direct connection between an unconnected module and the gateway. Further the communication lines allow calculating the location of additional modules, since the distance between the modules to maintain the required data transfer rate is calculated by the formula 2. From the obtained data, a common central communication line, indicated by black dots, is constructed, and for remote modules two connection options are offered (indicated by black squares): directly with the gateway and with the central communication line. One of the options is chosen from the tasks: reducing the number of additional modules or increasing the speed of data transmission to the gateway. Also, the location of additional modules for UAVs and mobile platforms is calculated. In the considered task, the paths of movement of the UAV and the mobile platform are known in advance. Therefore, it is proposed to divide the path into sections, each equal to the distance calculated by formula 2. At the boundaries of the calculated areas it is proposed to set additional wireless communication modules for continuous communication with the mobile platform and UAVs. Further, depending on the task, each of the additional radio modules is connected to the central communication line or directly to the gateway, or, which is much more efficient and less expensive. The modules are connected to each other in a network and this network is further connected to the central communication lines, or to the gateway.

The advantages of this method are the simplicity of implementation, which does not require large computing power, a small number of additional modules, the possibility of choosing between minimizing the number of additional modules and increasing the speed of communication with the gateway. Weak points of this solution are: it is not universal one, the resulting connection scheme can be hardly considered a mesh network; data transmission speed is reduced, the whole system is fragile. So, if one of the additional modules in the common central communication line fails, most or any other modules will have no communication with the gateway.

The second method is algorithmically presented in Fig. 3. This method is based on the step-by-step connection of all unconnected modules to the nearest module in the mesh network.

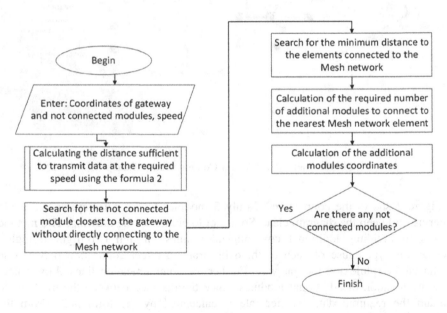

Fig. 3. Algorithm for connecting isolated modules into a network.

The coordinates of the gateway and any modules that need to be connected to the gateway, as well as data transfer rate to be established between the modules, are input data for the algorithm. Further, according to formula 2, using the known sensitivity of the receiver for the corresponding data rate, the maximum distance between the modules is calculated, needed to maintain the required data rate. In the third step, the nearest unconnected module is selected. Next, the distance to the gateway or to the mesh network modules that are connected to the gateway is calculated, and the minimum distance is selected. In the further steps of the algorithm, the number of required additional modules for connecting to the mesh network is calculated, as well their coordinates, and the presence of unconnected modules is checked. Should any unconnected modules remain, the algorithm returns to step 3, conversely, the algorithm terminates. Communication with the UAV and the mobile platform is provided similarly to the pattern, presented in Method 1. The coordinates of the location of additional radio modules are calculated on a known path of movement of robotic systems. The modules are located at a distance sufficient to maintain the required data transfer rate and the chain are connected to each other, forming a network. Next, the calculation of the distance from each network module moving the robotic system to each network mesh module connected to the gateway takes place. At the final step, the minimum distance is selected and the coordinates of the location of the additional modules are calculated.

The advantages of this method are simplicity, minimum number of modules in use, which reduces data transmission delay while communicating to the gateway. The downside of such system is poor reliability and high load on the modules by routing.

In the third method, the results of the second method are used together with clustering. At the beginning, all isolated modules are connected to each other by method 2, the coordinates of additional modules along UAV path and the coordinates of mobile platform are also calculated, while the additional modules along the track of the robotic systems have the same priority in connection to the mesh network as the unconnected modules. Further, all "non-connected" modules are clustered. The number of clusters depends on the tasks assigned for given data transfer rate and on system fault tolerance. security against module failure. Thus, the more reliable system we need, the more non-connected modules should be grouped into additional clusters. In each cluster, a central module is installed, to which all "unconnected" ones are bound; to that end additional modules are installed. The central modules of each cluster communicate with each other and are connected to the gateway. This connection scheme complicates network development, but enables mesh network design, secured from the failure of a large number of radio modules. Method 3 is charted in Fig. 4.

The advantages of this method are a high level of protection of the mesh network from the failure of radio modules, an increase in the speed of data transmission due to centralization in clusters and the possibility of storing routing tables in the central radio module of the cluster, a more universal model, the ability to use for complex systems. Cons: a large number of additional radio modules, which increases the cost of the network and contributes to the deterioration of the quality of communication due to interference from neighboring modules, the complexity of implementation. This method is suitable for large systems, where communication with each unconnected module is in priority, with a large number of unconnected radio modules located at long distances from each other.

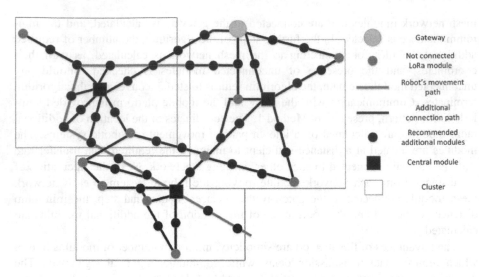

Fig. 4. Mesh clustering method.

4   Conclusion

The developed methods suit well for establishment of a mesh network together with radio modules for connecting all nodes to the network, permanently maintaining communication with the mobile platform and UAVs, and managing their local navigation. Each of the presented methods has certain advantages and disadvantages. The main advantage of the first two methods consists in achieving the smallest number of modules to connect all radio devices to the network. But, decreasing the number of modules we face a problem of reducing system reliability, i.e. if one of the modules fails, the entire system or any part of it may lose connection with the gateway. In terms of the third method this problem is solved by means of clustering, thus the reliability of the system increases. So, depending on the number of clusters, the system can tolerate the failure of a large number of additional modules, and the configuration itself becomes more similar to a mesh network. But when solving the problem using the third method, another complication appears, associated with a large number of radio modules. Such network suffers additional radio interference, communication quality drops, whereas the cost of the entire project increases. Also, these methods show poor performance for arbitrary movement of robotic systems. But you eventually will have to deploy a mesh network throughout the entire work area, that is, establish a radio sensor grid throughout the workspace to provide local navigation and maintenance of radio communication with the mobile platform and the UAV.

Acknowledgement. The present research was partially supported by project No. RFBR 18-58-76001 ERA_a.

References

1. Negrete, M., Savage, J., Contreras-Toledo, L.A.: A motion-planning system for a domestic service robot. SPIIRAS Proc. **5**, 5–38 (2018)
2. Popov, S.G., Zaborovsky, V.S., Kurochkin, L.M., Sharagin, M.P., Zhang, L.: Method of dynamic selection of satellite navigation system in the autonomous mode of positioning. SPIIRAS Proc. **18**(2), 302–325 (2019)
3. Merkulov, V.I., Sadovskiy, P.A.: Estimation of distance and its derivatives in the bistatic passive radar location system. SPIIRAS Proc. **1**, 122–143 (2018)
4. Magno, M., Rickli, S., Quack, J., Brunecker, O., Benini, L.: Combining LoRa and RTK to achieve a high precision self-sustaining geo-localization system. In: Proceedings of the 17th ACM/IEEE International Conference on Information Processing in Sensor Networks, pp. 160–161. IEEE Press (2018)
5. Pütz, S., Wiemann, T., Sprickerhof, J., Hertzberg, J.: 3d navigation mesh generation for path planning in uneven terrain. IFAC-PapersOnLine **49**(15), 212–217 (2016)
6. Rabie, T., Suleiman, S.: A novel wireless mesh network for indoor robotic navigation. In: 2016 5th International Conference on Electronic Devices, Systems and Applications (ICEDSA), pp. 1–4. IEEE (2016)
7. Nykorak, A., Hiromoto, R.E., Sachenko, A., Koval, V.: A wireless navigation system with no external positions. In: 2015 IEEE 8th International Conference on Intelligent Data Acquisition and Advanced Computing Systems: Technology and Applications (IDAACS), vol. 2, pp. 898–901. IEEE (2015)
8. Konieczny, M., Pawłowicz, B., Potencki, J., Skoczylas, M.: Application of RFID technology in navigation of mobile robot. In: 2017 21st European Microelectronics and Packaging Conference (EMPC) & Exhibition, pp. 1–4. IEEE (2017)
9. Malandra, F., Sansò, B.: A Markov-modulated end-to-end delay analysis of large-scale RF-mesh networks with time-slotted ALOHA and FHSS for smart grid applications. IEEE Trans. Wirel. Commun. **17**(11), 7116–7127 (2018)
10. Lavric, A., Popa, V.: Internet of things and LoRa™ low-power wide-area networks: a survey. In: 2017 International Symposium on Signals, Circuits and Systems (ISSCS), pp. 1–5. IEEE (2017)
11. Garrido-Hidalgo, C.: IoT heterogeneous mesh network deployment for human-in-the-loop challenges towards a social and sustainable Industry 4.0. IEEE Access **6**, 28417–28437 (2018)
12. Leon, E., Alberoni, C., Wister, M., Hernández-Nolasco, J.: Flood early warning system by Twitter using LoRa. In: Multidisciplinary Digital Publishing Institute Proceedings, vol. 2, no. 19, p. 1213 (2018)
13. Cagatan, G.K.B., Magsumbol, J.A.V., Baldovino, R., Sybingco, E., Dadios, E.P.: Connectivity analysis of wireless sensor network in two-dimensional plane using Castalia simulator. In: 2017 IEEE 9th International Conference on Humanoid, Nanotechnology, Information Technology, Communication and Control, Environment and Management (HNICEM), pp. 1–8. IEEE (2017)
14. Lavric, A., Popa, V.: A LoRaWAN: long range wide area networks study. In: 2017 International Conference on Electromechanical and Power Systems (SIELMEN), pp. 417–420. IEEE (2017)
15. Barriquello, C.H., et al.: Performance assessment of a low power wide area network in rural smart grids. In: 2017 52nd International Universities Power Engineering Conference (UPEC), pp. 1–4 (2017)

16. SHakhnovich, I.: Mif o zatukhanii svobodnogo prostranstva: chego ne pisal GT Friis [The Myth about Free Space Damping: What didn't GT write Friis]. Pervaya milya [First Mile] **2**, 40–45 (2014). (in Russian)
17. Kalinin, A.I., CHerenkova, E.L.: Rasprostranenie radiovoln i rabota radiolinij [The propagation of radio waves and the work of radio lines]. Svyaz'. Moskva [Connection Moscow] (1971). (in Russian)
18. Heltec Automation: WiFi LoRa 32. http://www.heltec.cn/project/wifi-lora-32/?lang=en. Accessed 01 Apr 2019

Review on Human–Robot Interaction During Collaboration in a Shared Workspace

Rinat Galin and Roman Meshcheryakov[✉]

V.A. Trapeznikov Institute of Control Sciences of Russian Academy of Sciences,
Moscow 117997, Russian Federation
rinat.r.galin@yandex.ru, mrv@ieee.org

Abstract. Collaboration humans and robots in close proximity in a shared workspace is a stimulating feature of Industry 4.0. Collaborative robotics solution provides for the production processes the benefits due to the characteristic properties of robots. These properties include high level of accuracy, speed and repeatability. In combination with the flexibility and cognitive skills of humans the process of human-robot interaction achieves an efficient human-robot collaboration. Today's topical issue research include problems of developing safer robots in human-machine systems. In considering the issue of safety human-robot interaction should be taken into account regulations and standards. A key challenge of human-robot collaboration is deciding how to distribute functions between human and robot to provide efficient interaction. This paper is a review on history of the robotic automation and modern research including Russian experience.

Keywords: Robotic automation · Collaborative robots · Cooperation · Coexistence · Human-robot collaboration · Safety · Efficient interaction

1 Introduction

Robotics in the modern world is one of the most important areas, the field of applications which is developing rapidly for year by year. The robotic automation process take place. It means system and process automation, when there is no need for human labor, and it is replaced by its automated version [1–3].

The robots design was preceded by the idea to replace a human in heavy work. A prototype for robots served as the physical capabilities of human. Over time, humanity began to entrust routine and hard work to computer algorithms. Today, the use of robots in the modern world is no surprise. Medicine, space, security systems, production, household and entertainment – these are the areas of human life, which is associated with the process of robotization.

The growing trend of the introduction of an increasing number of robotic equipment in the industry due to the high economic indicators: the quality and efficiency of the working process.

Today, the main area of use (application) of robots in the world remains industry (industrial and service robots). The first wave of robotics production in USSR began in the late 60 s: the first industrial robot "Universal-50" was created and after

A. Ronzhin et al. (Eds.): ICR 2019, LNAI 11659, pp. 63–74, 2019.
https://doi.org/10.1007/978-3-030-26118-4_7

few years first soviet robots were presented at the different exhibitions. Soviet engineers planned to introduce robotics in almost all areas of production: engineering, metallurgy, construction, agriculture, mining, light and food industries. In total, the Soviet Union produced more than a hundred thousand units of industrial robots and robotics solutions which later replaced more than a million workers [4].

2 Intelligent Robotic Systems of New Generation – Cobots

The robotic world going to achieve the position of comprehensive application of robots both in production and in everyday life. In some cases, they can completely replace a human. However, there are a number of jobs where they cannot replace human at all, but robots can speed up the production process. In such cases, robots have to work closely with people. Robots need to learn how to work with people together, distributing functions among themselves, allowing the creative potential of a person to manifest itself, not to waste time on monotonous activities to avoid difficult and dangerous moments of the working process. The use of robots in human life has great potential, so the interaction between humans and robots will eventually become closer.

Modern industrial robotic systems are used to save money and increase productivity. The robot has a number of limitations, such as load capacity, reach area, the need to pre-program each movement. Despite this, with proper operation, the manipulator is able to improve the quality and efficiency of the working process and provide production with a number of advantages:

- Improving productivity and quality of products or services: 24/7 work and without breaks and downtime, precise execution of complex technical operations at high speed.
- Fast return on investment. Replacing human labor, the robot significantly reduces the cost of specialists. There is no need to pay the wages for overtime work day and night, sick leave and vacation.
- Minimize workspace and service.
- Flexibility in system reconfiguration.
- Reducing the impact of harmful production factors on humans.

Automation of workplace processes looks like this: for each 10 automated workplaces will be one more workplace for job like programmer, designer, service or learning [5].

Over time, robotic automation became main part of human activity. Moreover, this arose a complex problem of human-robot interaction. At the junction of the solution of this problem, a new direction in robotics has appeared – collaborative robot (cobot) [3, 13].

The concept of cobot has undergone a number of changes due to the development of new technologies in the field of robotics. The term "collaborative robot" have applied to industrial manipulators in originally and the first used as part of a General Motors research project and it meant – "A robot that works with a human hand in hand" [6, 7].

International Organization for Standardization relates the modern understanding of the collaborative robot to the accepted requirements of international standards, and in particular to the satisfaction of technical specifications ISO/TS 15066:2016 [8]. According to these technical specification cobot is a robot designed for direct inter-action with a human within a certain joint space, subject to safety measures [9].

The following items will help you to understand the differences between cobots and other robotic solutions [8, 10, 11, 14, 15]:

- *Ability to interact safely with a human.* Industrial robots perform operations in accordance with a given program without taking into account the people working next to them. In order to prevent injuries when working with them, special fences and photo barriers are installing in work place. The collaborative robots designed specifically to work with people. When using them, no protective barriers are required. Cobots help to solve complex tasks that could not automated at full. For example, cobots pass parts to workers who then perform assembly or quality control operations.
- *Risk reduction in the implementation of hazardous tasks.* Collaborative robots perform operations that pose a risk to humans. These risks include a safety trans-portation of sharp and sharpened or hot items, tightening of bolts, etc. At this time, specialists can focus on less complex aspects of production.
- *Flexibility and learning.* Control of industrial robots requires special programming skills. Programming collaborative robots is easier. Some robots are capable of self-learning. For example, it is necessary to show such robot any movement and it is accurate to repeat it. Thus, employees can easily reprogram collaborative robots and use them to solve a variety of tasks.
- *Possibility of wide use and quick adjustment.* Collaborative robots are not only easy to reprogram, but also relatively easy to move and use at other points in the production chain. Many models of robots can be installing on any surface – hori-zontal, vertical and even on the ceiling. Often such automation solutions are quite easy and can be moving by only one person.

Modern robots no longer need enclosing perimeters, they become intelligent and flexible. There is a transition from cooperation and coexistence to collaboration. Now the usual understanding of robotics is identifying in the concept of socio-cyber physical systems. A human and a robot become partners, mutually reinforcing when working in a single workspace. Working in workplace is not only sequential, but also parallel. Collaborative robots bring automation where it was not before.

3   Human-Robot Interaction During Collaboration

Considering human-robot interaction (HRI), you should understand the taxonomy of human-robot interaction. Taxonomies of human-robot interaction, cooperation and collaboration proposed in these works [15, 17–19]. The main scenarios of human-robot interaction were showing on Fig. 1. Taxonomic classification for the level of shared interaction among agents can have one of eight following values [17]: one human – one robot (cobot); one human – robot (cobot) team; one human – multiple robots (cobots);

human team – one robot (cobot); multiple humans – one robot (cobot); human team – robot (cobot) team; human team – multiple robots (cobots) and multiple humans – robot (cobot) team.

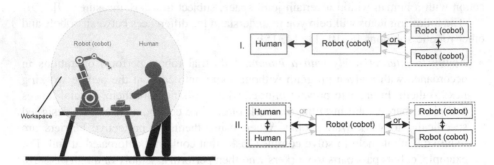

Fig. 1. The values of taxonomic classification for the level of shared interaction between human (s) and robot(s) during collaboration.

There is an important aspect related to human safety in HRI. First, human safety is providing by international standards and regulations. In HRI to the following take into account: the harm caused by the collision of a human and a robot, the psychophysiological effect of contact with a robot, not a safe approach to the robot in the workspace, setting robot's sensors and the correctness of the control algorithms of the robotic system. The development of a perfect taxonomy of standards will continue as the technology improves. It should assume that the period when the peak of technological progress will never come due to the complexity of knowledge of human nature and the limitless of his consciousness.

Next, consider the classification of safety standards and collaborative modes in human-robot collaboration (HRC) that developed and actuality for this time.

3.1   Standard Classification for Safety Human-Robot Collaboration

The purpose of the standards [8, 16] is to increase the interoperability of robots and their components, reduce the cost of their development and maintenance through standardization and harmonization of processes, interfaces and parameters.

This article discusses the international standards and their comparative analogues for the Russian Federation. Basic legislation in robotics area including classification of robots and spheres of their application, determining rights and duties of various subjects of relationships, grounds and procedure for accounting or registration of robot models and criteria of relating robots to sources of increased danger have been described in [29]. These regulations contribute to the system integration of safety measures in robotic systems for HRC.

The shared workspace not only does it involve the human and the robot but also other auxiliary devices like work table, electric screwdrivers, work tools etc. It means that safety needs to be address in an integrated manner for HRC.

Classification of General Safety Standards. Table 1 reports a review of general safety standards for robotic solutions classified three categories [15]. This helps to understand the basic legal framework of safety for human-robot interaction during collaboration.

Table 1. Review of general safety standards by types with description.

Type	Title	Description
A	ISO 12100	General principles for design. Risk assessment and risk reduction. Terminology and methodology
	IEC 61508	Functional safety of electrical, electronic, programmable electronic safety-related systems. General requirements
B		
B1	ISO 13849-1	Safety-related parts of control systems. Part 1. General principles for design. Specific safety aspects
	IEC 62061	Functional safety of electrical, electronic, programmable electronic safety-related systems
B2	ISO 13850	Emergency stop function - Principles for design
	ISO 13851	Two-hand control devices. Functional aspects and design principles
C	ISO 10218	Safety requirements for industrial robots
	ISO 10218-1, 2	Safety requirements for industrial robots: Part 1 – safety requirements for robot manufacturers (robot and controller). Part 2 – describes the basic hazards and hazardous situations identified with these systems, and provides requirements to eliminate or adequately reduce the risks associated with these hazards
	ISO TS 15066	Specifies safety requirements for collaborative industrial robot systems and the work environment, and supplements the requirements and guidance on collaborative industrial robot operation given in ISO 10218 1 and ISO 10218 2

This classification is not a complete description of safety standards. There are more than 700 different standards and regulations.

Collaborative modes. The main modes of a collaborative robot joint work that meet the technical specification of ISO/TS 15066 and ISO 10218-1, 2 [8–11, 16] are as follows:

- "Safety-rated monitored stop" – robot stops when human-operator enters the collaborative workspace and continues when workspace free (allows for direct operator interaction with the robot system under specific circumstances);
- "Hand guiding" – robot movements are controlled by human-operator (operator uses a hand-operated device to transmit motion commands);
- "Speed and separation monitoring" – operator and robot system may move concurrently in the collaborative workspace;

- "Power and force limiting" – contact forces between human-operator and moving robot are technically limited to safe level (physical contact between the robot system and a human-operator can occur either intentionally or unintentionally).

The organization of effective interaction between a person and cobot at work may have certain risks of harming both the person and the robot. Let us consider the risks presented in Table 2 that have described in detail in [10, 20].

Table 2. List of potential risks of hazardous from human-robot interaction during collaboration.

Type of risk of hazardous	Description
Risk of hazardous from robot	*Special attention is paid to*: • distance between human operator and robot in collaborative workspace; • trajectory traversed by the robot and obstacles in the path of the robot; • the speed of movement of the human operator and the slow response of the robot; • psycho-physiological state of a human operator
Risk of hazardous from the industrial process	*Special attention is paid to*: • the duration of the process and the transition from one action to the next; • lack of ergonomic solutions for operating activities and maintenance; • the complexity of the task in the collaborative work space; • human-operator influence
Risk of hazardous from robot control system malfunction	*Special attention is paid to*: • error of the human operator during the operation of the robot and at the time of completion of operational actions; • creating obstacles for the functioning of the robot sensors; • malfunction at the control level and impact on the control system from the outside (cyber-attack)

The above list of possible harm to the human health of the operator and his safety is comparable to the current level of organized human-machine interaction. For safe and effective interaction, collaborative robots should be equipped with integrated programs and additional sensors that will allow them to analyse, understand and predict human intentions in the collaborative workspace.

3.2 Safety Methods for Human-Robot Interaction During Collaboration

One of the most rapidly growing area of robotics research – is a human-robot interaction during collaboration. Robotic solutions became being in high demand on production and people's lives. Robots sort the goods on the conveyor line, preparing food in restaurants, carrying parcels in warehouse, taking part in rescue operations. The use of robots has no boundaries. However, there is an important issue to consider when developing robotic solutions – it is safe human-robot interaction.

In 1942, science fiction writer Asimov I. proposed three "Laws of Robotics" [21]:

1. First Law – A robot may not injure a human being or, through inaction, allow a human being to come to harm.
2. Second Law – A robot must obey the orders given it by human beings except where such orders would conflict with the First Law.
3. Third Law – A robot must protect its own existence as long as such protection does not conflict with the First or Second Laws.

Based on these laws, we can conclude that there are two distinct ways, in which a robot could inflict harm on a human being. They are - direct physical contact and psychological harm. The main causes of harm considered at list of potential risks of hazardous from HRI during collaboration (Table 2).

Next, the focus is on the major methods of providing safety in HRI. Researchers from MIT and NASA have done much work in this direction. The analysis of research works showed the actual division of methods for safety HRI during collaboration following to next directions [12, 13, 19].

Safety HRI during collaboration through control. Safety methods for HRI is through low-level control of robot motion. This type of safety is consider the simplest method of enabling safe human-robot coexistence. There are two ways of control methods for improving safety: before and after collision. In literature they also divisible into two categories: pre- and post-collision. Pre-collision control methods means to detect the danger before the human-robot collision during collaboration by monitoring either the human, the robot, or both of them. Post-collision control methods mean quickly detection the collusion after contact HRI and minimize harm to both of the human and the robot.

Table 3. Major methods of providing safety in HRI during collaboration

Methods	Subset	Details/Description
Pre-collusion	Quantitative limits	limiting a variety of parameters
	Speed and separation monitoring	Safety zones and separation distance
		Non-intrusive, real-time measurement
	Potential field methods	Human factors
		Robot features
Post-collusion	Collusion detection, localization and reaction	Non-collaboration contact
		Collaborative contact
		Evaluation
	Interactive control methods	Detection of collaborative intent
		Interaction strategies

The various approaches of pre- and post-collision methods are described on Table 3.

Quantitative limits a major subset of pre-collusion category that focused on providing quantitative guarantees that a robot cannot pose any threat to a human. This can be achieved by limiting a variety of parameters, such as the robot's joint velocity, energy, or potential exertion of force [21, 22]. In subset Speed and separation monitoring describes about slowing down or stopping the robot through the use of safety zones in workspace or distance of separation is another method of preventing collision through control in HRI during collaboration. Another method of prevention human-robot collusion is calculation of danger criteria and fields. For example, safety behaviors by defining a field of repulsive vectors that guide the robot's motion, modifying its trajectory in response to dynamically changing environmental factors. Usually, potential field approach used as a part of integrated safety frameworks.

In real tasks on production to aim a goal HRC can't reach without a certain level of physical contact. Thus, research in the field of post-collision became actually. It is necessary to develop a collision detection system for a prototype variable stiffness actuator that does not require torque sensing. An active reaction impulse that simultaneously moves the cobot arm and reduces its stiffness to allow the arm to gently bounce away from the human-robot collision and come to a stop. The research method consists in the study of external forces to limit torques and prevent exertion of force beyond a specified threshold. This method was worked out in an experiment on the condition when a person pushes a robot and when a person interferes with the robot [23]. Due important purpose of the method is to detect intentional or unintentional contact collisions. When intentional contact is detected, special safety measures and methodologies. Another than the "detection and response" paradigm are required: instead of simply moving away from the collision or switching control methods to minimize harm, the cobot take into account intention of the person and continue supporting interaction during collaboration. As interaction scenarios become increasingly complex, the ability to detect whether human-robot contact is intentional or accidental is a key to selecting an appropriate method to ensure safe interaction.

Overall, pre- and post-collision control methods have been shown as an effective approach for safe HRI during collaboration. In general, these methods do not require complex models of the environment and, in some cases, require limited or no tracking of the human. This quality improves robustness, as these approaches do not necessary to potentially faulty models.

Movement and prediction planning in HRI during collaboration. Providing safety interaction for human-robot interaction during collaboration in real-time can help to prevent harm to human and cobot. Pre-collision and post-collision techniques helps to prevent the cause and implication of collisions, but they are may become ineffective in some scenarios. The fact that, in certain scenarios, collision prevention and alleviation through low-level control to lead to poorer safety and efficiency compared with human-aware movement planning. This movement planning that directly consider human presence and motion when computing robot paths and motions. As well as motion planners capable of reasoning on both geometric and task-based constraints and supporting rapid, rescheduling in real-time.

In some HRI during collaboration situations the environment could be quasi-static and simply rely upon rescheduling motions quickly when the movement of human and robot in conflict situation with the initial plan. However, this approach is not appropriate for maintaining safety within more dynamic environments. In this context, motion plans based on a quasi-static assumption quickly become obsolete, and making reliance on rescheduling impractical – particularly if humans and robots are working in close proximity to one another, as there may not be sufficient time to replanning. As a result, the ability to anticipate the actions and movements of members of a human-robot team is critically important for providing safety within dynamic HRI environments during collaboration [12, 24].

Consider the methods of movement and prediction planning in HRI during collaboration in Fig. 2.

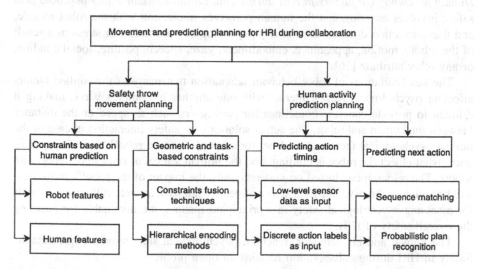

Fig. 2. Diagram depicting the methods of movement and prediction planning for HRI during collaboration. The diagram is built from work Lasota P. [12].

The primary method by which cobot movement planning can serve as a tool for HRI during collaboration is through direct consideration of constraints related to the presence of humans, such as distance of separation, human gaze direction, and robot motion legibility. By minimizing the inertia of the cobot throughout the movement path, the planner ensures that the cobot is already in a safe configuration in the event of an unanticipated collision. In order for cobot movement planning to be an effective method of improving safety in HRI during collaboration, the motion planner must be capable of rapid rescheduling and of taking both geometric and task-based constraints into consideration. On account of dynamic nature of any environment occupied by humans such planners must be able to rapidly recompute new paths and motions.

By predicting, which action a human might take next, cobot movement and activity planners such as those described in "Movement planning in HRI during collaboration" can identify actions and paths that will result in safe and efficient interaction.

The basis of human movement prediction can be divide into two distinct categories: goal intent and movement characteristics. For the former, action prediction can often serve to inform movement-level prediction by inferring humans' goals, which, in combination with an appropriate motion model, can be used to anticipate how a human will move. In the latter category instead utilizes techniques such as analysis of biomechanical predictors or reasoning on features of natural motion [25].

Furthermore, also utilize control-based safety methods, such as those highlighted in "Safety HRI during collaboration through control", as a safeguard against incorrect predictions.

Human psychological factors in HRI during collaboration. Maintaining psychological safety involves ensuring that the human perceives interaction with the robot as safe, and that interaction does not lead to any psychological discomfort or stress as a result of the robot's motion, appearance, embodiment, gaze, speech, posture, social conduct, or any other attribute [26].

The key limitations of robot behavior adaptation that many of the studied factors affecting psychological safety interact with one another in complex ways, making it difficult to provide concrete guidelines for parameters such as speed or the distance between the human and robot. The actual solutions for safety interaction in case of the human psychological factors should be, for example, can be robot's size and appearance, what object the robot is holding, and the human's level of prior experience with robots. The research conducted on understanding the impact of the robot's movement and behavior on the psychological safety of nearby humans, as well as the various tools for assessing psychological safety in a principled manner, are invaluable for ensuring the overall safety of HRI.

The human and his behavior, reaction, psychological state remain unpredictable. Safety in HRI during collaboration remains an open problem.

4   Conclusions and Future Work

In the future work, the development of collaborative robotics will be express by the close interaction of human and robot (cobot). In such conditions, the working space of the robot will intersect with the personal space of a person. To ensure a safe and effective interaction between a human operator and a robot(s), it is necessary to consider a complex task with a multitude of factors influencing the performance of production tasks. Industry 4.0 changes the structure of production processes, and human becomes the center of the human-robot system. Thanks to the emerging favorable conditions, cobots will become significantly smarter, demonstrate the benefits of reliable and safety cooperation, and increase the productivity and efficiency of performing tasks.

The purpose of the subsequent research will be to determine the maximum positive effect of the interaction between humans and the collaborative robot in a collaborative working environment [27, 28].

Acknowledgements. The reported study was partially funded by RFBR according to the research project № 19-08-00331.

References

1. Mihelj, M., et al.: Robotics, Chapter 12 - Collaborative Robots, pp. 173–187 (2019). https://doi.org/10.1007/978-3-319-72911-4_12
2. Bondareva, N.: The state and prospects of development of robotics in Russia and the world. Homepage. https://cyberleninka.ru/article/n/sostoyanie-i-perspektivy-razvitiya-robotizatsii-v-mire-i-rossii. Accessed 10 Mar 2019
3. Ermishin, K., Yuschenko, A.: Collaborative mobile robots - a new stage of development of service robotics. J. Robot. Tech. Cybern. 3(12), 3–9 (2016)
4. Molchalov, D.: How the advent of industrial robotics has forever changed the usual approach to production. Intelligent robot systems. 1 (2016)
5. Aaltonen, I., Salmi, T., Marstio, I.: Refining levels of collaboration to support the design and evalution of human-robot interaction in the manufacturing industry. Procedia CIRP 72, 93–98 (2018)
6. Pervez, A., Ryu, J.: Safe physical human robot interaction–past, present and future. J. Mech. Sci. Technol. 22, 469–483 (2008)
7. Robot or cobot: The five key differences. Hannover Messe, 18 October 2016. Homepage. http://www.hannovermesse.de/en/news/robot-or-cobot-the-five-key-differences.xhtml. Accessed 11 Apr 2019
8. ISO/TC 299 Robotics – "ISO/TS 15066:2016 Robots and robotic devices – Collaborative robots". Homepage. https://www.iso.org/standard/62996.html. Accessed 11 Apr 2019
9. Lazarte, M.: Robots and humans can work together with new ISO guidance. Homepage. https://www.iso.org/news/2016/03/Ref2057.html. Accessed 13 Apr 2018
10. Khalid, A., Kirisci, P., Ghrairi, Z., Thoben, K-D., Pannek, J.: Towards implementing safety and security concepts for human-robot collaboration in the context of Industry 4.0. In: 39th International MATADOR Conference on Advanced Manufacturing, pp. 0–7 (2017)
11. Robla-Gomez, S., et al.: Working together: a review on safe human-robot collaboration in industrial environments. IEEE Access 5, 26754–26773 (2017)
12. Lasota, P., Fong, T., Shah, J.: A survey of methods for safe human-robot interaction. Found. Trends Robot. 5(4), 261–349 (2014). https://doi.org/10.1561/2300000052
13. Colgate, J., Wannasuphoprasit, W., Peshkin, M.: Cobots: robots for collaboration with human operators. Proc. Int. Mech. Eng. Congr. Exhib. 58, 433–439 (1996)
14. Djuric, A., Urbanic, R., Rickli, J.: A framework for collaborative robot (cobot) in- tegration in advanced manufacturing systems. SAE Int. J. Mater Manuf. 9, 457–464 (2016)
15. Villani, V., Pini, F., Leali, F., Secchi, C.: Survey on human–robot collaboration in industrial settings: safety, intuitive interfaces and applications. Mechatronics 55, 248–266 (2018). https://doi.org/10.1016/j.mechatronics.2018.02.009
16. ISO 10218-1, 2:2011 "Robots and robotic devices – Safety requirements for industrial robots – Part 1, 2: Robot systems and integration", Geneva (2011)

17. Yanco, H., Drury, J.: Classifying human-robot interaction: an updated taxonomy. In: Proceedings of the IEEE International Conference Systems, Man and Cybernetics (SMC). vol. 3, pp. 2841–2846, IEEE (2004)

18. De Luca, A., Flacco, F.: Integrated control for HRI: Collision avoidance, detection, reaction and collaboration. In: Proceedings of the IEEE RAS & EMBS International Conference Biomedical Robotics and Biomechatronics (BioRob). IEEE; pp. 288–295 (2012)

19. Geravand, M., Flacco, F., De Luca, A.: Human–robot physical interaction and collaboration using an industrial robot with a closed control architecture. In: Proceedings of the IEEE International Conference Robotics and Automation (ICRA). IEEE; pp. 4000–4007 (2013)

20. Bragança, S., Costa, E., Castellucci, I., Arezes, P.: A brief overview of the use of collaborative robots in Industry 4.0: human role and safety. Wandel Durch Partizipation, pp. 641–650 (2019)

21. Asimov, I.: Runaround. In: Astounding Science Fiction (1942)

22. Broquere, D.S., Herrera-Aguilar, I.: Soft motion trajectory planner for service manipulator robot. In: Proceedings of IROS, pp. 2808–2813 (2008)

23. Vick, D., et al.: Safe physical human-robot interaction with industrial dual-arm robots. In: Proceedings of International Workshop on Robot Motion and Control (RoMoCo), pp. 264–269 (2013)

24. De Santis, A., Siciliano, B., De Luca, A., Bicchi, A.: An atlas of physical human–robot interaction. Mech. Mach. Theory 43(3), 253–270 (2008)

25. Pérez-D'Arpino, C., Shah, J.: Fast target prediction of human reaching motion for cooperative human-robot manipulation tasks using time series classification. In: Proceedings of ICRA (2015)

26. Lasota, P., Shah, J.: Analyzing the effects of human-aware motion planning on close-proximity human-robot collaboration. Hum. Factors 57(1), 21–33 (2015)

27. Chueshev, A., Melekhova, O., Meshcheryakov, R.: Cloud robotic platform on basis of fog computing approach. In: Interactive Collaborative Robotics: Third International Conference, ICR, pp. 34–43 (2018)

28. Zalevsky, A., Osipov, O., Meshcheryakov, R.: Tracking of warehouses robots based on the omnidirectional wheels. In: Interactive Collaborative Robotics: Second International Conference, ICR, pp. 268–274 (2017)

29. Arkhipov, V.V., Naumov, V.B.: Artificial intelligence and autonomous devices in legal context: on development of the first Russian law on robotics. SPIIRAS Proc. 6(55), 46–62 (2017). https://doi.org/10.15622/sp.55.2

A Signal Processing Perspective on Human Gait: Decoupling Walking Oscillations and Gestures

Adrien Gregorj[1,2], Zeynep Yücel[2(✉)], Sunao Hara[2], Akito Monden[2], and Masahiro Shiomi[3]

[1] Grenoble INP Ensimag, 681 Rue de la passerelle, Domaine universitaire, BP 72, 38402 Saint Martin d'Hères, France
adrien.gregorj@grenoble-inp.org

[2] Okayama University, 3-1-1 Tsushima-naka Kita-ku, Okayama 700-8530, Japan
{zeynep,hara,monden}@okayama-u.ac.jp

[3] ATR IRC, 2-2-2 Hikaridai, Keihanna Science City, Kyoto 619-0288, Japan
m-shiomi@atr.jp

Abstract. This study focuses on gesture recognition in mobile interaction settings, i.e. when the interacting partners are walking. This kind of interaction requires a particular coordination, e.g. by staying in the field of view of the partner, avoiding obstacles without disrupting group composition and sustaining joint attention during motion. In literature, various studies have proven that gestures are in close relation in achieving such goals.

Thus, a mobile robot moving in a group with human pedestrians, has to identify such gestures to sustain group coordination. However, decoupling of the inherent -walking- oscillations and gestures, is a big challenge for the robot. To that end, we employ video data recorded in uncontrolled settings and detect arm gestures performed by human-human pedestrian pairs by adopting a signal processing approach. Namely, we exploit the fact that there is an inherent oscillatory motion at the upper limbs arising from the gait, independent of the view angle or distance of the user to the camera. We identify arm gestures as disturbances on these oscillations. In doing that, we use a simple pitch detection method from speech processing and assume data involving a low frequency periodicity to be free of gestures. In testing, we employ a video data set recorded in uncontrolled settings and show that we achieve a detection rate of 0.80.

Keywords: Gesture · Pedestrian · Social robot · Group coordination

1 Introduction and Motivation

Nonverbal communication is a very complex and important part of human-human interaction, which relates facial expressions, postures, gestures etc. [30]. Among those, this study focuses on gestures, which may refer to different actions

© Springer Nature Switzerland AG 2019
A. Ronzhin et al. (Eds.): ICR 2019, LNAI 11659, pp. 75–85, 2019.
https://doi.org/10.1007/978-3-030-26118-4_8

or behaviors in different research fields. Namely, taking a *purely mechanical standpoint*, gestures can be defined as the deployment of -upper- limbs in interaction. On the contrary, taking a *social signal processing standpoint*, gestures can be dealt in regard to their implications [9][1]. Nevertheless, irrespective of the definition (being expressive or not), some of the most prominent body parts in gesture portrayal emerge as hands and arms [12].

Therefore, hand and arm gestures are studied in human-robot interaction (HRI) in a long time [3,20,26]. Specifically, human-robot collaboration treats gestures in a cooperation scenario. For instance, [27] examines common hand configurations of co-workers for ultimately building robots that work in collaboration with humans. Similar to [27], most human-robot collaboration studies address face-to-face communication in stationary settings (e.g. assembly line).

In this respect, we address a complex and dynamical interaction setting in a continuously evolving environment. Namely, we consider an outdoor scenario, where a robot-human pair interacts while walking. Such an interaction requires a complex coordination, where the peers stay in each other's field of view, avoid obstacles without breaking group composition and sustain their joint attention [5].

For achieving these goals, gestures are regarded to serve very useful [34]. Namely, Yucel et. al. demonstrate that pedestrian groups, which perform gestures along with their interaction, move in closer proximity, with a lower speed and sustain a firm configuration as compared to no-gesture groups [34]. In other words, for avoiding an obstacle no-gesture groups tend to interrupt their interaction, re-arrange for avoiding and subsequently recover the former arrangement, whereas gesture performing groups are more conservative.

In the light of these findings, we propose a method for identification of such gestures by a robot. We first assume that -manual- gestures involve the movement of the arms for making fine-grained parts (e.g. fingers) visible to the peer. Thus, as a first step in recognition of manual gestures, we propose decoupling inherent oscillations of the arms, i.e. arm swings, and gesture periods. To that end, we investigate common gesture and no-gesture arm motion patterns of human-human pedestrian pairs. We detect gestures by exploiting the fact that the oscillatory motion of upper limbs is not affected by the view angle or distance of the human to the camera[2]. Thanks to this independence, gestures can easily be identified as a disturbance on this oscillation. In testing, we employ a video data set recorded in uncontrolled settings and show that we achieve a detection rate of 0.80.

2   Background and Related Work

It is important to understand the dynamics of walking oscillations, to decouple arm gestures and arm swings. Arm swings are suggested to be an integral part of

---

[1] For instance, a hand waving gesture can refer to acceptance or rejection depending on the affective state or attitude of the performer.

[2] Although the amplitude of the oscillations vary with the view angle, we expect their frequency to be reasonably stable, provided that there is not significant (self)occlusion.

gait, possibly driven by central pattern generators arising from natural passive dynamics sustained with little active torque [13][3].

Despite their simplicity, arm swings are studied in a diverse range of research fields such as neuroscience [7], medicine and biomechanics [28], computer vision [29] etc. In humanoid robotics, gait is often analyzed for generating stable and natural biped locomotion focusing particularly on the oscillations of the lower body (i.e. hip, knee, foot) and representing upper body motion in a simple manner [6,8,17]. Moreover, gait issues are actively discussed in operator-exoskeleton interaction as well as programming of walking robots [10,32]. However, in human-robot social interaction, impact of hand/arm gestures is subject to a detailed treatment [3]. Most studies take a robot stand-point and address face-to-face communication between a robot and a human in stationary settings such as around a table [20]. In such scenarios, the aim is often recognizing and interpreting human gestures [27].

In this respect, Salem et al. differ from the mainstream studies by considering a more dynamical interaction, where the human-robot pair moves around in a domestic environment or classroom [25]. They show that a robot, which employs gestures along with speech, is perceived by humans as more friendly, engaged, and competent. Such effects of gestures are assumed to be pertinent in mobile human-robot interaction as well [11]. However, to the best of our knowledge there is yet no work on gesture recognition in mobile interaction. Therefore, this study tries to fill a void in literature initially by decoupling arm swings and arm gestures, which may then be recognized at a finer level (i.e. by distinguishing pointing, waving etc.)

3 Data Set

Although methodological experiments or simulations are very useful to test new tracking or detection algorithms, they do not provide workable data in studying social interaction [2]. Namely, target models or instructed subjects (acting deliberately) fail to interact in a natural way [1]. Therefore, the characteristic of human-human interaction is considered to be best depicted when the actors are observed in their ecological environment [35].

Therefore, we examined various pedestrian video data sets [21] and regarded the freely available DukeMTMC data set to be a well-match for our purposes due to several reasons [22]. Namely, DukeMTMC is filmed in the campus of Duke University depicting naturally interacting pedestrians at oblique view and involves a large quantity of data[4]. In addition, it provides several ground truth values including OpenPose estimations regarding each individual[5].

---

[3] Specifically, benefits of arm swings to gait economy involve decreasing shoulder and elbow joint torques, offsetting motion of the legs, reducing vertical ground reaction moments and attendant muscle forces, thereby reducing metabolic energy expenditure [18]. They also produce counter-rotations of the pelvis and thorax to maintain stability and a steady visual platform by minimizing head movements [19,31].

[4] 85 min of 1080p and 60 fps video from 8 cameras with more than 2700 identities.

[5] In addition, trajectories on image plane are provided in a piece-wise linear manner and relating real-world coordinates can be computed using homography matrices.

In addition, a subset of DukeMTMC is annotated for pedestrian groups and the DukeMTMC-Groups data set is introduced by [29], where 64 groups are tracked across 4 cameras for an average of ~400 frames per group (see Fig. 1).

Fig. 1. Frames from DukeMTMC-Groups. Group members are marked in yellow. (Color figure online)

In order to obtain a ground truth for the arm gestures in the DukeMTMC-Groups set, we carried out an additional annotation. Here, it is important to note that we do not contain ourselves to some well-defined symbolic gestures (e.g. waving) or deictic gestures (e.g. pointing) but also consider lexical gestures [16], which may be firmly interwoven with arm swings (see open palm pointing upwards in Fig. 5-(c)).

Two coders watched the clips and annotated such gestures for each individual in a group. We evaluated the reliability of the annotation process using an inter-rater agreement analysis based on Krippendorff's α coefficient [15], and found $\alpha = 0.80$, which indicates a substantial agreement (see [14] for significance of α).

4 Method

Principally, two kinds of joints play role in arm gestures[6], i.e. elbows and shoulders. The configuration of these joints is reflected by the four angles depicted in Fig. 2-(a). Therefore, we particularly focus on the limbs, which connect to these joints in the OpenPose estimations [4] provided as ground truth in [23].

We then compute the relative orientation of those limbs at every frame for each pedestrian in each group. As an example, Fig. 3 shows elbow and shoulder angles for a pedestrian, who does not perform any arm gestures. It appears that -sole- walking motion (i.e. without gestures) causes a certain periodicity in the signal and that is exactly what is intended to be identified. In addition, the values depicted in Fig. 3 are found to be in line with characteristics of common gait motion. Namely, in agreement with Van Emerik et al., shoulder flexion and extension is observed to vary roughly between 5 and 30° [31].

However, we also notice a certain instability in the estimation of the articulations, which are probably due to the errors in estimation of the joint coordinates

---

[6] Here, we exclude fine-grained gestures arising from finger and wrist motion.

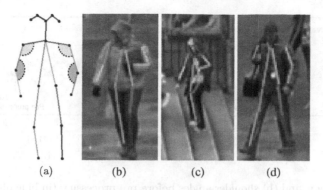

(a)   (b)   (c)   (d)

Fig. 2. (a) Skeleton representation of OpenPose together with elbow and shoulder angles; (b–d) Several examples of pose estimations.

(see Fig. 3-(a)). In order to eliminate such inconsistencies, we first perform a pre-processing operation as detailed in Sect. 4.1 and then apply a pitch detection algorithm to identify oscillatory motion as explained in Sect. 4.2.

4.1 Pre-processing

Suppose that $\alpha[n]$ denotes the articulation of an arbitrary joint (right or left elbow or shoulder) at frame n. For eliminating the noise or instability in the estimation of α, we apply a median filter

$$\bar{\alpha}[n] = m(\alpha[n-T], \ldots, \alpha[n], \ldots, \alpha[n+T]),$$

where $\bar{\alpha}$ denotes the pre-processed signal, $m(\cdot)$ stands for the median operator and $2T + 1$ is the size of the filter[7].

Obviously, due to the relative position of the pedestrians with respect to the camera or their partner, and occlusions with obstacles, some joints or limbs may not be visible at all frames. Thus, α is often defined as a piece-wise linear function. Should α be defined at some intervals shorter than the window size, we do not apply pre-processing to those intervals.

Note that this also introduces the need to deal with deficiencies due to missing data. So as to address this problem, we introduce an upper limit to the permissible rate of missing samples and consider only those joints with less than 15% missing estimations.

Figure 3 illustrates the outcome of the median filtering operation for a couple of elbow and shoulder joints. After carefully examining such pre-processed angles regarding all pedestrians, we decided to focus on elbow joints in our analysis for three reasons. Firstly, as seen in Figs. 3-(a) and (b), flexion and extension are inherently more pronounced for shoulders than elbows in gesture-free walking. Thus, gestures are easier to identify in terms of elbow angles, which are

---

[7] $T = 1$ is considered to give satisfactory results.

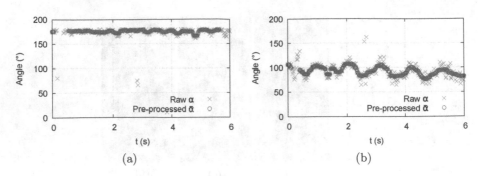

Fig. 3. (a) Elbow and (b) shoulder angles before pre-processing (in blue plus)and after pre-processing (in red cross). (Color figure online)

not subject to a variation as large as shoulder angles. Secondly, most gestures encountered in -pedestrian- interaction (e.g. metaphorical gestures) involve forearm motion to a more prominent degree than upper arm motion [12], which puts a bigger importance on elbow angles. Thirdly, since the region of the shoulder is broader than the region of the elbow, estimations of OpenPose are observed to vary more from one frame to the next regarding shoulders. This is particularly true since the footage is recorded outdoors in winter season and pedestrians often wear heavy clothes, which makes accurate identification of shoulders challenging.

4.2   Pitch Detection

Essentially, retrieval of the oscillations due to gait is very similar to pitch detection, where the goal is also to identify a low frequency periodicity from a noisy signal. Different methods exist to perform such tasks and in this study we opt for the average magnitude difference function (AMDF) introduced in [24]. AMDF concerning a discrete waveform $x[n]$ is defined as,

$$D[\tau] = \frac{1}{N - \tau - 1} \sum_{n=0}^{N-\tau-1} |x[n] - x[n + \tau]|,$$

where τ is the lag number and N is the number of samples. For mere walking action, $D[\tau]$ should be similar to a sine wave. Therefore, it is expected to have minimas at lags corresponding to the period of the walking oscillations and its multiples (see Fig. 4-(b)).

Based on this inference, we fit a sinusoidal waveform $y[\tau]$ to the obtained AMDF curve $D[\tau]$,

$$y[\tau] = A \sin[\omega \tau + \phi] + c,$$

where A is the amplitude, ω is the frequency, ϕ is the phase and c is the offset. In particular, we minimize the sum of squared error between D and y, i.e. ε

$$\varepsilon = \sum_{\tau} (D[\tau] - y[\tau])^2$$

using the Levenberg-Marquardt optimization algorithm. If the outcome of this optimization process is positive (i.e. there exist a solution), the underlying motion is considered to be periodic.

On the other hand, for walking actions involving arm gestures, oscillations are expected to have a disruption and the periodicity of $D[\tau]$ is supposed to be lost for a certain duration of time (see Fig. 4-(c)). In that case, overall periodicity is assumed to disrupted and an arm gesture is said to be performed.

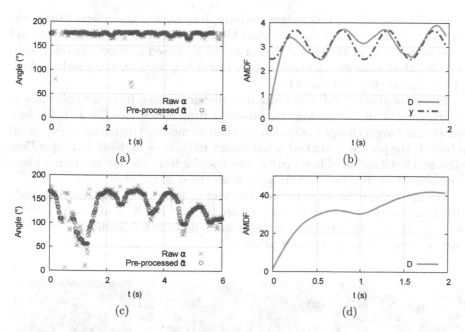

Fig. 4. (a) Elbow angles and (b) AMDF and corresponding sinusoidal model for a no-gesture case. (c) Elbow angles and (d) AMDF for a gesture case.

5   Results and Discussion

Running the proposed method on DukeMTMC-Groups data set, we obtained the results given in Table 1. Specifically, the proposed method achieves a precision of 0.65, a recall of 0.89, and an accuracy of 0.80. Considering the challenging nature of the set, these results are considered to be a promising start for the decoupling of walking oscillations and gestures. In what follows, we provide a discussion on possible sources of error and future work.

The principal cause of mistakes is considered to be the failures in accurate estimation of poses. Moreover, missing estimations due to occlusion (by objects, peers or other pedestrians) (see Fig. 5) are somehow an inevitable reason.

Table 1. Gesture detection results (in %).

		Estimation	
		Gesture	No gesture
Ground truth	Gesture	89	11
	No gesture	24	76

In addition, various pedestrians perform arm movements different than gestures (e.g. switch a cup from one hand to the other). Although the coders did not consider such movements as gestures, the proposed method identifies them as a disturbance on walking oscillations, which may explain the relatively high rate of false positives in Table 1.

There are also several fundamental challenges arising from the collection of the set. First of all, certain cameras provide a frontal view (see Fig. 1-(b)), where pedestrians have a change in depth more than 20 meters. Obviously, as explained in Sect. 1, the proposed method is indifferent to changes in depth but OpenPose relies on identification of body parts, which suffer from the low resolution views of targets when they are very far away from the camera.

Moreover, since the set is recorded in winter season, lots of pedestrians walk with their hands in pocket or with umbrellas (see Fig. 5-(b, d)), which limits the oscillations of the arms and makes it more difficult to identify an oscillatory pattern, even when no gesture is present.

| (a) | (b) | (c) | (d) |

Fig. 5. Occlusion due to (a) an object, (b) the partner (in the same group) and (c, d) other pedestrians (outside the group).

Future work includes improving pose estimations to correct errors and interpolate missing data. Graph convolutional neural networks, which generalize the convolution operation on 1D and 2D arrays to graph data structure, is a promising tool for skeleton pose estimations. The Spatio-Temporal Graph Convolutional Network by Yan et al. seem particularly beneficial in action classification, where the classier employs a graph model of the skeleton at multiple successive frames, each joint being linked to its detection on the preceding and succeeding frames [33]. Using this method, given a set of detections, it may be possible to estimate the locations of some missing joints. In addition, for the pitch detection step using a cepstrum analysis is considered to improve the results.

6 Conclusion

This study focuses on gesture recognition in mobile interaction settings, i.e. when the interacting partners are pedestrians. Here, the problem is that the pedestrians move their arms as part of their walking activity. Thus, a first step in recognition, would be to decouple this inherent oscillatory movement and gestures. To that end, we use a pitch detection method, identify the oscillatory motions and model them using a sinusoidal waveform. The signals which cannot be represented with this model, are assumed to involve a gesture action.

The proposed method achieves a considerable accuracy of 0.80. Besides, being based on video, it is noninvasive, which is very desirable in interaction studies. In addition, the oscillatory actions of the arms can be observed independent of the view angle or distance to the camera, which makes it independent of camera configurations. Moreover, video input is particularly favorable, since it can easily be collected and integrated into existing systems (e.g. security surveillance) in a large variety of environments (indoor or outdoor)[8].

Acknowledgments. This work was supported by JSPS KAKENHI Grant Number JP18K18168 and JP18H04121. We would like to thank S. Koyama, H. Nguyen, P. Supitayakul and T. Pramot for their help in annotation and F. Zanlungo for his invaluable discussion.

References

1. Berclaz, J., Fleuret, F., Turetken, E., Fua, P.: Multiple object tracking using k-shortest paths optimization. IEEE TPAMI **33**(9), 1806–1819 (2011)
2. Bochinski, E., Eiselein, V., Sikora, T.: Training a convolutional neural network for multi-class object detection using solely virtual world data. In: AVSS, pp. 278–285. IEEE (2016)
3. Breazeal, C., Kidd, C.D., Thomaz, A.L., Hoffman, G., Berlin, M.: Effects of non-verbal communication on efficiency and robustness in human-robot teamwork. In: IROS, pp. 708–713. IEEE (2005)
4. Cao, Z., Simon, T., Wei, S.E., Sheikh, Y.: Realtime multi-person 2D pose estimation using part affinity fields. In: CVPR, pp. 7291–7299 (2017)
5. Consortium for the physics and psychology of human crowd dynamics: a glossary for research on human crowd dynamics. Collect. Dyn. **4**, 1–13 (2019)

---

[8] With current depth sensors, observing the environments at the scale of the ones in Fig. 1 is perhaps not possible, if not with some very expensive equipment.

6. De-León-Gómez, V., Luo, Q., Kalouguine, A., Pámanes, J.A., Aoustin, Y., Chevallereau, C.: An essential model for generating walking motions for humanoid robots. Robot. Auton. Syst. **112**, 229–243 (2019)
7. Di Scala, G., et al.: Efficiency of sensorimotor networks: posture and gait in young and older adults. Exp. Aging Res. **45**, 41–56 (2019). https://doi.org/10.1080/0361073X.2018.1560108
8. Ferreira, J.P., Crisostomo, M.M., Coimbra, A.P.: Human gait acquisition and characterization. IEEE Trans. IM **58**(9), 2979–2988 (2009)
9. Goldin-Meadow, S.: Using our hands to change our minds. WIREs Cogn. Sci. **8**(1–2), e1368 (2017)
10. Gorobtsov, A., Andreev, A., Markov, A., Skorikov, A., Tarasov, P.: Features of solving the inverse dynamic method equations for the synthesis of stable walking robots controlled motion. In: SPIIRAS Proceedings, vol. 18, pp. 85–122, February 2019. https://doi.org/10.15622/sp.18.1.85-122
11. Haddington, P., Mondada, L., Nevile, M.: Interaction and Mobility: Language and The Body in Motion, vol. 20. Walter de Gruyter, Berlin (2013)
12. Karam, M.: A framework for research and design of gesture-based human-computer interactions. Ph.D. thesis, University of Southampton (2006)
13. Katz, P.S.: Evolution of central pattern generators and rhythmic behaviours. Philos. Trans. R. Soc. B **371**(1685), 20150057 (2016)
14. Krippendorff, K.: Reliability in content analysis: some common misconceptions and recommendations. Hum. Commun. Res. **30**(3), 411–433 (2004)
15. Krippendorff, K.: Content Analysis: An Introduction to Its Methodology. Sage, Thousand Oaks (2018)
16. McNeill, D.: Hand and Mind: What Gestures Reveal About Thought. University of Chicago Press, Chicago (1992)
17. Meng, S., Jin, S., Li, J., Hashimoto, K., Guo, S., Dai, S.: The analysis of human walking stability using ZMP in sagittal plane. In: 2017 IEEE International Conference on Cybernetics and Intelligent Systems (CIS) and IEEE Conference on Robotics, Automation and Mechatronics (RAM), pp. 496–501. IEEE (2017)
18. Meyns, P., Bruijn, S.M., Duysens, J.: The how and why of arm swing during human walking. Gait Posture **38**(4), 555–562 (2013)
19. Punt, M., Bruijn, S.M., Wittink, H., van Dieën, J.H.: Effect of arm swing strategy on local dynamic stability of human gait. Gait Posture **41**(2), 504–509 (2015)
20. Rautaray, S.S., Agrawal, A.: Vision based hand gesture recognition for human computer interaction: a survey. Artif. Intell. Rev. **43**(1), 1–54 (2015)
21. Riemenschneider, H.: YACVID (2018). http://yacvid.hayko.at/. Accessed 01 Apr 2019
22. Ristani, E., Solera, F., Zou, R., Cucchiara, R., Tomasi, C.: Performance measures and a data set for multi-target, multi-camera tracking. In: Hua, G., Jégou, H. (eds.) ECCV 2016. LNCS, vol. 9914, pp. 17–35. Springer, Cham (2016). https://doi.org/10.1007/978-3-319-48881-3_2
23. Ristani, E., Solera, F., Zou, R.S., Cucchiara, R., Tomasi, C.T.: DukeMTMC Project (2018). http://vision.cs.duke.edu/DukeMTMC/. Accessed 29 Mar 2019
24. Ross, M., Shaffer, H., Cohen, A., Freudberg, R., Manley, H.: Average magnitude difference function pitch extractor. IEEE Trans. ASSP **22**(5), 353–362 (1974)
25. Salem, M., Kopp, S., Wachsmuth, I., Rohlfing, K., Joublin, F.: Generation and evaluation of communicative robot gesture. IJSR **2**, 201–217 (2012)
26. Saponaro, G., Jamone, L., Bernardino, A., Salvi, G.: Interactive robot learning of gestures, language and affordances. In: GLU, pp. 83–87 (2017)

27. Sheikholeslami, S., Moon, A., Croft, E.A.: Cooperative gestures for industry: exploring the efficacy of robot hand configurations in expression of instructional gestures for human–robot interaction. IJRR **36**(5–7), 699–720 (2017)
28. Simon-Martinez, C., et al.: Age-related changes in upper limb motion during typical development. PLoS ONE **13**(6), e0198524 (2018)
29. Solera, F., Calderara, S., Ristani, E., Tomasi, C., Cucchiara, R.: Tracking social groups within and across cameras. IEEE Trans. Cir. Sys. Video Technol. **27**(3), 441–453 (2017). https://doi.org/10.1109/TCSVT.2016.2607378
30. Tracy, J.L., Randles, D., Steckler, C.M.: The nonverbal communication of emotions. Curr. Opin. Behav. Sci. **3**, 25–30 (2015)
31. Van Emmerik, R.E., Hamill, J., McDermott, W.J.: Variability and coordinative function in human gait. Quest **57**(1), 102–123 (2005)
32. Vorochaeva, L.Y., Yatsun, A.S., Jatsun, S.F.: Controlling a quasistatic gait of an exoskeleton on the basis of the expert system. Trudy SPIIRAN **52**, 70–94 (2017)
33. Yan, S., Xiong, Y., Lin, D.: Spatial temporal graph convolutional networks for skeleton-based action recognition. In: AAAI (2018)
34. Yücel, Z., Zanlungo, F., Shiomi, M.: Walk the talk: gestures in mobile interaction. In: ICSR, pp. 220–230 (2017)
35. Zanlungo, F., Yücel, Z., Brščić, D., Kanda, T., Hagita, N.: Intrinsic group behaviour: dependence of pedestrian dyad dynamics on principal social and personal features. PLoS ONE **12**(11), e0187253 (2017)

Dynamic Control of the Specialized Handling Robot for Installation of Cross Ties in the Subway

Sergey Tkalich, Vladimir Medvedev, Valerii Krysanov,
Viktor Burkovsky, Viktor Trubetskoy, Aleksander Danilov,
Pavel Gusev, and Konstantin Gusev[✉]

Voronezh State Technical University, 394026 Voronezh, Russia
gussev_konstantin@mail.ru

Abstract. Describing the design of the specialized handling robot for instal-lation of cross ties in the subway. For the reliable reproduction of the required trajectories at high movement speed of manipulator links the task was set to develop its dynamic model, and the particular microprocessor system of the dynamic control of the manipulator. The equations of a three-coordinate manipulator dynamics in the angular system of coordinates are obtained in a differential and vector form of record providing the solution of the return problem of dynamics. The structure of a microprocessor system for the dynamic control of the three-unit manipulator with angular system of coordinates is developed. It is expedient to use the three-coordinate manipulators with angular system of coordinates in a limited space of a subway. When the operating impact effects are formed of the on drives of the specialized robot for the installation of cross ties the most versatile and rational method is that of dynamic control, developing the dynamic model of the manipulator on the basis of its algorithm and Lagrange's method.

Keywords: Robot for installation of cross ties · The manipulator ·
Dynamic model · Dynamic control · Angular system of coordinates

1 Introduction

Operating conditions of the subways set up high requirements for quality of installation and the reliability of all elements of a railway. However, the characteristic features of a subway (viz., the constrained tunnel dimensions, existence of a contact rail and short technological "windows" for maintenance at night) do not allow to use on full scale the equipment which is usual on the surface, in the construction of common roads and the technology of construction, maintenance and track repair.

Whereas the road works in a tunnel are performed within a strictly limited time, the development of specialized high speed handling robots and the reduction of the expenses for labor, becomes not only a technical problem, but a social one connected with hard physical toil. At the same time it is expedient to use the three-coordinate manipulators with angular system of coordinates having the greatest possible

A. Ronzhin et al. (Eds.): ICR 2019, LNAI 11659, pp. 86–98, 2019.
https://doi.org/10.1007/978-3-030-26118-4_9

compactness due to their portability in the collapsible form which is very important in the conditions of limited space of a subway.

Characteristics and parameters of handling robots are defined both by their mechanical structure, and the particular realization of their control systems. Microprocessor implemented as the control system of a robot with angular system of coordinates allows to reduce twice or more the energy consumption concerning the system constructed on chips with small- and medium integration [11].

Time reduction of road works in a tunnel depends directly on higher speed of the specialized handling robots used there. To ensure the high-quality working off of the required trajectories at high movement speed of the manipulator links it is expedient to integrate to its the operating structure the dynamic model solving the problem of a return action dynamics [9, 12, 13].

2 Review of Literature

Formation of the operating action on the executive drives of the specialized robot should be repeated with substantially high frequency (at least 50 Hz or more) as the resonant frequency of the manipulator itself is about 10 Hz.

The first result which was used for the solution of both the direct, and reversed problem of dynamics was obtained by Wicker by means of Lagrange's method [19]. Kan [17] developed the algorithm for simulation of the opened kinematic chains. Young [21] realized this method in the form of the software package for the analysis of robot dynamics. Hollerbah [16] showed that the number of the operations of multiplication/addition used in these methods depends on n4 (where n is the number of the degrees of freedom) and the manipulators with three degrees of mobility should be able to perform over 5000 operations of multiplication and approximately the same number of addition operations at a time. Realization of these methods in the on-line mode dictates the use of high-speed computers.

Waters and Hollerbah developed the algorithms for the solution only of the problem of reversed dynamics only basing on the Kan-Wicker's method. The number of multiplication/addition operations in these algorithms was reduced to the number proportional to n [16]. However, in this case too, the performance of about 1000 operations of multiplication is a 'must' for three-coordinate manipulators.

In [8] the dynamic model is discussed of the PUMA-560 manipulator constructed on the basis of Newton-Euler's method as well as the simulation of the robot in the MATLAB environment. Themanipulator links were represented by the solid bodies described by sets of the kinematic Ki parameters and the dynamic Di parameters. Here the i index is the serial number of a link in a chain, from the support to the gripping device. Kinematic parameters were originally entered in relation to local systems of coordinates of the links. These are the Cartesian systems of coordinates connected with the centers of mass of the links and having the axes focused along their main axes of inertia. For the formation of matrixes of dynamic model the kinematic parameters of the manipulator links were defined in the absolute system of coordinates 0xyz. This kinematics problem was solved using the formula of final turns of vectors. Newton-Euler's method makes it possible to create the dynamic model of the manipulator with an arbitrary system of coordinates [7], i.e. it is universal.

Let's note the property which is universal for all methods mentioned above. These methods do not depend on the type of kinematic scheme of the manipulator and are based on the general laws of kinematics and the dynamics of solid bodies. For the manipulator with the particular kinematic scheme the creation of an analytical model requires a considerably smaller number of arithmetic operations. It is confirmed by [17, 20]. The creation of a model of the anthropomorphous three-coordinate manipulator demands no more than 44 multiplications and 23 additions. The manipulator with five degrees of freedom requires 352 operations of multiplication only [18]. Thus, during the on-line control of manipulators it is expedient to use of the methods focused on the particular kinematic schemes for purpose of economy of both hard- and software. Proceeding from it, we will build the dynamic model of the three-coordinate manipulator with angular system of coordinates on the basis of its computations routine, obtaining the expressions for both the kinetic and potential energy of the manipulator and using the Lagrange equations of the 2 order [4].

3 Development of the Dynamic Model of Manipulator with Angular System of Coordinates

The computation routine of the three-coordinate manipulator with angular system of coordinates is shown in Fig. 1. The link 1 has the mass $of\ m_1$ and the moment of inertia of J_1 concerning an axis of rotation O_{x2}. Through m_2, m_3 and m, respectively, the masses (weights) of the links 2, 3 and working body are designated. The lengths of the links are designated as l_1, l_2, l_3, the distances from the centers of masses m_1, m_2, m_3 to the centers of the joints are l_{01}, l_{02}, l_{03}. The manipulator discussed below has three rotary kinematic couples. The vector of the generalized coordinates of the manipulator consists of the angles of rotation in the joints of the links 1, 2, 3: $q =[\varphi_1, \varphi_2, \varphi_3]$. The Cartesian system of coordinates $0x_1x_2x_3$ is also shown in Fig. 1.

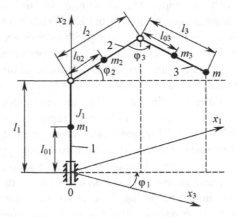

Fig. 1. The computation routine of the manipulator with angular system of coordinates.

When forming the dynamic model of the manipulator with angular system of coordinates we assume that the parameters of the manipulator links (length, weight, the moments of inertia, etc.) are known, and that they are the constants.

We assume that the coordinates of the joints (angles or linear movements of the links) and their derivatives are independent variables. All other values used in the formation of the mathematical models will be considered as functions of the coordinates of the joints (the generalized manipulator coordinates).

The Lagrange equations for the discussed three-coordinate manipulator look like:

$$\frac{d}{dt}\left(\frac{\partial W}{\partial \dot{\varphi}_j}\right) - \left(\frac{\partial W}{\partial \varphi_j}\right) + \left(\frac{\partial \Pi}{\partial \varphi_j}\right) = M_{\varphi j}, \quad j = 1,2,3, \tag{1}$$

where W – the kinetic energy of the manipulator; P – potential energy of the manipulator; $M_{\varphi}j$ – the moments developed by the electric drives in the joints of a rotary type.

The link 1 participates in the rotary motion only by the coordinate $\varphi 1$, therefore its kinetic energy is defined from the expression:

$$W_1(\dot{\varphi}) = \frac{J_1 \dot{\varphi}_1^2}{2}. \tag{2}$$

Links 2 and 3 make complex movements. Let's designate through V2, V3 and the V values of linear speeds of points in which the mass of m2, m3 and m are concentrated. Then to define the kinetic energy of links 2, 3 and weight m we write down the following expressions:

$$W_2 = m_2 V_2^2/2 = m_2 \sum_{s=1}^{3} x_{s2}^2/2,$$

$$W_3 = m_3 V_3^2/2 = m_3 \sum_{s=1}^{3} x_{s3}^2/2,$$

$$W_m = mV^2/2 = m\sum_{s=1}^{3} x_s^2/2, s = 1,2,3. \tag{3}$$

The square of speed of a point m_2 is defined from the equation:

$$V_2^2 = l_{02}^2(\dot{\varphi}_1^2 \cos^2 \varphi_2 + \dot{\varphi}_2^2). \tag{4}$$

The Cartesian coordinates xs3 of the m3 point are defined with the expression:

$$x_{13} = [l_2 \cdot \cos \varphi_2 - l_{03} \cdot \cos (\varphi_2 + \varphi_3)] \cdot \sin \varphi_1;$$
$$x_{23} = l_2 \cdot \sin \varphi_2 - l_{03} \cdot \sin(\varphi_2 + \varphi_3) + l_1; \tag{5}$$
$$x_{33} = [l_2 \cdot \cos \varphi_2 - l_{03} \cdot \cos(\varphi_2 + \varphi_3)] \cdot \cos \varphi_1.$$

Differentiating the xs3 coordinates by time, we receive:

$$\dot{x}_{13} = [-l_2\dot{\phi}_2 \cdot \sin\phi_2 + l_{03}(\dot{\phi}_2 + \dot{\phi}_3) \cdot \sin(\phi_2 + \phi_3)] \cdot \sin\phi_1$$
$$+ [l_2 \cdot \cos\phi_2 - l_{03} \cdot \cos(\phi_2 + \phi_3)] \cdot \cos\phi_1\dot{\phi}_1,$$
$$\dot{x}_{23} = l_2\dot{\phi}_2 \cdot \cos\phi_2 - l_{03}(\dot{\phi}_2 + \dot{\phi}_3) \cdot \cos(\phi_2 + \phi_3), \tag{6}$$
$$\dot{x}_{33} = [-l_2\dot{\phi}_2 \cdot \sin\phi_2 + l_{03}(\dot{\phi}_2 + \dot{\phi}_3) \cdot \sin(\phi_2 + \phi_3)] \cdot \cos\phi_1$$
$$- [l_2 \cdot \cos\phi_2 - l_{03} \cdot \cos(\phi_2 + \phi_3)] \cdot \sin\phi_1\dot{\phi}_1.$$

The square of point speed m3 is:

$$V_3^2 = \dot{x}_{13}^2 + \dot{x}_{23}^2 + \dot{x}_{33}^2. \tag{7}$$

Substituting in (7) the $\dot{x}_{13}$, $\dot{x}_{23}$ and $\dot{x}_{33}$ expressions for determination of speeds from (6), after a number of trigonometric transformations, we receive the following equation:

$$V_3^2 = l_2^2(\dot{\phi}_1^2 \cos^2\varphi_2 + \dot{\phi}_2^2) + l_{03}^2[(\dot{\phi}_2 + \dot{\phi}_3)^2 + \dot{\phi}_1^2 \cos^2(\varphi_2 + \varphi_2)]$$
$$-2l_2l_{03}[\dot{\phi}_2(\dot{\phi}_2 + \dot{\phi}_3)\cos\varphi_3 + \dot{\phi}_1^2 \cos\varphi_2 \cos(\varphi_2 + \varphi_3)]. \tag{8}$$

Similarly, we obtain the expression for a square of the point speed m which looks like:

$$V^2 = l_2^2(\dot{\phi}_1^2 \cos^2\varphi_2 + \dot{\phi}_2^2) + l_3^2[(\dot{\phi}_2 + \dot{\phi}_3)^2 + \dot{\phi}_1^2 \cos^2(\varphi_2 + \varphi_2)]$$
$$-2l_2l_3[\dot{\phi}_2(\dot{\phi}_2 + \dot{\phi}_3)\cos\varphi_3 + \dot{\phi}_1^2 \cos\varphi_2 \cos(\varphi_2 + \varphi_3)]. \tag{9}$$

The kinetic energy W of the manipulator is defined from the expression:

$$W = W_1 + W_2 + W_3 + W_m. \tag{10}$$

Basing on the Eqs. (2), (4), (8), (10) we obtain the following expression for kinetic energy of the manipulator:

$$W = J_1\dot{\phi}_1^2/2 + m_2l_{02}^2(\dot{\phi}_1^2 \cos^2\varphi_2 + \dot{\phi}_2^2)/2 + m_3\{l_2^2[\dot{\phi}_2^2 + \cos^2\varphi_2\dot{\phi}_1^2]$$
$$+ l_{03}^2[(\dot{\phi}_2 + \dot{\phi}_3)^2 + \cos^2(\varphi_2 + \varphi_3)\dot{\phi}_1^2] - 2l_2l_{03}[\cos\varphi_3\dot{\phi}_2(\dot{\phi}_2 + \dot{\phi}_3)$$
$$+ \cos\varphi_2 \cos(\varphi_2 + \varphi_3)\dot{\phi}_1^2]\}/2 + m\{l_2^2[\dot{\phi}_2^2 + \cos^2 j_2\dot{\phi}_1^2] + l_3^2[(\dot{\phi}_2 + \dot{\phi}_3)^2 \tag{11}$$
$$+ \cos^2(\varphi_2 + +\varphi_3)\dot{\phi}_1^2] - 2l_2l_3[\cos\varphi_3\dot{\phi}_2(\dot{\phi}_2 + \dot{\phi}_3)$$
$$+ \cos j_2 \cos(\varphi_2 + \varphi_3)\dot{\phi}_1^2]\}/2.$$

A partial derivative of kinetic energy W by speeds of the generalized coordinates is:

$$\partial W/\partial \dot{\phi}_1 = \dot{\phi}_1[J_1 + (m_2 l_{02}^2 + m l_2^2 + m_3 l_2^2)\cos^2 \phi_2 + (m_3 l_{03}^2$$
$$+ m l_3^2)\cos^2(\phi_2 + \phi_3) - 2l_2(m_3 l_{03} + m l_3)\cos \phi_2 \cos(\phi_2 + \phi_3)],$$
$$\partial W/\partial \dot{\phi}_2 = \dot{\phi}_2(m_2 l_{02}^2 + m l_2^2 + m_3 l_2^2) + (\dot{\phi}_2 + \dot{\phi}_3) \tag{12}$$
$$\times (m_3 l_{03}^2 + m l_3^2) - (2\dot{\phi}_2 + \dot{\phi}_3)l_2(m_3 l_{03} + m l_3)\cos \phi_3,$$
$$\partial W/\partial \dot{\phi}_3 = (\dot{\phi}_2 + \dot{\phi}_3)(m_3 l_{03}^2 + m l_3^2) - \dot{\phi}_2 l_2(m_3 l_{03} + m l_3)\cos \phi_3.$$

The partial derivatives of kinetic energy W by the generalized coordinates are:

$$\partial W/\partial \phi_1 = 0,$$
$$\partial W/\partial \phi_2 = -\dot{\phi}_1^2\{(m_2 l_{02}^2 + m_3 l_2^2 + m l_2^2)\sin 2\phi_2$$
$$+ (m_3 l_{03}^2 + m l_3^2)\sin[2(\phi_2 + \phi_3)] - 2(m_3 l_2 l_{03} + m l_2 l_3)$$
$$\times \sin(2\phi_2 + \phi_3)\}/2, \tag{13}$$
$$\partial W/\partial \phi_3 = -\dot{\phi}_1^2\{(m_3 l_{03}^2 + m l_3^2)\sin[2(\phi_2 + \phi_3)]/2$$
$$- l_2 \cos \phi_2 (m_3 l_{03} + m l_3)\sin(\phi_2 + \phi_3)\} + \dot{\phi}_2(\dot{\phi}_2 + \dot{\phi}_3)$$
$$\times (m_3 l_{03} + m l_3)l_2 \sin \phi_3.$$

The expression for potential energy Π of the manipulators looks like:

$$\Pi = m_1 g l_{01} + m_2 g(l_1 + l_{02}\sin \varphi_2)$$
$$+ m_3 g(l_1 + l_2 \sin \varphi_2 - l_{03}\sin(\varphi_2 + \varphi_3)] \tag{14}$$
$$+ m g[l_1 + l_2 \sin \varphi_2 - l_3 \sin(\varphi_2 + \varphi_3)].$$

The derivative of potential energy Π by the generalized coordinates is:

$$\partial \Pi/\partial \varphi_1 = 0; \partial \Pi/\partial \varphi_3 - g(m_3 l_{03} + m l_3)\cos(\varphi_2 + \varphi_3);$$
$$\partial \Pi/\partial \varphi_2 = g(m_2 l_{02} + m_3 l_2 + m l_2)\cos \varphi_2 - g(m_3 l_{03} + m l_3)\cos(\varphi_2 + \varphi_3). \tag{15}$$

Substituting to the system (1) the expressions (12), (13) and (15) for partial derivatives, having completed: the operation of differentiation by time, a number of trigonometric transformations, and the introduction of designations, we receive the following equations of dynamics of the manipulator with angular system of coordinates:

$$A_{\phi 1}(\phi_2, \phi_3)\ddot{\phi}_1 + B_{\phi 1}(\phi_2, \phi_3, \dot{\phi}_1, \dot{\phi}_2, \dot{\phi}_3)$$
$$= M_{\phi 1}, A_{\phi 2}(\phi_3)\ddot{\phi}_2 + A_{\phi 23}(\phi_3)\ddot{\phi}_3 + B_{\phi 2}(\phi_2, \phi_3, \dot{\phi}_1, \dot{\phi}_2, \dot{\phi}_3) + C_{\phi 2}(\phi_2, \phi_3)$$
$$= M_{\phi 2}, A_{\phi 3}\ddot{\phi}_3 + A_{\phi 32}(\phi_3)\ddot{\phi}_2 + B_{\phi 3}(\phi_2, \phi_3, \dot{\phi}_1, \dot{\phi}_2) \tag{16}$$
$$+ C_{\phi 3}(\phi_2, \phi_3) = M_{\phi 3}.$$

In system (16) the following designations are used:

$$A_{\phi 1}(\phi_2, \phi_3) = J_1 + (m_2 l_{02}^2 + m l_2^2 + m_3 l_2^2)\cos^2\phi_2$$
$$+ (m_3 l_{03}^2 + m l_3^2)\cos^2(\phi_2 + \phi_3)$$
$$- 2l_2(m_3 l_{03} + m l_3) \times \cos\phi_2\cos(\phi_2 + \phi_3),$$

$$B_{\phi 1}(\phi_2, \phi_3, \dot{\phi}_1, \dot{\phi}_2, \dot{\phi}_3) = \dot{\phi}_1\{-(m_2 l_{02}^2 + m l_2^2 + m_3 l_2^2)$$
$$\times \sin 2\phi_2 \cdot \dot{\phi}_2 - (m_3 l_{03}^2 + m l_3^2)\sin[2(\phi_2 + \phi_3)](\dot{\phi}_2 + \dot{\phi}_3)$$
$$+ 2l_2(m_3 l_{03} + m l_3)[\sin(2\phi_2 + \phi_3) \cdot \dot{\phi}_2 + \cos\phi_2$$
$$\times \sin(\phi_2 + \phi_3) \cdot \dot{\phi}_3\},$$

$$A_{\phi 23}(\phi_3) = m_3 l_{03}^2 + m l_3^2 - l_2\cos\phi_3 \cdot (m_3 l_{03} + m l_3),$$

$$A_{\phi 2}(\phi_3) = m_2 l_{02}^2 + m_3 l_2^2 + m l_2^2 + m_3 l_{03}^2 + m l_3^2$$
$$- 2\cos\phi_3 l_2(m_3 l_{03} + m l_3),$$

$$B_{\phi 2}(\phi_2, \phi_3, \dot{\phi}_1, \dot{\phi}_2, \dot{\phi}_3) = (2\dot{\phi}_2 + \dot{\phi}_3)l_2\sin\phi_3 \cdot \dot{\phi}_3 \times (m_3 l_{03} + m l_3)$$
$$+ \dot{\phi}_1^2\{(m_2 l_{02}^2 + m_3 l_2^2 + m l_2^2)\sin(2\phi_2)$$
$$+ (m_3 l_{03}^2 + m l_3^2)\sin[2(\phi_2 + \phi_3)] - 2(m_3 l_2 l_{03} + m l_2 l_3)$$
$$\times \sin(2\phi_2 + \phi_3)\}/2,$$

$$C_{\phi 2}(\phi_2, \phi_3) = g(m_2 l_{02} + m_3 l_2 + m l_2)\cos\phi_2$$
$$- g(m_3 l_{03} + m l_3)\cos(\phi_2 + \phi_3),$$

$$A_{\phi 3} = m_3 l_{03}^2 + m l_3^2,$$

$$A_{\phi 32}(\phi_3) = m_3 l_{03}^2 + m l_3^2 - l_2\cos\phi_3 \cdot (m_3 l_{03} + m l),$$

$$B_{\phi 3}(\phi_2, \phi_3, \dot{\phi}_1, \dot{\phi}_2) = \dot{\phi}_1^2\{(m_3 l_{03}^2 + m l_3^2)\sin[2(\phi_2 + \phi_3)]/2$$
$$- l_2(m_3 l_{03} + m l_3)\cos\phi_2 \cdot \sin(\phi_2 + \phi_3)\}$$
$$- \dot{\phi}_2^2(m_3 l_{03} + m l_3)l_2\sin\phi_3,$$

$$C_{\phi 3}(\phi_2, \phi_3) = -g(m_3 l_{03} + m l_3)\cos(\phi_2 + \phi_3).$$

(17)

The vector form of the record of a system of the Eq. (16) looks like:

$$A(q)\ddot{q} + B(q, \dot{q}) + C(q) = P,$$ (18)

Where $A(q), \ddot{q}$ – a matrix of inertial parameters and a vector column of accelerations; $B(q, \dot{q})$ – the vector column considering interference of coordinates; $C(q)$ – a vector column of forces of gravitation; P – a vector column of the generalized forces in manipulator joints.

The matrix $A(q)$ and vectors $\ddot{q}$, $PB(q,\dot{q})$, are defined *by* $C(q)$ as follows:

$$A(q) = \begin{bmatrix} A_{\varphi1}(\varphi_2,\varphi_3) & 0 & 0 \\ 0 & A_{\varphi2}(\varphi_3) & A_{\varphi23}(\varphi_3) \\ 0 & A_{\varphi32}(\varphi_3) & A_{\varphi3} \end{bmatrix}; \ddot{q} = \begin{bmatrix} \ddot{\varphi}_1 \\ \ddot{\varphi}_2 \\ \ddot{\varphi}_3 \end{bmatrix}; P = \begin{bmatrix} M_{\varphi1} \\ M_{\varphi2} \\ M_{\varphi3} \end{bmatrix};$$

$$B(q,\dot{q}) = \begin{bmatrix} B_{\varphi1}(\varphi_2,\varphi_3,\dot{\varphi}_1,\dot{\varphi}_2,\dot{\varphi}_3) \\ B_{\varphi2}(\varphi_2,\varphi_3,\dot{\varphi}_1,\dot{\varphi}_2,\dot{\varphi}_3) \\ B_{\varphi3}(\varphi_2,\varphi_3,\dot{\varphi}_1,\dot{\varphi}_2) \end{bmatrix}; \begin{bmatrix} 0 \\ C_{\varphi2}(\varphi_2,\varphi_3) \\ C_{\varphi3}(\varphi_2,\varphi_3) \end{bmatrix}. \tag{19}$$

4 Dynamic Control of the Manipulator

In system of dynamic control the mathematical model of dynamics of the manipulator is inserted directly into the structure of a control system. In [2, 3, 12, 13] the approach is shown providing the formation of the complete dynamic model of the robot in control process i.e. the calculation of a vector of the generalized forces according to the Eq. (18) when using the vectors of the measured values of the generalized coordinates $q(t)$ and speeds $\dot{q}(t)$ of the robot. The robot is asymptotically stable in the neighborhood of a nominal trajectory if a vector of the generalized forces is:

$$P(t) = A(q(t))\{\ddot{q}_{\text{зад}}(t) + K_0[q_{\text{зад}}(t) - q(t)] +$$

$$+ K_1[\dot{q}_{\text{зад}}(t) - \dot{q}(t)]\} + B(q(t),\dot{q}(t)) + C(q(t)), \tag{20}$$

where K_0 – a matrix with the $n \times n$ size of the feedback coefficients by position (location); *K1* – a matrix the $n \times n$ size of the coefficients of feedback by speed.

The scheme of formation of the operating impacts is constructed according to (20) and shown in Fig. 2. The vector $P(t)$ is calculated from the Eq. (20); the vector I (t) of the operating currents is calculated on the basis of a vector $P(t)$ taking into account the parameters of kinematic transfers. The parameters considered in the scheme are: the interference of links (matrix) $B(q,\dot{q})$, gravitational forces (a matrix *of C* (q)), change of the moments of inertia in the movement of the manipulator (in a matrix *of A(q)*).

5 Structure of a Control System of the Manipulator

The microprocessor system of dynamic control of the manipulator working in angular coordinates is formed according to the function diagram shown in Fig. 3.

As a part of the function diagram there are the following blocks:

- operating computer (OC);
- the communication module with sensors (МСД);
- input-output module (ИОМ);
- sources of the current of the robot's coordinates (ИТ1 – ИТn), $n = 1, 2, 3$;
- executive engines (M1 – Mn);

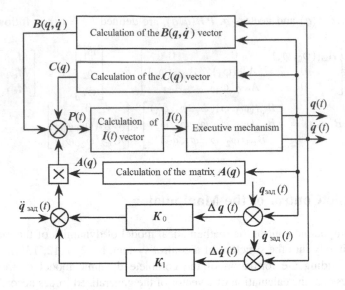

Fig. 2. The scheme of formation of the operating impacts.

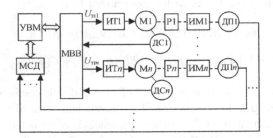

Fig. 3. Function diagram of the microprocessor system of the manipulator dynamic control.

- sensors of speeds (ДС1 – ДСn);
- reduction gears (P1 – Pn);
- executive mechanisms of the robot's coordinates (ИМ1 – ИМn);
- sensors of movements (ДП1 – ДПn).

A number of reference points is allocated for the trajectories of movement of the manipulator according to the required road works in a subway tunnel. Intermediate values of the coordinates between the reference points pay off as a result of interpolation of a trajectory by means of cubic splines [5, 6, 10, 14], using a run-through method [1] and the developed algorithm of interpolation [15].

The MBB module transforms the codes to the analog signals Uzt1 – Uztn which come in the ИТ1 – ИТn sources of current. Windings of anchors of the executive engines M1– Mn are fed by the preset currents, providing the working off of the required movements of the coordinates.

6 Results of Investigations of a Robot with an Angular Coordinate System

Experimental studies of the robot with an angular coordinate system were carried out in the mode of testing a given trajectory. Time diagrams of the task signals and actual movements of the generalized coordinates of the manipulator were formed with the help of a personal computer and the developed program. In accordance with the requirements for the trajectory of the manipulator consisting of eleven sections, an array of given values of generalized coordinates $q_1=\varphi_1$, $q_2=\varphi_2$, $q_1=\varphi_3$ at the reference points was formed (Fig. 4).

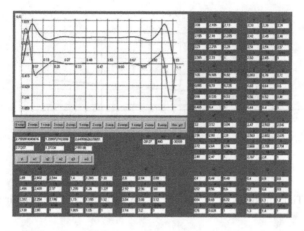

Fig. 4. Window of the program of formation of the setting signals and time diagrams.

On each of the eleven sections of the trajectory, the required displacements of the generalized coordinate at the reference points were introduced. The calculation of the reference signals of displacements, soon-scribed and accelerations of the coordinates between the reference points was carried out by the method of cubic splines, using the developed program of interpolation.

In addition, the specified boundary conditions (zero velocity and acceleration at the beginning and end of each section of the trajectory) were met (Fig. 5). The time diagram of the change in the given velocity is shown in Fig. 5 the blue line, the time diagram of change of the set acceleration – the green line.

Figure 6 shows the time diagrams of the change in the signal of the movement task (blue line) and the actual movement (green line) when the coordinate $q1$ changes monotonically.

Figures 7 and 8 show the time diagram of the change of the signal setting the variable (blue line) and the actual movement (green line) coordinates q2, q3 when changing the speed sign.

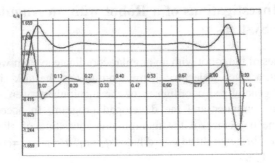

Fig. 5. Time diagrams of velocity and acceleration changes on the trajectory section.

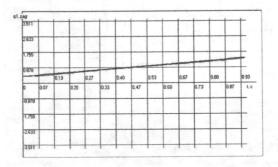

Fig. 6. Time diagrams of the change in the movement of the coordinate q1.

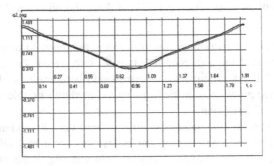

Fig. 7. Time diagrams of the change in the movement of the coordinate q2.

The results of experimental studies show that the dynamic control system provides reproduction with sufficient accuracy of the given trajectories of the robot under the action of dynamic effects associated with accelerated movement of links and mutual influence of coordinates, as well as gravitational forces.

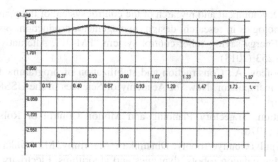

Fig. 8. Temporary diagrams of the change in the movement of the coordinate q3.

7 Conclusions

1. It is expedient to use in the limited space of a subway tunnel the three-coordinate manipulators with angular system of coordinates having the greatest compactness due to an opportunity to collapse practically without exceeding the basic dimensions of a robot.
2. When forming of the operating impacts to the executive drives of the specialized robot for the installation of cross ties, it is rational to use of the dynamic control method in which the dynamic model of the manipulator is included directly into the operating structure of the robot.
3. The equation of dynamics of the three-coordinate manipulator with angular system of coordinates obtained in a differential and vector form, on the basis of the computation routine and Lagrange's method of recording provide in their use as a part of microprocessor system the on-line control function of the manipulator.

References

1. Bahvalov, N.: Numerical Methods (analysis, algebra, ordinary differential equations). Nauka, Moscow (1975)
2. Vukobratovic, M., Stokic, D., Kircanski, N.: Non-adaptive and Adaptive Control of Manipulation Robots, vol. 5. Springer, Heidelberg (2013)
3. Vukobratovic, M., Stokic, D.: Control of Manipulation Robots: Theory and Application, vol. 2. Springer, Heidelberg (2012)
4. Krutko, P.: Control of Executive Systems of Robots. Nauka, Moscow (1991)
5. Marchuk, G.: Methods of Computational Mathematics. Nauka, Moscow (1980)
6. Medvedev, V.: Microprocessor control system of manipulator "PUMA-560". Bull. Voronezh State Tech. Univ. **13**(3), 34–38 (2017)
7. Medvedev, V., Novikov, A.: Modeling the dynamics of manipulators with arbitrary kinematic structures. Anal. Des. Robot. Autom. 139–142 (1999)
8. Medvedev, V., Petrenko, V., Kuzovkin, A.: The simulation Executive system of the robot PUMA 560 in MATLAB. Bull. Voronezh State Tech. Univ. **7**(12), 4–6 (2012)
9. Medvedev, V.: Simulation of robots and RTS.Voronezh State Technical University (2010)

10. Medvedev, V.: Development and research of the control system of the manipulator "PUMA-560". New technologies in research, design, management, production, pp. 311–315 (2017)
11. Medvedev, V.: Energy-saving robot control system "PM-01". Alternative and intellectual energy, pp. 252–253 (2018)
12. Pavlov, V., Timofeev, A.: Construction and stabilization of programmed movements of a movable robotic manipulator. News of Academy of Sciences of the USSR. Tech. cybernet. **6**, 91–101 (1976)
13. Pol, R.: Simulation, Trajectory Planning and Motion Control of Robotic Manipulator. Nauka, Moscow (1976)
14. Popov, E.: Manipulyacionnye roboty: Dinamika i Algoritmy. M.: Nauka (1978)
15. Shiyanov, A.: Manipulation robots: dynamics and algorithms. Elcctricity **5**, 40–42 (1998)
16. Hollerbach, J.: A recursive formulation of lagrangian manipulator dynamics. IEEE Trans. Syst. Man Cybern. **10**(11), 730–736 (1980)
17. Kahn, M., Roth, B.: The near-minimum-time control of open-loop articulated kinematic chains. J. Dyn. Syst. Meas. Contr. **93**, 164–172 (1971)
18. Renaud, N.: An efficient iterative analytical procedure for obtaining a robot manipulator dynamic model. In: Proceedings of First International Symposium of Robotics Research, pp. 749–762 (1983)
19. Uicker, J.: Dynamic force analysis of spatial linkages. Trans. ASME J. Appl. Mech. **34**, 418–424 (1976)
20. Vukobratovich, M.: New method for real-time manipulator dynamic model, forming on microcomputers. In: Proceeding of First Yugoslav-Soviet Symposium on Applied Robotics, pp. 60–65. Moscow (1983)
21. Yang, A.: Inertia force analysis of spatial mechanisms. Trans. ASME J. Eng. Ind. **93**, 39–46 (1971)

Distribution of Roles in a Dynamic Swarm of Robots in Conditions of Limited Communications

Donat Ivanov[1]([✉]) [iD], Sergey Kapustyan[2] [iD],
and Evgeny Petruchuk[1] [iD]

[1] Southern Federal University, 2 Chehova Street, 3479328 Taganrog, Russia
donat.ivanov@gmail.com
[2] Southern Scientific Center of the Russian Academy of Sciences,
41 Chehova Street, 344006 Rostov-on-Don, Russia

Abstract. The paper deals with the problem of the distribution of roles in coalition robots with limited communications. A formal formulation of the task of role distribution in the coalition of mobile robots is given. An analysis of existing approaches to the distribution of roles in groups of robots is given, such as solving the assignment problem by the Kuhn-Munkres algorithm, using the game theory apparatus, applying the methods of probability theory, and the method of propagating the control wave using a local conversion mechanism. An iterative approach to the distribution of roles in a group of robots, based on the strategy of decentralized control and the principles of swarm interaction, is proposed. A method for the distribution of roles in coalitions of mobile robots and an algorithm that implements this method for a separate coalition robot in the distribution of roles based on the proposed approach are described. The results of the study of the proposed approach, carried out with the help of computer simulation in coalitions of 100 robots in the distribution of three roles, are presented. The estimation of the error of the distribution of roles using the proposed algorithmically implemented method has been made and compared with the known approaches. The areas of possible practical application of the developed approach are shown.

Keywords: Swarm robotics · Distribution of roles · Distribution of tasks · Decentralized control · Multi-agent technologies · Limited communications

1 Introduction

The use of remotely controlled mobile robots is expedient and cost-effective when working in hard-to-reach and hazardous environments for humans. At the same time, the solution of many practical tasks requires the use of a large number of mobile robots united in a coalition, and their coordinated work (for example monitoring of coastal zones, woodlands [1–3], oil and gas pipelines [4–6], geological exploration of the seabed and shelf, etc.). Combining a certain number of robots to group in order to jointly perform a common group task (including one divided into subtasks) has in a number of works been called the coalition of robots. In this case, it is usually considered that the

© Springer Nature Switzerland AG 2019
A. Ronzhin et al. (Eds.): ICR 2019, LNAI 11659, pp. 99–108, 2019.
https://doi.org/10.1007/978-3-030-26118-4_10

robots of the group have the opportunity to enter into a coalition and leave it. As part of this work, we will assume that the coalition has already been formed and its composition does not change. Also, this article does not consider the formation task in a group of robots.

Decentralized control strategies and multi-agent [7] systems based on principles [8] of swarm intelligence [9] seem to be the most promising approaches to managing coalition robots.

When solving some tasks by coalitions of robots, the need arises for the functional differentiation of nodes, i.e. distribution of certain duties or roles in the coalition in such a way that some robots play one role and the other part others. The nature of the distribution of roles depends on the specifics of the task being performed.

In order to save on-board energy resources, the robots of the group are often impractical to assign computational and telecommunication tasks to the same robots. It is necessary to distribute the roles between the robots of the group so that in each individual area of the space covered by the mobile sensor network, there are both robots engaged in data collection and robots occupied in processing information and transferring the results to a remote server.

For example, all coalition robots are busy collecting data on the state of the environment using onboard sensor devices, however, some robots of the group (for example, 20%) additionally play the role of repeaters to ensure the transmission of the collected ones, another part of robots of the group (for example, 40%) performs preliminary processing of the data, and the remaining robots of the group provide backup storage of intermediate results.

Thus, the problem arises of the distribution of roles in a dynamic swarm of robots.

2   The Problem Statement

Consider the group R consisting of N mobile robots r_i where i is the ID of the robot, $i = 1, \ldots , N$. Each robot r_i at time t is described by a set of parameters: coordinates of the robot r_i in space $(x_i(t),\ y_i(t),\ z_i(t))$, velocity vector $\overline{v}_i(t)$, state (selected role) s_i from some set $\mathbf{s} = <s_0, s_1, \ldots , s_k>$ of available for the group roles. At the initial time t_0, all robots are in the state s_0. Each robot can independently change to any other state.

All robots of the R group move within a certain working zone Z with a width of Z_w, a length of Z_l and a height of Z_h, avoiding collisions between themselves. That is, there is a limit on the minimum allowable distance d_{min} between any pair of robots r_i and r_j in the group:

$$d_{min} \leq \sqrt{\left(x_j(t) - x_i(t)\right)^2 + \left(y_j(t) - y_i(t)\right)^2 + \left(z_j(t) - z_i(t)\right)^2}, \quad i,j = 1,\ldots,N; \quad i \neq j.$$

$$(1)$$

Onboard communications allows each robot to obtain data on the co-standing group of other robots that fall into its field of view is limited to a radius l_i of direct communication.

It is required to ensure the transition of the number n_m, $m = 1, \ldots, k$, robots of the group R to the state s_m, $m = 1, \ldots, k$, so that the percentage ratio is provided

$$c_m \in \left[\frac{n_m}{N} \cdot 100\% - \Delta_c\%, \frac{n_m}{N} \cdot 100\% + \Delta_c\% \right], \quad m = 1, \ldots, k, \tag{2}$$

where Δ_c – permissible error of the distribution of roles as a percentage of the total number of coalition robots. At the same time, $\sum\limits_{m=1}^{k} c_m = 100\%$. And also in any local area of space occupied by a coalition of robots, the dimensions of which exceed $2 \cdot l_i$, condition (2) is satisfied.

3 Review of Existing Approaches

It is possible to draw a parallel between the task of assigning roles in coalitions of robots and the task of distributing tasks (sub-tasks) in groups of robots, to which a fairly large number of scientific works are devoted (for example [4, 10, 11]). In general, when distributing targets, a certain set of robots and a set of targets are considered, and it is necessary to determine unambiguous correspondences between robots and targets with the required level of efficiency.

The task of target distribution can be represented as an assignment problem from the point of view of graph theory [12]. You can consider a bipartite graph, on the left side of which there are robots, on the right side there are targets, the edges of the graph determine the possible assignments of targets to robots, and the weights of the edges determine the "cost" of such assignments. Then the goal distribution problem is reduced to solving the assignment problem from the point of view of graph theory.

Known approaches to solving assignment problems, such as the Hungarian Algorithm (Kuhn-Mankres algorithm name is also found in scientific literature) [13, 14], defines assignments in a bipartite graph based on the cost matrix of the edges of the graph. However, the numerical evaluation of the cost of the graph edges in the distribution of roles is difficult, which prevents the use of the above methods of target distribution to solve the role assignment problem formulated in this article.

In game theory [15], back in the 60s of the 20th century, zero-sum games of two people were considered, when players only know the results of their games [16, 17]. However, these works do not take into account restrictions on communication and interaction with neighbors. In the considered problem statement, robots (automata) have access to information on which roles only neighboring robots have chosen.

In the simplest case, for each role, you can calculate a certain probability $P_m = c_m/100$, $m = 1, \ldots, k,$. Then, using the random number generator, each robot can choose one of the many roles in accordance with these probabilities. However, this approach is applicable only if the coalition robots are stationary, all coalition robots receive information about the required distribution at the same time, and further movements of the coalition robots and changes to the target role distributions are not provided. In practice, information about changes in the target distribution of roles will not be obtained by coalition robots at the same time; the fulfillment of a common group task can lead to movements of robots in space, including violations of the requirement for uniform distribution of roles in local areas.

An original approach to the distribution of roles in a static swarm based on the control wave propagation procedure was proposed in [18]. This method allows the distribution of roles in a static system in a relatively small number of iterations. The paper [18] presents the results of computer modeling, confirming the convergence of the re-ballot process when choosing a leader, and also showing that the number of re-ballots does not exceed the number N of the group R. However, it should be noted that this approach ensures the distribution of roles exclusively on the basis of the current network topology (which in turn depends on the configuration of the robots in space and the communication channels between them). Thus, it is impossible to obtain such a distribution of roles in a group in which the number n_0 of robots with a role s_0 exceeds unity. It is also impossible to set the number (or percentage) of robots with other roles in the group.

Thus, there is a need to develop a method and algorithm for solving the role distribution problem in coalitions of robots with limited communications, formulated above.

4   The Proposed Method

The materials proposed in this article are a continuation of the research carried out by a team of authors earlier and published in [19]. However, in the previous work, robots moved so slowly that the distribution of roles occurred before a change in the composition of the subgroups of neighbors occurred. In this paper, further studies have been conducted aimed at the distribution of roles in the dynamic swarms of robots. Robots make Brownian motion within the accessible area, avoiding collisions.

It is proposed to solve the problem iteratively. At each iteration, each robot r_i determines the number N_i of the sub-group R_i of the robots of group R that fall within its field of view limited to the radius l_i, i.e. robots neighbors. Then the robot counts the number of n_{mi}, $m = 1, \ldots, k$, in its subgroup (robots-neighbors), who have chosen one role s_m, $m = 1, \ldots, k$. With this information, the robot can calculate the current distribution of the roles of its subgroup R_i:

$$c_m^i = \frac{n_m^i}{N^i} \cdot 100\%, \quad m = 1, \ldots, k. \tag{3}$$

The robot then calculates the shortage Δc_{mi} (oversupply) robots for each role:

$$\Delta c_m^i = c_m - c_m^i, \quad m = 1, \ldots, k. \tag{4}$$

The robot then finds the maximum shortage max Δc_{mi} and chooses the appropriate role s_m.

If all roles are distributed in a group with an error of less than Δc, the task of assigning roles is considered completed. Otherwise, the next stage of the iterative process is repeated. The algorithm of actions of the robot r_i in the distribution of roles is shown in Fig. 1.

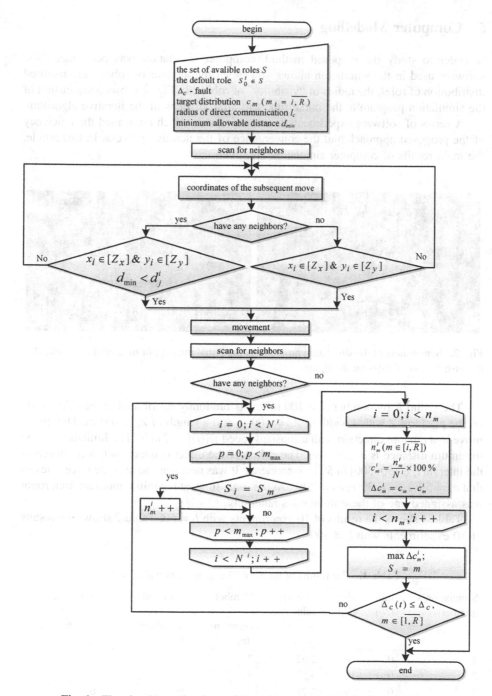

Fig. 1. The algorithm of actions of the robot r_i in the distribution of roles.

5   Computer Modelling

In order to study the proposed method, computer simulation was performed. The software used in the simulation allows you to set the number of robots, the required distribution of roles, the radius of "visibility" of robots. In Fig. 2 shows a screenshot of the simulation program at the initial time and after 20 steps of the iterative algorithm.

A series of software experiments were carried out, which confirmed the efficiency of the proposed approach and the convergence of the iterative process. In this article, the main results of computer simulation are given.

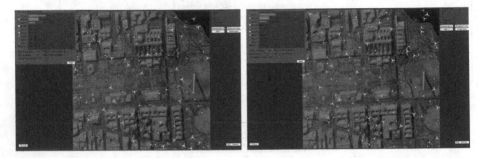

Fig. 2. Screenshots of the simulation program (at the initial moment of time on the left and after the distribution of roles on the right).

The group R by number $N = 100$ robots is randomly distributed at the initial time on the platform Z with a width of $Z_w = 500$ m and a length of $Z_l = 500$ m. The robots move in a random direction with a constant speed $|\bar{v}_i(t)| = 2$ m/s. The limitation on the minimum distance is $d_{min} = 5$ m. The radius of the direct connection l_i was chosen in the interval $l_i \in [50; 300]$ in 50 m increments. It was necessary to allocate three roles so that $c_1 = 50\%, c_2 = 30\%, c_3 = 20\%$. At the same time, at the initial moment each robot was assigned one of these three roles randomly.

Table 1 shows the results of 10 experiments with $l_i = 50$. Table 2 shows the results of 10 experiments with $l_i = 300$.

Table 1. The results of the first 10 experiments with $l_i = 50$.

Simulation's number	min (N_i)	max (N_i)	Average value N_i	Number of iteration steps	Minimum error of distribution, %	Maximum error of distribution, %
1	0	6	2,62	2	1	3
2	0	10	3,52	3	1	3
3	0	9	3,26	3	0	6
4	0	9	3,06	2	1	2
5	0	10	3,06	3	1	2

(*continued*)

Table 1. (*continued*)

Simulation's number	min (N_i)	max (N_i)	Average value N_i	Number of iteration steps	Minimum error of distribution, %	Maximum error of distribution, %
6	0	8	3,12	2	1	5
7	0	6	2,54	2	3	8
8	0	9	3,04	3	2	6
9	0	7	2,76	2	1	6
10	0	7	2,58	2	0	5

Table 2. The results of the first 10 experiments with $l_i = 300$.

Simulation's number	min (N_i)	max (N_i)	Average value N_i	Number of iteration steps	Minimum error of distribution, %	Maximum error of distribution, %
1	34	96	65,16	7	0	3
2	31	96	63,9	13	1	2
3	29	92	59,48	10	0	2
4	27	93	60,08	9	2	5
5	31	94	60,82	8	0	2
6	27	90	55,28	5	0	2
7	32	95	60,46	6	0	2
8	36	97	65,9	6	1	3
9	27	89	58,14	11	0	2
10	22	92	62,06	10	0	2

For each selected set of parameters, a series of model experiments was carried out. The minimum, maximum and average (for the whole group) number of robots falling into one subgroup, the number of repetitions of the iterative process required to perform the distribution of roles, the minimum and maximum error for individual roles was taken into account. When analyzing the current distribution in their subgroup, each robot took into account all robots of the subgroup, except for itself.

In the course of computer modeling, the distribution of roles was considered to be perfect if further iterations did not lead to redistribution of roles. So, Fig. 3 shows the distribution of roles changed in a coalition with 100 robots for $l_i = 300$.

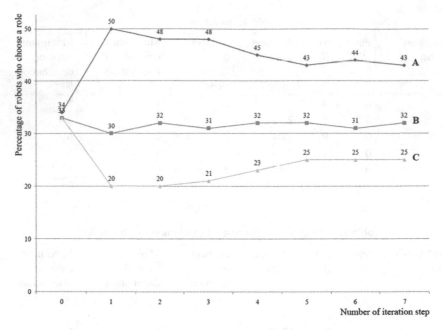

Fig. 3. The redistribution of roles when performing an iterative process in one of the experiments.

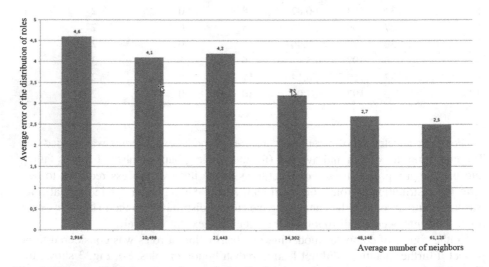

Fig. 4. The graph of the dependence of the distribution of roles on the average number of neighboring robots on the results of computer simulation

It should be noted that the results of computer simulation showed the convergence of the iterative process in the event that each robot takes into account the current distribution in its subgroup without taking into account its current role. Moreover, the number of iteration steps is relatively small (from 2 to 16 in the conducted model experiments) with the number of robots $N = 100$. At the same time, the distribution of roles in each individual local area was close to the target distribution.

6 Conclusions and Future Work

The results of computer simulation showed that, compared with the approach to the distribution of roles in groups of robots described in [18], the approach proposed in this work ensures convergence in a smaller number of iteration steps.

Given that the proposed method basically contains a probabilistic approach, it can be noted that the distribution error and the required number of iterative steps are less in cases when the number of local subgroups are higher (see Fig. 4).

Increasing the number of local subgroups without increasing the number of the coalition is possible either by increasing the radius of direct visibility, or by forming a more compact structure in the group of robots. Also in the future, we can consider the possibility of routing when transmitting messages about the status of those robots that are not part of one local subgroup. Further research will be devoted to finding methods and algorithms that will reduce the error in the distribution of tasks.

Acknowledgement. The reported study was funded by RFBR according to the research projects №17-29-07054, №19-07-00907, №18-05-80092, and the program of RAS presidium fundamental research I.29 "Actual problems of robotic systems" (progect №AAAAA18-118020190041-1).

References

1. Casbeer, D.W., Beard, R.W., Mehra, R.K., McLain, T.W.: Forest fire monitoring with multiple small UAVs. In: Proceedings of the 2005, American Control Conference, pp. 3530–3535. IEEE (2005). https://doi.org/10.1109/ACC.2005.1470520
2. Merino, L., Caballero, F., Martínez-de Dios, J.R., Ferruz, J., Ollero, A.: A cooperative perception system for multiple UAVs: application to automatic detection of forest fires. J. Field Robot. **23**, 165–184 (2006)
3. Sujit, P.B., Kingston, D., Beard, R.: Cooperative forest fire monitoring using multiple UAVs. In: 2007 46th IEEE Conference on Decision and Control, pp. 4875–4880 (2007)
4. Kalyaev, I., Kapustyan, S., Ivanov, D., Korovin, I., Usachev, L., Schaefer, G.: A novel method for distribution of goals among UAVs for oil field monitoring. In: 2017 6th International Conference on Informatics, Electronics and Vision & 2017 7th International Symposium in Computational Medical and Health Technology (ICIEV-ISCMHT), pp. 1–4 (2017)
5. Ondráček, J.: Intelligent Algorithms for Monitoring of the Environment Around Oil Pipe Systems Using Unmanned Aerial Systems (2014)
6. Ivanov, D., Korovin, I., Shabanov, V.: Oil fields monitoring by groups of mobile micro-robots using distributed neural networks. In: 2018 Joint 7th International Conference on Informatics, Electronics & Vision (ICIEV) and 2018 2nd International Conference on Imaging, Vision & Pattern Recognition (icIVPR), pp. 588–593 (2018)
7. Ferber, J.: Multi-agent Systems: An Introduction to Distributed Artificial Intelligence. Addison-Wesley, Reading (1999)

8. Kaliaev, I., Kapustjan, S., Ivanov, D.: Decentralized control strategy within a large group of objects based on swarm intelligence. In: 2011 IEEE 5th International Conference on Robotics, Automation Mechatronics, pp. 299–303 (2011). https://doi.org/10.1109/RAMECH.2011. 6070500
9. Dorigo, M., Birattari, M.: Swarm intelligence. Scholarpedia **2**, 1462 (2007)
10. Lerman, K., Jones, C., Galstyan, A., Matarić, M.J.: Analysis of dynamic task allocation in multi-robot systems. Int. J. Rob. Res. **25**, 225–241 (2006)
11. Batalin, M.A., Sukhatme, G.S.: Using a sensor network for distributed multi-robot task allocation. In: IEEE International Conference on Robotics and Automation. Proceedings, ICRA 2004, pp. 158–164 (2004)
12. Mulmuley, K., Vazirani, U.V., Vazirani, V.V.: Matching is as easy as matrix inversion. Combinatorica **7**, 105–113 (1987)
13. Kuhn, H.W.: The Hungarian method for the assignment problem. Nav. Res. Logist. Q. **2**, 83–97 (1955)
14. Kuhn, H.W.: The Hungarian method for the assignment problem. In: 50 Years of Integer Programming 1958–2008: From the Early Years to the State-of-the-Art, pp. 29–47 (2010). https://doi.org/10.1007/978-3-540-68279-0_2
15. Hajek, B.: An Introduction to Game Theory. Department of Electrical and Computer Engineering University of Illinois at Urbana-Champaign (2017)
16. Luce, R.D., Raiffa, H.: Games and Decisions: Introduction and Critical Survey. Wiley, New York (1958)
17. McKinsey, J.C.C.: Introduction to the Theory of Games. RAND Corporation, Santa Monica (1952)
18. Karpov, V., Karpova, I.: Leader election algorithms for static swarms. Biol. Inspired Cogn. Archit. **12**, 54–64 (2015)
19. Ivanov, D.Ya.: Distribution of roles in groups of robots with limited communications based on the swarm interaction. Procedia Comput. Sci. **150**, 518–523 (2019)

An Assist-as-Needed Impedance Controller for Rehabilitation Robots

Hamed Jabbari Asl[1]([✉]) [iD], Masashi Yamashita[2], and Tatsuo Narikiyo[1]

[1] Control System Laboratory, Toyota Technological Institute, 2-12-1 Hisakata, Tempaku-ku, Nagoya 468-8511, Japan
{hjabbari,n-tatsuo}@toyota-ti.ac.jp
[2] T-Frontier Division, Toyota Motor Corporation, Toyota-cho, Toyota, Japan
masashi_yamashita_ab@mail.toyota.co.jp

Abstract. This paper proposes an assistive control scheme for rehabilitation robots. The design objective is to develop a control strategy to follow a predefined path by maximizing the active participation of impaired subjects. For this purpose, we develop an impedance controller for velocity tracking and gain the assist-as-needed property by means of modulating the target impedance. The given method neither requires a compliant robot nor needs the dynamic model of the system. The approach also provides motion timing freedom due to working in the velocity domain. The performance of the controller is evaluated through experimental tests.

Keywords: Rehabilitation robots · Assist-as-needed control · Impedance control

1 Introduction

Robotic systems excel at repetitive training of patients suffering from neurological impairments, which is a key factor in the reorganization of nervous system. One of the challenges in gaining desired clinical outcomes from the rehabilitation robots is the controller design. For patients who have partial control on their limb, like post-stroke individuals, the minimal intervention of the controller (robot) delivers more promising results in robotic-assisted rehabilitation. The controllers which exert the minimum required assistance to the subject are called "assist-as-needed" (AAN) controller [11].

Different AAN control schemes have been proposed in the literature. Early AAN approaches are impedance controllers, in which a desired position trajectory is tracked [7,9]. These works consider a free moving area around the desired trajectory to achieve the AAN performance. However, the methods are developed under the assumption that the robotic system is fully back-drivable. The term back-drivable is used for the systems that can be moved compliantly without resistive torques, which is achievable at the cost of applying feedforward control compensators [11] and/or utilizing complex actuation systems [4].

© Springer Nature Switzerland AG 2019
A. Ronzhin et al. (Eds.): ICR 2019, LNAI 11659, pp. 109–118, 2019.
https://doi.org/10.1007/978-3-030-26118-4_11

A disturbance observer-based AAN controller is given in [11] and tested on an upper-limb robotic system. This method estimates the user inputs and cancels them through the controller. The AAN property, in this work, has been mainly achieved through adjusting the tracking error. This method also requires the dynamic model of the system.

An AAN controller is proposed in [13], which learns the dynamics of the systems through an adaptive scheme. The AAN property is injected into the controller by considering a forgetting factor in the adaptation law. Another adaptive neural network-based controller is given in [1], where the AAN property is featured by means of a dead-zone area as in [7,9] and a forgetting factor in the adaptation law as in [13]. Although these two adaptive methods have the advantage of providing a precise tracking for an uncertain system by tuning the forgetting factor, they still need a back-drivable system to deliver the desired AAN performance.

In this paper, we propose an impedance controller, which provides the AAN property by means of modulating a reference impedance model. The controller is designed in the velocity domain such that the robot follows desired velocity values encoding a desired path for the robot. Working in the velocity domain has the advantage of delivering freedom in the timing of movement, which is a crucial factor in maximizing the active participation of subjects during the rehabilitation process [5]. While tracking the velocity values, the proposed approach adjusts the impedance of the robot by monitoring the tracking error in a way to encourage the subject for active participation in the tests. In comparison to [6,7,9,12], which similarly utilize a variable impedance model, the proposed method provides timing freedom and also releases the assumption of having a fully back-drivable system or knowing the dynamics of the robot, hence it significantly reduces the mechanical and/or controller design complexity. The proposed scheme is validated through experiments conducted on a planar end-effector type upper-limb robot.

2 Equations of Motion

We assume that the studied rehabilitation robot consists of n revolute joints connected with rigid links. The kinematics of the robot is denoted here by $\mathcal{H}(\mathbf{q})$: $\mathbb{R}^n \to \mathbb{R}^l$, which determines the pose $\mathbf{x} \in \mathbb{R}^l$ of the end point from the known joint values as $\mathbf{x} = \mathcal{H}(\mathbf{q})$. The differential kinematics can then be written as $\dot{\mathbf{x}} = (\partial \mathcal{H}(\mathbf{q})/\partial \mathbf{q})\dot{\mathbf{q}} = \mathbf{J}(\mathbf{q})\dot{\mathbf{q}}$, where the matrix $\mathbf{J}(\mathbf{q}) \in \mathbb{R}^{l \times n}$ defines the analytical Jacobian, and gives a relation between the velocities in Cartesian space and joint space.

Assumption 1 *The Jacobian matrix* $\mathbf{J}(\mathbf{q})$ *is bounded and full-rank in the defined operational workspace such that its inverse exists.*

Denoting the position, velocity and acceleration of joints, respectively, as $\mathbf{q}, \dot{\mathbf{q}}, \ddot{\mathbf{q}} \in \mathbb{R}^n$, the dynamics of robot can be described as follows [2]:

$$\mathbf{M}(\mathbf{q})\ddot{\mathbf{q}} + \mathbf{C}(\mathbf{q}, \dot{\mathbf{q}})\dot{\mathbf{q}} + \mathbf{G}(\mathbf{q}) + \mathbf{F}(\dot{\mathbf{q}}) = \boldsymbol{\tau} + \mathbf{J}^\top \mathbf{f}_{\text{ext}}$$

where $\boldsymbol{\tau} \in \mathbb{R}^n$ denotes the vector of applied torques by actuators, $\mathbf{M}(\mathbf{q}) \in \mathbb{R}^{n \times n}$ is the inertia matrix, $\mathbf{C}(\mathbf{q}, \dot{\mathbf{q}}) \in \mathbb{R}^{n \times n}$ denotes the centrifugal and Coriolis matrix, $\mathbf{G}(\mathbf{q}) \in \mathbb{R}^n$ is the gravity vector, $\mathbf{F}(\dot{\mathbf{q}}) \in \mathbb{R}^n$ denotes the friction vector, and $\mathbf{f}_{\text{ext}} \in \mathbb{R}^l$ is the external force vector exerted by the user.

Considering *Assumption* 1 and assuming $l = n$, we can develop the dynamics based on the Cartesian space variable as follows:

$$\mathbf{M}_x(\mathbf{x})\ddot{\mathbf{x}} + \mathbf{C}_x(\mathbf{x}, \dot{\mathbf{x}})\dot{\mathbf{x}} + \mathbf{G}_x(\mathbf{x}) + \mathbf{F}_x(\dot{\mathbf{x}}) = \mathbf{J}^{-\top}\boldsymbol{\tau} + \mathbf{f}_{\text{ext}} \tag{1}$$

where the new dynamic terms are defined as $\mathbf{M}_x(\mathbf{x}) \triangleq \mathbf{J}^{-\top}\mathbf{M}(\mathbf{q})\mathbf{J}^{-1}$, $\mathbf{C}_x(\mathbf{x}, \dot{\mathbf{x}}) \triangleq \mathbf{J}^{-\top}[\mathbf{C}(\mathbf{q}, \dot{\mathbf{q}}) - \mathbf{M}(\mathbf{q})\mathbf{J}^{-1}\dot{\mathbf{J}}]\mathbf{J}^{-1}$, $\mathbf{G}_x(\mathbf{x}) \triangleq \mathbf{J}^{-\top}\mathbf{G}(\mathbf{q})$, and $\mathbf{F}_x(\dot{\mathbf{x}}) \triangleq \mathbf{J}^{-\top}\mathbf{F}(\dot{\mathbf{q}})$. As long as the Jacobian matrix is nonsingular, the dynamics (1) possess the following properties.

Property 1. The matrix $\mathbf{M}_x(\mathbf{x})$ is positive-definite and satisfies $\underline{m}\|\mathbf{y}\|^2 \le \mathbf{y}^\top \mathbf{M}_x(\mathbf{x})\mathbf{y} \le \overline{m}\|\mathbf{y}\|^2, \forall \mathbf{y} \in \mathbb{R}^l$, where $\|\cdot\|$ denotes the Euclidean norm, and $\underline{m}, \overline{m} \in \mathbb{R}^+$ are, respectively, defined as $\underline{m} \triangleq \min_{\forall \mathbf{x}}(\lambda_m(\mathbf{M}_x))$, and $\overline{m} \triangleq \max_{\forall \mathbf{x}}(\lambda_M(\mathbf{M}_x))$ with $\lambda_m(\cdot)$ and $\lambda_M(\cdot)$, respectively, denoting the minimum and maximum eigenvalues of a matrix.

Property 2. The matrix $\dot{\mathbf{M}}_x(\mathbf{x}) - 2\mathbf{C}_x(\mathbf{x}, \dot{\mathbf{x}})$ is skew-symmetric, and hence satisfies $\mathbf{y}^\top(\dot{\mathbf{M}}_x(\mathbf{x}) - 2\mathbf{C}_x(\mathbf{x}, \dot{\mathbf{x}}))\mathbf{y} = 0, \forall \mathbf{y} \in \mathbb{R}^l$.

3 Proposed Method

We aim to design a velocity tracking controller such that it generates a strong support when the user is not able to track the velocities, and it reduces the intervention of the robot when the user can perform the task. Our main goal is to gain this AAN performance without using the dynamic model of the system. The control objective has been achieved by assigning a desired impedance model for the robot, which is modulated according to the performance of the user. In comparison to the existing variable impedance methods in the literature [6,7,9, 12], the proposed one makes use of advantages of control in the velocity domain, and also does not necessarily require a fully back-drivable system.

First we design a precise impedance controller for tracking the desired velocity $\mathbf{v}_d \in \mathbb{R}^l$, and then a scheme will be proposed to modulate the reference impedance in order to achieve the AAN property. It is assumed that the velocity values in the work space, $\mathbf{v}_d$, are designed such that they encode a desired path for the robot; see [3] for the construction of velocity field. The desired impedance is defined as follows:

$$\mathbf{M}_i(\ddot{\mathbf{x}} - \dot{\mathbf{v}}_d) + \mathbf{D}_i(\dot{\mathbf{x}} - \mathbf{v}_d) = -\mathbf{f}_{\text{ext}} \tag{2}$$

in which $\mathbf{M}_i \in \mathbb{R}^{l \times l}$ and $\mathbf{D}_i \in \mathbb{R}^{l \times l}$ are positive-definite diagonal matrices. The controller design is based on the assumption that the applied torques by the user, $\mathbf{f}_{\text{ext}}$, are available through a force sensor, and the dynamics of the system is unknown. Due to the uncertainties in the system and to avoid using acceleration of the robot in the controller, inspired from [14], an intermediary impedance model is introduced as follows:

$$\mathbf{M}_i \left(\dot{\mathbf{v}}_i - \dot{\mathbf{v}}_d \right) + \mathbf{D}_i \left(\mathbf{v}_i - \mathbf{v}_d \right) = -\mathbf{f}_{\text{ext}} \tag{3}$$

where $\mathbf{v}_i \in \mathbb{R}^l$ is the state of the following reference model:

$$\mathbf{M}_i \dot{\mathbf{v}}_i + \mathbf{D}_i \mathbf{v}_i = \mathbf{M}_i \dot{\mathbf{v}}_d + \mathbf{D}_i \mathbf{v}_d - \mathbf{f}_{\text{ext}}. \tag{4}$$

If $\dot{\mathbf{x}}$ asymptotically converges to $\mathbf{v}_i$, then the intermediary target impedance (3) will converge to (2). The convergence of $\dot{\mathbf{x}}$ to $\mathbf{v}_i$ also means that $\dot{\mathbf{x}}$ will inherit the dynamics of $\mathbf{v}_i$ in (3), which is the desired impedance. Therefore a controller will be designed to reduce the error vector $\mathbf{r} \in \mathbb{R}^l$ defined as follows:

$$\mathbf{r} \triangleq \dot{\mathbf{x}} - \mathbf{v}_i.$$

Utilizing (1), the following dynamics can be developed for $\mathbf{r}$:

$$\mathbf{M}_x(\mathbf{x}) \dot{\mathbf{r}} = -\mathbf{C}_x(\mathbf{x}, \dot{\mathbf{x}}) \mathbf{r} + \mathbf{N} + \mathbf{J}^{-\top} \boldsymbol{\tau} + \mathbf{f}_{\text{ext}} \tag{5}$$

where $\mathbf{N}(\mathbf{x}, \dot{\mathbf{x}}, \mathbf{v}_i, \dot{\mathbf{v}}_i) \in \mathbb{R}^l$ is defined as

$$\mathbf{N} \triangleq -\mathbf{C}_x(\mathbf{x}, \dot{\mathbf{x}}) \mathbf{v}_i - \mathbf{G}_x(\mathbf{x}) - \mathbf{F}_x(\dot{\mathbf{x}}) - \mathbf{M}_x(\mathbf{x}) \dot{\mathbf{v}}_i \tag{6}$$

which includes the unknown dynamic terms. This function can be represented over a compact set Ω_N through a radial basis function (RBF) neural network with $\mathcal{L}$ neurons as follows [8]:

$$\mathbf{N}(\mathbf{z}) = \mathbf{W}^\top \boldsymbol{\sigma}(\mathbf{z}) + \boldsymbol{\varepsilon}(\mathbf{z}) \tag{7}$$

where $\mathbf{z} \triangleq [1 \ \mathbf{x}^\top \ \dot{\mathbf{x}}^\top \ \mathbf{v}_i^\top \ \dot{\mathbf{v}}_i^\top]^\top \in \mathbb{R}^m$ with $m = 4l + 1$, and $\mathbf{W} \in \mathbb{R}^{\mathcal{L} \times l}$ is a bounded constant ideal weight matrix. The function $\boldsymbol{\varepsilon}(\mathbf{z}) \in \mathbb{R}^l$ in (7) is the functional reconstruction error, and $\boldsymbol{\sigma}(\mathbf{z}) \in \mathbb{R}^{\mathcal{L}}$ is the vector of activation function. Considering the estimate of weight matrix as $\hat{\mathbf{W}} \in \mathbb{R}^{\mathcal{L} \times n}$, an estimate of $\mathbf{N}$ can be written as [8]

$$\hat{\mathbf{N}}(\mathbf{z}) \triangleq \hat{\mathbf{W}}^\top \boldsymbol{\sigma}(\mathbf{z}). \tag{8}$$

According to (7) and (8), the estimation error can be developed as

$$\mathbf{N} - \hat{\mathbf{N}} = \tilde{\mathbf{W}}^\top \boldsymbol{\sigma}(\mathbf{z}) + \boldsymbol{\varepsilon}(\mathbf{z}) \tag{9}$$

where $\tilde{\mathbf{W}} \triangleq \mathbf{W} - \hat{\mathbf{W}} \in \mathbb{R}^{\mathcal{L} \times l}$. Over the compact set Ω_N, the ideal weight matrix $\mathbf{W}$ is bounded such that $\|\mathbf{W}\|_F^2 \triangleq \text{tr}(\mathbf{W}^\top \mathbf{W}) \leq W_B$, where $\| \cdot \|_F$ denotes the Frobenius norm, $\text{tr}(\cdot)$ denotes the trace of a matrix, and $W_B \in \mathbb{R}^+$ is an unknown constant. Also, on Ω_N the functional reconstruction error $\boldsymbol{\varepsilon}(\mathbf{z})$ is bounded such that $\|\boldsymbol{\varepsilon}(\mathbf{z})\| \leq \varepsilon_N$, where $\varepsilon_N \in \mathbb{R}^+$ is a positive constant.

Having the estimate of unknown function $\mathbf{N}$, the controller is proposed as follows:

$$\boldsymbol{\tau} \triangleq -\mathbf{J}^\top \mathbf{K}_r \mathbf{r} - \mathbf{J}^\top \hat{\mathbf{N}} \tag{10}$$

where $\mathbf{K}_r \in \mathbb{R}^{l \times l}$ is a diagonal positive-definite gain matrix. Also, the adaptation law for the weight matrix is given as

$$\dot{\hat{\mathbf{W}}} \triangleq \varrho \boldsymbol{\sigma}(\mathbf{z}) \mathbf{r}^\top - \rho \varrho \hat{\mathbf{W}} \tag{11}$$

where, $\varrho, \rho \in \mathbb{R}^+$ are positive adjustable constants.

Substituting (10) into (5) and using (9), the closed-loop dynamics of the error system can be stated as

$$\mathbf{M}_x(\mathbf{x})\dot{\mathbf{r}} = -\mathbf{C}_x(\mathbf{x}, \dot{\mathbf{x}})\mathbf{r} - \mathbf{K}_r \mathbf{r} + \tilde{\mathbf{W}}^\top \boldsymbol{\sigma}(\mathbf{z}) + \boldsymbol{\varepsilon}(\mathbf{z}) + \mathbf{f}_{\text{ext}}. \tag{12}$$

Note that although $\mathbf{f}_{\text{ext}}$ is assumed to be available, it is not compensated through the controller. In fact, $\mathbf{f}_{\text{ext}}$ will be a supportive force to the controller if it is applied correctly, and it will otherwise be treated as a disturbance.

The stability result of the closed-loop system (12) is stated in the following theorem.

Theorem 1. *The controller (10) with the adaptation law (11) renders uniformly ultimately bounded (UUB) tracking under the condition that*

$$\lambda_{\min}(\mathbf{K}_r) > \frac{\kappa^2}{4} \tag{13}$$

where the parameters $\kappa \in \mathbb{R}^+$ is a known value defined in the proof.

Proof. The following Lyapunov function is considered:

$$L \triangleq \frac{1}{2}\mathbf{r}^\top \mathbf{M}_x(\mathbf{x})\mathbf{r} + \frac{1}{2\varrho}\text{tr}(\tilde{\mathbf{W}}^\top \tilde{\mathbf{W}}). \tag{14}$$

Using (12) and *Property* 2, and knowing that $\bar{\mathbf{a}}^\top \bar{\mathbf{b}} = \text{tr}(\bar{\mathbf{b}}\bar{\mathbf{a}}^\top)$, $\forall \bar{\mathbf{a}}, \bar{\mathbf{b}} \in \mathbb{R}^n$, we can develop the following time derivative for L:

$$\dot{L} = -\mathbf{r}^\top \mathbf{K}_r \mathbf{r} + \text{tr}\left(\tilde{\mathbf{W}}^\top \left(\boldsymbol{\sigma}(\mathbf{z})\mathbf{r}^\top - \frac{1}{\varrho}\dot{\hat{\mathbf{W}}}\right)\right) + \mathbf{r}^\top \left(\boldsymbol{\varepsilon}(\mathbf{z}) + \mathbf{f}_{\text{ext}}\right). \tag{15}$$

Substituting the adaptation law (11) into (15), we can develop the following upper bound for $\dot{L}$:

$$\dot{L} \leq -\lambda_{\min}(\mathbf{K}_r) \|\mathbf{r}\|^2 + \text{tr}(\rho \tilde{\mathbf{W}}^\top \hat{\mathbf{W}}) + \delta \|\mathbf{r}\|$$

where $\delta \triangleq \varepsilon_N + \|\mathbf{f}_{\text{ext}}\|$. Knowing the facts that

$$\delta \|\mathbf{r}\| \leq \frac{\kappa^2}{4}\|\mathbf{r}\|^2 + \frac{\delta^2}{\kappa^2}, \quad \forall \kappa \in \mathbb{R}^+$$

$$\text{tr}(\rho \tilde{\mathbf{W}}^\top \hat{\mathbf{W}}) \leq -\frac{\rho}{2}\left\|\tilde{\mathbf{W}}\right\|_F^2 + \frac{\rho}{2}\|\mathbf{W}\|_F^2$$

the following inequality can be written:

$$\dot{L} \leq -\left(\lambda_{\min}(\mathbf{K}_r) - \frac{\kappa^2}{4}\right)\|\mathbf{r}\|^2 - \frac{\rho}{2}\left\|\tilde{\mathbf{W}}\right\|_F^2 + \beta$$

where $\beta \triangleq \frac{\varrho}{2}\|\mathbf{W}\|_F^2 + \frac{\delta^2}{\kappa^2}$. We can also develop the following upper bound for $\dot{L}$:

$$\dot{L} \le -\eta L + \beta \tag{16}$$

where $\eta \in \mathbb{R}$ is defined as

$$\eta \triangleq \min\left\{ \frac{2}{m}\left(\lambda_{\min}(\mathbf{K}_r) - \frac{\kappa^2}{4}\right), \rho\varrho \right\}$$

which will be positive if the condition (13) is satisfied. Thus, from (14) and *Property* 1, and solving (16), the following inequalities can be concluded:

$$\frac{1}{2}\underline{m}\|\mathbf{r}\|^2 \le L(t) \le L(0)\,\mathrm{e}^{-\eta t} + \frac{\beta}{\eta}. \tag{17}$$

The inequalities in (17) indicate that the norm of tracking error eventually converges to the following compact set:

$$\Omega_e \triangleq \left\{ \mathbf{r} \mid \|\mathbf{r}\| \le \sqrt{\frac{2\beta}{\underline{m}\eta}} \right\}.$$

The proposed controller only satisfies the intermediary impedance model, and does not necessarily provide the AAN property. In the proposed scheme, this property can be achieved by considering a variable impedance model. For this purpose, we define the signal $\mathbf{e} \triangleq \dot{\mathbf{x}} - \mathbf{v}_d \in \mathbb{R}^l$ and decrease the intermediary impedance for small values of this signal and increase it otherwise by modulating the impedance matrices $\mathbf{M}_i$ and $\mathbf{D}_i$. Figure 1 shows an illustrative example of the impedance term modulation. In the figure, $D_i \in \mathbb{R}^+$ is set at its minimum value D_0 provided the signal $e \in \mathbb{R}$ is inside the admissible error range $|e| \le \gamma$ for some $\gamma \in \mathbb{R}^+$, and it increases toward its maximum value D_M for $|e| > \gamma$.

If the user inputs $\mathbf{f}_{\text{ext}}$ can minimize the error between $\dot{\mathbf{x}}$ and $\mathbf{v}_d$, the intervention of the robot would be significantly reduced. This is because of the reduced impedance terms, and also the fact that in this condition $\mathbf{v}_i$ will converge to $\mathbf{v}_d$; hence, according to (3), the total impedance will be reduced. If the user inputs are not correctly applied, the impedance terms will be increased and $\mathbf{f}_{\text{ext}}$ will act as a small perturbation for (4), which results in the convergence of $\mathbf{v}_i$ around $\mathbf{v}_d$. The increased impedance will yield strong support from the robot pushing the user in the correct direction. The error range, defined by γ in Fig. 1, provides admissible velocity values under low impedance, which means that the desired path can be freely tracked with different displacements in the time constant, i.e., timing freedom.

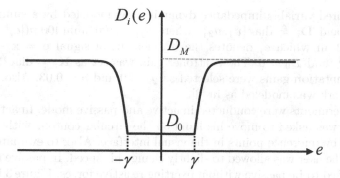

Fig. 1. Impedance term modulation for the AAN performance.

4 Resutls

In this section, we present experimental results conducted to evaluate the performance of the controller. The experiments were carried out on an end-effector type planar robot designed for moving shoulder, elbow, and hand of the user [see Fig. 2], and the subject was a healthy male volunteer. The robot includes two revolute joints and two links with the length of 0.25 m. The robot is equipped with a six-axis BL Autotec MINI 8/40 force sensor, which is attached to the end-effector. Actuators of the robot include harmonic drive servomotors of FHA-11C-100 series with the maximum continuous torque of 11 N m, maximum speed of 2π rads^{-1}, gear ratio of 100, incremental encoder resolution of 800,000 pulses per revolution, and can be driven via torque input commands. The controller was modeled in Simulink of MATLAB, running in real-time on xPC Target with the sampling frequency of 1 kHz. The experimental system includes a visual interface to provide qualitative information about the desired path, velocity and current position to the user.

A circular contour with a radius of 0.05 m was considered as the desired path. For this contour, assuming that the position vector $\mathbf{p} \in \mathbb{R}^2$ is given by $\mathbf{p} = [x\ y]^\top$, the desired velocity can be defined as follows [10]:

$$\mathbf{v}_d(\mathbf{p}) = -2k(\mathbf{p})u(\mathbf{p}) \begin{bmatrix} (x - x_c) \\ (y - y_c) \end{bmatrix} + 2c(\mathbf{p}) \begin{bmatrix} -(y - y_c) \\ (x - x_c) \end{bmatrix}$$

where $u(\mathbf{p}) \triangleq (x - x_c)^2 + (y - y_c)^2 - r_0^2$,

$$k(\mathbf{p}) \triangleq \frac{k_0}{|u(\mathbf{p})|\,\|\nabla u(\mathbf{p})\| + \epsilon_0}, \quad c(\mathbf{p}) \triangleq \frac{v_0 e^{-c_0|u(\mathbf{p})|}}{\|\nabla u(\mathbf{p})\|},$$

in which $\nabla u(\mathbf{p}) \triangleq [\partial u/\partial x\ \ \partial u/\partial y]^\top$. The parameters of the velocity field were set as $x_c = 0$ m, $y_c = 0.25$ m, $k_0 = 0.35$ m s^{-1}, $r_0 = 0.05$ m, $v_0 = 0.05$ m s^{-1}, $\epsilon_0 = 0.00075$ m^3, and $c_0 = 250$ m^{-2}.

The desired variable impedance dynamics was modeled by assuming $\mathbf{M}_i = \text{diag}\{1, 1\}$, and $\mathbf{D}_i \triangleq \text{diag}\{\vartheta_1, \vartheta_2\}$, where $\vartheta_j \triangleq 100 \tanh(400\varpi(|e_j|, \gamma)) + D_0$ for $j = 1, 2$, in which e_j denotes the ith element of signal $\mathbf{e} = \dot{\mathbf{x}} - \mathbf{v}_d$, $\gamma = 0.025$ m s^{-1}, and $D_0 = 0$. The controller gain was set as $\mathbf{K}_p = \text{diag}\{250, 250\}$, and the adaptation gains were selected as $\varrho = 50$ and $\rho = 0.03$. Also, the RBF neural network was modeled as in [3].

The experiments were conducted in active and passive mode. In active mode, the subject was asked to move his hand on the circular contour with the speed determined by reference points in the visual interface. Also, to evaluate freedom in motion, the user was allowed to slightly change his speed. In passive mode, the user was asked to be passive without exerting resistive forces. Figure 3 illustrates the trajectories of the end-effector in active and passive mode. The number of turns is different in each mode within a certain time period, which shows timing freedom. Also, the traveled path in passive mode is very close to the desired one, which demonstrates that the controller can complete the task whenever the user is not able. The tracking error signals are shown in Fig. 5, and Fig. 4 illustrates the measurements of the force sensor in two modes. As this figure shows, when the user can perform the task, the intervention of the robot is remarkably reduced.

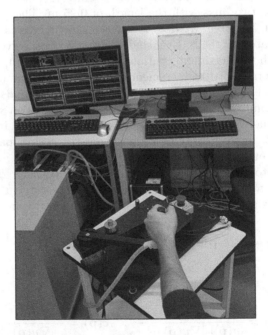

Fig. 2. Experimental setup: the system is a 2-DoF end-effector type upper-limb training robot, which is controlled using xPC Target platform.

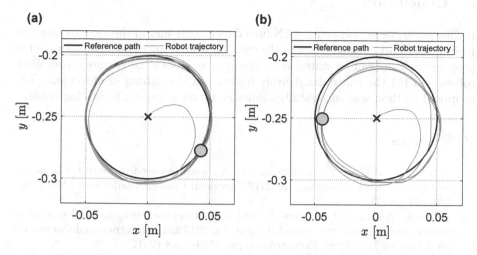

Fig. 3. Trajectories of the robot in (a) active mode, (b) passive mode.

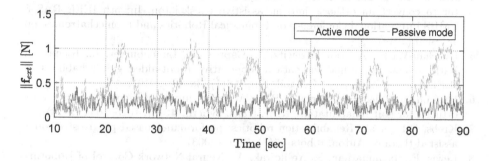

Fig. 4. Force sensor measurements.

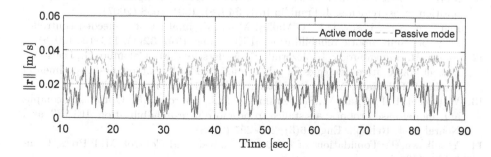

Fig. 5. Time evolution of tracking error in active and passive mode.

5 Conclusion

In this paper, we proposed an AAN impedance controller in the velocity domain. In summary and in comparison to the existing works, the main advantages of the proposed scheme can be stated as (i) the approach does not require a compliant robot, and (ii) the controller delivers freedom in the timing of movement. The proposed method was successfully evaluated on an upper-limb training robot.

References

1. Asl, H.J., Narikiyo, T., Kawanishi, M.: An assist-as-needed control scheme for robot-assisted rehabilitation. In: 2017 American Control Conference (ACC). pp. 198–203 (2017)
2. Asl, H.J., Narikiyo, T., Kawanishi, M.: Neural network velocity field control of robotic exoskeletons with bounded input. In: 2017 IEEE International Conference on Advanced Intelligent Mechatronics. pp. 1363–1368 (2017)
3. Asl, H.J., Narikiyo, T., Kawanishi, M.: An assist-as-needed velocity field control scheme for rehabilitation robots. In: 2018 IEEE/RSJ International Conference on Intelligent Robots and Systems (2018)
4. Brackx, B., et al., Lefeber, D.: Design of a modular add-on compliant actuator to convert an orthosis into an assistive exoskeleton. In: 5th IEEE RAS & EMBS International Conference on Biomedical Robotics and Biomechatronics. pp. 485–490 (2014)
5. Duschau-Wicke, A., von Zitzewitz, J., Caprez, A., Lunenburger, L., Riener, R.: Path control: a method for patient-cooperative robot-aided gait rehabilitation. IEEE Trans. Neural Syst. Rehabil. Eng. 18(1), 38–48 (2010)
6. Hussain, S., Xie, S.Q., Jamwal, P.K.: Adaptive impedance control of a robotic orthosis for gait rehabilitation. IEEE trans. cybern. 43(3), 1025–1034 (2013)
7. Krebs, H.I., et al.: Rehabilitation robotics: performance-based progressive robot-assisted therapy. Auton. robots 15(1), 7–20 (2003)
8. Lewis, F., Jagannathan, S., Yesildirak, A.: Neural Network Control of Robotmanipulators and Non-Linear Systems. CRC Press, Boca Raton (1998)
9. Mihelj, M., Nef, T., Riener, R.: A novel paradigm for patient-cooperative control of upper-limb rehabilitation robots. Adv. Rob. 21(8), 843–867 (2007)
10. Moreno-Valenzuela, J.: Velocity field control of robot manipulators by using only position measurements. J. Franklin Inst. 344(8), 1021–1038 (2007)
11. Pehlivan, A.U., Losey, D.P., O'Malley, M.K.: Minimal assist-as-needed controller for upper limb robotic rehabilitation. IEEE Trans. Rob. 32(1), 113–124 (2016)
12. Riener, R., Lunenburger, L., Jezernik, S., Anderschitz, M., Colombo, G., Dietz, V.: Patient-cooperative strategies for robot-aided treadmill training: first experimental results. IEEE Trans. Neural Syst. Rehabil. Eng. 13(3), 380–394 (2005)
13. Wolbrecht, E.T., Chan, V., Reinkensmeyer, D.J., Bobrow, J.E.: Optimizing compliant, model-based robotic assistance to promote neurorehabilitation. IEEE Trans. Neural Syst. Rehabil. Eng. 16(3), 286–297 (2008)
14. Yoshikawa, T.: Foundations of Robotics: Analysis and Control. MIT Press, Cambridge (1990)

Distributed Ledger Based Workload Logging in the Robot Swarm

Igor Kalyaev[1], Eduard Melnik[2], and Anna Klimenko[3(✉)]

[1] Southern Federal University, Rostov-on-Don, Russia
[2] Southern Scientific Center of Russian Academy of Sciences,
Rostov-on-Don, Russia
[3] Scientific Research Institute of Multiprocessor Computer Systems
of Southern Federal University, Taganrog, Russia
anna_klimenko@mail.ru

Abstract. In this paper a new application of the distributed ledger technology is proposed. The swarm robotics is a rapidly developing area due to the numerous advantages of the swarm. Yet there can be situations when some additional functional tasks should be relocated from one robot to another, for example, if there is a need to offload one of the robots. For such resource allocation tasks the robot reliability must be taken into account. This causes the importance of the robot workload logging in the swarm, because it is not sufficient to take into account the current workload to estimate the reliability level. In the paper the technique of the distributed-ledger-based workload logging is presented as well as information propagation methods are considered and the peculiarities of the robot swarm has been taken into account.

Keywords: Robot swarm · Distributed ledger · Blockchain ·
Information propagation · Consensus · Distributed systems

1 Introduction

Swarm robotics, originating from the unification of the swarm intelligence and robotics, is an extremely popular and growing area nowadays.

Robot swarm behavior and intelligence are inspired by the various natural phenomena, e.g., flocks of birds, ant colonies, bee hives, schools of fish and others [1–3]. As is mentioned in [4] swarm can be defined as a large group of locally interacting individuals with common goals. Actually, one of the key advantages of the robot swarm consists in the fact that very complex tasks can be solved by some relatively cheap robots in a fault-tolerant and robust manner.

The review of contemporary state of the art in the field of swarm robotics is presented in [2]. As is mentioned, there are some issues in this area, which can be solved for particular conditions. For example, should the swarm be heterogeneous or not, or should the monitoring and control of the robot swarm be centralized or fully distributed. There is a considerable amount of papers, proposing particular techniques, for example [5, 6]. In the current paper we consider the situation, when the computational task, which has been solved by one robot of the swarm, is to be relocated to

A. Ronzhin et al. (Eds.): ICR 2019, LNAI 11659, pp. 119–128, 2019.
https://doi.org/10.1007/978-3-030-26118-4_12

another robot (or robots), assuming that all robots in the swarm are equal in terms of computational capabilities and there is some performance reserve.

The situation is quite possible due to the advent of new Internet of Robotic Things growing and popularity. The comprehensive examples of such workload relocation are presented in [7–11]. Yet, it must be mentioned that no attention has been paid to the robots reliability issues.

The simplest way to change the computational role of the robot (and so to change its functional behaviour) is to launch the additional task on the robot computational element (CU), and, doubtless, it will work. But such a method does not consider the reliability perspective of the robot control system, which is connected with the robot CU reliability, while the mission success of the robot depends on the dependability of its control system [12]. So, the reliability function of the robot CU is of a high importance and should be logged as a chain of functional workload measurements. Some particular constraints can be created on the basis of workload log, and the task of the computational resources allocation can be solved taking into account the calculated reliability function values.

In this paper the distributed ledger based workload logging is proposed. Blockchain is an integral part of the so-called distributed ledger technologies described in [13–15]. Some new trends of distributed ledger and blockchain usage in robotics are proposed in [16]. According to the studies published, the distributed ledger usage focuses on security robustness, collective decision making and commercial issues.

We consider the distributed ledger - based workload logging as a means to enhance the robots reliability. In the sections of the paper the following questions will be discussed:

- the interdependence of the computational units reliability and their workload;
- a brief review of information propagation and distributed information storing in cryptocurrencies;
- a new technique of the distributed ledger based workload-logging in the swarm.

2   Reliability of the Robot Computational Units

The CU reliability dependency on the workload is determined by the following equation [17, 18]:

$$\lambda = \lambda_0 \cdot 2^{\Delta T/10}, \tag{1}$$

where λ – is a failure rate of the element; λ_0 – is a nominal failure rate considering the temperature of the object is equal 20 °C; ΔT – is a temperature increase while the element is functioning.

Assuming $\Delta T = kD$, where k is a ratio between temperature and workload, D is the element workload, the Eq. (1) can be presented as follows:

$$\lambda = \lambda_0 \cdot 2^{kD/10}.$$

Reliability is a probability that an element will be functioning on the time period [0; T]. Reliability function is calculated according to the exponential distribution law, which is appropriate for the computation facilities.

$$P(t) = e^{-\int_0^t \lambda(t)dt}.$$

Consider D is a variable, $D(t)$, and is a piecewise function. As a consequence, $\lambda(t)$ will be a piecewise function too (the example is shown in Fig. 1).

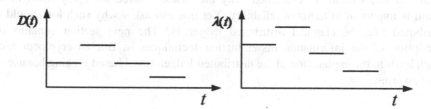

Fig. 1. A failure rate depending on the workload.

It is obvious that the reliability function value calculated on the historical data differs from one calculated on the basis of the current workload, as is shown in Fig. 2. Also, one can see that the basis of the current workload is insufficient for the reliability estimation because of its inappropriate value.

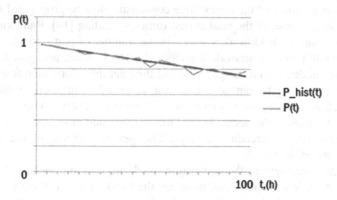

Fig. 2. The comparison of the reliability function values based on the current workload only and on the historical workload data.

So, the historical data-based reliability estimation seems to be more fair and must be considered if the constraints of robots reliability take place.

Yet there is another important feature of the workload relocation within the swarm. Consider a part of robots are rather new, and the other part is used for a while, and, perhaps, some of them are finishing their lifetime. Some computational tasks must be launched on a particular robots, which save the historical data of their workloads. The solution of the problem highly depends on the aim to be reached. For example, if the aim is to launch the computational task on the most reliable robot, then, the strategy is to analyze the historical data of the robots, choose the most reliable one, the reliability function of which meets some reliability constraints. After that the task can be launched on the robot chosen. Yet there can be another aim, e.g., to maximize the possible robots reliability function values in the far prospect of the swarm functioning. Then there must be another strategy of choosing the robot with the acceptable estimation of its reliability from the set of the worn out ones.

So, in this section we explained, why the history, saved for every robot in the swarm is important in terms of reliability. Yet one can ask – why such log should be distributed like the classical distributed ledger is? The next section contains the description of the information dissemination techniques in Bitcoin cryptocurrency, which leads to the explanation of the distributed ledger-based based logging bonuses in robot swarms.

3   Information Propagation in Blockchain and the Advantages of the Distributed Ledger in Terms of History Collecting and Storing

As is mentioned in [14], the structure of Bitcoin network is a random graph, and the pieces of information propagating through the network are transactions and blocks. Transactions are verified by participants of the system and added to the blocks. The block, which is a winner of the competitive consensus must be propagated through the network too in a manner of the randomized rumor spreading [19]. Randomized rumor spreading is estimated as O(ln n), where n is the number of participants.

When a node joins the network, it queries the DNS server, and gets a knowledge about the other nodes from its neighbours, and they get the information from theirs. As is estimated, a running bitcoin node has an average 32 connections, which is much more than default pool size of 8 connections. Those connections do not depend on the geographical location of the nodes, and the transactions and blocks spread according to the randomized rumor spreading concept. The general scheme of the information spreading is shown in Fig. 3.

This mechanism prevents the duplicating block propagation; message "inv" allows to get preliminary information if the node has the block or not. If there is no block on the node, the node sends the message "getdata", and after that receives the block. After that the node sends the "inv" message to its neighbors and continues the data propagation if it is needed.

Such a mechanism of the information propagation guarantees the awareness of each node about the overall state of the system. In our case every node possesses the knowledge about the workload history of other participants of the swarm.

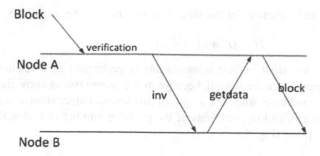

Fig. 3. Block dissemination process in the bitcoin network.

The historical workload data, which is collected and stored in a manner of distributed ledger, allows to decrease the time of resources allocation in comparison with the situation, when historical data are stored in individual local logs.

Consider the following example: a piece of workload must be launched at some node of the robot swarm. In the first case, there is a subsystem, which delivers the distributed ledger functioning, and all nodes have the knowledge about the workload history of the others. In the second case, every node has its own local history.

In general, to perform the workload relocation, the following steps are supposed to be done, considering the existence of the node, which initiates the offloading or the need to launch the additional functional task somewhere in the swarm.

Distributed Ledger based history

1. The node, which tries to offload, analyzes its instance of the ledger.
2. Chooses the node with appropriate geographical location, resources and reliability function value according to the priorities chosen;
3. Has a kind of dialog with the node chosen, and after this, in case of successful dialog, the workload is relocated.

Local history

1. The initial node sends request to all the participants of the swarm;
2. Every participant, receiving the request, checks its resources and the workload history to estimate the reliability function;
3. Participants send the answers to the initial node.

Consider the following rough estimates for the schemes given above.

Let n be the number of the nodes in the swarm, l is the size of blockchain, h is the local history size and t is the time of data transmission between two nodes. Then, for the Distributed Ledger based history the time estimation of the workload relocation process will be as follows:

$$Tb = O(l) + t$$

And the time estimation for the local history case will be as follows:

$$Tl = O(\ln n) \cdot t + kh + t + k \cdot (n - l),$$

assuming that the initial request transmission is performed in a randomized rumor spreading manner. It is quite natural, because in the swarm robots know their neighbors only. Then, in conditions when the length of distributed ledger storage is two times of local storage length, and in conditions of the growing number of nodes, the following tendency takes place (Fig. 4).

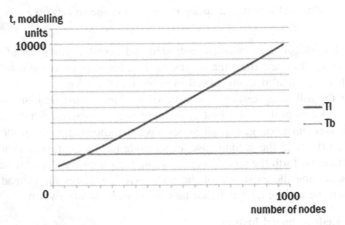

Fig. 4. The time of workload relocation with the growing number of the nodes, while DLT-based storage gives the constant time relating to the time of ledger analysis

Yet, with the distributed ledger size growth another situation takes place (see Fig. 5).

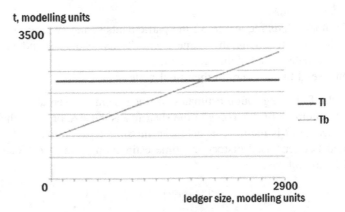

Fig. 5. The time of workload relocation with the growing DL size and the fixed node number

One can see, that with the ledger size increase and the fixed size of local storage there is a critical ledger size, when it is more expedient to analyze the local storages.

Then, consider the same situations in the slow data transmission conditions (Figs. 6, 7).

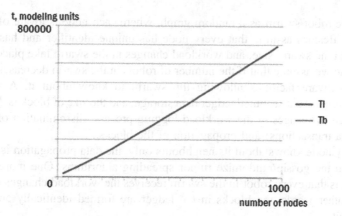

Fig. 6. The time of workload relocation with the growing number of the nodes in conditions of slow data transmission.

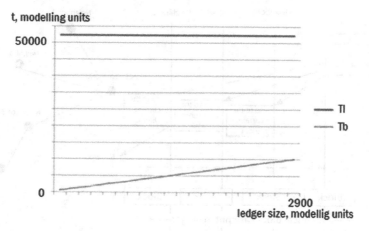

Fig. 7. The time of workload relocation with the growing ledger size in conditions of slow data transmission.

So, estimates made allow to consider the distributed ledger – based workload history to be prospective in terms of time, which is needed for resource allocation in the robot swarm.

We have shown that the workload history collecting and storing are important for the robot swarms, as well as the distributed ledger technologies are quite promising for this purpose in terms of time needed for the resource allocation. The following section of this paper contains the rough scheme of the workload historical data logging in the swarm of robots.

4 A Distributed Ledger Based Logging Technique

Consider the robot swarm as a random graph, where each node is aware of its neighbours only. Besides assume that every node has unique identifier and has the information about the swarm size, and workload changes in the swarm take place relatively seldom. Also we assume that if the number of robots in the swarm decreases, there is a particular software facilities allowing the swarm to know about it. A blockchain structure is used as a distributed ledger data storage, and the size of block is determined.

There are two stages in the workload logging process: dissemination of workload changes (via transactions) and propagation of the blocks.

As every node knows about its neighbours only, the data propagation is conducted according to the gossip/randomize rumor spreading algorithms. One more important assumption is that every robot in the swarm receives the workload changes of all other robots. In other words, the blocks in the ledger are formed identically and with the same content.

The scheme of workload logging technique is presented below (Fig. 8).

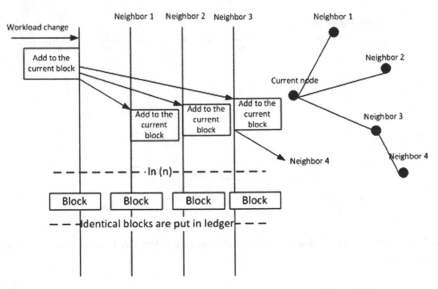

Fig. 8. The generic scheme of workload logging via distributed ledger.

One can see that as the content of blocks is supposed to be identical, there is no need in consensus, or it can be the simplest one, like "round-robin", for example. In case of new events, that is some workload changes take place during the block committing procedure, the local queues are used for the temporary history-transactions storing.

So, each of the robots receives its own replica of the ledger, and as a result, one can use the historical data from the ledger to affect the reliabilities of the robots in the swarm by means of appropriate workload distribution.

5 Conclusion

In the current paper a new application area for the distributed ledger technologies in the swarm robotics is presented. As the reliability issue of the robotic control system is rather important for the overall robot mission, it is also important to provide the appropriate level of the robot CU reliability function.

So, the key question is where in the swarm the additional functional tasks must be launched, while the reliability function is a serious constraint.

Paper presented contains the hypothesis that it is important to log the robot workload data and to do it by means of the distributed ledger. By some rough estimations we have shown that the blockchain-based workload logging has some advantages, such as:

- the reliability function value in the moment of resource allocation request is calculated more precisely;
- the overall vision of the swarm state in terms of reliability allows to decrease the time of searching the robot with appropriate resources.

All together the spotlighted advantages make the distributed ledger based workload logging to be promising for such procedures, as resources allocation in the swarms of robots, and the task relocation in case of robot failures.

Acknowledgements. The current study is granted by the RFBR project 18-29-03229 and the GZ SSC RAS N GR project AAAA-A19-119011190173-6.

References

1. Şahin, E.: Swarm robotics: from sources of inspiration to domains of application. In: Şahin, E., Spears, William M. (eds.) SR 2004. LNCS, vol. 3342, pp. 10–20. Springer, Heidelberg (2005). https://doi.org/10.1007/978-3-540-30552-1_2
2. Mohan, Y., Ponnambalam, S.G.: An extensive review of research in swarm robotics. In: 2009 World Congress on Nature and Biologically Inspired Computing, NABIC 2009 – Proceedings, pp. 140–145. IEEE Xplore (2009)
3. Sharkey, A.J.C.: Robots, insects and swarm intelligence. Artif. Intell. Rev. **26**(4), 255–268 (2006)
4. Brambilla, M., Ferrante, E., Birattari, M., Dorigo, M.: Swarm robotics: a review from the swarm engineering perspective. Swarm Intell. **7**(1), 1–41 (2013)
5. Prorok, A., Hsieh, M.A., Kumar, V.: Formalizing the impact of diversity on performance in a heterogeneous swarm of robots. In: Proceedings - IEEE International Conference on Robotics and Automation, Stockholm, Sweden, pp. 5364–5371. IEEE (2016)

6. Stranieri, A., et al.: Self-organized flocking with a heterogeneous mobile robot swarm). In: Lenaerts, T., et al. (eds.) Proceedings of ECAL 2011, pp 789–796, MIT Press, Cambridge (2011)
7. Verbelen, T., Simoens, P., De Turck, F.: AIOLOS: middleware for improving mobile application performance through cyber foraging. J. Syst. Softw. **85**(11), 2629–2639 (2012)
8. De Coninck, E., Bohez, S., Leroux, S.: Middleware platform for distributed applications incorporating robots, sensors and the cloud. In: 5th IEEE International Conference on Cloud Networking (CloudNet), Pisa, Italy, pp. 218–223. IEEE (2016)
9. Bacciu, D., Chessa, S., Gallicchio, C.: A general purpose distributed learning model for robotic ecologies. In: 10th International IFAC Symposium on Robot Control (SYROCO), Proceedings, Dubrovnik, Croatia, vol. 45, no. 22, pp. 435–440. IEEE (2012)
10. Verstraeten, D., Schrauwen, B., D'Haene, M.: An experimental unification of reservoir computing methods. Neural Netw. **20**(3), 391–403 (2007)
11. Zhang, K., Collins, E.G., Shi, D.: Centralized and distributed task allocation in multi-robot teams via a stochastic clustering auction. ACM Trans. Autonom. Adapt. Syst. **7**(2), 21 (2012)
12. Crestani, D., Godary-Dejean, K.: Fault tolerance in control architectures for mobile robots: fantasy or reality? In: 7th National Conference on Control Architectures of Robots, Nancy, France (2012)
13. Wüst, K., Ritzdorf, H., Karame, G.O., Glykantzis, V., Capkun, S., Gervais, A.: On the security and performance of proof of work blockchains. In: Proceedings of the 2016 ACM SIGSAC Conference, Vienna, Austria, pp. 3–16 (2016)
14. Crosby, M., Nachiappan, Pattanayak, P., Verma, S., Kalyanaraman, V.: Blockchain technology - beyond bitcoin. Berkley Engineering, p. 35 (2016)
15. Nguyen, G.T., Kim, K.: A survey about consensus algorithms used in blockchain. J. Inf. Process. Syst. **14**(1), 101–128 (2018)
16. Castello, E.: The blockchain: a new framework for robotic swarm systems. https://www.researchgate.net/publication/305807446_The_blockchain_a_new_framework_for_robotic_swarm_systems. Accessed 05 Apr 2019
17. Melnik, E.V., Klimenko, A.B.: Informational and control system configuration generation problem with load-balancing optimization. In: 10th International Conference on Application of Information and Communication Technologies, Azerbaijan, Baku, pp. 492–496. IEEE (2016)
18. Melnik, E., Klimenko, A., Ivanov, D.: The model of device community forming problem for the geographically-distributed information and control systems using fog-computing concept. In: Proceedings of the 4th International Research Conference "Information Technologies in Science, Management, Social Sphere and Medicine", Tomsk, Russia, vol. 72, pp. 132–136. Atlantis-Press (2017)
19. Decker, C., Wattenhofer, R.: Information propagation in the Bitcoin network. In: 13th IEEE International Conference on Peer-to-Peer Computing Proceedings, Trento, Italy, pp. 1–10. IEEE (2013)

Smartphone-Based Driver Support in Vehicle Cabin: Human-Computer Interaction Interface

Alexey Kashevnik[1,2]([✉]), Igor Lashkov[1], Dmitry Ryumin[1], and Alexey Karpov[1]

[1] SPIIRAS, St. Petersburg, Russia
{alexey, igla, ryumin, karpov}@iias.spb.su
[2] ITMO University, St. Petersburg, Russia

Abstract. The paper proposes an approach to driver support in vehicle cabin oriented to dangerous states determination and recommendation generation. To determine dangerous states, we propose to analyze images from smartphone front-facing camera as well as analyze information from accessible sensors. We identified two main dangerous states that are most important to identify to prevent the possible accidents in the roads: drowsiness and distraction. In scope of the approach determined dangerous states are used to generate recommendations for the driver to notify him/her about drowsiness and distraction. Since the attention of the driver should be in the road during the driver, we propose the human-computer interaction interface that is based on speech recognition to interact the driver. Using the interface, the driver interacts with the driver support system to increase the quality of the dangerous state determination and recommendation generation.

Keywords: Driver support · Dangerous driving ·
Human-computer interaction · Vehicle · Smartphone

1 Introduction

Driver support systems becomes more and more popular last years. Increasing the amount of accidents in public roads causes the research and development in transport sector that is aimed to reduce them and save human lives. At the moment, the research community in the area of intelligent transportation systems (ITS) is concentrated on the two main topics: automated vehicles and driver support. Automated vehicles topic is the popular research direction that will completely change the situation in the future and significantly reduce the amount of accidents. But, at the moment, ITS community understands that automated vehicles can not come tomorrow in people daily life instead of all human-driving transport. There are a lot of problems have to be solved before. In this case research and development in the area of driver support still actual task.

Vehicle manufacturing companies such as Volvo, Mercedes, BMW, and etc. provide a lot of functions to the customers that help driver such as: adaptive cruise control, lane keeping, and etc. Systems that implement such functions are called advanced

© Springer Nature Switzerland AG 2019
A. Ronzhin et al. (Eds.): ICR 2019, LNAI 11659, pp. 129–138, 2019.
https://doi.org/10.1007/978-3-030-26118-4_13

driver assistant systems (ADAS). However, at the moment modern vehicles do not provide the functions that determine the in-cabin dangerous states.

In scope of the paper, we propose an approach to driver support system aimed at dangerous states determination in vehicle cabin based on mobile video measurement as well as smartphone sensors analysis and recommendation generation. We identified two main dangerous states that are most important to identify to prevent the possible accidents in the roads: drowsiness and distraction. Since the attention of the driver should be in the road during the driver, we propose the human-computer interaction interface that is based on speech recognition to interact the driver [1]. Utilizing this interface, the driver interacts with the driver support system increase the quality of the dangerous state determination and recommendation generation.

The rest of the paper is organized as follows. Section 2 presents a related work in the area of driver support and speech based human-computer interfaces. Section 3 describes the proposed driver support system. Section 3 is concentrated on human-computer interface based on speech recognition. Section 4 presents evaluation in the real driving situations. Conclusion summarizes the paper.

2   Related Work

The section proposes a related work in the area of driver support systems as well as modern human-computer interfaces and their applicability to utilize in vehicle cabin.

The study [2] demonstrates that detection of blinks can be affected by the driver state, level of automation, the measurement frequency, and the algorithms used. It proposes the evaluation of the performance of an electrooculogram- and camera-based blink detection algorithms in both manually and conditionally automated driving conditions under various constraints. During the experiment, the participants were requested to rate their subjective drowsiness level with the Karolinska Sleepiness Scale every 15 min.

The main goal of the existing smartphone-based research studies and solutions is to early warn driver about recognized dangerous state and eliminate the risk of drowsy or distracted driving. Let's consider driver's drowsiness determination related studies. This study [3] demonstrates a monitoring system developed to detect and alert the vehicle driver about the presence of the drowsiness state. To recognize whether the driver is drowsy, the visual indicators that reflect the driver's condition, comprising the state of the eyes, the head pose and the yawning, were assessed. The number of tests were proposed to assess the driver's state, including yawning, front nodding, blink detection, etc. Although the proposed recognition method gets 93% of total drowsiness detections, its unclear which dataset was utilized to evaluate the system and whether the detection method was tested under different light conditions. In this study the Android-based smartphone was utilized to assess the driver's state.

Another study [4] presents the developed smartphone mobile application "Drowsy Driver Scleral-Area" related to driver's drowsiness detection. The proposed mobile application includes a Haar cascade classifier, provided by the computer vision framework OpenCV [5] for driver's face and eyes detection; and a module written in Java and responsible for image processing and alerting driver about potential hazards while driving. The developed application is configured to detect prolonged eyelid closure exceeding three seconds indicating drowsiness state. Also, it was tested on a static photo sequence, person in a laboratory and in a vehicle. The paper highlights that the pixel density analysis method was used that eliminates the need to manually count pixels and determine a threshold for drowsiness. It involves the calculation of the ratio of white pixels to maximum white pixels (corresponding to full eye opening) in the region of detection. The authors of the study consider that additional tests need to be conducted under more dynamic motion and reduced light conditions.

One more paper proposes the three-stage drowsiness detection framework for vehicle drivers, developed for Android-based smartphones [6]. The first stage uses the PERCLOS (percentage of eyes closure) obtained through images captured by the front-facing camera with an eye state classification method. The system uses near infrared lighting for illuminating the face of the driver while night-driving. The next step uses the voiced to the unvoiced ratio calculated based on the speech data taken from the built-in smartphone microphone, in the event PERCLOS crosses the threshold. A final stage is used as a touch response within a specified time to declare the driver as drowsy and subsequently alert with an audible alarm. According to the received results of the study the developed framework for smartphones demonstrates 93% drowsiness state classification. The final measurement indicators used in this study include PERCLOS, the voiced-unvoiced ratio and a reaction test response of the driver on the smartphone screen.

Other more sophisticated approach is related to the detection of sleep deprivation by evaluating a short video sequence of a driver [7]. It utilizes the OpenCV Haar Caascades to extract the driver's face from every frame and classify it by the deep learning framework into two classes: "sleep derived" and "rested". In detail, this approach is based on the use of the trained model formed by the non-linear models MobileNets, adapted specifically for mobile applications on smartphones. The output of MobileNet for camera frame is the estimation of the probability of the frame to belong to "sleep deprived" class. In case the probability of this class is more than 0.5, the driver in the frame is classified as "sleep deprived". The real experiments have been conducted with aid of prototype implemented as an Android-based mobile application for smartphone. TensorFlow lite framework was utilized to compile the MobileNet model previously trained on a standalone laptop.

Another major cause for road accidents is driver's distraction. The paper [8] proposes a smartphone camera-based driver fatigue and distraction monitoring system while driving. This study heavily relies on monitoring driver's eyes and mouth, and detecting eye rub due to irritation in eye and yawning through intensity sum of facial region. The evaluation of the proposed approach is done using the developed mobile application for Android platform with Xiaomi Redmi 1s smartphone. The authors of the study conducted the experiments and only evaluated the CPU load and the battery consumption of the developed system. They concluded their system consumed 12% of battery of continuous use for a one hour. The paper highlights that the proposed approach is not suitable for work under low/no light conditions.

Another study [9] is focused on developing Driver Fatigue Detection System aimed at monitoring driver behavior and alerting him to prevent from falling asleep while driving. The proposed solution is adapted for working on the smartphone, utilizing built-in camera for recording video and processing it for real-time eye-tracking. The authors of the study admit that their solution is limited due to external illumination conditions and wearing sunglass by a driver.

Other paper [10] evaluates the pertinence of using the driver head rotation movements to automatically predict the smartphone usage while driving. The duration a driver spends looking down from a reference neutral direction is used as a parameter to predict the smartphone usage. According to the conducted experiments, a smartphone usage detection system based on real-time video analysis of head movements is implemented in this study. It performs the real-time video analysis of the driver's face, evaluates its head rotation deviation from neutral orientation when the driver is looking at the road, and detects whether the percentage of these deviations exceeds a threshold.

To monitor the driver's vigilance level and recognize its fatigue state, the study relies on multiple visual indicators, including eye blinking, head nod and yawning [11]. Real-time detection is based on the use of the face and eye blink detection with Haar-like technique and mouth detection for yawning state with canny active contour finding method. The proposed approach was implemented using Java programming language and OpenCV framework responsible for image processing that is supported by Android platform. According to the conducted experiments, the performance of the proposed method for face and eye tracking was tested under variable light conditions.

In the paper [12], a strategy and system to detect driving fatigue based on machine vision and machine learning AdaBoost algorithm is proposed. The entire detection strategy consists of the following operations: detection of the face using classifiers of the front and deflected face; extraction of eye region according to geometric distribution of facial organs; and, finally, trained classifiers for open and closes eyes are used to detect eyes in the selected regions. As a result, the PERCLOS measure is calculated and used as a measure for fatigue rate as well as the duration time of eye-closed state. Underneath, the OpenCV library was utilized to analyze frames for face recognition. In case the driver's fatigue state is recognized, the system will make an audible alert for a driver or dial the emergency center or police. The performance of the proposed system may decrease up to 10 frames per second. The developed Driving Fatigue Detection System is compatible with Android smartphones. It should be highlighted that the study misses the experiments in conditions under poor illumination.

A recent research study utilizing the smartphone camera-based solution [13] is focused on the driver monitoring and recognizing drowsiness, distraction and gaze direction. The presented approach uses facial landmarks to detect eye closure via eye aspect ratio and PERCLOS metrics and yawns via the ratio of the height of the mouth to its width. Distraction state is recognized whether the driver is talking on the phone while driving. This recognition is based on the use of a pre-trained deep neural network YOLOv2 [14] on the COCO dataset.

3 Driver Support System Description

We developed the reference model of the driver support system (Fig. 1). The reference model includes two main modules: vehicle cabin and cloud. The vehicle cabin module includes a driver, a smartphone, and a vehicle infotainment system. We use the driver face as a main source of information to determine the dangerous states [15]. Based on image processing from the front-facing camera we identify the face direction angles as well as mouth and eyes openness/closeness and based on this information conclude about drowsiness and distraction dangerous states. Every time when the system determines a dangerous state it generated the recommendation to the driver [16]. We propose to convert the generated recommendation to the speech using the smartphone supported text to speech function since the showing to the driver text information is not safely. Speech recommendation is transferred to the vehicle infotainment system via the Bluetooth protocol and presented to the driver. If the smartphone does not have a connection the vehicle infotainment system, its loud speakers can be used instead of the vehicle speakers. Together with the recommendation the system asks the driver about a question (Table 1) based on the context situation. We use the smartphone microphone sensor to record the driver answer and the developed speech recognition interface (Sect. 4) to recognize it. Based on the recognized answer the system changes its behavior.

When the driver installs the system, it proposes him/her to switch on the training mode that provides possibilities to record the labeled statistics to the cloud. Based on the driver estimation the system knows if a dangerous state has been estimated correctly or the error has been occurred. If the system recognizes the drowsiness dangerous situation several times it checks the rest of the driver trip and tries to find a gas station or cafes where the driver can have a rest. If the rest of the trip is further than a predefined distance specified in the driver profile (by default 100 km) and a place is found, it proposes the drivers to change the trip and stay in a cafe or gas station. If the driver say "Yes" it means that he/she is drowsy, but the changing trip is not confirmed. If the driver says "No" then the he/she is not drowsy. If the driver confirms to change its route then the system automatically changes the route in the navigation system. The system can also propose the driver to play with the system a question/answer game if it recognizes drowsiness dangerous states several times.

Table 1. Examples of the questions the system generates for the driver.

Question for a driver	Context situation	Possible answers
Are you drowsy?	Training mode	Yes/No
Are you distracted?	Training mode	Yes/No
Are you drowsy? Would you like to have a cup of coffee in a cafe/gas station (say change route)?	Drowsiness dangerous states has been determined several times, rest of the driver trip more that one hour, a cafe or gas station is found nearby	Yes/No/Change route
Are you drowsy? Would you like to play with the system?	Drowsiness dangerous states has been determined several times	Yes/No/Play

In this game the system asks the driver questions and the driver should answer yes or no. Such kind of interaction prevents the driver sleepiness since if a person has a

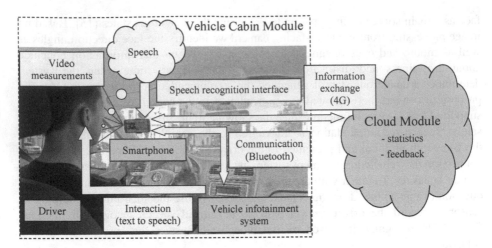

Fig. 1. Reference model of the proposed driver support system.

dialog it reduces the level of drowsiness. We propose the cloud service module to store the driver related information and use it to enhance the system quality in dangerous states recognition and recommendations and questions generation. Dangerous event statistics includes all information acquired and processed by the system from front-facing camera and sensors and determined dangerous states as well as confirmation of these dangerous states by the driver (driver feedback). Detailed information about statistics is presented in evaluation section.

4 Speech Recognition Interface

The voice input using the dictionary of limited size in natural language significantly improves the usability and efficiency of interaction with the driver [17]. The smart interaction with the driver based on speech recognition is the preferred option while driving due to relatively small number of commands available for interaction and no need to be distracted of looking down at the smartphone's touch screen or key pad [18].

The Android mobile platform provides an access to application interfaces for third-party developers and provides automatic speech recognition of the natural language, allow to estimate the reaction speed since the system voice request is sent to a driver [19], as well as further calculation of the average level of the incoming audio signal. The reference model of the proposed speech recognition interface is presented in Fig. 2.

Before the first attempt of capturing driver's voice, the system analyzes the language model of the natural language and a pre-defined dictionary of words/phrases that need to be recognized. As soon this analysis is completed, the speech recognition interface is activated and the system waits for the voice request from a driver that has a textual presentation included in a dictionary. When the system will start to listen for driver's speech, the countdown of reaction speed begins.

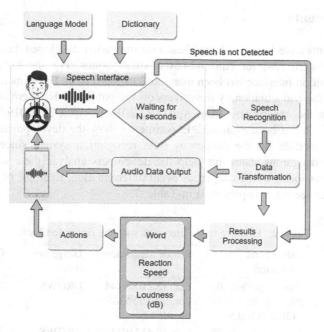

Fig. 2. Reference model of the proposed speech recognition interface.

As soon as the speech is ready to be recognized, the timer of reaction speed stops and, therefore, the calculation of the average volume (the level of loudness, measured in dB) of speech and speech recognition are activated. When the speech ends, the speech recognition process is considered completed, the data transformation is performed to provide audible data for a driver and further processing of the output results. In case the driver does not respond within the specified period of time, the system takes an action for the current situation [20]. Thereby, the driver pronounces a voice command, and at this point the system generates a data bundle including the reaction speed, the average volume of input command loudness, as well as text representation of speech with the result code for further actions [21].

The current approach allows to recognize the driver's speech with minimum error threshold in the conditions, when there is no background noise. The direct reason for this situation may be related to the fact that the data for training models did not contain the driver's speech while being in the cabin of the vehicle, or their component was minimum [22]. This concern can be addressed by utilizing the wireless headset or developing the advanced speech recognition technologies for natural language processing under the conditions of significant noise component of input signal, that is proposed to be implemented in the following research studies [23].

5   Experiments

The experiments have been conducted based on the earlier developed dangerous states recognition system [24] for Android-based smartphones. For the experiments the speech recognition interface has been integrated to the system. Experiments have been conducted in the real situation by the drivers on the public roads. There are 38 drivers participated in the experiments from April 01, 2019 to April 21, 2019. The driving statistics of 8.3 h has been evaluated. Experiments show the development interface is an important module for the dangerous state recognition system since the drivers decline some dangerous states that help the developers analyze these situations and increase the possibility of the dangerous event determination. Example of the statistics with the driver feedback is presented in Table 2.

Table 2. Example of the statistics with the driver feedback.

Date/time	Driver head parameters	Sensor parameters	Dangerous state	Confirmation
02/04/2019 11:54	Yaw angle: −8.80 Pitch angle: −19.08 PERCLOS: 0.5	Lat: 32.21099144 Long: 50.78536576 Speed: 11	DROWS.	No
09/04/2019 11:15	Yaw angle: −10.05 Pitch angle: −4.58 PERCLOS: 0.125	Lat: 58.4321911 Long: −3.0893319 Speed: 11	DROWS.	Yes
09/04/2019 11:18	Yaw angle: −36.40 Pitch angle: −1.17 PERCLOS: 1.0	Lat: 58.4321643375 Long: −3.089416280 Speed: 18	DISTR.	Yes

6   Conclusion

The paper presents a reference model for driver support system in vehicle cabin that determines dangerous states and generates recommendations & questions for a driver using the presented human-computer interaction interface. The interface has been developed based on speech recognition technology. Since the proposed system does not require to recognize a large dictionary of words, the recognition in vehicle cabin works well. Authors conducted experiments with real drivers that shows that such interface is important to the dangerous event recognition system since the driver can leave feedback and the recognition can be further improved based on this information.

Acknowledgements. The work has been partially financially supported by grants: #17-29-03284, #16-07-00462, and #16-37-60100 of Russian Foundation for Basic Research; by Government of Russian Federation, Grant #08-08; and by the Russian State Research #0073-2019-0005.

References

1. Markovnikov, N., Kipyatkova, I.: An analytic survey of end-to-end speech recognition systems. SPIIRAS Proc. **3**(58), 77–110 (2018)
2. Schmidt, J., Laarousi, R., Stolzmann, W., Karrer, K.: Eye blink detection for different driver states in conditionally automated driving and manual driving using EOG and a driver camera. Behav. Res. Meth. **50**(3), 1088–1101 (2018)
3. Galarza, E.E., Egas, F.D., Silva, F.M., Velasco, P.M., Galarza, E.D.: Real time driver drowsiness detection based on driver's face image behavior using a system of human computer interaction implemented in a smartphone. In: Rocha, Á., Guarda, T. (eds.) ICITS 2018. AISC, vol. 721, pp. 563–572. Springer, Cham (2018). https://doi.org/10.1007/978-3-319-73450-7_53
4. Mohammad, F., Mahadas, K., Hung, G.K.: Drowsy driver mobile application: development of a novel scleral-area detection method. Comput. Biol. Med. **89**, 76–83 (2017)
5. Bradski, G., Kaehler, A.: Learning OpenCV: Computer Vision in C ++ with the OpenCV Library, 2nd edn. O'Reilly Media Inc, Sebastopol (2013)
6. Dasgupta, A., Rahman, D., Routray, A.: A smartphone-based drowsiness detection and warning system for automotive drivers. In: IEEE Transactions on Intelligent Transportation Systems, pp. 1–10 (2018)
7. García-García, M., Caplier, A., Rombaut, M.: Sleep deprivation detection for real-time driver monitoring using deep learning. In: Campilho, A., Karray, F., ter Haar Romeny, B. (eds.) ICIAR 2018. LNCS, vol. 10882, pp. 435–442. Springer, Cham (2018). https://doi.org/10.1007/978-3-319-93000-8_49
8. Ramachandran, M., Chandrakala, S.: Android OpenCV based effective driver fatigue and distraction monitoring system. In: 2015 International Conference on Computing and Communications Technologies (ICCCT), pp. 262–266 (2015)
9. Abulkhair, M., et al.: Mobile platform detect and alerts system for driver fatigue. Procedia Comput. Sci. **62**, 555–564 (2015)
10. García-García, M., Caplier, A., Rombaut, M.: Driver head movements while using a smartphone in a naturalistic context. In: 6th International Symposium on Naturalistic Driving Research, pp. 1–5 (2017)
11. Qiao, Y., Zeng, K., Xu, L., Yin, X.: A smartphone-based driver fatigue detection using fusion of multiple real-time facial features. In: 2016 13th IEEE Annual Consumer Communications & Networking Conference (CCNC), pp. 230–235 (2016)
12. Kong, W., et al.: A system of driving fatigue detection based on machine vision and its application on smart device. J. Sens. **2015**, 1–11 (2015)
13. Nambi, A.U., et al.: HAMS: Driver and driving monitoring using a Smartphone. In: Proceedings of the 24th Annual International Conference on Mobile Computing and Networking. MobiCom 2018, pp. 840–842. ACM (2018)
14. Redmon, J., Farhadi, A.: YOLO9000: better, faster, stronger. In: 2017 IEEE Conference on Computer Vision and Pattern Recognition (CVPR), pp. 6517–6525 (2017)
15. Smirnov, A., Kashevnik, A., Lashkov, I., Parfenov, V.: Smartphone-based identification of dangerous driving situations: algorithms and implementation. In: Proceedings of the 18th Conference of Open Innovations Association FRUCT, St.Petersburg, pp. 306–313 (2016)
16. Smirnov, A., Kashevnik, A., Lashkov, I.: Human-smartphone interaction for dangerous situation detection and recommendation generation while driving. In: Ronzhin, A., Potapova, R., Németh, G. (eds.) SPECOM 2016. LNCS (LNAI), vol. 9811, pp. 346–353. Springer, Cham (2016). https://doi.org/10.1007/978-3-319-43958-7_41

17. Kopinski, T., Geisler, S., Handmann, U.: Contactless interaction for automotive applications. In: Mensch & Computer Workshopband, pp. 87–94 (2013)
18. Huang, Z., Huang, X.: A study on the application of voice interaction in automotive human machine interface experience design. In: AIP Conference Proceedings, vol. 1955, no. 1, p. 040074 (2018)
19. Hua, Z., Ng, W.L.: Speech recognition interface design for in-vehicle system. In: Proceedings of the 2nd International Conference on Automotive User Interfaces and Interactive Vehicular Applications, pp. 29–33 (2010)
20. Nass, C., et al.: Improving automotive safety by pairing driver emotion and car voice emotion. In: CHI 2005 Extended Abstracts on Human Factors In Computing Systems, pp. 1973–1976 (2005)
21. Peissner, M., Doebler, V., Metze, F.: Can voice interaction help reducing the level of distraction and prevent accidents. In: Meta-Study Driver Distraction Voice Interaction, p. 24 (2011)
22. Owens, J.M., McLaughlin, S.B., Sudweeks, J.: On-road comparison of driving performance measures when using handheld and voice-control interfaces for mobile phones and portable music players. SAE Int. J. Passeng. Cars-Mech. Syst. **3**, 734–743 (2010)
23. Meng, L.J., Wang, Z.Z.: Design and implementation of wireless voice controlled intelligent obstacle-avoiding toy car system. In: 2011 International Conference on Electronics, Communications and Control (ICECC), pp. 1982–1984 (2011)
24. Kashevnik, A., Lashkov, I.: Decision support system for drivers & passengers: Smartphone-based reference model and evaluation. In: Proceedings of the 23rd Conference of Open Innovations Association FRUCT, pp. 166–171 (2018)

Household Objects Pick and Place Task for AR-601M Humanoid Robot

Kamil Khusnutdinov[1], Artur Sagitov[1], Ayrat Yakupov[1],
Roman Lavrenov[1(✉)], Edgar A. Martinez-Garcia[2], Kuo-Hsien Hsia[3],
and Evgeni Magid[1]

[1] Higher Institute for Information Technology and Intelligent Systems (ITIS),
Kazan Federal University, 35 Kremlyovskaya Street, Kazan, Russian Federation
{KaSHusnutdinov,AjrAYakupov}@stud.kpfu.ru,
{sagitov,lavrenov}@it.kfu.ru, dr.e.magid@ieee.org
[2] Universidad Autonoma de Ciudad Juarez, 32310 Cd. Juarez, Chihuahua, Mexico
edmartin@uacj.mx
[3] Department of Electrical Engineering, Far East University,
Zhonghua Road 49, Xinshi District, Tainan City, Taiwan
khhsia@mail.feu.edu.tw

Abstract. Humanoid robots are created to facilitate many facets of daily life, both in scenarios when humans and robots collaborate and when robot completely replaces human. One of such more important cases is the household assistance for older people. When a robot operates in home environments the needs to interact with various household objects, of different shape and size. A humanoid end-effector is typically modeled to have from two to five configuration of fingers designed specifically for grasping. By making fingers flexible and using dexterous arm one could operate objects in many different configurations. If one chooses to provide a finger control by actuating each of the finger's phalanxes by using separate motor, humanoid hand becomes costly and overall size of the hand will significantly increase to accommodate necessary hardware and wiring. To address this issue, many engineers prefer to employ mimic joints to reduce a cost and size, while keeping acceptable levels of finger's dexterity. This paper presents a study on household objects pick and place task being implemented for AR-601M humanoid robot that is using mimic joints in his fingers. Experiments were conducted in a Gazebo simulation with 5 model objects, which were created to be representations of real typical household items.

Keywords: Grasping · Grasp planning algorithm
Pick and place task · Humanoid robot · Mimic joint
Gazebo simulation · Grasp modelling

1 Introduction

At present, humanoid robotic assistants' development is gaining momentum [22] and the target is to create the most accurate human replica that could perform

© Springer Nature Switzerland AG 2019
A. Ronzhin et al. (Eds.): ICR 2019, LNAI 11659, pp. 139–149, 2019.
https://doi.org/10.1007/978-3-030-26118-4_14

dexterous locomotion and manipulation with the ability to complete some of intellectual tasks. We already seen significant progress that had been already achieved in many areas, including locomotion [5], self-protection at loosing balance [16], collaboration [11], manipulation [17] and others, but in general, modern humanoid robots are yet far away from the functionality that fully conforms to human functionality. Therefore, there is a need for their comprehensive development, including arm movements and vision improvements. Humanoid robots are created to facilitate the work of a human in a variety of environments or to replace a human completely when possible. Humanoids are constructed to operate both in environments without human presence and in social environments when interaction and collaborative activities with multiple humans may be required. One of such environments is a household environment and a humanoid robot is supposed to interact with objects of various shapes, sizes and weights. In addition, environment conditions should be considered. There may appear a high degree of clutter in a grasp scene [10] as well numerous occluding objects [18] that require searching for the target items before they could be picked. Objects may have various qualitative characteristics of their surface material, e.g., the surface of an object may be wet, which may contribute to slipping of an object within the hand grasp. With object that deformed easily (e.g. a sponge for dishwashing) as more force is applied to a gripper during a grasp of such object, the more it will be deformed; therefore, for such objects it is important to find a balance between an applied force and a preservation of the object shape.

A humanoid end-effector is typically constructed to have two to five fingers being designed for grasping household objects. For this reason, it is well suited for grasping household objects, taking into account the above mentioned environmental conditions. Due to the fact that fingers are flexible and dexterous, a robot hand can take a large variety of forms to grasp an object. These advantages have already been taken into account in developing solutions [3], [24] for grasping objects.

The flexibility and dexterity of the fingers of a humanoid robot is achieved by using a large number of joints. They set in motion phalanges of fingers, with combined motion of phalanges representing finger movement. There are two ways to control finger movement: controlling all of its joints or only some of them. When all joints are controlled, fingers can move with a greater accuracy, their movements will be more deterministic and easier to control. But in this case, the humanoid hand may become expensive, and a size of fingers may significantly increase. Increasing the size will affect the success of object grasping: enlarged fingers could either fail to grasp objects, or during a grasp, unintentionally significantly modify a grasp scene while pushing objects as the hand moves toward its target object through the grasp scene. For these reasons, many manufacturers prefer using mimic joints.

The basic idea of a mimic joint is to replace some finger joints with a joint, which movement depends on other joints movement (that are referred as active joints). Thus, only active joints are directly controlled, and a finger is set in motion via these active joints. With this approach, a finger movement accuracy is rather lower and, respectively, it is more difficult to carry out a robust grip. And because of using a significantly smaller number of motors within a finger, this approach results in lower cost and smaller size of a finger.

This article is devoted to pick and place task execution for household objects by humanoid robot AR-601M, which employs mimic joints fingers. The task algorithm verification was performed in Gazebo simulation. The rest of the paper is organized as follows. Section 2 presents a literature review. Section 3 describes kinematics of AR-601M manipulators and the fingers of the robot. Section 4 describes the modelling and simulation. Section 5 presents the results and our future work.

2   Literature Review

This section provides overview of the relevant articles, information from which were used to implement pick and place task execution for robot.

The article [23] investigated the problem of the implementation of an object manipulation with the participation of only fingers, without hand movements. The urgency of this problem is due to the fact that during the manipulation a situation may arise when the hand may lose the ability to move due to the limits in movement space. In such situation, further manipulation can only be carried out with the fingers of the hand, so the robotic hand must be trained in this type of manipulation. To solve this problem, the authors of the article proposed a set of principles for the design of fingers that allows fingertips to grasp objects and manipulate them. An analytical framework is introduced to accurately assess a dexterous workspace for manipulating objects at the fingertips.

In [7], an algorithm for calculating the optimal configuration for the grasp of a robotic hand was proposed. It can predict the movement of gripping fingers and determine their configuration using information about the size of an object and its position. The metrics used to describe the calculated grasp configuration can be reproduced on a robotic hand.

To solve the problem of obtaining feedback on manipulation while it executes, the authors of article [4] proposed a single model for evaluating the manipulation of the hand and an object. It allows determining the type of grasp and the attributes of an object, with help of which it becomes possible to determine the optimal type of grasp for an object of a certain form, to make their correlation.

The article [12] presents a description of the robot Team Delft that won the competition for the pick and place task. The paper presents information about the robot functionality, its software. The performance of the system and the results of its work in the final competition are discussed.

In [19], a method for planning a powerful grasp for a human-like hand is presented. First, it determines the surface of an object in order to find the best places to perform the opposite grasp with two or three fingers, and then aligns the other fingers to match the local curvature of object surface [15]. The method also creates a database of grasps for the current object that satisfy the force closure condition. Different setting strategies are considered depending on the size of an object in relation to the hand and on the location of the obstacles in the manipulation environment.

To solve the problem of determining a grasp strategy that is capable of ensuring the compatibility of an object determination tasks and carrying out its grasp, a study [21] of analytical and empirical approaches to building a grasp strategy was conducted. As a result, a review of algorithms for synthesizing the grasp of three-dimensional objects was prepared.

The article [20], using the Atlas humanoid robot as an example, demonstrates the use of an object manipulation approach that allows the robot to use any object located in its environment to accomplish manipulation task. The approach allows the robot to understand how to recognize new objects and adapt them for the manipulation task.

In [1], a methodology for teaching humanoid robots to manipulation by demonstration is presented. This approach, according to the authors of the article, will allow humanoid robots to more easily master various techniques of manipulating objects and eventually use and change them at their discretion without human help.

3   Kinematics of an Arm and Fingers

This section presents a description of the AR-601M humanoid robot arms and fingers and the calculation of their working areas. Because of the task in a simulation in the Gazebo simulator, a 3D model of AR-601M humanoid robot manipulator shown in Fig. 1 was used. It is reproduce in details real robot manipulator.

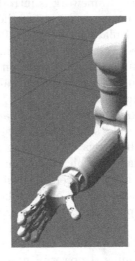

Fig. 1. 3D model manipulator of AR-601M humanoid robot in its default position.

The humanoid robot AR-601M is a Russian development created by the research and production association "Android Technology" [14]. The functionality of the robot allows to manipulate objects, move along a given route, perform local object orientation etc. Each robot arm, including its hand, has 20 DOFs. An arm itself has 7 DOFs, the fingers of each hand have 13 DOFs. To control the movements of the 3D model manipulator, its configuration framework MoveIt! [6] was created and the API of framework was used. For planning motion trajectory of a model, the RRTConnect algorithm was used.

To provide 3D model manipulator ability to move, it was necessary to solve inverse kinematics problem for it. Currently, there are libraries that allow programmatically solving the problem of inverse kinematics. They provide both an analytical solution [9] and a numerical one [2]. Based on them, various plugins are created to solve the inverse kinematics problem for manipulators that use the MoveIt! to control their movements. Therefore, solution of inverse kinematics problem is to select a plugin suitable for 3D model manipulator.

Due to the fact that 3D model manipulator has 7 DOFs, the analytical solution of the inverse kinematics problem is difficult to find for it. Moreover, it may not exist. Therefore, it necessary to find a plugin for the MoveIt! framework that provided a numerical solution of this problem for 3D model manipulator. The plugin "kdl_kinematics_plugin" is a suitable plugin. Figure 2 show the position of 3D model manipulator achieved using this plugin and the MoveIt! framework API.

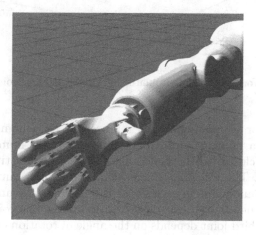

Fig. 2. Applying inverse kinematics plugin to the 3D model of right manipulator.

To prepare the simulation scene, it is necessary to calculate the workspace of manipulator in order to find space on scene for placing an objects, so that the humanoid robot hand could reach and grasp them. To calculate it, is needed to solve the problem of forward kinematics. Then, using obtained solution and taking into account the range of angles of rotation of each joint, a manipulator must be set in motion. During the movement, a manipulator end-effector can reach different points in space. The set of reached points can be accepted as a workspace [13].

To calculate the workspace of 3D model manipulator of the AR-601M robot, according to the above scenario, the Matlab software platform and the software package for performing robotic calculations Robotics Toolbox [8] are suitable. Figure 3 shows calculated workspace for manipulator of AR-601M humanoid robot.

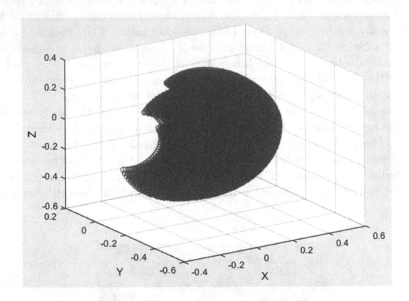

Fig. 3. Workspace of manipulator of AR-601M humanoid robot.

The end-effector of manipulator is represented by a humanoid hand with fingers similar to a human hand. Robot fingers are use mimic joints. For all fingers, the joints closest to the hand's base are the first active joints and are controlled directly. The remaining finger connections are mimic. The principle of movement of mimic joints in each finger is as follows: the angle of rotation of the second joint depends on the angle of rotation of the first joint, and the angle of rotation of the third joint depends on the angle of rotation of the second. The thumb and pinkie have 2 joints. The index, middle and ring have 3 joints.

The fingers workspace calculation is based on the principle similar to calculation of manipulator workspace. Figure 4 shown fingers workspaces calculated using Matlab software package.

4   Simulation in Gazebo

Due to the inability to work with a real robot, pick and place task execution was modelled in a Gazebo simulation. To perform simulation, it is necessary to select 5 real household objects for creating their 3D models and task execution with them further. Figure 5 shown photographs of real household objects.

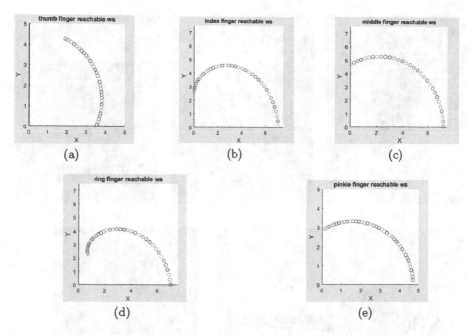

Fig. 4. Reachable workspace for: (a) thumb, (b) index, (c) middle, (d) ring and (e) pinkie. Unit measurements is centimeters (cm).

The 3D models of the selected objects were created using the SketchUp tool. Their dimensions exactly correspond to the real objects dimensions.

To perform simulation, it is necessary to determine the coordinates of the target point for reaching it and grasping object, and the angles of rotation of active finger joints. These values were determined empirically during the experiments according following scenario.

First, it is necessary to determine the height with regard to object that the hand must take to grasp it. Taking into account the height of each object, it is necessary to divide by 5 in order to get 5 points with the same x and y coordinates, but different z coordinates. Getting 5 points due to the need to find out position the fingers take relative to the object when the hand reaches each point in space. Such movements of the manipulator must be carried out in order to avoid situations when the trajectory of movement of only some of the fingers is able to pass through the object. Thus, the z coordinate of the target point is determine.

After that is needed to determine the x and y coordinates of the target point. According to the calculated fingers workspaces, presented in Fig. 4, it becomes clear that the trajectory of the movement of the fingers during their flexion has the direction of movement from the initial, straightened position, in the direction of their attachment to the arm, along a curved line. For this reason, when the hand reaches such a point in space, being in which the ends of fingers can be in the middle of the object, for example, bottles, the fingers can not be able to

Fig. 5. Household objects selected for creating their 3D models: (a) bottle, (b) box of vitamins, (c) juice box, (d) ladle and (e) plastic cup.

grasp an object in the middle as in the case of performing a simple antipodal grip using parallel grippers. Therefore, it is necessary to determine the distance between an object and the inside of the palm of the hand, suitable for gripping, taking into account the peculiarities of the movement of the fingers described above.

To determine the desired distance, in the XY plane, it is necessary to move the hand to an object so that between the object and the inside of the palm of the hand 4 different distances can be obtained for comparison. In all 4 cases, the beginning of the distance is necessary to establish the inner part of the palm. Its end is determined by the position of the object in which its side, to which the movement of the arm:

– For 1 distance is located on the same line with the beginning of the third, extreme phalanx of the middle finger

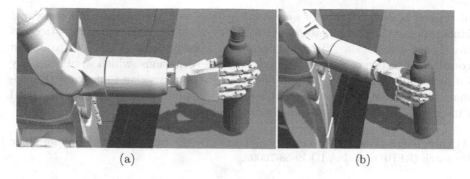

(a)   (b)

Fig. 6. Pick and place task performing for 3D model of bottle

- For 2 distances it is located on the same straight line with the beginning of the second phalanx of the middle finger
- For 3 distances it is located on the same straight line with the beginning of the first phalanx of the middle finger, which is set in motion by the active joint
- For 4 distances, it is located as close as possible to the inside of the palm, to prevent empty space between the surface of an object and parts of the hand.

To determine the x and y coordinates of the hand target point the middle finger was selected for the following reasons. The end of the middle finger is located farther than the ends of the other fingers. Because of this the end of the hand is determined by the coordinates of the end of the middle finger. Such estimation of the end of hand allows to cover the maximum surface of an object during its grasping, this contributes to a greater fixation of an object in the hand.

After calculating the desired coordinates of the target point, necessary to achieve by hand and grasping an object, it is necessary to determine the angles of rotation of the fingers for the grasp implementation. Due to the use of mimic joints in the fingers of a humanoid hand, this task comes down to finding the angles of rotation of the first joints of each finger located closest to the center of the hand. The angles of rotation of the connections of each finger must be set to their successive increase and choose such values of the angles of rotation at which it becomes possible to implement a reliable grasp an object without slipping it. Figure 6 shows the results of the pick and place task execution for the 3D model of the bottle, obtained by performing the calculations presented above, as well as using the 3D model manipulator of AR-601M humanoid robot. Video about task execution for other objects is available at: https://tinyurl.com/y5mbfhya.

5   Conclusions

This paper described pick and place task that was performed in Gazebo simulation by a 3D model of AR-601M humanoid robot right arm. Five 3D models of typical household objects were used for the task verification. We presented kinematics of the manipulator and its fingers, including their characteristics and workspace calculation. Virtual experiments were performed in order to obtain coordinates of target points and angles of finger rotations, which were necessary for pick and place tasks. As a part of our future work we plan to provide an automatic calculation of target points for object grasping employing robot on-board cameras, and to validate our approach via experiments with the real robot.

Acknowledgments. This work was supported by the Russian Foundation for Basic Research (RFBR), project ID 19-58-70002.

References

1. Ahmad, H., Yao, X., Muddassir, M., Chiragh, J., Ali, Y.: Humanoid robots object grasping and manipulation learning by demonstration. In: 2017 3rd International Conference on Control, Automation and Robotics (ICCAR), pp. 158–161, April 2017. https://doi.org/10.1109/ICCAR.2017.7942678
2. Beeson, P., Ames, B.: TRAC-IK: an open-source library for improved solving of generic inverse kinematics. In: 2015 IEEE-RAS 15th International Conference on Humanoid Robots (Humanoids), November 2015. https://doi.org/10.1109/HUMANOIDS.2015.7363472
3. Bonilla, M., et al.: Grasping with soft hands. In: 2014 IEEE-RAS International Conference on Humanoid Robots 2015, pp. 581–587, February 2015. https://doi.org/10.1109/HUMANOIDS.2014.7041421
4. Cai, M., Kitani, K., Sato, Y.: Understanding hand-object manipulation with grasp types and object attributes. In: Robotics Conference: Science and Systems 2016, June 2016. https://doi.org/10.15607/RSS.2016.XII.034
5. Caron, S., Kheddar, A., Tempier, O.: Stair climbing stabilization of the HRP-4 humanoid robot using whole-body admittance control. In: IEEE International Conference on Robotics and Automation, September 2018
6. Coleman, D., Sucan, I., Chitta, S., Correll, N.: Reducing the barrier to entry of complex robotic software: a MoveIt! case study. CoRR, April 2014
7. Cordella, F., Zollo, L., Salerno, A., Accoto, D., Guglielmelli, E., Siciliano, B.: Human hand motion analysis and synthesis of optimal power grasps for a robotic hand. Int. J. Adv. Robot. Syst. **11**(3), 37 (2014). https://doi.org/10.5772/57554
8. Corke, P.I.: Robotics, Vision & Control: Fundamental Algorithms in MATLAB, 2nd edn. Springer, Cham (2017). https://doi.org/10.1007/978-3-319-54413-7. ISBN 978-3-319-54412-0
9. Diankov, R., Kuffner, J.: OpenRAVE: a planning architecture for autonomous robotics. Technical report CMU-RI-TR-08-34, Carnegie Mellon University, Pittsburgh, PA, July 2008
10. Fischinger, D., Vincze, M., Jiang, Y.: Learning grasps for unknown objects in cluttered scenes. In: 2013 IEEE International Conference on Robotics and Automation, pp. 609–616, May 2013. https://doi.org/10.1109/ICRA.2013.6630636
11. Gomilko, S., Zhulaeva, D., Rimer, D., Yakushin, D., Mescheryakov, R., Shandarov, E.: Robot soccer team for RoboCup humanoid kidsize league. In: Ronzhin, A., Rigoll, G., Meshcheryakov, R. (eds.) ICR 2016. LNCS (LNAI), vol. 9812, pp. 181–188. Springer, Cham (2016). https://doi.org/10.1007/978-3-319-43955-6_22

12. Hernandez, C., et al.: Team delft's robot winner of the Amazon picking challenge 2016. In: Behnke, S., Sheh, R., Sariel, S., Lee, D.D. (eds.) RoboCup 2016. LNCS (LNAI), vol. 9776, pp. 613–624. Springer, Cham (2017). https://doi.org/10.1007/978-3-319-68792-6_51

13. Kawamura, S., Svinin, M. (eds.): Advances in Robot Control. Springer, Berlin Heidelberg (2006). https://doi.org/10.1007/978-3-540-37347-6

14. Khusainov, R., Sagitov, A., Klimchik, A., Magid, E.: Arbitrary trajectory foot planner for bipedal walking. In: Proceedings of the 14th International Conference on Informatics in Control, Automation and Robotics, ICINCO 2017, Madrid, Spain, 26–28 July 2017, vol. 2, pp. 417–424 (2017). https://doi.org/10.5220/0006442504170424

15. Li, H., Liu, W., Kawashima, K.: Development of a human-arm like laparoscopic instrument. In: 2016 IEEE International Conference on Robotics and Biomimetics (ROBIO), pp. 68–70, December 2016. https://doi.org/10.1109/ROBIO.2016.7866299

16. Magid, E., Sagitov, A.: Towards robot fall detection and management for Russian humanoid AR-601. In: Jezic, G., Kusek, M., Chen-Burger, Y.-H.J., Howlett, R.J., Jain, L.C. (eds.) KES-AMSTA 2017. SIST, vol. 74, pp. 200–209. Springer, Cham (2018). https://doi.org/10.1007/978-3-319-59394-4_20

17. Murooka, M., Nozawa, S., Kakiuchi, Y., Okada, K., Inaba, M.: Whole-body pushing manipulation with contact posture planning of large and heavy object for humanoid robot. In: 2015 IEEE International Conference on Robotics and Automation (ICRA), pp. 5682–5689. IEEE (2015)

18. Oikonomidis, I., Kyriazis, N., Argyros, A.A.: Full DOF tracking of a hand interacting with an object by modeling occlusions and physical constraints. In: 2011 International Conference on Computer Vision, pp. 2088–2095, November 2011. https://doi.org/10.1109/ICCV.2011.6126483

19. Roa, M., J. Argus, M., Leidner, D., Borst, C., Hirzinger, G.: Power grasp planning for anthropomorphic robot hands. In: Proceedings - IEEE International Conference on Robotics and Automation, pp. 563–569, May 2012. https://doi.org/10.1109/ICRA.2012.6225068

20. Romay, A., Kohlbrecher, S., Conner, D.C., von Stryk, O.: Achieving versatile manipulation tasks with unknown objects by supervised humanoid robots based on object templates. In: 2015 IEEE-RAS 15th International Conference on Humanoid Robots (Humanoids), pp. 249–255, November 2015. https://doi.org/10.1109/HUMANOIDS.2015.7363543

21. Sahbani, A., El-Khoury, S., Bidaud, P.: An overview of 3d object grasp synthesis algorithms. Robot. Auton. Syst. 60, 326–336 (2012). https://doi.org/10.1016/j.robot.2011.07.016

22. Stasse, O., Flayols, T.: An overview of humanoid robots technologies. In: Venture, G., Laumond, J.-P., Watier, B. (eds.) Biomechanics of Anthropomorphic Systems. STAR, vol. 124, pp. 281–310. Springer, Cham (2019). https://doi.org/10.1007/978-3-319-93870-7_13

23. Odhner, L.U., Dollar, A.M.: Stable, open-loop precision manipulation with underactuated hands. Int. J. Robot. Res. 34, (2015). https://doi.org/10.1177/0278364914558494

24. Odhner, L.U., Ma, R., Dollar, A.M.: Open-loop precision grasping with underactuated hands inspired by a human manipulation strategy. IEEE Trans. Autom. Sci. Eng. 10, 625–633 (2013). https://doi.org/10.1109/TASE.2013.2240298

Hierarchical Psychologically Inspired Planning for Human-Robot Interaction Tasks

Gleb Kiselev[1] and Aleksandr Panov[1,2(✉)]

[1] Artificial Intelligence Research Institute FRC CSC RAS, Moscow, Russia
kiselev@isa.ru
[2] Moscow Institute of Physics and Technology, Moscow, Russia
panov.ai@mipt.ru

Abstract. This paper presents a new algorithm for hierarchical case-based behavior planning in a coalition of agents – HierMAP. The considered algorithm, in contrast to the well-known planners HEART, PANDA, and others, is intended primarily for use in multi-agent tasks. For this, the possibility of dynamically distributing agent roles with different functionalities was realized. The use of a psychologically plausible approach to the representation of the knowledge by agents using a semiotic network allows applying HierMAP in groups in which people participate as one of the actors. Thus, the algorithm allows us to represent solutions of collaborative problems, forming human-interpretable results at each planning step. Another advantage of the proposed method is the ability to save and reuse experience of planning – expansion in the field of case-based planning. Such extension makes it possible to consider information about the success/ failure of interaction with other members of the coalition. Presenting precedents as a special part of the agent's memory (semantic network on meanings) allows to significantly reduce the planning time for a similar class of tasks. The paper deals with smart relocation tasks in the environment. A comparison is made with the main hierarchical planners widely used at present.

Keywords: Cognitive agent · Sign · Sign-based world model ·
Human-like knowledge representation · Behavior planning · Spatial planning ·
Pseudo-physical logic · Task planning

1 Introduction

In connection with the development of robotics and automation of the management of complex technical means, the activity of research in the direction of artificial intelligence increases. The actual problem in this area is the complexity of the transition from a symbolic description of the environment to objects which perceptual images are directly observed by the agent. Existing symbolic planning algorithms do not allow the agent to synthesize an action plan based on sensor data from the real environment state. Currently, the most common architecture of robotic agents is the hybrid architecture [1, 2], which responds to the dynamics [3] of the environment and updates the previously synthesized action plan. The hybrid architecture implies the presence of several levels of abstract representations of agent actions in the plan, for example, the HFSM

© Springer Nature Switzerland AG 2019
A. Ronzhin et al. (Eds.): ICR 2019, LNAI 11659, pp. 150–160, 2019.
https://doi.org/10.1007/978-3-030-26118-4_15

structure (parallel hierarchical finite state machine) used in WillowGarage allows the implementation of robot's actions such as delivering food from a refrigerator, playing chess, moving over rough terrain. HFSM considers both a general view of task actions and specific implementations of agent actions. The hierarchy of abstractions of action representation helps reduce time and resource costs for building a plan [4], lowers the level of dissemination of personal information of an agent [5], provides an opportunity to parallelize actions [6], allows you to find and process possible risks of the plan [7], and also allows partially re-planning activities in the environment dynamics [8].

In modern architectures, the hierarchy of abstractions of actions is represented using plans of various levels of detail. Abstract plans generated using classical planning approaches can be refined in the implementation process, and experience describing detailed actions can be reused in subsequent tasks. In this paper, we propose to use the representation of the agent knowledge in the form of a semiotic network, a part of which can be saved at the end of the activity and used in solving subsequent problems. The developed mechanism for limiting the used set of knowledge allows you to deal with a decrease in the rate of search for a plan in the current situation due to the dependence of the dimension of variations of substitutions when planning actions only on the description of the problem being solved. After the completion of the planning process, all the actions found are saved as a subnet of the global knowledge network of the agent, and access to this subnet can be accomplished by moving from the element designating the task to be solved. (This process is described in more detail in Sect. 2). Strictly structuring the sequence of sub-actions is used in modern HTNPlan-P [9], PANDA [10] planners, based on the HTN planning approach, improvements of which provide the ability to partially re-plan [11] in a dynamic environment and limit time execution processes as elementary, and complex actions [12] of the agent. But, unlike the above planners, the approach in question does not contain predefined descriptions of abstract actions (methods, if we speak in terms of HTN), but generates these sequences dynamically based on the task and the available planning precedents.

The behavior planning approach described in this paper allows an agent to use a complex, previously detailed action to select coalition members with whom there have already been successful interaction cases [13]. The HierMAP algorithm uses information both about the capabilities of the planning agent itself and about the capabilities of other team agents. Based on the knowledge of the capabilities of another agent and the experience of previous interactions with him, the decision on the activity's implementation is made. Since the described algorithm performs the planning of the cognitive agent's activity, an appropriate communication protocol is used, transmitting messages between actors in a manner understandable to humans. After the planning process is completed, an auction of plans is carried out in which agents select the final goal plan. This process is described in more detail in Sect. 3.

Modern robotic agents are designed to perform actions in a real environment and require an internal representation of spatial and quantitative relations with respect to each other and the objects with which they interact. Human's spatial relations are directly related to the significances of the objects themselves [14] and with their entry into the focus of attention [15], in which elementary actions are carried out. Forming the focus of a person's attention is based on the concepts of "Left", "Right", "Here", "There", "Close", "Far" and others, which contribute to the awareness of the fact that

"I am here" and the rest of the world is "there". The described algorithm, in contrast to traditional approaches [16, 17], is based on a psychologically-similar way of representing knowledge and uses spatial pseudo-physical logic [18, 19], typical to planners [20, 21] which are commonly used by cognitive agents. A characteristic feature of agents whose actions are synthesized on the basis of psychologically or biologically [22–24] of such ways of representing knowledge in the planning process is the presence of intelligent terrain marking. The agent needs to assess its location and purposefully act by implementing a synthesized plan. The main problem of modern cognitive agents is the accumulation too much knowledge about the environment, which makes it possible to draw a conclusion that a person can understand a real state of an agent [25], but leads to a significant slowdown in his activity. To eliminate this problem, various types of spatial semantic hierarchy [19, 26] are used, allowing robotic agents to act on large maps [27] in a dynamically changing environment. The planning approach presented in this paper allows an agent to have different levels of focus abstraction of attention (situations) and to carry out activities based on the local location of subjects and objects of activity. The possibility of preserving the experience of intersecting a plot of terrain in which a clarification of the situation was required allows one to reuse an abstract action of moving in a similar situation without slowing down the planning process. This process is described in more detail in Sect. 4.

Further article is organized as follows. Section 2 describes the basic principles of the used method of knowledge representation and describes the logic of the HierMAP algorithm. Section 3 presents a description of the multi-agent component of the approach, discloses the principles of agent reflection, role distribution. Section 4 describes the pseudo-physical logic used in the intellectual movement of agents. In Sect. 5, the results of experiments and their discussion are given.

2 Cognitive Agent Subject Activity

The HierMAP algorithm uses a semiotic representation of the agent knowledge [28, 29] the base element is the sign [30–32]. Using the sign structure as a way of presenting knowledge about the elements of the environment was chosen on the basis of research by neurophysiologists and psychologists [33, 34] regarding the representation of knowledge by human. In addition, the possibility of combining different ways of representing knowledge about the same object to move from the classical for artificial intelligence symbolic way of representing knowledge to a hybrid one that meets the principles of robotics of the present time was considered.

2.1 Psychologically Inspired Knowledge Representation

The sign is described by a tuple, which includes 4 main components $s = <n, p, m, a>$, where n is the name component, which is used to define the sign, p is the image component, m is the significance component, and a is the personal meaning component. Each of the components of the sign is responsible for its type of presentation of information about the described entity. Component p is a description of the characteristic features of an entity (in HierMAP, this is a description of the coordinates of a terrain segment, or a sequence of sub-actions of an abstract action). Component m - is responsible for the available generalized scenarios for the use of an entity by a group of agents, and component a - determines the role of the represented entity in the action of the planning entity. Personal meanings of the sign are synthesized in the process of the agent with the described entity. A sign can be either a static object or an action.

The components of the sign are represented by a special structure – the causal matrix [35], which allows to connect the components of signs and form semantic networks, the relations on each of which are different. The causal matrix has a structure divided into two parts, the left side is responsible for the conditions of the matrix, and the right side for effects. In the simplest case, the causal matrix can be described using a tuple of length t of events ei. Each of the events on the images network describes the recognized element at the moment of time t1, on the networks of significances and personal meanings – a link to another sign, feature or function of the agent. The described structure of the matrix contributes to the division of matrices into two types: objective and procedural. Procedural matrices describe various actions and processes, therefore, unlike object matrices, they have a non-empty set of effects events.

An example of relations on a images network is the "part-whole" relationship; in the algorithm described, this relationship is used when checking the intersection of the agent's focus and the global part of the map, or the description of the connection between actions of a lower level of abstraction and the action of a larger one due to the connection "action-sub action". On the significances network, characteristic connections are "class-subclass" or "scenario-role" relationships. An example of the implementation of relations of this type can be considered in the task of the well-known domain "Blocks world", in which the block class has subclasses "huge block", "red block", and the role of blocks "block?x" and "block?y" are included in action scenarios "stack". On the network of personal meanings there are "situation-participant of the situation" links, allowing to limit the description of a specific situation to agents who are directly involved in it.

The sign world model is the five elements tuple $\langle W_p(s), W_m(s), W_a(s), R_n, \Theta \rangle$, where W_m, W_a, W_p – are semantic and causal significances, personal meanings and images networks, respectively, $R = \langle R^m, R^a, R^p \rangle$ are relations on components sign, and Θ - operations on a set of signs. Relationships on the components of a sign allow you to implement the processes of propagation of activity presented in the HierMAP by selecting matrices of a higher level of abstraction (if activity extends upward) or matrices of a lower level of abstraction (if activity extends downward) on the significances network. On the network of personal meanings, the processes of propagation of activity allow the agent to choose the actions that it can make with existing objects, and on the images network to get the sensory data of objects.

2.2 Plan Synthesis Algorithm

Synthesis of the cognitive agent behavior plan is the result of the HierMAP algorithm. The algorithm allows you to build a chain of actions with different levels of abstraction from the initial state to the goal. The planning process begins with the grounding procedure, with the help of which the replenishment of the subject's world model with knowledge of this task takes place. In the grounding procedure, the agent activates signs of objects and subjects, creates a set of rules and substitutions that allow the synthesis of a behavior plan. At the stage of synthesis of the plan, the agent recursively creates all possible plans for reaching the matrix of the goal situation on the network of personal meanings, which describes the goal location of the agent on the map. To do this, the agent searches for a semiotic network from a sign describing the current situation and activates the network elements associated with this sign. Those signs that were received during the spreading of activity "downward» from the situation sign are included in its description (causal matrix), as well as contained in the description (causal matrix) of actions that can be performed in this situation. When extending the activity «upward» from the sign of the current situation, the signs of activity precedents (complex actions) are activated, the performance of which brings the agent much closer to the goal situation than the elementary actions. After activation of the signs of elementary actions, heuristics are applied, which reduce the combinatorial complexity of the algorithm. The heuristic is the procedure in which the signs of actions activate the sign of the next situation, which is compared with the goal situation. The most similar to the goal situation is added to the plan and becomes a new starting point for the activity distribution process.

The described algorithm allows you to save the constructed plan of action as a sign of a complex action (experience) in the agent's world model. The sign of a complex action contains causal matrices on networks of personal meanings and images, the significances of the sign remain empty. The conditions of the matrix contain a reference to the sign of the initial situation, and the effects refer to the sign of the goal situation. Each of the columns of the conditions of the matrix contains a reference to the sign of the action that is performed at the present plan step (see Fig. 1).

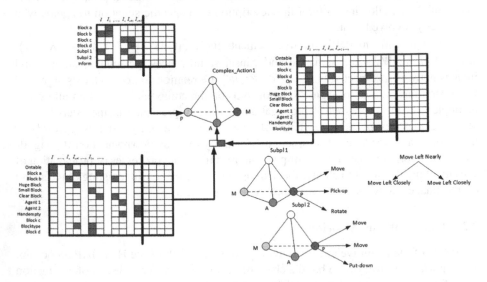

Fig. 1. Complex action's sign with its causal matrices.

3 Multiagent Knowledge Representation

In the process of activity, the agent may face tasks that cannot be done alone. Situations in which there is a physical limitation of the planning agent (someone can fly, and someone can lift large loads), the lack of sufficient resources to accomplish the goal on their own (battery of the robot, time limit on the task) lead to functional addition of agents to each other, which allows you to optimally solve the problem. Coalition activity of agents requires appropriate multi-agent planning and creation of communication protocols. The spectrum of classical planning problems is significantly expanded due to the need for dynamic re-planning during the plan implementation, the need to consider the redundancy of information about other team members, which in all cases of agent interaction without a coalition contributes to disrupting the activities of other agents for personal gain or the acquisition of additional resources.

In the simplest case, the agents are united in a coalition to achieve the goal. When planning actions in a coalition, an agent must have not only an idea about his capabilities, but also about the capabilities of other members of the coalition. The construction of a multi-agent plan by each of the agents is accompanied by reflexive planning, followed by a joint sampling of a general plan of action. The selection of the general plan of actions by agents is achieved using the methods of reaching agreements such as: auctions [36], contract networks [37] and so on. The plans of each of the agents, as well as in the case of non-group planning, consist of actions of different levels of abstraction, the actions of which can be either specified or not specified plans of other agents. Since coalitions may consist of a heterogeneous set of agents, the synthesis of the plan must consider the role composition of actions and the ability of agents of the current coalition to implement the activities of all the required roles. In many situations, the same action can be performed by different coalition agents, which allows us to talk about the ways to assign roles in coalitions [38].

In the HierMAP algorithm, the sign representation of the agent's knowledge allows one to describe the agent's knowledge of himself with the "I" sign, and the knowledge of other coalition participants as agents of "Agent1", "Agent2". The fact that the agent was aware of the fact "I am here", and everything else "There" made it possible to create an anthropomorphic unified description of all other coalition members using the "They" sign, including references to the signs of other agents in the matrix of personal meanings of this sign. The object representation of other coalition agents provides an opportunity to implement a dynamic process of assigning roles in a coalition, based on the study of precedents of activity. After finding all the available plans, the agents select the most appropriate plan, in the simplest case, based on a set of heuristics:

- Plans of the smallest length are selected.
- Plans are selected with the most uninterrupted sequence of actions by one agent (the communication channel may not be stable).
- Plans are selected with the fewest agents involved.
- Plans are selected in which the planning agent is involved.
- Randomly select one of the remaining plans.

Depending on the number of coalition participants, a meta-action is added to the agent's plan for communicating with other agents. If the coalition includes more than 2 agents, then the procedural matrix on the network of personal meanings of the "Broadcast" sign is activated, otherwise the procedural matrix of the "Notify" sign. The object sign representation of the ways of communication allows not only to activate the corresponding functions of compiling a message adapted for a person and the process of its transmission, but also allows preserving the used method of communication in the experience of the agent. The availability of information about the previous methods of communication of agents provides an opportunity to evaluate the implementation of the plan and change the way of communication with the negative termination of agents' activities.

4 Spatial Logic Representation

Purposeful activity of agents both in a real environment and in a simulation implies the execution of certain actions on the manipulation of environmental objects and on moving around the map. Next, we consider the specific application of the HierMAP algorithm for the problem of smart relocation tasks [39–41].

In the HierMAP algorithm, agents synthesize a plan using a spatial knowledge representation of the environment, which is described by dividing the surrounding space into 9 cells of the agent's attention focus, which dynamically changes its size depending on the presence of surrounding objects and 9 map regions whose dimensions remain static throughout the construction and implementation of the plan by the agent. The focus of the agent and the terrain map is formed using the causal matrixes of the "Location" and "Content" signs, which contain references to the spatial and quantitative relations of the surrounding objects relative to the central cell in which the agent is located. An example of spatial descriptions are the matrices of the signs "Nearly", "Closely" and "Far Away". The semiotic representation of environmental knowledge allows you to create a hierarchy of spatial relationships that are understandable to human. The representation used is consistent with the statement that spatial representations are dependent on the subject matter and scope. For example, if we describe to our friend the distance from the research institute to the nearest metro station within our city, then the entrance to the metro will be far from the institute, and if we describe the same distance, but within the dialogue about the distances between cities and countries, then the distance to the subway becomes insignificant. In addition, the hierarchy of spatial relations is observed by the fact that a relation to a weakly remote point of space is a relation to some close point and the same relation from that close point to a close point from it in the same direction.

5 Experiments

As part of the demonstration of the features of the use of the sign approach in complex problems, an experimental study was presented. The main criterion for the selection of tasks was the presence of subplans in the plans synthesized by agents. The agents-built plans for intellectual movement, which at the elementary level consisted of the actions "pick-up block", "put-down block", "rotate", "move" and "Inform". The domain of the tasks under consideration is a spatial extension of the classical "Blocks world" problem. In the hierarchical case, the set of actions is replenished by the actions "Abstract" and "Clarify", which allow dynamic changes in the dimension of the agent's focus, as well as the case-law actions of movements and previously synthesized plans.

Experiments are made on the PC AMD FX ™ - 6300 Six – Core Processor 3.76 GHz with 16 Gb RAM.

Since the comparison of our algorithm occurred with single-agent algorithms, the following are experiments with a single agent. The differences between these experiments and experiments with a multitude of agents will not be strongly expressed, since each agent in our algorithm is independent and calculates plans at its own facilities. In the framework of this study, only tasks related to planning within the framework of knowledge already existing in the agent's world picture were considered, all plans could be found and no additional acquisition of environmental knowledge by agents was required.

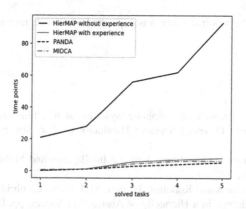

Fig. 2. Comparison with HTN planners.

Figure 2 shows the dependence of the solution time on the number of objects and obstacles in the path of the agent (narrow hallways, transitions, etc.) – black graph and elapsed time when using experience – gray graph. The dotted line denotes the PANDA algorithm, the dash point line denotes the MIDCA algorithm. 5 tasks were considered:

1. Move from one end of the card to another. Detour obstacles in the form of a table.
2. Move from one end of the card to the other. Avoiding multiple obstacles.
3. Departure from the narrow corridor to the large room. The presence of obstacles in the form of a wall.
4. Travel through a narrow corridor and check into a small room. The presence of obstacles in the form of a set of walls.
5. Moving a block from one table to another. Movement with the object.

Methods greatly speed up the planning process, but if there are precedents of activity, the HierMAP algorithm produces a result that does not differ much in time, even considering the fact of much better detail of actions (1 classically defined action for moving in the HTN planner equals from 1 to 12 action to move in HierMAP).

6 Conclusion

The paper presents a psychologically plausible approach to the problem of hierarchical multi-agent behavior planning. An example is given of applying the developed algorithm as a method for calculating an agent's intelligent movement plan, at each step of which an agent can explain his actions to a person. A model example of accelerating the process of synthesizing a plan through the use of activity precedents is given, and a comparison with other hierarchical planning algorithms was also given. In the further work, cases of co-operation of agents and the transfer of entire scenarios of activities will be considered in more detail, and robotic examples for the claimed algorithm will be given.

Acknowledgments. The reported study was supported by RFBR, research Project No. 17-29-07051.

References

1. Kortenkamp, D., Simmons, R.: Robotic systems architectures and programming. In: Siciliano, B., Khatib, O. (eds.) Springer Handbook of Robotics, pp. 187–206. Springer, Berlin (2008)
2. Gat, E.: On three-layer architectures. Artificial Intelligence and Mobile Robots. MIT Press, Cambridge (1998)
3. Arkin, R.C.: Behavior-based Robotics, 1st edn. MIT Press, Cambridge (1998)
4. Ellman, T.: Hillclimbing in a Hierarchy of Abstraction Spaces, pp. 0–12 (1974)
5. Brafman, R.I.: A privacy preserving algorithm for multi-agent planning and search. In: Proceedings of the Twenty-Fourth International Joint Conference on Artificial Intelligence (IJCAI 2015), pp. 1530–1536 (2015)
6. Rovida, F., Grossmann, B., Kruger, V.: Extended behavior trees for quick definition of flexible robotic tasks. IEEE International Conference on Intelligent Robots and Systems, pp. 6793–6800 (2017)
7. Grea, A., Matignon, L., Aknine, S.: HEART. In: International Conference on Automated Planning and Scheduling, pp. 17–25 (2018)
8. Bechon, P., et al.: Integrating planning and execution for a team of heterogeneous robots with time and communication constraints, pp. 1091–1097 (2018)
9. Sohrabi, S., Baier, J.A., McIlraith, S.A.: HTN planning with preferences. In: IJCAI International Joint Conference on Artificial Intelligence, pp. 1790–1797 (2009)
10. PANDA homepage. https://www.uni-ulm.de/en/in/ki/research/software/panda/panda-planning-system/
11. Daniel, H., Bercher, P., Behnke, G., Biundo, S.: HTN Plan Repair Using Unmodified Planning Systems, pp. 26–30 (2018)

12. Boerkoel, J.C., Planken, L.R., Wilcox, R.J., Shah, J.A.: Distributed algorithms for incrementally maintaining multiagent simple temporal networks. In: Proceedings of the Autonomous Robots and Multirobot Systems Workshop (at AAMAS-12), vol. 59, pp. 256–263 (2012)
13. Kiselev, G.A., Panov, A.I.: Sign-based approach to the task of role distribution in the coalition of cognitive agents. In: SPIIRAS Proceedings, pp. 161–187 (2018)
14. Tversky, B.: Functional significance of visuospatial representations. In: Shah, P., Miyake, A. (eds.) Handbook of Higher-Level Visuospatial Thinking, pp. 1–34. Cambridge University Press, Cambridge (2005)
15. Lakoff, G., Johnson, M.: Philosophy in the Flesh. Basic Books, New York (1999)
16. Erdem, U.M., Hasselmo, M.E.: A biologically inspired hierarchical goal directed navigation model. J. Physiol. Paris 108(1), 28–37 (2014)
17. Daniel, K., et al.: Any-angle path planning on grids. J. Artif. Intell. Res. 39, 533–579 (2010)
18. Pospelov D.A.: Situacionnoe upravlenie. Teoria i praktika. Nauka. p. 288 (1986)
19. Aitygulov, E., Kiselev, G., Panov, A.I.: Task and spatial planning by the cognitive agent with human-like knowledge representation. In: Ronzhin, A., Rigoll, G., Meshcheryakov, R. (eds.) Interactive Collaborative Robotics, pp. 1–12. Springer International Publishing, New York (2018)
20. Epstein, S.L., Aroor, A., Sklar, E.I., Parsons, S.: Navigation with Learned Spatial Affordances, pp. 1–6 (2013)
21. Epstein, S.L., et al.: Spatial abstraction for autonomous robot navigation. Cogn. Process. 16, 215–219 (2015)
22. Erdem, U.M., Hasselmo, M.E.: A biologically inspired hierarchical goal directed navigation model. J. Physiol. Paris 108(1), 28–37 (2014)
23. Milford, M., Wyeth, G.: Persistent navigation and mapping using a biologically inspired slam system. Int. J. Robot. Res. 29(9), 1131–1153 (2010)
24. Milford, M., Schulz, R.: Principles of goal-directed spatial robot navigation in biomimetic models. Philos. Trans. R. Soc. B: Biol. Sci. 369(1655), 20130484 (2014)
25. Huang, S.H., Held, D., Abbeel, P., Dragan, A.D.: Enabling Robots to Communicate their Objectives (2017)
26. Kuipers, B., Byun, Y.T.: A robot exploration and mapping strategy based on a semantic hierarchy of spatial representations. Robot. Auton. Syst. 8, 47–63 (1991)
27. Milford, M.J., Wyeth, G.F., Prasser, D.P.: Rat- SLAM on the edge: revealing a coherent representation from an overloaded rat brain. In: Proceedings of the International Conference on Robots and Intelligent Systems, pp. 4060–4065 (2006)
28. Osipov, G.S., Panov, A.I.: Relationships and operations in a sign-based world model of the actor. Sci. Tech. Inf. Process. 45, 317–330 (2018)
29. Panov, A.I.: Behavior planning of intelligent agent with sign world model. Biol Inspired Cogn. Archit. 19, 21–31 (2017)
30. Osipov, G.S., Panov, A.I., Chudova, N.V.: Behavior control as a function of consciousness. I. world model and goal setting. J. Comput. Syst. Sci. Int. 53, 517–529 (2014)
31. Osipov, G.S., Panov, A.I., Chudova, N.V.: Behavior control as a function of consciousness. II. synthesis of a behavior plan. Journal of Computer and Systems Sciences International 54, 882–896 (2015)
32. Osipov, G.S.: Sign-based representation and word model of actor. In: Yager, R., Sgurev, V., Hadjiski, M., Jotsov, V. (eds.) 2016 IEEE 8th International Conference on Intelligent Systems (IS). p. 2226. IEEE (2016)
33. Leontyev, A.N.: The Development of Mind. Erythros Press and Media, Kettering (2009)
34. Vygotsky, L.S.: Thought and Language. MIT Press, Cambridge (1986)

35. Panov, A.I.: Goal setting and behavior planning for cognitive agent. Scientific and Technical Information Processing. **6**, (In press) (2019)
36. Primeau, N., et al.: Improving task allocation in risk-aware robotic sensor networks via auction protocol selection. In: 2016 IEEE 20th Jubilee International Conference on Intelligent Engineering Systems (INES). pp. 21–26 (2016)
37. Holodkova, A.V.: Application of agents is in model of contractual network. Inf. Process. Syst. **4**(102), 142–145 (2012)
38. Kiselev, G., Kovalev, A., Panov, A.I.: Spatial reasoning and planning in sign-based world model. In: Kuznetsov, S., Osipov, G.S., Stefanuk, V. (eds.) Artificial Intelligence, pp. 1–10. Springer, Berlin (2018)
39. Panov, A.I., Yakovlev, K.: Behavior and path planning for the coalition of cognitive robots in smart relocation tasks. In: Kim, J.H., et al. (eds.) Robot Intelligence Technology and Applications, vol. 4, pp. 3–20. Springer, Berlin (2016)
40. Panov, A.I., Yakovlev, K.S.: psychologically inspired planning method for smart relocation task. Procedia Comput. Sci. **88**, 115–124 (2016)
41. Emel'yanov, S., Makarov, D., Panov, A.I., Yakovlev, K.: Multilayer cognitive architecture for UAV control. Cogn. Syst. Res. **39**, 58–72 (2016)

The Fog-Computing Based Reliability Enhancement in the Robot Swarm

Iakov Korovin[1], Eduard Melnik[2], and Anna Klimenko[3]([✉])

[1] Autonomous Federal State Institution of Higher Education
«Southern Federal University», Rostov-on-Don, Russia
[2] Southern Scientific Center of Russian Academy of Sciences,
Rostov-on-Don, Russia
[3] Scientific Research Institute of Multiprocessor Computer Systems of Southern
Federal University, Taganrog, Russia
anna_klimenko@mail.ru

Abstract. The current paper deals with the swarm robots reliability. Cloud robotics, fog robotics and the Internet of the Robotic Things are the fast growing scientific fields nowadays, yet the terms "cloud" and "fog" relate to the network facilities and devices rather than the swarm. In this paper the new approach is proposed, to place a fog-like structure into the swarm and so to affect the reliability of those robots, which need the reliability correction. To show the potential of the approach proposed, simple models are developed, as well as some simulations have been made. Based on the simulation results, "greedy" and "egoistic" strategies are proposed to affect the robots reliability.

Keywords: Robot swarm · Fog robotics · Fog-computing · Reliability · Cloud robotics · Optimization

1 Introduction

A swarm robotics is an extremely popular and growing area in the robotic field. There is a wide range of key advantages to use a swarm, for example, scalability, fault tolerance, cost, adaptivity, configurability and others [1]. The robot swarm has its own features, which distinguish it from multi-robot groups, e.g., the autonomy of robots, large number of robots in the swarm, homogeneity of the swarm, insufficiency of the single robot to solve the problem chosen, and local R2R communication. The latter plays quite an important role in the data transmission to the base station, making swarm locate in a way to transmit sensor data with routing through the swarm members.

At the same time, robots have to solve the tasks of a high computational complexity frequently. The examples of those tasks are so-called SLAM (simultaneous localization and mapping) [2], map merging or other tasks of data processing [3–5], which needs high computational capacities. Yet the swarm robots are cheap and possess relatively low computational resources. It led to the efforts of distributed problem solving, including the robot clusters [6, 7] usage and the so-called cloud robotics [8–10]. Cloud robotics, providing the scalable and agile computational resources for the data processing, has met an obstacle in recent years: in conditions of data amount increase, the

© Springer Nature Switzerland AG 2019
A. Ronzhin et al. (Eds.): ICR 2019, LNAI 11659, pp. 161–169, 2019.
https://doi.org/10.1007/978-3-030-26118-4_16

cloud has shown such issues as: insufficient scalability, high latency, overloaded communication channels, security problems and others. The obvious solution was to locate the data processing near the data sources. The fog- and edge-computing paradigms, intersected with robotics, resulted in the new paradigm called the Internet of Robotic Things [11, 12].

Yet the swarm and the cloud combined sometimes can not generate an appropriate effect. In case of large amounts of raw data, routing through the swarm to the cloud, the system has an obvious issues:

Data transmitted through the swarm generate the additional workload of the transitional nodes, and as the amount of data is bigger, the bigger additional load is;

The need to transmit data to the cloud through the swarm increases the system latency, which is highly undesirable.

Besides, there is another specific feature, which is rarely considered in the papers devoted to the swarm robotics. This particular feature is reliability, which is closely interconnected to the dependability as one of its components. Actually, the reliability issue is observed poorly in the robotic and fog-computing research papers: relating to the swarm, the study [13] considers the reliability in terms of virtual robot controller placement in the set of fog-nodes of a network.

So, the reliability enhancement problem is considered in this paper.

In order to estimate the interconnection between the reliability and the data processing in the swarm, we generated some simplified models, which help to demonstrate, how the placement of information processing affects the robot computational nodes loading and the reliability as a consequence. On the basis of research conducted some strategies of reliability enhancement are proposed. The main contribution of this research to the robotic field is to show that the fog- and edge computing paradigms are appropriate for reliability enhancement in the robot swarm. It must be mentioned, that in the context of this paper the fog-layer is shifted from some gateways of any other network facilities to the swarm, and the members of the swarm play the roles of the fog-nodes.

2 Multi-robot Groups, Robot Swarms and Robot Clusters

Before the consideration of the problem, some historical and terminological review must be made.

Multi-robot group consists of several robots working together to achieve a certain application objective [14].

The usage of multirobot groups brings lots of benefits, such as:

- multiple robots can concurrently work on the task to achieve it faster;
- robots can be heterogenous in their capabilities to provide a cost-effective solution to achieve a task where each robot handles specific components of the task matching its capabilities;
- multiple robots can effectively deal with a task that is inherently distributed over a wide area;

- using multiple robots for achieving a task provides fault tolerance as the presence of multiple robots capable of similar processes can be used to compensate when any of them fails [15, 16].

A comprehensive definition of the robot swarm is presented in [17]: swarm robotics is the study of how large number of relatively simple physically embodied agents can be designed so that a desired collective behaviour emerges from the local interactions among agents and between the agents and the environment.

There is a set of criteria [17], which distinguishes the swarm from other multi-robot types of systems:

- the robots of the swarm must be autonomous robots, able to sense and actuate in a real environment;
- the number of robots in the swarm must be large or at least the control rules allow it;
- robots must be homogeneous in terms of type and capabilities;
- the robots must be incapable or inefficient in relation to the main task they have to solve, so, they need to collaborate in order to succeed or to improve the performance;
- robots have only local communication and sensing capabilities. It ensures the coordination is distributed, so scalability becomes one of the properties of the system.

From the terminological point of view one can see that the swarm can be considered as a multi robot group with certain constraints. At the same time, with the increasing of data to be processed and the geographical distribution of the swarm, the problem of data transmission and processing emerges.

The analysis of the studies published has shown that in 2012 the first paper was produced defining the robot cluster from the resource sharing point of view [6].

In this study the new definition of robot cluster is proposed: robots share their own processing resources to establish a computer cluster and solve the computational problem. Some later works use the term "robot cluster" in the same way, but the number of those papers is rather small [3].

In the later years, the field of cloud and fog robotics took started to prevail with the considerable amount of research papers and implementations. The cloud- and fog-based information processing was proposed: the information is transmitted to the cloud, or is preprocessed on some fog-nodes of the network.

3 Cloud and Fog Robotics

As the computational complexities of the task solving by robots have increased, the new concept has emerged, the so-called cloud robotics. The large amount of studies has been published until recently in the field of cloud computing, fog computing, edge computing, including studies in the area of Internet of Robotic Things [18].

Briefly, the overall idea of the cloud robotics is to place the complex computations to the cloud, while the key idea of the fog- and edge computing is to put some preliminary data processing as near to the data source as possible.

Cloud robotics is coined by [19], declaring that robots are independent with unlimited computational power.

Cloud robotics is centered around benefits of shared service and converged infrastructure using cloud computing, cloud storage, and other Internet technologies. It provides detachment between physical and software aspects of robotics. One of the comprehensive examples of cloud robotic project is the RoboEarth [20] platform. It provides the following advantages:

- cooperation facilitation: cloud helps to facilitate cooperation among device nodes;
- the possibility to computation offloading: computationally intensive tasks like planning, probabilistic inference, and mapping can be offloaded to cloud;
- datastore providing: scalable storage provided by cloud layer database can be used to store and share information;
- multiple robots can learn about the environment using other's experience, this is a method of learning by sharing experiences;
- instead of individually programming robot, a developer can create robot task instruction.

The Fog robotics is determined in [21]: this is an architecture, which consists of storage, networking functions, control with decentralized computing closer to robots.

The integral parts of such an architecture are: Fog Robot Server, Robots and Cloud. If a robot requests some resources, then it will first query the Fog Robot Server. If there are sufficient resources, the cloud remains unused. In opposite case, the resources will be allocated in the cloud.

Yet it must be mentioned that fog is supposed to be distributed in the network infrastructure. In the following section the new approach is proposed as to place the fog-layer directly into the robot swarm.

In the next section of this paper the simple model based estimations are conducted to show how the fog-layer placement in the swarm affects the robot nodes workload and reliability.

4 A Simplified Model of Workload Distribution Through the Swarm with Fog-Computing Concept Application

Consider the simplified swarm model, which is chain-like. Every robot, say, gathers the graphical information about the landscape and transmits this information to the base, using other robots as a route. Assume that all robots perform their functional tasks, so, information transmitting and functional tasks performing simultaneously.

The scheme of such a swarm is presented in the Fig. 1.

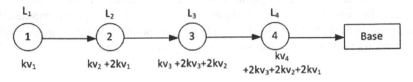

Fig. 1. The scheme of a swarm and the information transmission route.

Assume the overall computational load of a robot node consists of its own computational load and the effort to receive and send the information from and to the other robots. So, the overall workload of the robot computational nodes will be as follows:

$$L_{01} = L_1 + kv_1;$$
$$L_{02} = L_2 + 2kv_1 + kv_2;$$
$$L_{03} = L_1 + 2kv_1 + 2kv_2 + kv_3;$$
$$L_{04} = L_1 + 2kv_1 + 2kv_2 + 2kv_3 + kv_4,$$

where L_{0i} is an overall node workload, k is a ratio determining the effort of data transmission, v_i is a transmitted data volume.

One can see that the nearer the node is to the base, the bigger volume of information it transfers.

Consider another situation: assume that every robot in our chain preprocess its own information and so the volume of the information to be transferred is less than in previous case.

Consider the variable η as ratio determining the dependency between the volume of preprocessed information and the volume of transmitted information.

Then, the equations describing the overall workload of the nodes will be as follows:

$$L_{01} = (1+\eta)L_1 + (1-\eta)kv_1;$$
$$L_{02} = (1+\eta)L_2 + (1-\eta)2kv_1 + (1-\eta)kv_2;$$
$$L_{03} = (1+\eta)L_1 + (1-\eta)2kv_1 + (1-\eta)2kv_2 + (1-\eta)kv_3;$$
$$L_{04} = (1+\eta)L_1 + (1-\eta)2kv_1 + (1-\eta)2kv_2 + (1-\eta)2kv_3 + (1-\eta)kv_4,$$

where η is a share of information to be preprocessed.

The results of simulation are presented in Fig. 2.

Yet with the increasing of the volume of preprocessed information, the nodes far from the edge have less workload than the nodes in case of no preprocessing. At the same time preprocessing loads the edge nodes, and so affects the workload and reliability negatively.

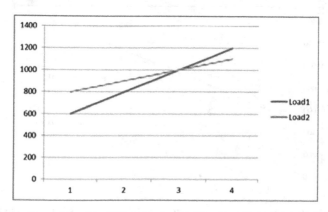

Fig. 2. Relatively high computational load, high volumes of information to be transferred, $\eta = 0.5$.

Then consider the case when there is a kind of a fog-layer in the chain of robots, e.g., the node №1 preprocesses its own information, and none of them preprocesses it as well. For the example considered, the equations will be as follows:

$$L_{01} = (1+\eta)L_1 + (1-\eta)kv_1;$$
$$L_{02} = L_2 + 2(1-\eta)kv_1 + kv_2;$$
$$L_{03} = L_1 + 2(1-\eta)kv_1 + 2kv_2 + kv_3;$$
$$L_{04} = L_1 + 2(1-\eta)kv_1 + 2kv_2 + 2kv_3 + kv_4.$$

Consider another example for comparison is to place the fog-layer and the information preprocessing to the node №2. Assume that node №2 preprocess not only its own information, but the information of the node №1, too.

$$L_{01} = L_1 + kv_1;$$
$$L_{02} = (1+\eta_1+\eta_2)L_2 + 2(1-\eta_2)kv_1 + (1-\eta_1)kv_2;$$
$$L_{03} = L_3 + 2(1-\eta_2)kv_1 + 2(1-\eta_1)kv_2 + kv_3;$$
$$L_{04} = L_4 + 2(1-\eta_2)kv_1 + 2(1-\eta_1)kv_2 + 2kv_3 + kv_4.$$

Adding the trend to the diagram, one can see Fig. 3.

One can see that the workloads of the nodes 1, 3, 4 are less then ones of the other strategies of information preprocessing placement.

So, such simple estimations allow to make a conclusion that the application of the fog-concept within the robot swarm affects the workloads of the robot nodes and so affects their reliability.

Hence, shifting the fog-layer within the swarm, we can enhance the reliability of particular swarm members, requesting the partial information preprocessing from the previous robots in the information transmission route. It must be mentioned that there can be situations, for example, when more than one node has to become "a fog-layer". It is possible when the reliability constraints of the nodes don't allow to run all the presupposed information processing.

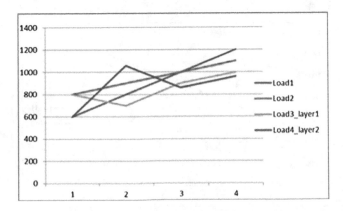

Fig. 3. Trends with no-preprocessing, overall preprocessing and fog-layers within the swarm (load3_layer1, load4_layer2).

5 Strategies and Algorithms of the Information Preprocessing Placement in the Swarm

In this section two generic strategies are proposed, the first one being "greedy", and the other one – "egoistic".

Consider the node in the swarm, who transmits the information and performs its own computational tasks. In some time periods it checks its reliability level, and, for example, if it exceeds the threshold predetermined, some steps must performed to offload the computational node. In the scope of this paper we consider the case, when each robot in the swarm knows only about its neighbors.

5.1 The "Greedy" Strategy

1. The initiator node estimates the workload volume to be offloaded and sends the request to the previous nodes of the information transmission route.
2. Node received the request:
   estimates its own reliability and failure rate, using the equation:

$$\lambda = \lambda_0 \cdot 2^{\Delta T/10}, \tag{1}$$

where λ – is a failure rate of the element; λ_0 – is a nominal failure rate considering the temperature of the object is equal 20°C; ΔT – is a temperature increase while the element is functioning.

As $\Delta T = kD$, where k is a ratio between temperature and workload, D is the element workload, the Eq. (1) can be presented as follows:

$$\lambda = \lambda_0 \cdot 2^{kD/10}.$$

3. Compares the current failure rates or the reliability function to its reliability constraints:

   - if the constraints meet the additional workload, the node performs its information preprocessing;
   - if it is not enough for the initial node reliability constraints satisfaction, the node forms the request on the remainder of the offload and sends it to the previous node in the route.

   This strategy is called "greedy" because each node takes as much workload, which is the information preprocessing, as possible due to the reliability constraints existence.

5.2 Egoistic Strategy

While in the previous case every predecessor node in the information transmission route takes as much information preprocessing as it can, the "Egoistic" strategy, on the contrary, presupposes that every node tries to take as little additional workload as it can.

To perform such procedure, the following steps are to be done:

1. The initiator node estimates its own reliability constraints and, if it is needed, sends the request to the previous node.
2. The node received the request, estimates its capabilities in terms of reliability constraints satisfaction, and retranslates the request and this data to the previous node. This repeats until the edge robot in the swarm is reached.
3. The set of nodes involved to the offloading process solve the problem of workload distribution, paying attention to the information transmission process and its computational complexity. This task can be solved as an optimizational one, with n objective functions, such as:

$$F_i = \min_{\eta_i}(\lambda_i), i = 1..n, \qquad (2)$$

The overall workload for each node is estimated as is shown in equations above (2).
4. If the multicriteria optimization problem is solved by each node in a randomized search manner, then the consensus must be achieved. The way to achieve the consensus is out of the scope of this paper.

If the problem has no solution, the swarm is supposed to change the route of information transmission.

6   Conclusion

In the current paper the problem of swarm node reliability is considered. If the swarm is formed of the robots with different exploitation history, there are situations, when the reliability of some robots must be corrected by the offloading procedure, because it is expedient to save as much robots performing as possible. Inspired by fog-computing concept, the authors of this paper propose to enhance the capabilities of the fog to the swarm, organizing the computational process as the fog-computing concept proposes. With the simple models and estimations it is shown that the placement of the information preprocessing affects the overall load distribution in the swarm and so can be applied to the reliability enhancement of the particular nodes.

In the current research two fog-layer forming strategies are proposed, the "greedy" and the "egoistic" ones. Both of them presuppose only robot-to-robot communication between the nodes without any overall knowledge, and all of them presuppose that the initial nodes offloading takes place by the "fog-nodes" placement before the initial nodes on the information transmission route. As the "fog-nodes" begin the information preprocessing, the offload process takes place and so the reliability of the particular nodes improves.

Acknowledgements. The current study is granted by the RFBR projects 19-07-00907 and 17-08-01605.

References

1. Brambilla, M., Ferrante, E., Birattari, M., Dorigo, M.: Swarm robotics: a review from the swarm engineering perspective. Swarm Intell. **7**(1), 1–41 (2013)
2. Gouveia, B.D., Portugal, D., Silva, D.C., Marques, L.: Computation sharing in distributed robotic systems: a case study on SLAM. IEEE Trans. Autom. Sci. Eng. **12**(2), 410–422 (2015)
3. León, A., et al.: SLAM and map merging. J. Phys. Agents **3**(1), 13–23 (2009)
4. Konolige, K., et al.: Map merging for distributed robot navigation. In: Intelligent Robots and Systems Proceedings, vol. 1, pp. 212–217. IEEE, Las Vegas (2004)
5. Carpin, S.: Fast and accurate map merging for multi-robot systems. Auton. Robots **25**(3), 305–316 (2008)
6. Marjovi, A., Choobdar, S., Marques, L.: Robotic clusters: multi-robot systems as computer clusters a topological map merging demonstration. Rob. Auton. Syst. **60**(9), 1191–1204 (2012)
7. Kehoe, B., Patil, S., Abbeel, P., Goldberg, K.: A survey of research on cloud robotics and automation. IEEE Trans. Autom. Sci. Eng. **12**(2), 1–12 (2015)
8. Hu, G., Tay, W.P., Wen, Y.: Cloud robotics: architecture, challenges and applications. IEEE Network **26**(3), 21–28 (2012)
9. Wang, X.V., Wang, L., Mohammed, A., Givehchi, M.: Ubiquitous manufacturing system based on cloud: a robotics application. Robot. Comput. Integr. Manuf. **45**, 116–125 (2017)
10. Dey, S., Mukherjee, A.: Robotic SLAM: a review from fog computing and mobile edge computing perspective. In: Adjunct Proceedings of the 13th International Conference on Mobile and Ubiquitous Systems: Computing Networking Services, pp. 153–158 (2016)
11. Ray, P.P.: Internet of robotic things: concept, technologies, and challenges. IEEE Access **4**, 9489–9500 (2016)
12. Inaltekin, H., Gorlatova, M., Mung, C.: Virtualized control over fog: interplay between reliability and latency, CoRR. https://arxiv.org/pdf/1712.00100.pdf. Accessed 5 Apr 2019
13. Jawhar, I., Mohamed, N., Wu, J., Al-Jaroodi, J.: Networking of multi-robot systems: architectures and requirements. Sens. Actuator Netw. Feature Papers **7**(52), 1–16 (2018)
14. Parker, L.E.: Multiple mobile robot systems. In: Siciliano, B., Khatib, O. (eds.) Springer Handbook of Robotics, pp. 921–941. Springer, Heidelberg (2008). https://doi.org/10.1007/978-3-540-30301-5_41
15. Zlot, R., Stentz, A., Dias, M.B., Thayer, S.: Multi-robot exploration controlled by a market economy. In: Proceedings of the IEEE International Conference on Robotics and Automation, ICRA 2002, vol. 3, pp. 3016–3023. IEEE, Washington, DC (2002)
16. Şahin, E.: Swarm robotics: from sources of inspiration to domains of application. In: Şahin, E., Spears, W.M. (eds.) SR 2004. LNCS, vol. 3342, pp. 10–20. Springer, Heidelberg (2005). https://doi.org/10.1007/978-3-540-30552-1_2
17. Simoens, P., Dragone, M., Saffiotti, A.: The internet of robotic things: a review of concept, added value and applications. Int. J. Adv. Rob. Syst. **15**(1), 1–11 (2018)
18. Kuffner, J.J.: Cloud-enabled robots. In: Proceedings of the IEEE-RAS International Conference on Humanoid Robots, Nashville, TN, USA, pp. 176–181 (2010)
19. Waibel, M., et al.: Robo earth – a World Wide Web for robots. Robot. Autom. Mag. **18**(2), 69–82 (2011)
20. Krishna, S.L., et al.: Fog robotics for efficient, fluent and robust human-robot interaction. In: 17th IEEE International Symposium on Network Computing and Applications (NCA 2018). https://arxiv.org/abs/1811.05578. Accessed 5 Apr 2019

Generation of Walking Patterns for Biped Robots Based on Dynamics of 3D Linear Inverted Pendulum

Artem Kovalev⬤, Nikita Pavliuk⬤, Konstantin Krestovnikov⬤,
and Anton Saveliev$^{(\boxtimes)}$⬤

St. Petersburg Institute for Informatics and Automation of the Russian Academy
of Sciences (SPIIRAS), 14th Line, 39, 199178 St. Petersburg, Russia
saveliev.ais@yandex.ru

Abstract. Biped humanoid robot dynamics is approximated by dynamics of 3D linear inverted pendulum, which can be derived from dynamics of ordinary 3D inverted pendulum. Based on this approximation of biped robot dynamics we can generate walking patterns, which are specified by step parameters, that specify desired zero moment point (ZMP) trajectory. To track desired center of mass (CoM) trajectory, modified foot positions are calculated by minimizing an error function in closed form. Different forces acting on biped robot are taken into account during calculation of robot dynamics for plain surface as well for uneven terrain. Some walking patterns and walking primitives are expressed algorithmically for different 3D cases in terms of ground-fixed coordinate frame. Some dynamic constraints applicable in this setting are presented.

Keywords: Linear inverted pendulum · Walking pattern generation · Biped robots

1 Introduction

Legged robot dynamics is similar to dynamics of inverted pendulum, where its pivot point is located at the ZMP in the supporting foot (see Fig. 1), and its center of mass is the center of mass of biped robot [1–3]. By deriving 3D linear inverted pendulum from general 3D inverted pendulum, we can represent biped robot dynamics with limited parameters [4–6]. We can control center of mass (CoM) trajectory of the humanoid robot in real-time by controlling CoM trajectory of the linear inverted pendulum, which approximates biped humanoid robot dynamics [3, 7].

ZMP (Zero Moment Point) – a concept, first defined by Vukobratovic and Stepanenko [8–10]. Ground reaction force of the foot in XZ plane can be decomposed into

A. Ronzhin et al. (Eds.): ICR 2019, LNAI 11659, pp. 170–181, 2019.
https://doi.org/10.1007/978-3-030-26118-4_17

its horizontal $\sigma(x)$ and vertical components $\rho(x)$. Horizontal component of the ground reaction force exists because of the friction between the ground and the sole of the foot:

$$f_x = \int_{x_1}^{x_2} \sigma(x)dx; \qquad f_z = \int_{x_1}^{x_2} \rho(x)dx,$$

where $\sigma(x)$ – horizontal component of the ground reaction force per unit length of the sole, $\rho(x)$ – vertical component of the ground reaction force per unit length of the sole.

The moment at a certain sole point p_x can be calculated as:

$$\tau(p_x) = -\int_{x_1}^{x_2} (x - p_x)\rho(x)dx.$$

By setting $\tau(p_x) = 0$ we can obtain p_x:

$$p_x = \frac{\int_{x_1}^{x_2} x\rho(x)dx}{\int_{x_1}^{x_2} \rho(x)dx}.$$

Thus, p_x is the center of pressure and ZMP. For 2D case, ZMP is a point where the moment of ground reaction force becomes zero. If the ground reaction force doesn't become negative, then $x_1 \leq p_x \leq x_2$.

For 3D case, ground reaction force can be decomposed into horizontal and vertical components. Reaction forces are distributed over the surface of the sole. By integrating them over the area S (contact area) between the sole and the ground, we can substitute them by the force $\mathbf{f} = [f_x \quad f_y \quad f_z]^T$.

$$f_x = \int_S \sigma_x(x,y)dS; \qquad f_y = \int_S \sigma_y(x,y)dS; \qquad f_z = \int_S \rho(x,y)dS.$$

The moment $\tau(p) = \tau_n(p) + \tau_t(p)$ about point p is the sum of the moment τ_t of the horizontal ground reaction force and the moment τ_n of the vertical ground reaction force. The moment $\tau_n(p) = [\tau_{nx} \quad \tau_{ny} \quad \tau_{nz}]^T$ of the vertical ground reaction force about the point p can be calculated as:

$$\tau_{nx} = \int_S (y - p_y)\rho(x,y)dS; \qquad \tau_{ny} = -\int_S (x - p_x)\rho(x,y)dS.$$

Assuming $\tau_{nx} = 0$ and $\tau_{ny} = 0$ we can find the point p:

$$p_x = \frac{\int_S x\rho(x,y)dS}{\int_S \rho(x,y)dS}; \qquad p_y = \frac{\int_S y\rho(x,y)dS}{\int_S \rho(x,y)dS}.$$

The moment $\tau_t(p) = [0 \quad 0 \quad \tau_{tz}]^T$ of the horizontal ground reaction force about the point p can be calculated as:

$$\tau_{tx} = 0; \qquad \tau_{ty} = 0;$$

$$\tau_{tz} = \int_S [(x - p_x)\sigma_y(x,y) - (y - p_y)\sigma_x(x,y)]dS.$$

The moment of the ground reaction force about the point p is $\tau(p) = \tau_n(p) + \tau_t(p) = [0 \ \ 0 \ \ \tau_{tz}]^T$. The point p is the ZMP for 3D case, i.e. the point where the horizontal components of the moment of the ground reaction force become zero.

2 2D Inverted Pendulum

Walking robot can be approximated as an inverted pendulum. Inverted pendulum consists of the CoM of the robot, CoM is connected to leg support point or leg pivot point O, which is located at the ZMP in the supporting foot.

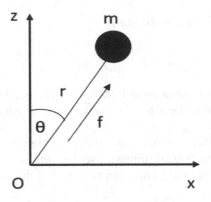

Fig. 1. 2D inverted pendulum model, approximating a walking robot.

Differential equations, describing the dynamics of inverted pendulum, can be derived with Lagrange's method:

$$\begin{cases} r^2\ddot{\theta} + 2r\dot{r} - gr\,sin\theta = \tau/m \\ \ddot{r} - r\dot{\theta}^2 + g\,cos\theta = f/m \end{cases},$$

where r – distance between pivot point and CoM.

Linear inverted pendulum is controlled by τ – torque at contact point O and leg thrust force f [2, 11]. In practice, we cannot command big torques because of hardware limitations, and it's assumed that torque $\tau = 0$. If torque is zero, unless we apply a leg thrust force, then the pendulum will fall down (see Fig. 2). To control the behavior of pendulum we need to command a leg thrust force. If we apply leg thrust force of $f = mg/cos\theta$, then pendulum will be moving horizontally (see Fig. 3). This mode is called Linear Inverted Pendulum Mode [12–15] and can be described by the following differential equation

$$\ddot{x} = \frac{g}{z}x,$$

where x – CoM position, g – gravity acceleration, z – CoM height (constant).

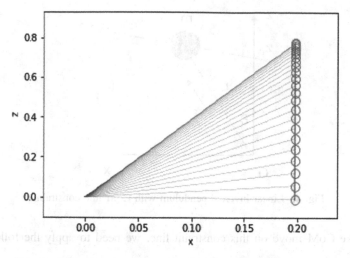

Fig. 2. Inverted pendulum behavior with leg thrust force $f = 0$.

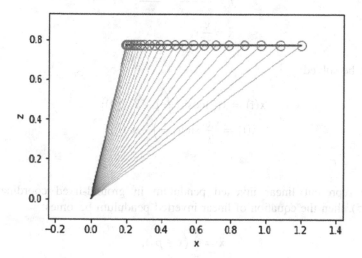

Fig. 3. Inverted pendulum behavior with leg thrust force $f = f = mg/cos\theta$.

To extend linear inverted pendulum for uneven terrain, we can introduce a constraint line (see Fig. 4), along which CoM can move:

$$z = kx + z_c,$$

where k – line slope, z_c – point of intersection with Z axis.

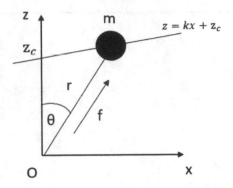

Fig. 4. Linear inverted pendulum with CoM line constraint.

To make CoM move on this constraint line, we need to apply the following leg thrust force:

$$f = \frac{mgr}{z - kx} = \frac{mgr}{z_c};$$
$$\ddot{x} = \frac{g}{z_c}x,$$

which can be solved:

$$x(t) = x(0)\cosh\left(\frac{t}{T_c}\right) + T_c\dot{x}(0);$$
$$\dot{x}(t) = \frac{x(0)}{T_c}\sinh\left(\frac{t}{T_c}\right) + \dot{x}(0),$$

where $T_c = \sqrt{\frac{z_c}{g}}$.

If we represent linear inverted pendulum in ground-fixed coordinate frame (see Fig. 5), then the equation of linear inverted pendulum becomes:

$$\ddot{x} = \frac{g}{z_c}(x - p_x),$$

where p_x – foot ZMP position. It is solved as:

$$x(t) = (x(0) - p_x)\cosh\left(\frac{t}{T_c}\right) + T_c\dot{x}(0)\sinh\left(\frac{t}{T_c}\right) + p_x;$$
$$\dot{x}(t) = \frac{x(0) - p_x}{T_c}\sinh\left(\frac{t}{T_c}\right) + \dot{x}(0)\cosh\left(\frac{t}{T_c}\right),$$

where $T_c = \sqrt{\frac{z_c}{g}}$.

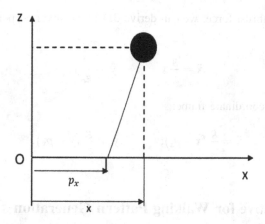

Fig. 5. Linear inverted pendulum in ground-fixed coordinate frame.

3   3D Linear Inverted Pendulum

For 3D linear inverted pendulum [16, 17], leg thrust force can be decomposed into its x, y, z components:

$$f_x = \left(\frac{x}{r}\right)f; \qquad f_y = \left(\frac{y}{r}\right)f; \qquad f_z = \left(\frac{z}{r}\right)f.$$

Since we assumed $\tau = 0$, only gravity and leg thrust force will act on CoM. CoM dynamics in 3D can be described as:

$$m\ddot{x} = \left(\frac{x}{r}\right)f; \qquad m\ddot{y} = \left(\frac{y}{r}\right)f; \qquad m\ddot{z} = \left(\frac{z}{r}\right)f - mg.$$

Instead of constraint line, for 3D linear inverted pendulum we must introduce a constraint plane

$$z = k_x x + k_y y + z_c.$$

To derive the leg thrust force, that will make CoM move on this plane, we need to solve the following equation

$$\left[\left(\frac{x}{r}\right)f \quad \left(\frac{y}{r}\right)f \quad \left(\frac{z}{r}\right)f - mg \right] \begin{bmatrix} -k_x \\ -k_y \\ 1 \end{bmatrix} = 0.$$

By solving this equation, we obtain leg thrust force:

$$f = \frac{mgr}{z - k_x x - k_y y} = \frac{mgr}{z_c}.$$

Under this leg thrust force, we can derive 3D linear inverted pendulum dynamics equations:

$$\ddot{x} = \frac{g}{z_c}x; \qquad \ddot{y} = \frac{g}{z_c}y$$

or in ground-fixed coordinate frame:

$$\ddot{x} = \frac{g}{z_c}(x - p_x); \qquad \ddot{y} = \frac{g}{z_c}(y - p_y).$$

4 Walk Primitive for Walking Pattern Generation

Walk primitive [16] is a 3D linear inverted pendulum trajectory [18, 19], which is symmetric about Y axis in a time period of $[0 \quad T_{sup}]$, where T_{sup} – leg support time. Because walk primitive is symmetric, we can easily determine its terminal position $(\bar{x}, \bar{y})$ and it's terminal velocity $(\bar{v}_x, \bar{v}_y)$. Given T_{sup} and z_c, we can determine terminal position and terminal velocity from the analytic solution of linear inverted pendulum. Terminal position and velocity for x component of walk primitive with initial condition $(-\bar{x}, \bar{v}_x)$:

$$\bar{x} = -\bar{x}\cosh\left(\frac{T_{sup}}{T_c}\right) + T_c\bar{v}_x\sinh\left(\frac{T_{sup}}{T_c}\right);$$
$$\bar{v}_x = \bar{x}(\cosh\left(\frac{T_{sup}}{T_c}\right) + 1)/T_c\sinh\left(\frac{T_{sup}}{T_c}\right);$$
$$T_c = \sqrt{\frac{z_c}{g}}.$$

Terminal position and velocity for y component of walk primitive with initial condition $(\bar{y}, -\bar{v}_y)$:

$$\bar{y} = \bar{y}\cosh\left(\frac{T_{sup}}{T_c}\right) + T_c(-\bar{v}_y)\sinh\left(\frac{T_{sup}}{T_c}\right);$$
$$\bar{v}_y = \bar{y}(\cosh\left(\frac{T_{sup}}{T_c}\right) - 1)/T_c\sinh\left(\frac{T_{sup}}{T_c}\right);$$
$$T_c = \sqrt{\frac{z_c}{g}}.$$

5 Generation of Walking Patterns for Producing Walk Trajectories

Using walking primitives, we can produce a variety of walk trajectories by varying step length parameters (s_x, s_y) and the heading angle s_θ, using which we specify the direction change. To generate a walking pattern, we specify a sequence of foot positions as a sequence of step parameters $\left(s_x^0, s_y^0, s_\theta^0\right) \ldots \left(s_x^N, s_y^N, s_\theta^N\right)$. We also need to specify initial foot position $\left(p_x^0, p_y^0\right)$ and T_{sup} – leg support time. We can change step direction using the following rotation matrix:

$$R(\theta) = \begin{bmatrix} cos\theta & -sin\theta \\ sin\theta & cos\theta \end{bmatrix}$$

Step 1. We integrate differential equations of linear inverted pendulum (in earth-fixed coordinate frame) from current time t to $t + T_{sup}$.

Step 2. we calculate the next foot position. If the first support foot was the left foot, then the position of n-th footstep can be calculated as:

$$\begin{bmatrix} p_x^n \\ p_y^n \end{bmatrix} = \begin{bmatrix} p_x^{n-1} \\ p_y^{n-1} \end{bmatrix} + R(s_\theta^n) \begin{bmatrix} s_x^n \\ (-1)^n s_y^n \end{bmatrix}.$$

If the first support foot was the right foot:

$$\begin{bmatrix} p_x^n \\ p_y^n \end{bmatrix} = \begin{bmatrix} p_x^{n-1} \\ p_y^{n-1} \end{bmatrix} + R(s_\theta^n) \begin{bmatrix} s_x^n \\ -(-1)^n s_y^n \end{bmatrix}.$$

Step 3. Using step parameters, we can calculate required walk primitive for n-th step:

$$\begin{bmatrix} \bar{x}^n \\ \bar{y}^n \end{bmatrix} = R(s_\theta^{n+1}) \begin{bmatrix} 0.5 * s_x^{n+1} \\ 0.5 * (-1)^n s_y^{n+1} \end{bmatrix}.$$

Terminal velocity of a walk primitive:

$$\begin{bmatrix} \bar{v}_x^n \\ \bar{v}_y^n \end{bmatrix} = R(s_\theta^{n+1}) \begin{bmatrix} \bar{y}^n \left(\cosh\left(\frac{T_{sup}}{T_c}\right) + 1\right)/T_c \sinh\left(\frac{T_{sup}}{T_c}\right) \\ \bar{y}^n \left(\cosh\left(\frac{T_{sup}}{T_c}\right) - 1\right)/T_c \sinh\left(\frac{T_{sup}}{T_c}\right) \end{bmatrix};$$

$$T_c = \sqrt{\frac{z_c}{g}}.$$

Step 4. Desired position can be calculated by representing walk primitive in the ground coordinate frame

$$\begin{bmatrix} x^d \\ y^d \end{bmatrix} = \begin{bmatrix} p_x^n + \bar{x}^n \\ p_y^n + \bar{y}^n \end{bmatrix}.$$

Desired velocity:

$$\begin{bmatrix} \dot{x}^d \\ \dot{y}^d \end{bmatrix} = \begin{bmatrix} \overline{v}_x^n \\ \overline{v}_y^n \end{bmatrix}.$$

To track state vectors $(x^d, \dot{x}^d)$ and $(y^d, \dot{y}^d)$ we need to modify our foot placement (p_x, p_y). We need to define some error function, which measures deviation from desired state

$$E = \alpha\left(x^d - x^n\right)^2 + \beta\left(\dot{x}^d - \dot{x}^n\right)^2,$$

where α, β – weights. $(x^n, \dot{x}^n)$ – position of linear inverted pendulum after step 1.

By solving $\frac{\partial E}{\partial p_x} = 0$, we obtain required foot position (ZMP), which minimizes this error function:

$$p_x = -\frac{\alpha\left(\cosh\left(\frac{T_{sup}}{T_c}\right) - 1\right)}{D}\left(x^d - \cosh\left(\frac{T_{sup}}{T_c}\right)x_i^n - T_c\sinh\left(\frac{T_{sup}}{T_c}\right)\dot{x}_i^n\right)$$

$$-\frac{\beta\sinh\left(\frac{T_{sup}}{T_c}\right)}{T_c D}\left(\dot{x}^d - \frac{\sinh\left(\frac{T_{sup}}{T_c}\right)}{T_c}x_i^n - \cosh\left(\frac{T_{sup}}{T_c}\right)\dot{x}_i^n\right);$$

$$D = \alpha\left(\cosh\left(\frac{T_{sup}}{T_c}\right) - 1\right)^2 + \beta\left(\sinh\left(\frac{T_{sup}}{T_c}\right)/T_c\right)^2.$$

where $(x_i^n, \dot{x}_i^n)$ – position of linear inverted pendulum after step 1. Position p_y is calculated using corresponding linear inverted pendulum state $(y^n, \dot{y}^n)$ and corresponding desired state $(y^d, \dot{y}^d)$.

To obtain a smoother pattern, we can introduce a double support phase with a period T_{double} at the moment of support leg exchange.

We repeat steps 1–4 for all step parameters. Figure 6 shows the result of walking pattern generation. By adjusting step parameters, we can achieve diagonal walking, and rotation about Z axis, which is shown in Fig. 6. Table 1 and Figs. 7 and 8 show differences between target ZMP trajectories and modified ZMP trajectories, as a result of error function minimization.

Table 1. X and Y squared errors.

Step sequence #	0	2	4	6	8	10
X squared error	0.000	3.153E-04	6.000E-05	1.265E-09	2.542E-05	3.326E-04
Y squared error	0.000	9.495E-05	3.474E-01	4.098E-07	2.762E-05	4.115E-03

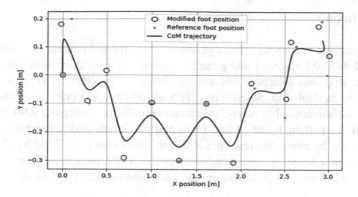

Fig. 6. Linear inverted pendulum walking pattern generation result.

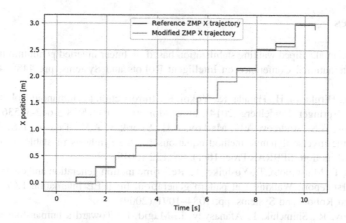

Fig. 7. Reference and modified ZMP X CoM trajectory.

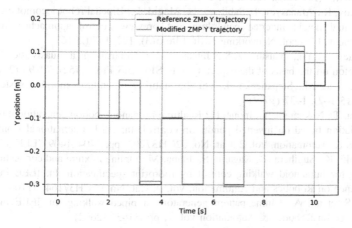

Fig. 8. Reference and modified ZMP Y CoM trajectory.

6 Conclusion

By approximating humanoid robot dynamics with inverted pendulum dynamics, we can control its CoM trajectory and generate walking patterns using a sequence of step parameters. Required foot positions are calculated by minimizing an error function, which can be evaluated in closed form. By varying step parameters, we can achieve walking in any direction. Intuitively, step parameters define a reference ZMP trajectory, and the walking pattern, based on linear inverted pendulum model, generates a desired CoM trajectory, by modifying reference ZMP trajectory (see Figs. 7 and 8), [5, 11]. We can say that in a linear inverted pendulum model, CoM motion is generated by the ZMP, or a linear inverted pendulum inputs ZMP and outputs CoM motion [2, 11].

Acknowledgment. This research is supported by RSF grant No. 16-19-00044P.

References

1. Kajita, S., et al.: Biped walking stabilization based on linear inverted pendulum tracking. In: IEEE International Conference on Intelligent Robots and Systems, pp. 4489–4496. IEEE (2010)
2. Kajita, S., Hirukawa, H., Harada, K., Yokoi, K.: Introduction to Humanoid Robotics. STAR, vol. 101. Springer, Heidelberg (2014). https://doi.org/10.1007/978-3-642-54536-8
3. Gorobtsov, A.S., Andreev, A.E., Markov, A.E., Skorikov, A.V., Tarasov, P.S.: Features of solving the inverse dynamic method equations for the synthesis of stable walking robots controlled motion. SPIIRAS Proc. **18**(1), 85–122 (2019)
4. Taenaka, T., Matsumoto, T., Yoshiike, T.: Real time motion generation and control for biped robot - 1st report: Walking gait pattern generation. In: IEEE International Conference on Intelligent Robots and Systems, pp. 1084–1091 (2009)
5. Khusainov, R., Shimchik, I., Afanasyev, I., Magid, E.: Toward a human-like locomotion: modelling dynamically stable locomotion of an anthropomorphic robot in simulink environment. In: 2015 12th International Conference on Informatics in Control, Automation and Robotics (ICINCO), vol. 2, pp. 141–148. IEEE (2015)
6. Khusainov, R., Afanasyev, I., Sabirova, L., Magid, E.: Bipedal robot locomotion modelling with virtual height inverted pendulum and preview control approaches in Simulink environment. J. Robot. Networking Artif. Life **3**(3), 182–187 (2016)
7. Vorochaeva, LYu., Yatsun, A.S., Jatsun, S.F.: Controlling a quasistatic gait of an exoskeleton on the basis of the expert system. SPIIRAS Proc. **3**(52), 70–94 (2017)
8. Vukobratovic, M., Stepanenko, J.: On the stability of anthropomorphic systems. Math. Biosci. **15**(1–2), 1–37 (1972)
9. Sugihara, T., Nakamura, Y., Inoue, H.: Realtime humanoid motion generation through ZMP manipulation based on inverted pendulum control. In: IEEE International Conference on Robotics & Automation, vol. 2, Cat. No. 02CH37292, pp. 1404–1409. IEEE. (2002)
10. Nishiwaki, K., Sugihara, T., Kagami, S., Inaba, M.: Online mixture and connection of basic motions for humanoid walking control by footprint specification. In: IEEE International Conference on Robotics and Automation, vol. 4, Cat. No. 01CH37164, 4110–4115 (2001)
11. Kajita, S. et al.: A realtime pattern generator for biped walking. In: IEEE International Conference on Robotics & Automation vol. 1, pp. 31–37 (2002)

12. Yokoi, K., et al.: Experimental study of humanoid robot HRP-1s. Int. J. Robot. Res. **23**(4–5), 351–362 (2004)
13. Kajita, S., Tani, K.: Experimental study of biped dynamic walking in the linear inverted pendulum mode. In: IEEE International Conference on Robotics and Automation, vol. 3, pp. 2885–2891. IEEE (1995)
14. Englsberger, J., Ott, C.: Integration of vertical COM motion and angular momentum in an extended capture point tracking controller for bipedal walking. In: IEEE International Conference on Humanoid Robots, pp. 183–189. IEEE (2012)
15. Pratt, J.E., Drakunov, S.V.: Derivation and application of a conserved orbital energy for the inverted pendulum bipedal walking model. In: IEEE International Conference on Robotics and Automation, pp. 4653–4660. IEEE (2007)
16. Kajita, S., Kanehiro, F., Kaneko, K., Yokoi, K., Hirukawa, H.: The 3D linear inverted pendulum mode: a simple modeling for a biped walking pattern generation. In: IEEE International Conference on Intelligent Robots and Systems, vol. 1, Cat. No. 01CH37180, 239–246 (2001)
17. Koolen, T., Posa, M., Tedrake, R.: Balance control using center of mass height variation: limitations imposed by unilateral contact. In: IEEE International Conference on Humanoid Robots, pp. 8–15. IEEE (2016)
18. Denisov, A., Iakovlev, R., Mamaev, I., Pavliuk, N.: Analysis of balance control methods based on inverted pendulum for legged robots. In: MATEC Web of Conferences, vol. 113, p. 02004. EDP Sciences (2017)
19. Denisov, A.V., Iakovlev, R.N.: Methods to ensure the stability of the movement of an anthropomorphic robot based on the reverse pendulum. Zavalishinsky Readings **17**, 227–231 (2017)

Design of a Graphical User Interface for the Structural Synthesis of Parallel Manipulators with Single Platform

Mertcan Koçak$^{(\boxtimes)}$, Fatih Cemal Can, and Erkin Gezgin

Izmir Katip Celebi University Mechatronics Engineering, 35620 Izmir, Turkey
mertcan.kocak@ikc.edu.tr

Abstract. Structural synthesis of parallel manipulators is the first step of design process when new parallel manipulators are needed to be designed. Structural synthesis can be obtained by using structural synthesis formulations. Furthermore, structural synthesis of parallel manipulators can be quickly solved by computer programs. These type of programs are referred as "Automatic Sketching of Mechanism and Manipulators". In this paper, a new Graphical User Interface (GUI) is presented to obtain structural synthesis of parallel manipulators. Two distinct mobility formulations are used to calculate joints on the limbs of parallel manipulators. Apart from other automatic sketching of mechanisms and manipulators, variable general constrained loops were used for the first time in this study. Manipulators with single platform are used in the example designs for the first program runs. After the total number of joints are calculated by the program and they can be placed manually or automatically. This makes proposed program to be user friendly and easy to use. Algorithm can be extended for the design of multi-platform parallel manipulators.

Keywords: Structural synthesis · Automatic sketching ·
Parallel manipulators · Computer aided design

1 Introduction

Structural synthesis of parallel manipulators plays a critical role for designing new parallel manipulator structures. The design procedure of parallel manipulators starts from limb configuration designs to kinematic and dynamic analysis of the manipulators. When number of joints and number of independent loops are increased, structural synthesis of parallel manipulators become harder as it is difficult to get all possible solutions in these situations. Independent loops that are created by the limbs of the manipulator can also be variable for that manipulator. Lots of researches have been presented for structural synthesis of mechanisms and manipulators.

Computer aided structural synthesis of 5-DoF parallel manipulators having different limb configurations which are stored in a database was proposed by Ding et al. [1]. In the study, a human–computer interactive graphical user interface (GUI) can illustrate sketching of parallel manipulator structures according to possible limb configuration selections. Crossley's contribution to the number and type synthesis is graph-based algorithms as presented by Pennestri and Belfiore [2]. Automatic sketching of kinematic

© Springer Nature Switzerland AG 2019
A. Ronzhin et al. (Eds.): ICR 2019, LNAI 11659, pp. 182–192, 2019.
https://doi.org/10.1007/978-3-030-26118-4_18

chains and mechanisms is part of this graph theory contribution. Structural synthesis of planar 3-DoF Closed Loop mechanisms or robots was realized automatically by Ding et al. [3]. In this research, planar 3-DoF heavy-load hydraulic robots are automatically designed by using the complete atlas database. A methodical way of automatic sketching, based on the information provided by the mechanism link–link adjacency matrix, was proposed by Mauskar and Krishnamurty [4]. The algorithm of automatic sketching in this study was developed only for planar mechanisms. Yan and Chiu [5] introduced a new algorithm to improve the efficiency of their algorithm in previous research [6] by deleting generalized kinematic chains with cut-links and nonplanar chains utilizing the concepts of a multiple link adjacency matrix and the Kuratowski graph. A new algorithm, which is a combination of loop-based algorithm and force-directed algorithms, was presented by Pucheta et al. [7]. The loop-based algorithm finds an adequate initial position of graph vertices with minimal edge crossings. The force-directed algorithms are constructed by spring repulsion and electrical attraction. Software written in the C++ language Qt environment is developed by using both algorithms in sequence to generate a representative layout of the graph. Several studies on automatic sketching of mechanisms and robots are presented by Ding et al. [8–13]. Automatic sketching of a planar closed kinematic chain is proposed with a presented C++ program by Huang et al. [14]. In their method, automatic connectivity, automatic distance by using the Floyd–Warshall algorithm, and automatic minimum mobility matrices are calculated. All matrices, topological graphs, and kinematic chain sketching are shown in the GUI. After drawing a topological graph with hand drawing or code reading, several examples such as a 12-link 3-DoF kinematic chain with four independent loops, are given to demonstrate the efficiency of the method in the program. A new method for automatic sketching of a planar closed kinematic chain which can include more than 12 links is presented by Yang et al. [15]. The user enters the number of links and DoF from the user interface for drawing possible kinematic chains. The proposed systematic method has been verified with 6 to 19 links. The method includes extraneous edges' elimination by sequencing the joints in the multiple links. Their method can detect and eliminate concave angles in the multiple links. The program generates mechanisms by minimizing link crossings, maximizing symmetry, avoiding bends, and concave polygons.

This research proposes a new graphical user interface for structural synthesis of parallel manipulators. User is able to enter design parameters in interface for getting new designs on the GUI canvas. Furthermore, throughout the automatic sketching field, concept of loops with variable general constraint were used for the first time in this study. This feature enables designer to get a large variety of structural synthesis. Mobility equations that are used in the algorithm were presented in Sect. 2. Graphical User interface for structural synthesis was represented in Sect. 3. In Sect. 4, examples of parallel manipulators' structural synthesis with design parameters were shown in Figures. Finally, conclusions were discussed at the end of the study.

2   Mobility Equations

The mobility of a mechanism is a quantity that corresponds to number of the independent actuators in order to control the position. In the work of Freudenstein and Alizade [16], general universal mobility equation was defined for the mechanisms with variable or fixed general constraints. Also In the work of Alizade, Bayram and Gezgin [17], mobility equations throughout the related literature were tabulated in a compact table. In the light of these, in order to be utilized for the current study following mobility formulation was decided to be used as the first design equation of the study

$$M = \sum_{i=1}^{N} F_i - \lambda L,$$
(1)

where M is the mobility, N is the number of total joints, λ is the space or subspace of the mechanism, L is the number of the independent loops. This equation works when the term general constraint is constant, since the space or subspace of the mechanism is always the same for each independent loop. In order to make Eq. 1 more generic, it could be modified for the manipulators that have loops from various subspaces as

$$M = \sum_{i=1}^{N} F_i - \sum_{j=1}^{L} \lambda_j,$$
(2)

where λ_j is the space or subspace of each independent loop. As seen from the modified equation, different space or subspace values are used for each independent loops, thus the term general constraint becomes variable. Note that in this work, Eq. 1 is used for the design with fixed space or subspace systems, while the Eq. 2 is used for the design with variable general constraint systems.

Since the software deals with the single platforms, the number of independent loops defines directly the type of the platform.

$$P = L + 1,$$
(3)

where L is the number of the independent loops and P is the type of the platform, which can be up to six (hexagonal platform) in this software.

Since the platform type is 1 more than the number of the independent loops, the remaining loop becomes the dependent one. In the case of fixed space or subspace, the dependent loop is also the same as the other fixed space or subspace, however, if the case is variable general constraint, then the space or subspace of the dependent loop is considered as the maximum possible value of it, six, for avoiding the inconsistency.

In the software, in order to implement the parallel manipulator design rules, some assumptions were made. Firstly, it was considered that all the actuators are connected to the ground, which means that the mobility of the system cannot be greater than the platform type. Since there will be no floating actuated joints on any of the limbs, the number of joints on each limb cannot be greater than the space or subspace of the loop of the related limb. Otherwise, the actuated limb cannot be actuated properly [18].

3   Graphical User Interface for Structural Synthesis

3.1   Views

There are two fundamental design options, which are visualized on a combo box for users to choose. One of which is designed for constant space or subspace value, which uses the Eq. 1, while the other one is designed for variable general constraint systems, which uses the Eq. 2. User is free to choose one of the design options according to design criteria (see Fig. 1).

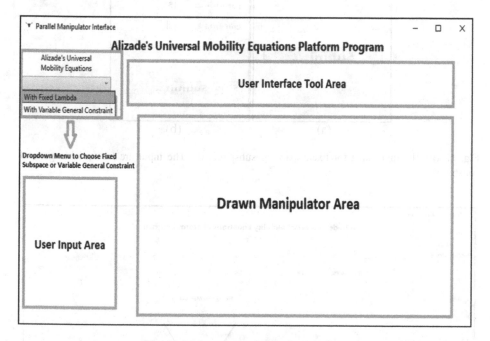

Fig. 1. Main screen of the user interface.

According to user's selection, new panel is opened, which can be filled with the requirements of the Eqs. 1 and 2. This section needs the inputs for design constraints, such as the mobility, number of independent loops and the space or subspace values. If the variable general constraint case is chosen, the user has to enter the multiple space or subspace values for each independent loops (see Fig. 2). In this part of the flow, for executing the equations without any problem, logical inputs are expected from the user, therefore a control process takes place. This process manages the inputs in terms of being digits as well as maximum and minimum constraints. The nature of space or subspace values forces the maximum value of it to be six, as well as it cannot be smaller than three. Also, the graphical interface can handle a platform up to six limbs (hexagonal platform), so the maximum independent loops of the system cannot be greater than five (see Fig. 3). In order to avoid from the bugs in the software, control mechanism plays an important role here.

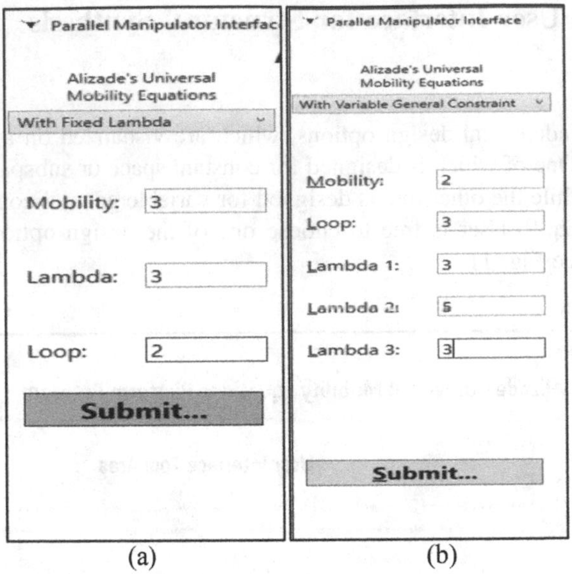

Parallel Manipulator Interface

Alizade's Universal
Mobility Equations

With Fixed Lambda

Mobility: 3

Lambda: 3

Loop: 2

Submit...

Parallel Manipulator Interface

Alizade's Universal
Mobility Equations

With Variable General Constraint

Mobility: 2

Loop: 3

Lambda 1:   3

Lambda 2:   5

Lambda 3:   3

Submit...

(a)   (b)

Fig. 2. (a) The input area for fixed space or subspace. (b) The input are for variable general constraint.

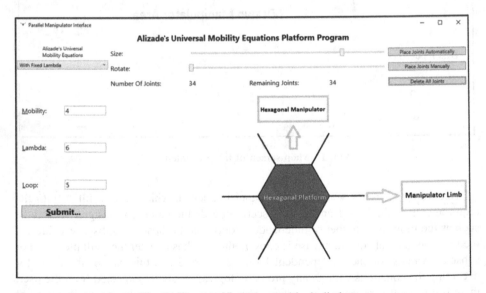

Fig. 3. Hexagonal platform with six limbs

After the user's inputs, the program waits to be pressed on submit button, which is actually executes the main program to construct the visualization on the user interface. However, another control process is taken place on this event, which is related to the possibility for constructing the manipulator with given inputs. As mentioned on the

Sect. 2, number of joints on the limbs cannot be greater than the space or subspace of the independent loop. Because of this constraint, the user's input has to be controlled whether it is possible to construct the manipulator with calculated number of joints by Eq. 1 or Eq. 2. For any limb of the manipulator, if the calculated number of joints is greater than the space of subspace of the related independent loop, the control process returns a warning message to user about the impossible design inputs.

If the warning process is not returned, then the platform and the limbs are created on visual interface. The type of the platform depends on the number of the independent loop as in the Eq. 4.

After the platform is visualized, another user interaction interface is created as well, which includes the sliders for sizing and rotating, text boxes for total number of joints and remaining number of joints, as well as the buttons for user to choose to place the joints by automatically or manually (see Fig. 3).

In order to place the joints automatically on the limbs, number of joints per limb is calculated and the remaining joints are added to the limbs in sequence. In this event, it is not possible to create an asymmetric design. If the user choose to place the joints manually, drag and drop event is expected. The text box of the remaining joints gives to user feedback about the joints that can be placed on limbs. This makes the software flexible to be used in custom designs such as asymmetric if the system can handle it.

3.2 Code Behind

The software is created on the structure of Model-View-View Model (MVVM) by using the Microsoft Visual Studio C# Windows Presentation Foundation (WPF), which supports the object oriented coding. MVVM structure gives the opportunity to control and show different views on one main window with its easy and well oriented structure.

The main idea behind the code structure is to keep all the information of the limbs in a matrix, whose dimension is nx5 and the matrix is updated when any event is called. Here, n represents the number of the limbs that is directly depend on the number of the independent loops. The columns keep the basic information about the each limb such as spaces or subspaces, number of joints on the limbs, lengths of the limbs and the rotation angles of the limbs.

$$Limb\ Data = \begin{bmatrix} \lambda_1 & \lambda_n & j_1 & l & \emptyset \\ \lambda_2 & \lambda_1 & j_2 & l & \emptyset \\ \lambda_3 & \lambda_2 & j_3 & l & \emptyset \\ \vdots & \vdots & \vdots & \vdots & \vdots \\ \lambda_n & \lambda_{n-1} & j_n & l & \emptyset \end{bmatrix}, \tag{4}$$

In matrix form above, the carried information about the limbs are revealed. Here, in the first and the second columns, λ_x represents the related space or subspace values, since one limb is affected by two loops. In the third column, j_x represents the number of joints on each limb. In the fourth and fifth columns, l and $\emptyset$ are limb length and rotation angle respectively, and they both depend directly on the sliders in user interface about size and rotation. Using this structure is useful when updating the inputs, while the visual output is bind to the matrix data.

4   Structural Synthesis of Parallel Manipulators

In this chapter several case studies of the structural synthesis of parallel manipulators with the software will be shown.

4.1   Loops with Fixed Space or Subspace

Let's design a three degrees of freedom manipulator with a single platform with two independent loops form subspace three (planar mechanism). Normally, the design should be started by calculating the number of joints to be shared by the limbs of the platform by using the Eq. 1. Here, since the design is not considered as asymmetric, the graphical interface can be used with the option of placing joints automatically.

As seen from the figure (Fig. 4), with the given design requirements, the system should have a triangular platform with nine joints. All the joints are shared in the limbs equally by placing joints automatically.

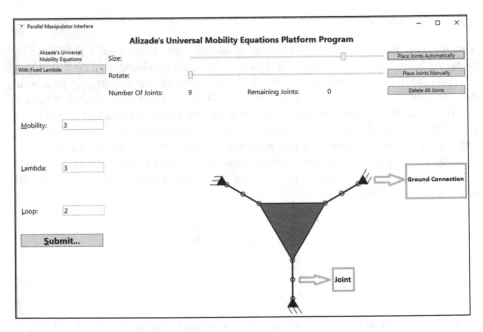

Fig. 4. Triangular platform with mobility and subspace three.

Let's design a four degrees of freedom manipulator with a single platform with three independent loops from the space six (spatial mechanism) with asymmetric design. In this example, since one of the constraints is the asymmetry, it is impossible to be created with placing joints automatically. Instead, the manual joint placing will be used in order to create the system visually.

In Fig. 5, three of the limbs share six joints while one limb has four joints on it, which makes the design asymmetric.

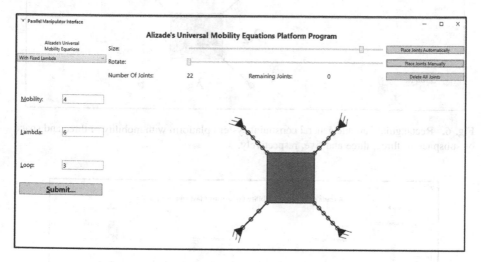

Fig. 5. Rectangular platform with mobility of four and space or subspace of six.

4.2 Loops with Variable Subspaces

Let's design a three degrees of freedom manipulator with a single platform with three independent loops and the each independent loops has different space or subspace numbers as three, three and five, respectively. The designed manipulator is shown in Fig. 6.

Since all the independent loops has different space or subspace values, the specific space or subspaces are defined on the interface with a visual interface.

As last example, let's design a three degrees of freedom manipulator with a single platform with two independent loops and each independent loops has different space or subspaces as three and five, respectively. The output of the program is illustrated in Fig. 7.

With fixed space or subspace and variable general constraint, all possible platform types are summarized and visualized in Table 1.

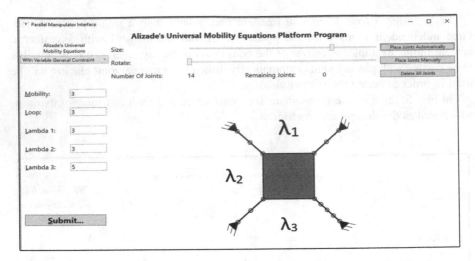

Fig. 6. Rectangular variable general constraint system platform with mobility of three and space or subspace of three, three and five, respectively.

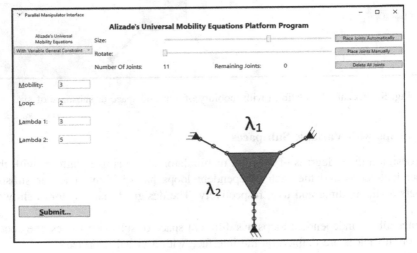

Fig. 7. Triangular variable general constraint system platform with mobility of three and space or subspace of three, and five, respectively.

Table 1. Examples of all possible parallel manipulators

	2 Independent Loops (Triangular Platform)	3 Independent Loops (Rectangular Platform)	4 Independent Loops (Pentagonal Platform)	5 Independent Loops (Hexagonal Platform)
Fixed Subspace				
	$\lambda=3$, Mobility=2	$\lambda=3$, Mobility=2	$\lambda=6$, Mobility=3	$\lambda=3$, Mobility=2
VGC				
	$\lambda_1=3$, $\lambda_2=5$, Mobility = 2	$\lambda_1=3,\lambda_2=3$, $\lambda_3=4$, Mobility = 3	$\lambda_1=3,\lambda_2=3$, $\lambda_3=5,\lambda_4=6$ Mobility = 3	$\lambda_1=5,\lambda_2=5,\lambda_3=3$, $\lambda_4=3,\lambda_5=3$, Mobility = 3

5   Conclusion and Discussion

A new GUI was proposed for the structural synthesis of parallel manipulators. This interface enable us to design parallel manipulators with single platform using different parameters in mobility formulations. Several parallel manipulator examples are illustrated in figures to show effectiveness of the program. This interface can be improved to design multi-platform parallel manipulator with variable general constraint. This will give to designer a large number of possible configurations for parallel robot manipulator.

References

1. Ding, H., Cao, W., Cai, C., Kecskeméthy, A.: Computer-aided structural synthesis of 5-DOF parallel mechanisms and the establishment of kinematic structure databases. Mech. Mach. Theory **83**, 14–30 (2015). https://doi.org/10.1016/j.mechmachtheory.2014.08.013
2. Pennestrì, E., Belfiore, N.P.: On Crossley's contribution to the development of graph based algorithms for the analysis of mechanisms and gear trains. Mech. Mach. Theory **89**, 92–106 (2015). https://doi.org/10.1016/j.mechmachtheory.2014.09.001
3. Ding, H., Huang, P., Liu, J., Kecskeméthy, A.: Automatic structural synthesis of the whole family of planar 3-degrees of freedom closed loop mechanisms. J. Mech. Robot. **5**, 041006 (2013). https://doi.org/10.1115/1.4024919
4. Mauskar, S., Krishnamurty, S.: A loop configuration approach to automatic sketching of mechanisms. Mech. Mach. Theory **31**(4), 423–437 (1996). https://doi.org/10.1016/0094-114X(95)00090-L

5. Yan, H.S., Chiu, Y.T.: An improved algorithm for the construction of generalized kinematic chains. Mech. Mach. Theory **78**, 229–247 (2014). https://doi.org/10.1016/j.mechmachtheory. 2014.03.015
6. Yan, H.S., Chiu, Y.T.: An algorithm for the construction of generalized kinematic chains. Mech. Mach. Theory **62**, 75–98 (2013). https://doi.org/10.1016/j.mechmachtheory.2012.11.005
7. Pucheta, M.A., Ulrich, N.E., Cardona, A.: Automated sketching of non-fractionated kinematic chains, esthetics. Mech. Mach. Theory **68**, 67–82 (2013). https://doi.org/10.1016/j.mechmachtheory.2013.04.013
8. Ding, H., Huang, P., Huang, Z., Kecskeméthy, A.: An automatic method for sketching of planar simple and multiple joint kinematic chains. In: ASME 2015IDETC/CIE 2015, Boston Massachusetts USA, 2–5 August 2015, DETC2015-47216, 1–10. https://doi.org/10.1115/detc2015-47216
9. Ding, H., Huang, P., Zi, B., Kecskeméthy, A.: Automatic synthesis of kinematic structures of mechanisms and robots especially for those with complex structures. Appl. Math. Model. **36**, 6122–6131 (2012). https://doi.org/10.1016/j.apm.2012.01.043
10. Ding, H., Huang, Z., Mu, D.: Computer-aided structure decomposition theory of kinematic chains and its applications. Mech. Mach. Theory **43**, 1596–1609 (2008). https://doi.org/10.1016/j.mechmachtheory.2007.12.011
11. Ding, H., Huang, P., Yang, W., Kecskeméthy, A.: Automatic generation of the complete set of planar kinematic chains with up to six independent loops and up to 19 links. Mech. Mach. Theory **96**, 75–93 (2016). https://doi.org/10.1016/j.mechmachtheory.2015.09.006
12. Ding, H., Cao, W., Kecskeméthy, A., Huang, Z.: Complete atlas database of 2-DoF kinematic chains and creative design of mechanisms. J. Mech. Des. **134**(031006), 1–10 (2012). https://doi.org/10.1115/1.4005866
13. Ding, H., Hou, F., Kecskeméthy, A., Huang, Z.: Synthesis of the whole family of planar 1-DOF kinematic chains and creation of their atlas database. Mech. Mach. Theory **47**, 1–15 (2012). https://doi.org/10.1016/j.mechmachtheory.2011.08.011
14. Huang, P., Ding, H., Yang, W., Kecskeméthy, A.: An automatic method for the connectivity calculation in planar closed kinematic chains. Mech. Mach. Theory **109**, 195–219 (2017). https://doi.org/10.1016/j.mechmachtheory.2016.10.004
15. Yang, W., Ding, H., Kecskeméthy, A.: A new method for the automatic sketching of planar kinematic chains. Mech. Mach. Theory **121**, 755–768 (2018). https://doi.org/10.1016/j.mechmachtheory.2017.11.028
16. Freudenstein, F., Alizade, R.: On the degree of freedom of mechanisms with variable general constraint. In: IV World IFToMM Congress, England, pp. 51–56 (1975)
17. Alizade, R., Bayram, Ç., Gezgin, E.: Structural synthesis of serial platform manipulators. Mech. Mach. Theory **42**, 580–599 (2007)
18. Gezgin, E.: Structural synthesis of parallel manipulators based on a different approach. DEUFMD **21**(61), 225–234 (2019)

Wireless Power Transmission System Based on Coreless Coils for Resource Reallocation Within Robot Group

Konstantin Krestovnikov[✉] ⓘ, Ekaterina Cherskikh ⓘ, and Petr Smirnov ⓘ

Laboratory of Autonomous Robotic Systems, St. Petersburg Institute for Informatics and Automation of the Russian Academy of Sciences, 14-th Linia, VI, no. 39, St. Petersburg 199178, Russian Federation
open56it@gmail.com

Abstract. This paper analyzes modern solutions in wireless charging system development. The main energy transfer standards, prototypes and experimental assemblies and their characteristics are considered. We present circuits and engineering solutions of the transmitting and receiving parts of the developed wireless energy transfer system. The results of testing the prototype are discussed, as well as obtained dependencies of the efficiency from the transmitted power and characteristic curve for various energy transfer distances. The presented prototype ensures magnetic insulation and features energy transfer up to 76.47% and can be used in swarm robotic systems for balancing energy resources of swarm and wireless power transfer between agents of swarm and in other different robotic complexes.

Keywords: Wireless charging system · Energy transfer · Synchronous rectifier · Wireless transfer control system

1 Introduction

Wireless energy transfer technology conceptually based on inductively-coupled circuits offers wide range of potential applications. One of the current areas of research in modular robotics is to solve the problem of the distribution of energy resources in a group of robots. The energy resources of the agent group are limited, therefore, the agents are forced to interrupt the task and go to the charging station, spending time on energy replenishment. In this case, the task execution time by a group of robots can be significantly increased. The wireless power transfer system will allow the redistribution of energy resources among the agents of the group and the robots will be able to perform the task much faster. Currently several energy transfer standards exist, based on this principle. Further, we consider experimental systems and standardized solutions for wireless energy transfer devices and briefly describe their composition and features, such as transmitted power and efficiency.

Rezence standard allows to charge several devices from one transmitter simultaneously, what is profoundly different from Qi and PMA standards [1]. The system

© Springer Nature Switzerland AG 2019
A. Ronzhin et al. (Eds.): ICR 2019, LNAI 11659, pp. 193–203, 2019.
https://doi.org/10.1007/978-3-030-26118-4_19

works at frequency of 6.78 MHz and allows to transmit power up to 50 W. Connection between receiver and transmitter is ensured via Bluetooth Smart technology at frequency of 2.4 GHz. Magnetic resonance principle is used here. Efficiency of the system is between 25-50%, consequently, lower, as per Qi and PMA standards. Such system allows to charge multiple devices from a single transmitter simultaneously [2].

In papers [3, 4] authors developed and tested battery charging system for a hybrid bicycle E-bike. By supply voltage 46 V, output voltage 36 V, transmitted power 96 W, system efficiency makes up 79%. In this study magnetic field analysis has been performed. According to the requirements and guidelines of International Commission on Non-Ionizing Radiation Protection (ICNIRP) safe radius around the developed system is 0.25 m. The developed system is a power part of an energy transmission device via magnetic induction and isn't equipped with any control, management, protection and user interaction subsystems.

In [5] authors describe a system for wireless charging of EDLC-capacitor (super-capacitor), used as a power supply for a hybrid bike. Research showed, that the highest efficiency is pertinent to a system with parallel-resonant circuit in the transmitting part. Experimental results were obtained with the following settings: energy transmission distance 50 mm, transmitted power 100 W, load resistance 50 Ω, outer diameter of the transmitting and receiving coil 200 mm. One of the peculiarities of the system is, that the receiving and transmitting coils are implemented as conductors on a two-sided printed circuit board (PCB). Efficiency of the system with the parallel resonant circuit at energy transmission frequency 1.1 MHz was 72–73%, whereas for a system with series resonant circuit it reached 70% at frequency 2.3 MHz.

In [6] authors present development and practical testing of a wireless energy transfer system with planar magnetic-coupled coils. Circuit design of the transmitting part of the system is exemplified with an E-class two-channel transmitter. Test bench was assembled on MOSFET transistors IRFP21N60L at the transmitting part; at the receiving part diodes MUR420 were used as part of bridge rectifier. The sizes of receiving and transmitting coil are 13×13 and 21×21 cm respectively. The transmitting coil contains 10 wire loops, the receiving one – 5 loops. The maximum efficiency by energy transfer was 77% by transmitted power 295 W, using forced cooling of the system. The maximum transmitted power by natural cooling was 69 W, and energy transfer efficiency was 74%.

In [7] authors present a robotic system for battery and charging system replacement. Experimental results show, that peak current in wireless charging system is about 725 mA. Charge duration for a battery of 4000 mAh capacity is about 8 h by mean charging efficiency of 46.4%.

In [8, 9] is presented a wireless energy transfer system based on magnetic resonance. Authors propose a system with two transmitting coils and a single receiving one. They also presented an equivalent design of a transmitting or receiving coil, which is a serial RLC-resonant circuit with internal resistance R, self-inductance, capacity resistance; mathematical equations for dissipation parameters were acquired. The proposed configuration is modelled with in-circuit simulators, as well with electromagnetic simulators. Coupling effect between coils is studied with aid of modeling. The proposed configuration has been implemented with solenoid coils and tested to approve the modelling outcomes. Maximum working efficiency of the system was 60.01%.

In [10] a structure U-WPT is proposed, consisting of three resonant circuits: transmitting, receiving, intermediate. In this paper, based on mutual inductance theory, analytic function of energy transmission was obtained. Contrasting U – WPT (wireless power transfer) system and a traditional system with two resonant circuits, authors formulated a condition to increase energy transfer efficiency. On example of U-WPT system they studied influence of the intermediate resonance circuit on the energy transfer efficiency. The system efficiency was 74.83%.

In [11] authors presented a wireless charging system, intended to power the group interactive m3Pi robot. Conceptually this system is based on magnetically-coupled resonance circuits. The energy is transferred via magnetic induction. Robots are situated on a tabletop 17.7 mm thick, whereas the energy transmission device is under the table. Controlling the output voltage of the down-converter, it's also possible to control the transmitted power. The receiving part of the system consists of a rectifier and a step-up DC-DC converter for power regulation during battery charging. Nominal transmitted power is 7 W, nominal battery voltage – 1.2 V, nominal charging current – 0.4 A.

In the research papers considered here authors present prototypes and experimental models of wireless energy transfer systems. Prototypes have high enough values of transmitted power and system efficiency. Among the downsides of the presented solutions are absence of control systems [12], security, user interaction. In [11] the nominal transmitted power is too low compared with other considered prototypes, as well with the prototypes, presented in this paper. Here we omit the problem of magnetic shielding in wireless energy transfer systems, which are based on inductive transfer mechanisms.

2 Conceptual Models of Power Unit and Control System of Transmitting Part

The power unit of the transmitting part of Wireless Electric Transmission System, second prototype, (WETS-2) consists of self-excited oscillator with trigger and operating frequency control circuits. The respective diagram is presented in Fig. 1.

The operating principle of the system is as follows. After the logic high signal in "START" circuit, transistor VT3 opens, and current begins to flow in base-to-emitter circuit of the VT4 transistor, opening it. Current begins to flow through VT4 transistor to the gates of both field-effect transistors, charging the gate capacitances through resistors R3 and R4. Because dynamical characteristics of transistors are something different, one of them (e.g., VT1) opens faster and begins to conduct, at the same time discharging the gate of the other transistor VT2 through diode, while VT2 remains closed. Voltage at drain of the closed transistor VT2 increases at first, and later (when the current growth is limited in the smoothing choke) decreases, crossing zero. When crossing the null value, the gate of the open transistor VT1 discharges, and transistor VT1 locks. Because VT1 has been locked, positive potential emerges on its drain. The gate of the transistor VT2 charges through resistor R4. VT2 opens, thus completely discharging the gate of the transistor VT1 through diode D2. In a half-time the whole sequence repeats in reverse order: VT2 will close and VT1 will open. Consequently, sinusoidal self-oscillations arise in the circuit. Choke L3 limits supply current surges

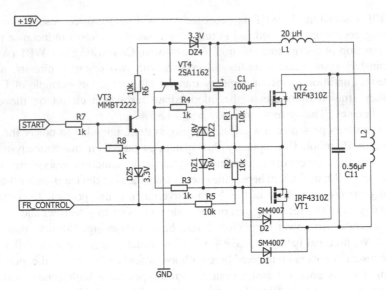

Fig. 1. Self-excited oscillator.

when switching transistor keys. Transistor locking occurs by source-drain voltage near zero, when the current in the circuit coil is at its maximum. This allows to minimize switching losses. The "FR_CONTROL" circuit, implemented in elements DZ5 and R5 is required to control the operating frequency of the oscillator. This allows to track and to exclude off-nominal self-oscillator performance.

Resonance self-oscillator with zero voltage switching (ZVS) was chosen based on original research, described in [13] and [14]. Efficiency of ZVS-oscillator in wireless energy transfer system is considered in [15].

Control system of transmitting part implements the power unit, the operating parameters of the system, displaying of actual parameters and diagnostic messages on screen. The controlled parameters are: consumed current of the power part, supply voltage level, self-oscillator operating frequency. The conceptual model of the control system is presented in Fig. 2.

The control system of the transmitting part of the wireless energy transfer system is implemented on Atmel ATMEGA328P-PU microcontroller [16]. On microcontroller IC3 are implemented, particularly, the following aspects: control of the power unit of the transmitting part, overload and off-nominal condition protection algorithms, reading and displaying of actual performance parameters and diagnostic messages.

The developed prototype employs OLED-display with 128×32 resolution, connected via i2c bus. Display is plugged into J3 jack. Jack J1 is intended to load control programs and debugging routines into the microcontroller. Lines, tagged as "I_CONTROL" and "V_CONTROL", lead to the current sensor on ACS712 base [17] and to the voltage divider, installed on the supply circuit to measure the supply voltage level and consumption current of the transmitting part of WETS-2. This part of the circuitry is presented in Fig. 3.

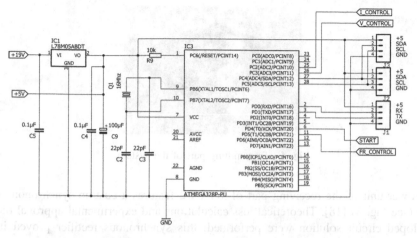

Fig. 2. Conceptual model of the control system.

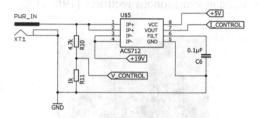

Fig. 3. Conceptual model of current sensor.

The power supply of the transmitting part of the system is carried out via the XT1 male connector with a diameter of 2.5 mm.

3 Transmitting and Receiving Resonance Circuits of WETS-2

The transmitting part consists of a power unit (the main functional block of which is a resonant self-excited oscillator with trigger circuit) and a control system, which maintains performance characteristics, protects the system from off-nominal operation modes and output of actual parameters and diagnostic messages onto the screen.

The case of the transmitting part (see Fig. 4) is made of aluminum alloy, used for insulation of magnetic fields of the transmitting resonance circuit of the system. The dimensions of the designed case are $173 \times 219.5 \times 24$ mm. Side shielding panels of the case are divided by a plastic insulator, which allows to avoid closed loop formation.

The socket for the coil, coated with insulating varnish, is made of ABS plastic. Plastic pad is mounted on 4 mm plexiglas sheet, which has a special cutout on it. The plexiglas sheet also is the top side of the case. Such solution facilitates laying of resonance circuit cable and assembly of the receiving part of the system.

Fig. 4. Transmitting part of the system.

Power unit of the receiving part of WETS-2 features a custom synchronous rectifier (see Fig. 5) [18]. Theoretical loss calculations and experimental approval of the developed circuit solution were performed; this synchronous rectifier proved itself efficient and robust in any operation modes. Before developing the synchronous rectifier and using it on WETS-2 we performed comparative performance analysis of various synchronous and non-synchronous rectifiers [19].

Fig. 5. Synchronous rectifier board.

Theoretical loss calculation for this rectifier was performed; based on it, full losses by output current of 7.5 A are 0.909 W. By output voltage 19 V estimated performance efficiency was 99.3%.

The case of the receiving part (see Fig. 6) is made of the same materials, as the transmitting part case. The design and structural parts are also similar to the ones from the transmitting part. The coil socket has the same dimensions, as in the transmitting part.

At the top side of the case the synchronous rectifier board is positioned. Case dimensions are $173 \times 173 \times 23$ mm. Plastic insulators between side shielding case elements are made of ABS, just as in the transmitting part.

When using a self-excited oscillator, where the frequency-setting circuit is the transmitting one, we can maintain resonance in the transmitting circuit, altering the inductivity of the transmitting coil without additional frequency adjustment systems.

Fig. 6. Case of the receiving part of the system

Transmitting and receiving parts of WETS-2 have identical resonance circuits. It allows to work without additional systems of receiving circuit adjustment systems, though, maintain resonance in it. Because mutual positioning of the receiving and transmitting coils equally influence the inductivity and goodness of the resonance circuits in the receiving and transmitting parts, and the transmitting circuit is the frequency-setting one, the both circuits of the system (transmitting as well receiving ones) remain in resonance. This allows achieve the best levels of efficiency and transmitted power in any mutual configurations of the receiving and transmitting device parts.

To suppress the skin effect, resonance coils (see Fig. 7) are made of litz wires.

Fig. 7. Resonance coil of litz wires

Resonance coils of WETS-2 were made of 4.21mm^2 wires, where every single conductor was 0.071 mm thick. The coil base was manufactured with 3D printing.

The best performance results of the wireless energy transfer system were achieved using film capacitors of metal polypropylene (MPP) film in resonance circuits [20]. Capacitors of this type were used in all wireless energy transfer prototypes.

4 Experimental Results of Testing Prototype WETS-2

The graphical dependencies of the power and efficiency parameters for different working distances of the wireless power transmission system are shown in Fig. 8. The presented graph allows you to visually assess the effect of the energy transfer distance on the efficiency and maximum transmit power for a given distance.

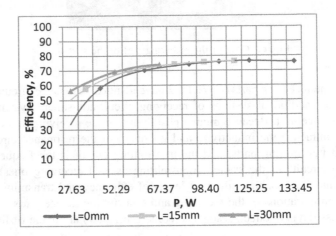

Fig. 8. Dependency of efficiency from transmitted power by various L.

At the distance L = 0 mm (close proximity between the transmitting and receiving system parts) the maximum load power is 133.45 W. Such limitation is pertinent to the unified secondary power supply, used in the prototype. Efficiency reaches its maximum – 76.47%. Increasing load power over 125.25 W, we get minor efficiency decrease in the system, caused by growing power losses by the active resistance of the resonant circuits, growing static and dynamic losses on the keys of resonant self-oscillator of the transmitting part, as well of the synchronous rectifier in the receiving part of wireless energy transfer system. By transmitted power values greater than 50 W system efficiency decreases because of high value of leakage flux. Leakage flux returns not only through air gap, but also through shielding elements, inducing eddy currents there and causing hysteresis losses.

At energy transfer distance of 30 mm maximum load power was 67.37 W, with respective system performance efficiency of 73.91%. Increasing load power, we decrease the ratio of leakage flux losses to useful load power, what contributes to overall system efficiency growth.

The presented chart (Fig. 8) also suggests that the efficiency of the wireless energy transfer system is over 70% by transmitted power over 55 W at energy transfer distance up to 30 mm.

External characteristic of WETS-2 by different energy transfer distances is presented in Fig. 9.

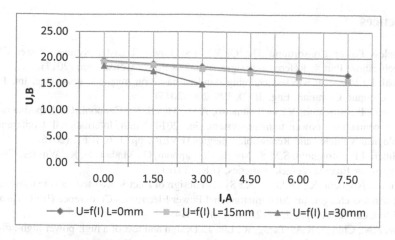

Fig. 9. External system characteristic for various L.

As follows from the chart, presented in Fig. 9, increasing the energy transfer distance, rigidity of the external characteristic of the system decreases. The underlying reason of this is high resistance of air gap, influencing the magnetic flux. As the distance grows, the ratio of the leakage flux to the magnetic flux inducing EMF in receiving coil increases, what further decreases its amplitude.

5 Conclusion

The presented wireless energy transfer prototype has high performance efficiency and transmitted power level. In context of limited power consumption and rechargeable batteries usage, the prototype of wireless power transmission presented in this work can be applied in systems of mobile robots operating in groups [21]. The principles, outlined above, equally apply in systems with a rotation of the composition for charging batteries of the agents in group during task execution without using charging stations [22], which can shorten the task execution time by a group of robots. As opposed to the analogous energy transfer systems without magnetic field shielding, our prototype is a ready device, enclosed in a case, shielding electromagnetic fields in working system, causes no noise for electronic devices, which are in close proximity with our device. System performance efficiency decreases slightly, when the distance between coils reaches 30 mm and more and remains over 70% by transmitted power 55 W. Further research goals will be concerned with development of data communication system between receiving and transmitting parts; optimization of sockets for receiving and transmitting resonance coils.

References

1. Wireless Power Consortium. The Qi Wireless Power Transfer System, Power Class 0 Specification; Part 4: Reference designs. Wireless Power Consortium (2017)
2. Dubal, P.: Rezence: wireless charging standard based on magnetic resonance. Int. J. Adv. Res. Comput. Commun. Eng. 4(12), 198–200 (2015)
3. Pellitteri, F., Boscaino, V., Di Tommaso, A.O., Miceli, R., Capponi, G.: Experimental test on a contactless power transfer system. In: 2014 Ninth International Conference on Ecological Vehicles and Renewable Energies (EVER), pp. 1–6. IEEE (2016)
4. Pellitteri, I.F., Mongiovì, S.M.S., Miceli, R., Capponi, G., Madawala, K.: Wireless Charging Systems for Electric Vehicle Batteries. U.K. (2016)
5. Itoh, J.I., Noguchi, K., Orikawa, K.: System design of electric assisted bicycle using EDLCs and wireless charger. In: 2014 International Power Electronics Conference (IPEC-Hiroshima 2014-ECCE ASIA), pp. 2277–2284. IEEE (2014)
6. Low, Z.N., Chinga, R.A., Tseng, R., Lin, J.: Design and test of a high-power high-efficiency loosely coupled planar wireless power transfer system. IEEE Transactions on Industrial Electronics, 56(5), 1801–1812. IEEE (2009)
7. Zhang, J., Song, G., Li, Y., Qiao, G., Li, Z.: Battery swapping and wireless charging for a home robot system with remote human assistance. IEEE Trans. Consum. Electron. 59(4), 747–755 (2013)
8. Yu, C., Lu, R., Cui, S., Su, C.: Research on resonance based wireless energy transfer device for small mobile equipments. In: 2011 International Conference on Electrical Machines and Systems, pp. 1–3. IEEE (2011)
9. Skaik, T.F., AlWadiya, B.O.: Design of wireless power transfer system with triplet coil configuration based on magnetic resonance. IU-JEEE 17(1), 3169–3174 (2017)
10. Sun, Y., Zhao-Hong, Ye.: Power transfer efficiency analysis of U-WPT system. In: 2016 Asia-Pacific International Symposium on Electromagnetic Compatibility (APEMC), vol. 1, pp. 858–861. IEEE (2016)
11. Ota, J.: Multi-agent robot systems as distributed autonomous systems. Adv. Eng. Inform. 20(1), 59–70 (2006)
12. Sun, Y., Zhao-Hong Ye.: Power transfer efficiency analysis of U-WPT system. In: Asia-Pacific International Symposium on Electromagnetic Compatibility (APEMC), vol. 1, pp. 858–861. IEEE, China (2016)
13. Saveliev, A., Krestovnikov, K., Soleniy, S.: Development of a wireless charger for a mobile robotic platform. Intellectual Energy Systems, works of the V International Youth Forum, pp. 197–201 (2017)
14. Krestovnikov K., Soleniy S.: Wireless charging system for mobile robots. In: 12th International Conference on Electromechanics and Robotics "Zavalishin's Readings", youth section, SUAI, pp. 71–76, Saint Petersburg (2017)
15. Low, Z.N., Chinga, R.A., Tseng, R., Lin, J.: Design and test of a high-power high-efficiency loosely coupled planar wireless power transfer system. IEEE Trans. Ind. Electron. 56(5), 1801–1812 (2009)
16. ATmega328P [DATASHEET], Rev.: 7810D–AVR–01/15. Atmel Corporation (2015)
17. ACS712. Fully Integrated, Hall Effect-Based Linear Current Sensor with 2.1 kV RMS Voltage Isolation and a Low-Resistance Current Conductor, Rev. 7. Allegro MicroSystems (2006)
18. Krestovnikov, K., Cherskikh, E., Pavliuk, N.: Concept of a synchronous rectifier design for wireless power transfer, Eurocon 2019, in press

19. Krestovnikov, K., Saveliev, A., Shabanova, A.: Comparative study of synchronous and non-synchronous rectifiers for use in the receiving part of a wireless charging system. Zavalishin's Readings ER(ZR)-2019, in press
20. General Technical Information about film capacitors. https://www.vishay.com/docs/26033/gentechinfofilm.pdf. Accessed 9 Mar 2019
21. Bychkov, I.V., Kenzin, MYu., Maksimkin, N.N.: A two-level evolutionary approach to the routing of a group of underwater robots under conditions of periodic rotation of the composition. SPIIRAS Proc. **18**(2), 267–301 (2019). https://doi.org/10.15622/sp.18.2.267-301
22. Pshikhopov, V.K.H., Medvedev, MYu.: Group control of the movement of mobile robots in an uncertain environment using unstable modes. SPIIRAS Proc. **5**(60), 39–63 (2018). https://doi.org/10.15622/sp.60.2

Discrete Model of Mobile Robot Assemble Fault-Tolerance

Eugene Larkin[1(✉)], Alexey Bogomolov[1], and Aleksandr Privalov[2]

[1] Tula State University, Tula 300012, Russia
elarkin@mail.ru
[2] Tula State Lev Tolstoy Pedagogical University, Tula 300026, Russia
privalov.61@mail.ru

Abstract. Mobile robots, operated in hard environments, are investigated. It is shown, that in order to ensure the required reliability parameters of the onboard equipment, it should have the fault-tolerance properties. The task of designing fault-tolerant assembles can be properly solved only if there is an adequate model of reliability parameters estimation. A two-stage method of reliability parameters estimation is proposed, in which at the first stage the "lifetime" of one unit in a complex failure-restoration cycle is determined, and at the second stage, the "lifetime" of the fault-tolerant assemble as a whole, is determined. To solve the problem of the second stage "lifetime" density sampling procedure is envisaged. The method of evaluation of the fault-tolerant assembles reliability parameters, with use of discrete model, is worked out.

Keywords: Failure · Restoration · Reliability · Redundancy · Fault-tolerance · Semi-Markov process · Sampling · "Lifetime" · Competition

1 Introduction

The main task to be solved when creating mobile robots, operated in hard environment [1–3], is to ensure the uninterrupted functioning of onboard equipment during preset time. When reliability parameters [4–6] of detached equipment unit are restricted, this task may be solved only systematically, using fault-tolerant structures [7–9]. The general principle of fault-tolerance involves the introduction of a redundancy into the system structure to substitute the failed assemble unit during operation. This technical solution increases both the weight and size characteristics of the robot, and its power consumption. Therefore, a necessary design stage is a preliminary modeling of the redundant system from point of view of reliability. There is a general approach to simulation of the system reliability, based on the theory of Markov [10, 11] or semi-Markov [12–14] processes, which allows to describe the single equipment unit "life-cycle". When modeling redundant structures, competition effect arises, and semi-Markov models are replaced by more coarse Markov models, which reduce the accuracy of simulation procedure. So, there is an idea to replace coarse Markov model with unregulated exactness by the model, exactness of which one can to estimate and increase/decrease, in accordance with solvable reliability problem. Below utilization of discrete semi-Markov models instead of Markov models for description of competition

© Springer Nature Switzerland AG 2019
A. Ronzhin et al. (Eds.): ICR 2019, LNAI 11659, pp. 204–215, 2019.
https://doi.org/10.1007/978-3-030-26118-4_20

in fault-tolerant assembles is proposed and discussed, in which one can control the accuracy by means of changing number of samples at the distribution densities. The theory of discrete parallel semi-Markov processes is currently insufficiently used to analyze the fault-tolerant structures of mobile robots, which explains the necessity and relevance of this investigation.

2 The Approach to Simulation of Fault-Tolerant Systems

Mobile robot assembly, in which fault-tolerance principle is realized, may be considered as M units, operated in parallel [15]. Fault/recoveries in assembly units develop in parallel, so such abstraction as M-parallel semi-Markov process may be obtained to describe a reliability of the assembly as follows;

$$\boldsymbol{\mu} = [\mu_1, \ldots, \mu_m, \ldots, \mu_M]. \tag{1}$$

where μ_m, $1 \leq m \leq M$, is the ordinary semi-Markov process [12, 13].

In turn, ordinary semi-Markov process μ_m is characterized with set of structural states A_m and semi-Markov matrix $\mathbf{h}_m(t)$:

$$\mu_m = \{A_m, \mathbf{h}_m(t)\}, \tag{2}$$

where t is the time; $A_m = \{a_{0(m)}, \ldots, a_{j(m)}, \ldots, a_{J(m)}\}$; $a_{0(m)}$ simulates the start of m-th unit exploitation when it surely able to work; $a_{J(m)}$ is the absorbing state, which simulates the fully destroyed unit. $a_{j(m)}$, $1(m) \leq j(m) < J(m)$, simulate other physical states (able to work, short-time failed, under recovering, etc.);

$$\mathbf{h}_m(t) = \left[h_{j(m),k(m)}(t)\right] = \mathbf{p}_m \otimes \mathbf{f}_m(t); \tag{3}$$

$\mathbf{p}_m = \lfloor p_{j(m),k(m)} \rfloor$ and $\mathbf{f}_m(t) = \lfloor f_{j(m),k(m)}(t) \rfloor$ are $[J(m)+1] \times [J(m)+1]$ stochastic matrix; and matrix of pure time densities, correspondingly.

Semi-Markov matrix (4) has the next features (Fig. 1): elements of the matrix $\mathbf{h}_m(t)$ zero column, $J(m)$-th row and diagonal elements are equal to zeros. Physically it means, that unit cannot return to the beginning of exploiting, cannot return from the state of complete destruction and cannot switch to the same state, as before switching. Weighted time densities $h_{j(m),k(m)}(t)$ describe both time of sojourn in the state $a_{j(m)}$, and prior probabilities of switching into conjugative states. Due to there is the only absorbing state in μ_m, for elements of rows from $0(m)$-th till $[J(m) - 1]$-th the next expression is true:

$$\sum_{k(m)=1(m)}^{J(m)} \int_0^\infty h_{j(m),k(m)}(t)dt = 1, \; 0(m) \leq j(m) \leq J(m); \tag{4}$$

Both probabilities of $\mathbf{p}_m$-matrix and parameters of $\mathbf{f}_m(t)$-matrix (expectation, dispersion, initial and central moments of higher orders) depend on the substance, of

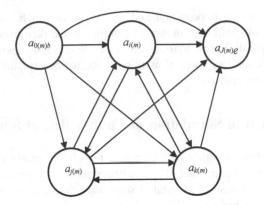

Fig. 1. The structure of elementary failure/recovery process

which the element is made, a quality of element manufacturing and assembling, an exploiting conditions, side effects, etc., and define parameters of reliability.

There are only three tasks, which one should to decide, when reliability parameters evaluation:

calculation of the time till failure (wandering from $a_{0(m)}$ till $a_{J(m)}$);
calculation of the time and probability of wandering from arbitrary $a_{j(m)} \neq a_{0(m)} \neq a_{J(m)}$ till arbitrary $a_{k(m)} \neq a_{0(m)} \neq a_{J(m)}$;
calculation of the time and probability of returning to $a_{j(m)} \neq a_{0(m)} \neq a_{J(m)}$.

In common time till failure may be define as follows [15, 16]:

$$\tilde{f}_{0(m),J(m)}(t) = L^{-1}\left[\mathbf{I}^R_{0(m)} \cdot \sum_{w=1}^{\infty} \{L[\mathbf{h}_m(t)]\}^w \cdot \mathbf{I}^C_{J(m)} \right], \tag{5}$$

where $\mathbf{I}^R_{0(m)}$ is the $[J(m) + 1]$-size row-vector, in which $0(m)$-th element is equal to one, and other elements are equal to zeros; $\mathbf{I}^{\tilde{N}}_{0(m)}$ is the $[J(m) + 1]$-size column-vector, in which $J(m)$-th element is equal to one, and other elements are equal to zeros; $L[\ldots]$ and $L^{-1}[\ldots]$ are direct and inverse Laplace transforms, correspondingly.

To solve the second task one should transform $\mathbf{h}_m(t)$ as follows:

$$\mathbf{h}_m(t) \rightarrow \mathbf{h}'_m(t). \tag{6}$$

When transformation the only restriction, imposed onto wandering trajectories, is that neither to state $a_{j(m)}$, nor to state $a_{k(m)}$ process should not fall twice. To form $\mathbf{h}'_m(t)$ with such properties in semi-Markov matrix $\mathbf{h}_m(t)$ all elements of $j(m)$-th column and

$k(m)$-th row should be replaced by zeros. Elements $h_{i(m),l(m)}(t)$ should be recalculated as follows:

$$h'_{i(m),l(m)}(t) = \frac{h_{i(m),l(m)}(t)}{\sum\limits_{k(m)=0(m),\, k(m)\neq j(m)}^{J(m)} P_{i(m),k(m)}}\,;\; 0(m) \leq i(m) \leq J(m);\; i(m) \neq k(m). \quad (7)$$

Stochastic summation of densities, formed on all possible wandering trajectories gives next expression:

$$\tilde{h}'_{j(m),k(m)}(t) = \mathbf{I}^R_{j(m)} \cdot L^{-1}\left[\sum_{w=1}^{\infty} \{L[\mathbf{h}'_m(t)]\}^w\right] \cdot \mathbf{I}^C_{k(m)}, \quad (8)$$

where $\mathbf{I}^R_{j(m)}$ is the row-vector, in which $j(m)$-th element is equal to one, and other elements are equal to zeros; $\mathbf{I}^{\tilde{N}}_{0(m)}$ is the column-vector, in which $k(m)$-th element is equal to one, and other elements are equal to zeros.

In the semi-Markov process $\mathbf{h}'_m(t)$ there are as minimum two absorbing states, namely $a_{k(m)}$ and $a_{J(m)}$, so group of events of reaching $a_{k(m)}$ from $a_{j(m)}$ is not full, and in common case $\tilde{h}'_{j(m),k(m)}(t)$ is weighted, but not pure density. The state $a_{k(m)}$ from the state $a_{j(m)}$ may be reached with probability [17]:

$$\tilde{p}'_{j(m),k(m)} = \int_0^{\infty} \tilde{h}'_{j(m),k(m)}(t)dt, \quad (9)$$

and pure time density of wandering from the state $a_{j(m)}$ to the state $a_{k(m)}$ may be defined as follows:

$$\tilde{f}'_{j(m),k(m)}(t) = \frac{\tilde{h}'_{j(m),k(m)}(t)}{\tilde{p}'_{j(m),k(m)}}. \quad (10)$$

When solving the third task one should execute the following transformation:

$$\mathbf{h}_m(t) \rightarrow \mathbf{h}''_m(t). \quad (11)$$

When doing (11): one row and one column should be added to the matrix; added, $[J(m)+1]$-th, row should be fulfilled with zeros; $j(m)$-th column at first should be carried to the $[J(m)+1]$-th column, and then it should be fulfilled with zeros.

Stochastic summation of densities, formed on all possible wandering trajectories gives next expression:

$$\tilde{h}''_{j(m),k(m)}(t) = \mathbf{I}^R_{j(m)} \cdot L^{-1}\left[\sum_{w=1}^{\infty}\{L[\mathbf{h}''_m(t)]\}^w\right] \cdot \mathbf{I}^C_{J(m)+1}, \tag{12}$$

where $\mathbf{I}^R_{j(m)}$ is the $[J(m) + 2]$-size row-vector, in which $j(m)$-th element is equal to one, and other elements are equal to zeros; $\mathbf{I}^{\tilde{N}}_{J(m)+1}$ is the $[J(m) + 2]$-size column-vector, in which $[J(m)+1]$-th element is equal to one, and other elements are equal to zeros.

In the semi-Markov process $\mathbf{h}''_m(t)$ there are two absorbing states, namely $a_{J(m)}$ and $a_{J(m)+1}$, so group of events of reaching $a_{J(m)+1}$ from $a_{j(m)}$ is not full and in common case $\tilde{h}''_{j(m),J(m)+1}(t)$ is weighted, but not pure density. The state $a_{J(m)+1}$ from the state $a_{j(m)}$ may be reached with probability:

$$\tilde{p}''_{j(m),J(m)+1} = \int_0^{\infty}\tilde{h}''_{j(m),J(m)+1}(t)dt, \tag{13}$$

and pure time density

$$\tilde{f}''_{j(m),J(m)+1}(t) = \frac{\tilde{h}''_{j(m),J(m)+1}(t)}{\tilde{p}''_{j(m),J(m)+1}}. \tag{14}$$

3 Sampling of Time Densities

Let us consider generalized density

$$\phi_m(t) \in \left\{\tilde{f}_{0(m),J(m)}(t), \tilde{f}'_{j(m),k(m)}(t), \tilde{f}''_{j(m),J(m)+1}(t)\right\} \tag{15}$$

In the most general case $\phi_m(t)$ is continual function, with the next common properties:

$$0 \le t_{\min} \le \arg[\varphi_m(t)] \le t_{\max} < \infty. \tag{16}$$

Time density $\phi_m(t)$ may be represented as a histogram. For this purpose domain $[t_{\min}, t_{\max}]$ should be divided onto X intervals, $0 \le t < \tau_1, \ldots, \tau_{x-1} \le t < \tau_x, \ldots, \tau_{X-1} \le t < \infty$, as it is shown on the Fig. 2. For simplification of the model it is advisable to do both borders τ_x between histogram digits, and sampling points θ_x, representing digits, uniform for all $1 \le m \le M$.

Histogram digits width Δ is the next:

$$\Delta = \frac{\tau_1 - \tau_{X-1}}{X - 2},\qquad(17)$$

where X is the quantity of histogram digits; τ_1 and τ_{X-1} are the right border of first digit and the left border of X-th digit.

Values of digits are equal to

$$\pi_{m,x} = \int_{l(x)}^{r(x)} \phi_m(t)dt,\qquad(18)$$

where $l(x) \leq t \leq r(x)$ are left and right limits of integration interval;

$$l(x) = \begin{cases} \tau_1 + \Delta(x-2), & \text{when } 2 \leq x \leq X; \\ 0, & \text{when } x = 1; \end{cases}\qquad(19)$$

$$r(x) = \begin{cases} \tau_1 + \Delta(x-1), & \text{when } 1 \leq x \leq X - 1; \\ \infty, & \text{when } x = X. \end{cases}\qquad(20)$$

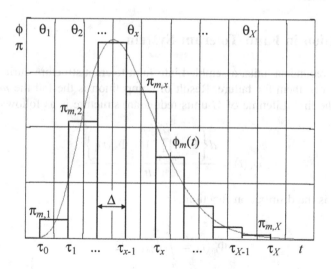

Fig. 2. Time density sampling

Sampling points, representing digits, are as follows

$$\theta_x = \tau_x - \frac{\Delta}{2}; 1 \leq x \leq X.\qquad(21)$$

In sampled model every digit of histogram is represented as weighted shifted degenerative distribution law, so function, described histogram, is as follows:

$$\tilde{\phi}_m(t) = \sum_{x=1}^{X} \pi_{m,x} \cdot \delta(t - \theta_x),$$ (22)

where $\delta(\ldots)$ is the Dirac δ-function; $\pi_{m,x}$ is the weight of Dirac function:

$$\sum_{x=1}^{X} \pi_{m,x} = 1.$$ (23)

Error of digitizing is as follows:

$$\varepsilon_m = \int_{0}^{l(0)} \varphi_m(t)dt + \sum_{x=1}^{X} \int_{l(x)}^{r(x)} |\varphi_m(t) - \pi_{m,k}|dt + \int_{\tau(K)}^{\infty} \varphi_m(t)dt,$$ (24)

One would to admit, that there are no restrictions, imposed on $\phi_m(t)$, besides $\arg[\phi_m(t)] \geq 0$. Expression (22) satisfies this restriction, so process μ still remains the semi-Markov one.

4 Interaction in Fault-Tolerant System

Mobile robot redundant units, assembled into fault-tolerant structure during operation, compete between them for failure. Result of competition is the fail the m-th unit the first, or not the first. Lifetime of M-units redundant structure is as follows [15, 17]:

$$\varphi_v(t) = \frac{d\left\{1 - \prod_{m=1}^{M} [1 - \Phi_m(t)]\right\}}{dt},$$ (25)

where $\Phi_m(t)$ is the distribution function;

$$\Phi_m(t) = \int_{0}^{t} \phi_m(\xi)d\xi.$$

The weighted time density, the probability and the pure time density of winning the competition for failure by the m-th unit are as follows:

$$\vartheta_{v,m}(t) = \phi_m(t) \prod_{l=1,l\neq m}^{M} [1 - \Phi_l(t)];$$ (26)

$$\pi_{v,m} = \int_0^\infty \vartheta_{v,m}(t)dt; \tag{27}$$

$$\varphi_{v,m}(t) = \frac{\vartheta_{v,m}(t)}{\pi_{v,m}}, \tag{28}$$

where $\vartheta_{v,m}(t)$ is the weighted time density; $\pi_{v,m}$ is the probability; $\varphi_{v,m}(t)$ is the pure time density of winning by the m-th unit.

When $\varphi_m(t)$ is transformed into its discrete analogue $\tilde{\varphi}_m(t)$, as it is shown in (22), time distribution function is transformed to $\tilde{\Phi}_m(t)$:

$$\tilde{\Phi}_m(t) = \int_0^t \tilde{\varphi}_m(\xi)d\xi = \sum_{x=1}^{X} \pi_{m,x} \cdot \eta(t - \theta_x), \tag{29}$$

where $\eta(t - \theta_x)$ is the shifted Heaviside function.

Dependence (29) may be transformed into sequence of samples as follows:

$$\tilde{\Phi}_m(t) \to \bar{\Phi}_m(t) = \sum_{x=1}^{X} \left[\left(\sum_{y=1}^{x} \pi_{m,y} \right) \cdot \delta(t - \theta_x) \right], \tag{30}$$

where $\sum_{y=1}^{x} \pi_{m,y}$ is the nomination of the function $\bar{\Phi}_m(t)$ sample at the point θ_x.

Accordingly, function $1 - \Phi_m(t)$ may be transformed into discrete form as follows:

$$\overline{[1 - \Phi_m(t)]} = \sum_{x=1}^{X} \left[\left(\sum_{y=x+1}^{X} \pi_{m,y} \right) \cdot \delta(t - \theta_x) \right]. \tag{31}$$

Combinations of $\tilde{\varphi}_m(t)$ and $\overline{[1 - \Phi_m(t)]}$ permit construct the discrete analog $\bar{\vartheta}_{v,m}(t)$ of function (26). It is necessary to admit, that when time intervals are described with continual functions $\varphi_m(t)$, $1 \le m \le M$, then there may be only one winner in the competition (25) due to the fact, that probability of competition draw, even in the case of paired races, is too small in comparison with probabilities of winning by one of participants. Where time intervals are described with discrete function the probabilities, when draw effect emerging, is comparable with probabilities of one unit winnings due to the fact, that time interval $\tau_{x-1} \le t < \tau_x$ may include number of events. To determine possible combinations $\tilde{\varphi}_m(t)$ and $\overline{[1 - \Phi_m(t)]}$ it is necessary to consider data, which includes M binary digits:

$$n = \langle n(1), \ldots, n(m), \ldots, n(M) \rangle, \tag{32}$$

where inside triangle brackets there is the code, obtained by means of Cartesian exponentiation to M-th degree the set $\{0, 1\}$; $n(m) \in \{0, 1\}$ is binary digit; $0 \leq n < 2^M$.

All codes n may be gathered onto set N, which is divided onto subsets N_l:

$$N = \{N_0, \ldots, N_l, \ldots, N_M\}, \tag{33}$$

where N_l is the subset of codes, which include l "nulls" and $M - l$ "ones".

In turn,

$$N_l = \{n_{1(M,l)}, \ldots, n_{c(M,l)}, \ldots, n_{C(M,l)}\}, \tag{34}$$

where $n_{c(M,l)}$ is $c(M, l)$-th M-digits code, including l "nulls" and $M - l$ "ones"; $C(M, l)$ is common quantity of such codes, equal to l-th of M binary coefficient; $c(M, l)$ is the index, which numerates codes in the set N_l;

$$C(M, l) = \frac{M!}{l! \cdot (M - l)!}; \tag{35}$$

$$n_{c(M,l)} = \langle n[1, c(M, l)], \ldots, n[m, c(M, l)], \ldots, n[M, c(M, l)]\rangle, \tag{36}$$

$$n[m, c(M, l)] \in \{0, 1\}. \tag{37}$$

Function of two parameters < namely, time and m-th code digit state $n[m, c(M, l)]$ should be introduced to describe distribution:

$$\psi\{t, n[m, c(M, l)]\} = \begin{cases} \tilde{\phi}_m(t), & \text{when } n[m, c(M, l)] = 0; \\ [1 - \Phi_m(t)], & \text{when } n[m, c(M, l)] = 1. \end{cases} \tag{38}$$

A competition outcome, alike (26), when l units of M failure during time interval $\tau_{x-1} \leq t < \tau_x$, may be expressed as:

$$\tilde{\vartheta}_{v,l/M}(t) = \sum_{m=1}^{M} \prod_{c(M,l)=1}^{C(M,l)} \psi\{t, n[m, c(M, l)]\}. \tag{39}$$

The probability and pure discrete time distribution and mean time of l/M units simultaneous failure are as follows:

$$\tilde{\pi}_{v,l/M} = \int_0^\infty \tilde{\vartheta}_{v,l/M}(t)dt; \tag{40}$$

$$\tilde{\varphi}_{v,l/M}(t) = \frac{\tilde{\vartheta}_{v,l/M}(t)}{\tilde{\pi}_{v,l/M}(t)}; \tag{41}$$

$$\tilde{\tau}_{v,l/M} = \int_0^\infty t \cdot \tilde{\phi}_{v,l/M}(t)dt. \tag{42}$$

Let some robot fault-tolerant assemble is workable until all M units at least one unit stay "alive". There are 2^{M-1} combinations of reaching unworkable state, f. e., 3-units assemble may fail as $1 + 1 + 1$, $1 + 2$, $2 + 1$, 3. Analysis of every combination gives different probabilities and pure time densities for evaluation of assemble "lifetime". So it is necessary to evaluate time till failure for every combination, and then stochastically summarize them.

5 Digital Calculation of Reliability Parameters

From the above theoretical calculations follows the method of fault tolerant system reliability parameters estimation.

(1) Working out the model of single unit failure/recovery process and calculation time density till failure of this unit accordingly (5), (7), (13).
(2) Transformation time density into discrete form accordingly Fig. 2.
(3) With use the formulae (22), (31), (38) (39) calculation discrete distribution of assemble "lifetime" for different combinations of units failures/recoveries.
(4) Estimation of reliability parameters the fault-tolerant assemble as a whole.

Let us apply the method describes above to estimation of time to failure of mobile robot dubbed control system for the case, when "lifetime" of single unit is defined with uniform distribution law as follows:

$$f_1(t) = f_2(t) = \begin{cases} 2, & \text{when } |t - 1| \leq 0,25; \\ 0, & \text{when } |t - 1| > 0,25. \end{cases} \tag{43}$$

Sampling of (43) gives the following expression:

$$\tilde{f}_1(t) = \tilde{f}_2(t) = 0,2 \cdot \sum_{x=-2}^{2} (t - 1 - x \cdot 0, 1), \tag{44}$$

where $0, 1$ is the sampling interval; $0, 2$ is the probability of hitting the failure into proper interval, the same for all samples.

Every unit has time-to-failure equal to 1 [time]. Simple calculations show, that units, operated in parallel, have time-to-failure equal to 1,074 [time], so "lifetime" of the control system assembly increases by 7,4% in comparison to sole control system unit. Sometime it is sufficient for the mobile robot to return "alive" to the point of departure after completion a task, when operated under hard environment.

6   Conclusion

In result, the simulation of fault-tolerant systems has been proposed to be divided into two stages. On the first stage ordinary semi-Markov models of separate units should be developed, and time intervals obtained should be transformed into discrete distribution density. On the second stage parallel discrete semi-Markov process should be analyzed to obtain reliability parameters the fault-tolerant assemble as a whole. The approach proposed permits to create model of redundant system with any degree of accuracy.

Further research in this area may be directed to simulation the great number of practical redundant systems with complex interactions between components and complex algorithms of "lifecycle". Also method of fault-tolerant system optimization, based on discrete model approach may be worked out too.

Acknowledgements. The research was carried out within the state assignment of the Ministry of Education and Science of Russian Federation (No 2.3121.2017/PCH).

References

1. Tzafestas, S.: Introduction to Mobile Robot Control. Elsevier, Amsterdam (2014)
2. Landau, I., Zito, G.: Digital Control Systems, Design, Identification and Implementation. Springer, London (2006). https://doi.org/10.1007/978-1-84628-056-6
3. Aström, J., Wittenmark, B.: Computer Controlled Systems: Theory and Design. Tsing-hua University Press, Prentice Hall (2002)
4. Rousand, M.: Reliability of Safety-Critical Systems: Theory and Applications. Wiley, Hoboken (2014)
5. Sánchez-Silva, M., Klutke, G.-A.: Reliability and Life-Cycle Analysis of Deteriorating Systems. Springer, Switzerland (2016). https://doi.org/10.1007/978-3-319-20946-3
6. O'Conner, P., Kleyner, A.: Practical Reliability Engineering. Willey, Hoboken (2012)
7. Koren, I., Krishna, M.: Fault Tolerant Systems. Morgan Kaufmann Publishers, San Francisco (2007)
8. Dubrova, E.: Fault-Tolerant Design. Springer, New York (2013). https://doi.org/10.1007/978-1-4614-2113-9
9. Zhang, Y., Jiang, J.: Bibliographical review on reconfigurable fault-tolerant control sys-tems. Annu. Rev. Control 2(32), 229–252 (2008)
10. Bielecki, T.R., Jakubowski, J., Niewęgłowski, M.: Conditional Markov chains: properties, construction and structured dependence. Stoch. Process. Appl. **127**(4), 1125–1170 (2017)
11. Ching, W.K., Huang, X., Ng, M.K., Siu, T.K.: Markov Chains: Models, Algorithms and Applications. International Series in Operations Research & Management Science, vol. 189. Springer, New York (2013). https://doi.org/10.1007/978-1-4614-6312-2
12. Howard, R.: Dynamic Probabilistic Systems. vol. 1: Markov Models. Vol. II: Semi-Markov and Decision Processes. Courier Corporation (2012)
13. Janssen, J., Manca, R.: Applied Semi-Markov Processes. Springer, New York (2006). https://doi.org/10.1007/0-387-29548-8
14. Larkin, E.V., Malikov, A.A., Ivutin, A.N.: Petri-Markov model of fault-tolerant computer systems. In: 2017 4th International Conference on Control, Decision and Information Technologies (CoDIT), pp. 416–420. IEEE (2017)

15. Ivutin, A.N, Larkin, E.V.: Simulation of concurrent games. Bull. South Ural. State University. Ser. Math. Model. Program. Comput. Software. Chelyabinsk **8**(2), 43–54 (2015)
16. Petersen, P.: Linear Algebra. Springer, New York (2012). https://doi.org/10.1007/978-1-4614-3612-6
17. Bauer, H.: Probability Theory. Walter de Gruyter, Berlin (1996)

DCEGen: Dense Clutter Environment Generation Tool for Autonomous 3D Exploration and Coverage Algorithms Testing

Evgeni Denisov[1] , Artur Sagitov[1] , Roman Lavrenov[1]([✉]) , Kuo-Lan Su[2] ,
Mikhail Svinin[3] , and Evgeni Magid[1]

[1] Higher Institute for Information Technology and Intelligent Systems (ITIS),
Kazan Federal University, 35 Kremlyovskaya street, Kazan, Russian Federation
evdenisov@stud.kpfu.ru, {sagitov,lavrenov,magid}@it.kfu.com
[2] Department of Electrical Engineering, National Yunlin University of Science
and Technology, Tainan, Taiwan
sukl@yuntech.edu.tw
[3] Robot Dynamics and Control Laboratory, College of Information Science
and Engineering, Ritsumeikan University,
Noji Higashi 1-1-1, Kusatsu 525-8577, Japan
svinin@fc.ritsumei.ac.jp

Abstract. Autonomous exploration and coverage in 3D environments
recently has became a rapidly developing research field. Emerging 3D
reconstruction methods, designed specifically for exploration and coverage, allows capturing an environment in a greater details. However,
not much work addresses certain difficulties inherent to dense clutter
environments. We observed those difficulties and made an attempt that
seeks to expand the applicability of such methods to more demanding
scenarios. Automating the process of testing and evaluation by designing
a dense clutter environment generation algorithm (DCEGen) allows us
to measure comparative performance of available algorithms. We focus
on path-planning algorithms used in an unmanned ground vehicles. The
algorithm was implemented and verified using Gazebo simulator.

Keywords: Mobile robot · Gazebo simulation · ROS ·
Dense clutter environment · 3D environment reconstruction ·
Autonomous exploration and coverage algorithm · Next-best-view

1 Introduction

Modern 3D reconstruction systems have developed methods that are able to
produce highly-detailed and largely accurate reconstructions of real environments using online processing even with monocular cameras [8]. 3D Reconstruction systems have found their applications in autonomous navigation of mobile

© Springer Nature Switzerland AG 2019
A. Ronzhin et al. (Eds.): ICR 2019, LNAI 11659, pp. 216–225, 2019.
https://doi.org/10.1007/978-3-030-26118-4_21

robots [19], 3D scanning [25] and augmented reality [27], that include consumer software. However, some issues have not been yet resolved, e.g. operating in various dynamic environments, small range of sensing, operation in a featureless monotone environments, presence of reflective surfaces, dynamic lighting conditions, etc. Efforts that amend those issues lead to the fully autonomous 3D scanning and possibility learning and reasoning about of 3D space. Complex environments are especially important for evaluation of autonomous 3D exploration algorithms that are used in urban search and rescue robotics (USAR), which is often constrained to non-typical environments, such as tunnels, caves, forests, mountains, mines, construction sites, collapsed buildings, junkyards, etc [16]. Even for applications within collaborative robotics [21], the task of finding objects with known geometry specified by human in a house environments represents an exploration and coverage task [9], where the robot indicates successful discovery. Motivation for this work is the lack of general evaluation methodology for existing algorithms in dense cluttered environments. Majority of development and testing work for 3D exploration and coverage planning algorithms are undertaken in well-controlled environments, majority of researchers test their algorithms in their laboratory rooms that have simple underlying 3D structure [4, 15, 20]. In general, behavior of an algorithm is not validated against a complex geometry environment. Creating a dense clutter environment for real experiments is a challenging task, especially if we are required to have fragile objects that are coming out from walls or hanging down from a ceiling [14, 26]. We propose an algorithm for testing environment generation for evaluation of existing and our own exploration and coverage planning algorithms.

In this paper, we present the first version of DCEGen - an environment generation algorithm that produces random dense clutter unstructured environments as a 3D model with information of possibly visible voxels from a given robot configuration. DCEGen is designed to aid development of new algorithms for tasks of autonomous exploration and coverage in dense clutter 3D environments. DCEGen was developed using Python programming language and is targeting for usage within Robot Operating System (ROS) framework [3].

The rest of this paper is organized as follows. Section 2 overviews related work and highlights limitations of existing solutions. Section 3 describes problem definition, system setup and our proposed solution approach. Finally, we conclude in Sect. 4 and discuss our future work plans.

2 Related Work

The problem of autonomous exploration and coverage in 3D space appeared fairly recently as a scientific research, but there already significant progress has been made. This research area have started and still mostly concentrate on algorithms for UAVs, as UAVs usually have limited teleoperation control and low capacity batteries that require more automation in area coverage jobs. Exploration and coverage path-planning problem for 3D and 2D (see [10]) spaces have similar goal of developing a globally optimal solution that provides total coverage of all visible environment in free configuration space without a-priori knowledge.

One of the first research groups who have successfully combined exploration and coverage goals for 3D space were [11]. They indicated that previous research on exploration were ignorant of 3D space, works on coverage were based on a-priori knowledge of the entire environment map, while next-best-view algorithms assumed only single objects of known size (further discussed in [11]). They presented an information gain-based heuristic solution for unmanned aerial vehicles (UAVs), which relies on selection of closest frontiers with high information gain (called next-best-view gain) (see Sect. 4.2). Next-best-view gain remains highly popular measure in existing solutions for 3D space exploration and coverage problems. Another early take on this problem was made by [2] with a similar next-best-view solution, although addressing 3-DoF unmanned ground vehicle (UGV) with omnidirectional depth sensor.

Another notable solution to the problem was proposed by [5] using RRT* path-planning algorithm [13] replacing typical frontier-based algorithms. They improved RRT* algorithm with execution of the current best branch that stops after one node, which have improved the result and resilience to changes compared to existing solutions. Authors augmented their approach in [6] with the ability to explore visible space by surfaces instead of voxels.

Other works in this area also contains some notable ideas: [22] use search for edges of known surfaces instead of unobserved frontiers, which is a good idea for orthogonal environment; [17] take into account the paths that provide the gain in quality to model results inside voxels; [7] implement human-inspired visual attention model that plan the exploration towards visually salient parts of RGB image. [18] use genetics algorithms as an extra step to refine the movement of the robot between selected frontier viewpoints.

We assuming that most of these algorithms are not well suited for a goal of getting total coverage in dense clutter environments due to their stochastic based approach. Althrough most algorithms in this area are suitable for any robot configurations, we designed DCEGen to use with basic 3-DoF UGV, without considering applicability to other configurations.

3   Overview

This section describes our approach in detail. After formal problem definition, an overview for random environment generation algorithms is presented.

3.1   Formal Definition of Autonomous Exploration and Coverage Problem in 3D

Usually the problem's goal in this research field is to autonomously explore a bounded 3D space $V \subset R^3$ while minimizing the time to achieve total coverage. Volume V is partitioned into voxels, each categorized as free, occupied, non-observed or residual (not observable) type. The goal of exploration is considered achieved when $V_{free} \cup V_{occ} = V \backslash V_{res}$.

We start addressing specifics goal of dense clutter environment exploration with formal definition by adding extra "hard to observe" voxel type, indicated as V_{hto}. We consider environment as densely cluttered if it contains a large portion of voxels that are only observable from limited view points in free configuration space.

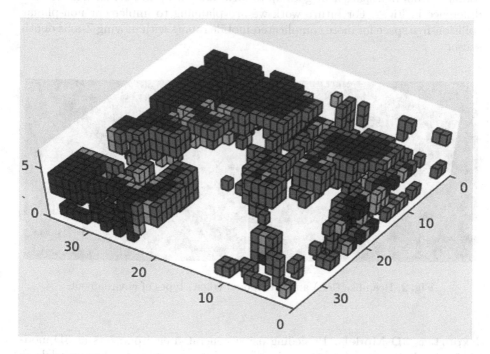

Fig. 1. Labeled generated environment. Green voxels are observable voxels, red are non-observable voxels and yellow are "hard to observe" voxels (V_{hto}). Walls and voxels above the robot head are omitted for better visualization. Visualized in MATLAB environment using [23]. (Color figure online)

In addition, V_{hto} can be used as a performance indicator for more successful algorithms during early iterations, as top performing algorithms must not skip close V_{hto} for later. We also suggest using V_{hto} for real environment experiment quality assessment by juxtaposing automatic and manual coverage for those areas, as an alternative to entirety of the environment.

3.2   Random Dense Clutter Environment Generation

The core contribution of this paper is description of algorithm DCEGen used for generation of cluttered environment for 3-DoF UGV robot configuration. Our algorithm composed of two steps. First, sample a random set of point tuples defining lines of random width in 2D space that are joined together in a single figure. Resulted figure is defines as collision-free path in space. Second, placing random voxels onto 3D space outside the collision-free space with the addition of random cuboids. Example of a generated environment is presented in Fig. 1.

DCEGen includes option to make environment to look more rugged or more structured like urban environment. Another options controls dilation of the environment from free space as it goes up to form more heap-like structures. See the difference in Fig. 2. For future work we are planning to implement non-planar collision-free space for more complicated mobile robots with moving Z-axis depth sensor.

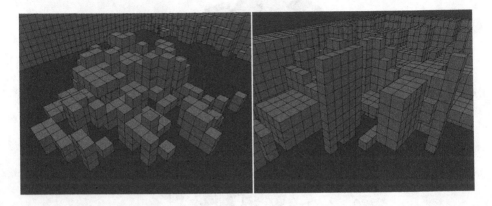

Fig. 2. Heap-like (left) and orthogonal (right) types of environment.

Export as 3D Models. Preceding using generated environments as 3D models in simulation experiments, we have to apply smoothing to those models to reduce voxel-based appearance. Smoothing is done in such a way that the resulting model does not touch 3D grid. This is required to negate noise factor and also to make a dense clutter environment looks more realistic when voxel size is quite high. Our solution for smoothing is to move away voxel faces in the opposite direction to their normals, repeated for several steps in Blender [1]. We subdivide faces by 2, thus every face is now splitted to 4 faces. Smoothing vertices are then applied with user-defined multiplier value. Further inset faces operation are executed with negative depth and resulting model is exported to DAE file format for use in Gazebo simulator. For convenience, we supply a Python script using Blender that make whole process automatic. Figure 3 shows a simple example of a hole that gets transformed after execution of our smoothing process. Depending on your goals, the result can be less or more smoothed. Fully generated environment is presented in Fig. 5.

Count Visible Voxels. The core feature of DCEGen analyzer is the ability to count number of observable and hard to observe voxels of free space in a generated environment. For this process we use octomap_mapping package [12] which

Fig. 3. The proposed solution for smoothing voxels in a simple case of a hole. Note that there are V_{hto} inside the hole (considering that viewpoints are located only around the model).

Fig. 4. The results of octomap_mapping package that brings scans back to voxel form. Different colors are used only for demonstration purposes to emphasize voxels' height.

translates scanned 3D reconstruction back to voxel form, usage shown in Fig. 4. Possible coverage for a map is assessed by counting every visible voxel from every view point with detail summarization. If a voxel was seen from limited amount of viewpoints below HTO threshold from the whole environment, then it is considered V_{hto}. Robot is teleported to viewpoints to speed ups observation process and controlled by changing robot model position in Gazebo via pause_physics service that is accessable through ROS interface. After processing a viewpoint the script resets octomap_mapping package but before that it increments the visibility of covered voxels.

Fig. 5. Example of a generated environment with a robot. A user can define an environment size.

Free space is a continuous space, so it is not possible to sample all free space for viewpoints. Therefore, we propose sampling of viewpoints as more dense 2D grid than initial robot's free space 2D grid with density multiplier parameter. The quality of voxel visibility can be double-checked by projecting covered voxels into a 3D model [20,24].

4 Conclusions and Future Work

In this paper we have presented an algorithm for generating dense clutter environment DCEGen, which was designed for assessment of autonomous exploration and coverage algorithms that are employed for UGVs. We implemented the algorithm in Python programming language and it works within Robot Operating System framework inside Gazebo simulator. We presented a novel metric of space point visibility that is based upon a number of "hard to observe" voxels and will serve as a useful assessment tool in simulation and real world experiments. Our next goal is to create an algorithm that improves upon existing solutions for dense clutter environments. The Python code is available for public use in our Gitlab repository.[1]

Acknowledgments. This work was supported by the Russian Foundation for Basic Research (RFBR), project ID 19-58-70002.

References

1. Blender: Free and open source 3d creation. https://www.blender.org/
2. Adán, A., Quintana, B., Vázquez, A.S., Olivares, A., Parra, E., Prieto, S.: Towards the automatic scanning of indoors with robots. Sensors (Basel) **15**(5), 11551–11574 (2015)
3. Afanasyev, I., Sagitov, A., Magid, E.: ROS-based SLAM for a Gazebo-simulated mobile robot in image-based 3D model of indoor environment. In: Battiato, S., Blanc-Talon, J., Gallo, G., Philips, W., Popescu, D., Scheunders, P. (eds.) ACIVS 2015. LNCS, vol. 9386, pp. 273–283. Springer, Cham (2015). https://doi.org/10.1007/978-3-319-25903-1_24
4. Andreychuk, A., Yakovlev, K.: Path finding for the coalition of co-operative agents acting in the environment with destructible obstacles. In: Ronzhin, A., Rigoll, G., Meshcheryakov, R. (eds.) ICR 2018. LNCS (LNAI), vol. 11097, pp. 13–22. Springer, Cham (2018). https://doi.org/10.1007/978-3-319-99582-3_2
5. Bircher, A., Kamel, M., Alexis, K., Oleynikova, H., Siegwart, R.: Receding horizon "next-best-view" planner for 3D exploration. In: IEEE International Conference on Robotics and Automation (ICRA) (2016)
6. Bircher, A., Kamel, M., Alexis, K., Oleynikova, H., Siegwart, R.: Receding horizon path planning for 3D exploration and surface inspection. Auton. Robot. **42**(2), 291–306 (2018)

---

[1] https://gitlab.com/LIRS_Projects/Simulation-3d-reconstruction/tree/master/autonomous_exploration_and_coverage. Note for reviewers: The access will be opened after the conference if the paper is accepted.

7. Dang, T., Parachristos, C., Alexis, K.: Visual saliency-aware receding horizon autonomous exploration with application to aerial robotics. In: IEEE International Conference on Robotics and Automation (ICRA) (2018)
8. Engel, J., Schöps, T., Cremers, D.: LSD-SLAM: large-scale direct monocular SLAM. In: IEEE European Conference on Computer Vision (ECCV), pp. 834–849 (2014)
9. Galceran, E., Carreras, M.: A survey on coverage path planning for robotics. Robot. Auton. Syst. **61**(12), 1258–1276 (2013)
10. González-Banos, H.H., Latombe, J.C.: Navigation strategies for exploring indoor environments. Int. J. Robot. Res. **21**(10–11), 829–848 (2002)
11. Heng, L., Gotovos, A., Krause, A., Pollefeys, M.: Efficient visual exploration and coverage with a micro aerial vehicle in unknown environments. In: IEEE International Conference on Robotics and Automation (ICRA) (2015)
12. Hornung, A.: Octomap_mapping ros package. wiki.ros.org/octomap_mapping/
13. LaValle, S.M.: Rapidly-exploring random trees a new tool for path planning. Technical report (1998)
14. Lavrenov, R., Matsuno, F., Magid, E.: Modified spline-based navigation: guaranteed safety for obstacle avoidance. In: Ronzhin, A., Rigoll, G., Meshcheryakov, R. (eds.) ICR 2017. LNCS (LNAI), vol. 10459, pp. 123–133. Springer, Cham (2017). https://doi.org/10.1007/978-3-319-66471-2_14
15. Lavrenov, R., Zakiev, A.: Tool for 3D Gazebo map construction from arbitrary images and laser scans. In: 2017 10th International Conference on Developments in eSystems Engineering (DeSE), pp. 256–261. IEEE (2017)
16. Magid, E., Tsubouchi, T., Koyanagi, E., Yoshida, T.: Static balance for rescue robot navigation: losing balance on purpose within random step environment. In: 2010 IEEE/RSJ International Conference on Intelligent Robots and Systems, pp. 349–356. IEEE (2010)
17. Mendez, O., Hadfield, S., Pugeault, N., Bowden, R.: Taking the scenic route to 3D: optimising reconstruction from moving cameras. In: IEEE International Conference on Computer Vision (ICCV) (2017)
18. Meng, Z., Qin, H., Chen, Z., Chen, X., Sun, H., Lin, F., Ang Jr., M.H.: A 2-stage optimized next view planning framework for 3-d unknown environment exploration and structural reconstruction. IEEE Robot. Autom. Lett. **2**(3), p1680–1687 (2017)
19. Panov, A.I., Yakovlev, K.: Behavior and path planning for the coalition of cognitive robots in smart relocation tasks. In: Kim, J.-H., Karray, F., Jo, J., Sincak, P., Myung, H. (eds.) Robot Intelligence Technology and Applications 4. AISC, vol. 447, pp. 3–20. Springer, Cham (2017). https://doi.org/10.1007/978-3-319-31293-4_1
20. Rodríguez-Teiles, F.G., Pérez-Alcocer, R., Maldonado-Ramírez, A., Torres-Méndez, L.A., Dey, B.B., Martínez-García, E.A.: Vision-based reactive autonomous navigation with obstacle avoidance: towards a non-invasive and cautious exploration of marine habitat. In: 2014 IEEE International Conference on Robotics and Automation (ICRA), pp. 3813–3818. IEEE (2014)
21. Ronzhin, A., Saveliev, A., Basov, O., Solyonyj, S.: Conceptual model of cyberphysical environment based on collaborative work of distributed means and mobile robots. In: Ronzhin, A., Rigoll, G., Meshcheryakov, R. (eds.) ICR 2016. LNCS (LNAI), vol. 9812, pp. 32–39. Springer, Cham (2016). https://doi.org/10.1007/978-3-319-43955-6_5
22. Senarathne, P.G.C.N., Wang, D.: Towards autonomous 3D exploration using surface frontiers. In: IEEE International Symposium on Safety, Security, and Rescue Robotics (SSRR) (2016)

23. Shabat, Y.B., Fischer, A.: Design of adaptive porous micro-structures using curvature analysis for additive manufacturing. In: the 25th CIRP Design conference, Haifa, Israel (2015)
24. Shimchik, I., Sagitov, A., Afanasyev, I., Matsuno, F., Magid, E.: Golf cart prototype development and navigation simulation using ROS and Gazebo. In: MATEC Web of Conferences, vol. 75. EDP Sciences (2016)
25. Weise, T., Leibe, B., Van Gool, L.: Fast 3D scanning with automatic motion compensation. In: 2007 IEEE Conference on Computer Vision and Pattern Recognition, pp. 1–8. IEEE (2007)
26. Yakovlev, K., Khithov, V., Loginov, M., Petrov, A.: Distributed control and navigation system for quadrotor UAVs in GPS-denied environments. In: Filev, D., Jabłkowski, J., Kacprzyk, J., Krawczak, M., Popchev, I., Rutkowski, L., Sgurev, V., Sotirova, E., Szynkarczyk, P., Zadrozny, S. (eds.) Intelligent Systems 2014. AISC, vol. 323, pp. 49–56. Springer, Cham (2015). https://doi.org/10.1007/978-3-319-11310-4_5
27. Yang, M.D., Chao, C.F., Huang, K.S., Lu, L.Y., Chen, Y.P.: Image-based 3D scene reconstruction and exploration in augmented reality. Autom. Constr. 33, 48–60 (2013)

Investigation of Movements of Lower-Limb Assistive Industrial Device

Sergey Jatsun, Andrei Malchikov[(✉)], and Andrey Yatsun

Southwest State University, 305040 Kursk, Russia
zveroknnp@gmail.com

Abstract. The present paper deals with the topical issues of the control system development for electric drives of the powered (active) lower-limb exoskeleton device designed for industrial applications. The article explores ways to assist in walking and running modes. Use of special types of the measuring complex allowing to evaluate the operator's activity and to form the driving signals for electric drives. Particular attention is paid to the simulation of non-linear properties of the electric drive and the measuring system. To assess the results of numerical simulations, a comprehensive criterion for evaluating the quality indicators of the control system, was developed and optimization possibilities for the control system parameters were studied. A comparative analysis of different modes of human moving in assistive industrial device has been presented, and a few proposals for their practical application have been outlined in the article.

Keywords: Assistive device · Industrial assistive device ·
Human-machine interaction · Control system

1 Introduction

Currently, various devices are widely used which feature systems consisting of two main elements: a human and a controlled machine. The interaction of these elements determines the quality of functioning of the system as a whole. These devices include objects called the exoskeleton (exoskeleton – an external skeleton) and are used to expand the functionality of a human. Exoskeletons increase human capabilities in terms of facilitating movement, carrying weights and various types of activities that require considerable effort [1–12].

One of the most promising areas for the use of assistive device systems is to ease the operation of workers of industrial enterprises. Industrial exoskeletons are designed to reduce the operator's fatigue, expand his functionality, reduce the rate of injuries and increase comfort.

Nowadays, there is a large number of diverse passive exoskeleton systems, in which the load is compensated by various elastic elements, balances, stops, etc. The disadvantage of such devices is their narrow specialization and the impossibility of using external sources of energy – all the power consumption for making movements falls on the operator. In view of this, becomes actual the task of creating active exoskeletons, where assistance in the process of performing an operation is carried out at the expense of electric drives located in the most loaded hinges.

The most common design scheme is the scheme with the location of electric drives in the hip joints [13–15]. Such a scheme allows for lifting the cargo, retention during transfer, etc.

The present paper approaches the walking mode in an industrial exoskeleton with assistance in the femoral joint.

2 Description of HMI as Part of the ACS in the Walking-Running Mode

Within the scope of this work, a scheme is proposed according to which the interaction of an exoskeleton suit and a person is carried out by means of a measuring cuff, which is fixed movably on the link of the exoskeleton. The cuff is equipped with a sensor that measures the value of force between the person and the exoskeleton. A human-machine interface diagram for a single managed link is shown in Fig. 1.

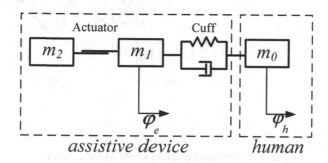

Fig. 1. Human – machine interface diagram.

The control task is reduced to minimizing the elastic deformation of the cuff suspension in master-slave modes and transferring additional force from the exoskeleton during the assistive mode.

3 Description of the Scheme and the Operation Principle of the Model of the Exoskeleton System

The computational diagram describing the operation of the industrial assistive device in a walking mode is shown in Fig. 2.

The system functions in the following way. The operator's leg acts on the measuring cuff, which is attached to the device link by means of a linear guide, with the force τ_0, which is determined by the effort of the operator, as well as by the stiffness and viscosity of the soft tissues of the leg (c_{01}, b_{01}), the given force displaces the cuff, while, between the cuff and the link of the exoskeleton, there is only the friction force

τ_{fr} of the linear cuff guide. The displacement of the cuff relative to the link is determined by the displacement sensor that forms a residual for the master-slave control system $(x_2 - x_1)$. The regulator R based on the microcontroller, forms the signal u^*, which is enhanced by the driver D, after which the signal u enters the drive, which displaces the exoskeleton's link by the output link. An important feature of the design is an additional elastic element (c_{12}, b_{12}) located between the drive and the unit link. External force P_1 also acts on the device link.

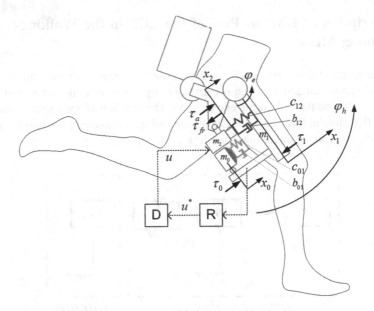

Fig. 2. Computational diagram of the assistive device.

Based on the described model, a block diagram of the ACS of one leg of the exoskeleton system is proposed, which is shown in Fig. 3.

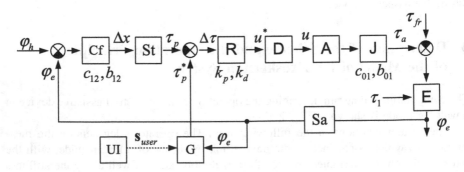

Fig. 3. Block diagram of the control system of the industrial assistive device.

In this diagram, the following notation is agreed: R – the proportional-differential regulator, D – motor driver, A – the electric actuator of the device, J – active joint, E – the exoskeleton femoral link attached to a human through the intelligent cuff Cf, Sa, St – the sensors, respectively, of the exoskeleton link angle of rotation, and the torque between the human and the exoskeleton link, G – the generator of the master control, determining the master-slave and assistive modes.

The system works as follows. The displacement of the operator's foot to the angle φ_h, relative to the exoskeleton link $\varphi_e - \Delta\varphi$, causes deformation of the elastic suspension of the cuff $-\Delta x$. As a result of the deformation the force τ_P, registered by the sensor St, is created. From the master control generator **G**, the required force τ_p^* is received (during the master-slave mode $\tau_p^* = 0$).

The force error $\Delta\tau$ – enters the PD-regulator, which forms the control voltage u for the drive. Sum of torques (τ_1) formed by the electric drive, gravity, viscous friction and torque from the side of the cuff set in motion the link of the exoskeleton, which moves by the angle φ_e.

To implement the required mode of operation, the user parameter vector s_{user} arrives at the generator unit.

The proposed scheme allows for the implementation of various control strategies by the assistive exoskeleton. The selection and adjustment of the mode is carried out through the user interface.

In the general case, the voltage across the motor is determined by the equation:

$$u = e \cdot kp + \dot{e} \cdot kd - \tau_a \cdot kp_\tau + \left(\frac{d((e \cdot kp + \dot{e} \cdot kd) - \tau_a)}{dt}\right) \cdot kd_\tau, \qquad (1)$$

Where kp, kd – determines the coefficients of the PD-controller in the force control loop on the cuff, kp_τ, kd_τ – stand for the coefficients of the PD-controller in the control loop of the torque on the drive of the device. The current moment value τ_a, determined by the force – torque sensor (or through the motor winding current sensor), e – the error ($\dot{e}$ error derivative) of response (force) between the exoskeleton and the operator.

In the master - slave mode, when the movements of link 2 repeat the movements of the limb of operator, minimizing the force between the human and the device $(\tau_p^* = 0)$:

$$e = 0 - \tau_p. \qquad (2)$$

For the implementation of the assistive mode, in the simplest case, $\tau_p^* = f(\varphi_e)$ can be represented as a function of the angle of displacement. Thus, it is possible to carry out gravitational compensation of the mass of the exoskeleton. In more complex modes, the response value can be a function of several variables $\tau_p^* = f(\varphi_e, \tau_a \ldots)$. In this case, the decision - taking block G can include a mathematical model of the control object, which can be used to compensate for the moments of inertia of the exoskeleton limb. Herewith, the error is:

$$e = \tau_p^* - \tau_p. \tag{3}$$

For convenience of recording, let us assume the original set of controller parameters as the vector:

$$\mathbf{s}_{user}^T = \bar{b}(kp, kd, kp_\tau, kd_\tau ka, \phi_{\min}, \phi_{mid}, \phi_{\max}). \tag{4}$$

During simulation, to describe the motion of the mechanical system, we use the equations:

$$J_e \ddot{\phi}_e = \tau_p l_e - \tau_e, \tag{5}$$

Where l_e – the length of the exoskeleton link, τ_p – the force between the exoskeleton and the operator, determined by the elastic-viscous properties of the cuff and the limb of the operator:

$$\tau_p = c_{01}(\phi_h - \phi_e) + b_{01}\frac{d(\phi_h - \phi_e)}{dt}, \tag{6}$$

where c_{01}, b_{01} – denote the reduced coefficients of rigidity and viscosity of the man – exoskeleton system.

4   Results of the Mathematical Simulation of Walking

We will show the results of simulation of the operation of the control system in various modes with the following model parameters (Table 1).

Table 1. Main parameters of the simulated system.

Parameter	Value
Weight of the link	1200 g
Length of the link	0,4 m
Drive power	205 W
Elasticity of the cuff suspension	3000 N/m
Viscosity of the suspension	200

In the current implementation, the assistive force is determined according to:

$$\tau_p^* = \begin{cases} 0 \ \text{if} \ \phi_e < \phi_{\min} \\ (\phi_e - \phi_{\min})k_a^B sign(\dot{\phi}_e) \ \text{if} \ (\phi_{\min} < \phi_e < \phi_{mid}) \wedge \left(\dot{\phi}_e < 0\right) \\ (\phi_e - \phi_{\min})k_a^F sign(\dot{\phi}_e) \ \text{if} \ (\phi_{\min} < \phi_e < \phi_{mid}) \wedge \left(\dot{\phi}_e > 0\right) \\ (2\phi_{mid} - \phi_e)k_a^B sign(\dot{\phi}_e) \ \text{if} \ (\phi_{mid} < \phi_e < \phi_{\max}) \wedge \left(\dot{\phi}_e < 0\right) \\ (2\phi_{mid} - \phi_e)k_a^F sign(\dot{\phi}_e) \ \text{if} \ (\phi_{mid} < \phi_e < \phi_{\max}) \wedge \left(\dot{\phi}_e > 0\right) \\ 0 \ \text{if} \ \phi_e < \phi_{\max} \end{cases}, \tag{7}$$

$\varphi_{\min}$, φ_{mid}, $\varphi_{\max}$ – the values of the angles that specify the operation range of the assistive mode, determined by the walking parameters, k_a^F, k_a^B – the proportional coefficients for forward and reverse leg movement.

Thus, the vector of system parameters is defined as follows:

$$\mathbf{s}_{user}^T = \left\{\phi_{\min}, \ \phi_{mid}, \ \phi_{\max}, k_a^F, \ k_a^B\right\}. \tag{8}$$

In the simulation, the periodic law of torque variation in the human hip joint was used when walking about 4 (km/h).

Figure 4 shows the master – slave operation mode of the ACS of the exoskeleton system, where the control task is to minimize the force arising between the operator and the exoskeleton.

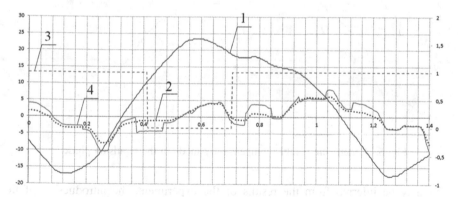

Fig. 4. Experiment results: master - slave mode.

In this and the following figures, the following notation is accepted
On the main (left) vertical axis:

1. the absolute angle of rotation of the femoral part of the exoskeleton relative to the back in the sagittal plane (degree),
2. the force received from the intelligent cuff force sensor (N),
3. binarized graph of the normal reaction in the foot.

4. the integral value of the voltage across the motor (W),
5. the value of the assisting force in (N)
   On the auxiliary (right) vertical axis:

As can be seen from the simulation results: when walking, there is a force between the operator and the exoskeleton system link, defined by the curve (2), which determines the magnitude of the supply voltage (4), the drive puts in motion the link, which rotates by the angle (1), trying to minimize this force. The elastic suspension of the measuring cuff, on the one hand, minimizes the impact effects of the interaction between the operator and the exoskeleton system caused by transport delays and the accuracy of the ACS setting. On the other hand, the presence of deformable elastic links can lead to the oscillatory nature of the movement of the cuff, which can be compensated for by the viscous component in the suspension and the differential component of the PD – regulator.

As shown by the results of the simulation of the master – slave mode, the maximum force does not exceed 7 (N), which allows the operator to perform walking in the usual mode.

Next, we consider the effect of the assistive impetus in the repulsion phase with straightening the leg until separation from the support (Fig. 5).

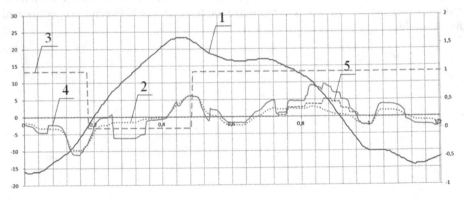

Fig. 5. Experiment results: compensatory mode in the repulsion phase.

As may be inferred from the results of the experiment, the introduction of the assistive impetus (5) at the moment of repulsion allowed for the limitation of the force values at the given moment 5 (N). In addition, the integral value of force is reduced by more than 40%. Such system parameters correspond to the compensatory mode of the exoskeleton system ACS operation.

Let us consider the impact of the assistive impetus during the phase of carrying the leg forward (Fig. 6).

The specified experiment also characterizes the reduction of the force almost up to zero at the time of the assistive impetus (5) action, which can also indicate the compensating nature of the control system – a mode, in which the force necessary for a

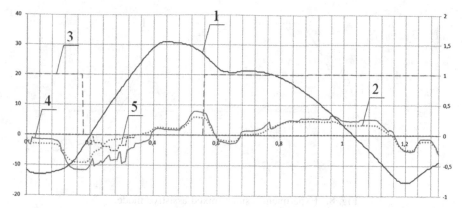

Fig. 6. Experiment results: compensatory mode in the phase of carrying the leg forward.

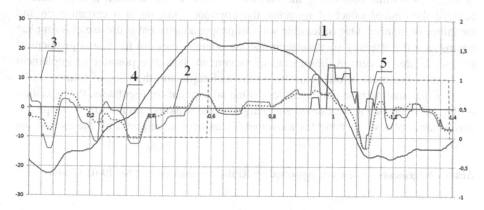

Fig. 7. Experiment results: assistive mode in the repulsion phase.

human to change the position of exoskeleton links, is minimized. Let us consider two examples of the assistive mode.

Figure 7 shows the implementation of the assistive mode of the exoskeleton system, operating in the repulsion phase.

As may be inferred from the results of the simulation, at the time 1.05 s, the force created on the cuff changes the sign and reaches the peak value 12.6 (N), this assistive impetus "pushes" the operator's leg, increasing the effectiveness of the leg straightening in this phase. As can be seen from the graph, the link in the repulsion phase moves faster than in the previous experiments, which is felt by the operator, as the impact contributing to the increase in the width of the step and the walking pace.

A similar result was obtained in the process of the assistive mode study in both phases (Fig. 8).

In the case under consideration, the positive impact on the operator from the exoskeleton is realized in both phases: when the leg moves forward and while repulsion. As shown on the results of the experimental research, by varying the parameters

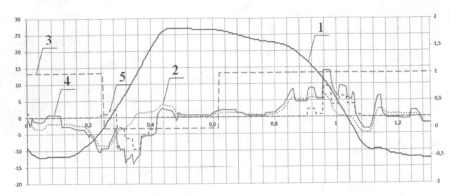

Fig. 8. Experiment results: mixed assistive mode.

of the ACS – while controlling the magnitude of the assistive force, it is possible to achieve the desired effect of reducing the operator's fatigue at a certain pace and technique of running. One of feasible ways of proper adjustment is the use of a simplest controller – the intensity of assistance that the operator can use for fine adjustment of the exoskeleton system in the process of movement. It is also possible to implement automatic adjustment of the controller to the technique and the pace of running.

It is important to note that regardless of the adjustments of regulators, the algorithm of the ACS allows for the immediate change of the walking -running pace, stoppage, performance of a set of complex movements that may be required by the carried out task.

Acknowledgements. The work supported by RFBR, research project No 19-01-00540.

References

1. Jatsun, S., Savin, S., Yatsun, A., Malchikov, A.: Study of controlled motion of exoskeleton moving from sitting to standing position. In: Borangiu, T. (ed.) Advances in Robot Design and Intelligent Control. AISC, vol. 371, pp. 165–172. Springer, Cham (2016). https://doi.org/10.1007/978-3-319-21290-6_17
2. Vorochaeva, L.Y., Yatsun, A.S., Jatsun, S.F.: Controlling a quasistatic gait of an exoskeleton on the basis of the expert system. SPIIRAS Proc. 3(52), 70–94 (2017)
3. Jatsun, S., Savin, S., Yatsun, A., Turlapov, R.: Adaptive control system for exoskeleton performing sit-to-stand motion. In: 2015 10th International Symposium on Mechatronics and Its Applications (ISMA), pp. 1–6. IEEE (2015)
4. Jatsun, S., Savin, S., Yatsun, A.: Parameter optimization for exoskeleton control system using sobol sequences. In: Parenti-Castelli, V., Schiehlen, W. (eds.) ROMANSY 21 - Robot Design, Dynamics and Control. CICMS, vol. 569, pp. 361–368. Springer, Cham (2016). https://doi.org/10.1007/978-3-319-33714-2_40
5. Zoss, A.B., Kazerooni, H., Chu, A.: Biomechanical design of the Berkeley lower extremity exoskeleton (BLEEX). IEEE/ASME Trans. Mechatron. 11(2), 128–138 (2006)

6. Sankai, Y.: HAL: hybrid assistive limb based on cybernics. In: Kaneko, M., Nakamura, Y. (eds.) Robotics research, vol. 66, pp. 25–34. Springer, Heidelberg (2010). https://doi.org/10.1007/978-3-642-14743-2_3
7. Kazerooni, H., Steger, R., Huang, L.: Hybrid control of the Berkeley lower extremity exoskeleton (BLEEX). Int. J. Robot. Res. 25(5–6), 561–573 (2006)
8. Banala, S.K., Agrawal, S.K., Kim, S.H., Scholz, J.P.: Novel gait adaptation and neuromotor training results using an active leg exoskeleton. IEEE/ASME Trans. Mechatron. 15(2), 216–225 (2010)
9. Rosen, J., Brand, M., Fuchs, M.B., Arcan, M.: A myosignal-based powered exoskeleton system. IEEE Trans. Syst. Man. Cybern. Part A Syst. Hum. 31(3), 210–222 (2001)
10. Veneman, J.F., et al.: Design and evaluation of the LOPES exoskeleton robot for interactive gait rehabilitation. IEEE Trans. Neural Syst. Rehabil. Eng. 15(3), 379–386 (2007)
11. Pratt G.A., Williamson, M.M.: Series elastic actuators. In: IEEE/RSJ International Conference on Intelligent Robots and Systems 95. 'Human Robot Interaction and Cooperative Robots'. Proceedings, vol. 1, pp. 399–406. IEEE (1995)
12. Ortega, R., Kelly, R., Loria, A.: A class of output feedback globally stabilizing controllers for flexible joints robots. IEEE Trans. Robot. Autom. 11(5), 766–770 (1995)
13. Yamamoto, K., Hyodo, K., Ishii, M., Matsuo, T.: Development of power assisting suit for assisting nurse labor. JSME Int. J. Ser. C 45(3), 703–711 (2002)
14. Anam, K., Al-Jumaily, A.A.: Active exoskeleton control systems: state of the art. Proc. Eng. 41, 988–994 (2012)
15. Aguirre-Ollinger, G., Colgate, J.E., Peshkin, M.A., Goswami, A.: Active-impedance control of a lower-limb assistive exoskeleton. In: IEEE 10th International Conference on Rehabilitation Robotics, ICORR 2007, pp. 188–195. IEEE (2007)

Experience of Developing a Multifunctional Tethered High-Altitude Unmanned Platform of Long-Term Operation

Vladimir Vishnevsky and Roman Meshcheryakov[(⊠)]

V.A. Trapeznikov Institute of Control Sciences of Russian Academy of Sciences,
Moscow 117997, Russian Federation
vishn@inbox.ru, mrv@ieee.org

Abstract. The paper provides a brief overview of the state-of-the-art of development of tethered high-altitude unmanned telecommunication platforms. It is described an architecture, scientific and technical issues and the designing principles of such platforms which can be used to expand the capabilities of ground-based electronic warfare. The experience of Institute of Control Sciences (ICS RAS) on the development and implementing the tethered platform is also presented.

Keywords: Tethered high-altitude platform · Power transmission system · Unmanned aerial vehicle · Differential equations system · Mobile complex

1 Introduction

At present, high-altitude telecommunication platforms implemented on autonomous unmanned aerial vehicles and underwater robots have been widely developed. The main disadvantage of the autonomous unmanned vehicles (UAVs) is a limited time of operation due to the small battery resource of UAVs equipped with electric motors or the fuel reserve for internal combustion engines. In this regard, these UAVs cannot be effectively used in systems that require long-term operation, for example, in the safety management systems and counter-terrorist surveillance systems, protecting critical facilities (nuclear power plants, airports, extended bridges and sections of the border, etc.) from the terrorist threats. Long-term operation can be provided by tethered high-altitude unmanned platforms in which the power supply of engines and payload equipment is provided from the ground-based energy sources [1–6]. In [1] shows modeling and design of tether powered multicopter by construction with crews powered AC. Some approach for power optimization of tethered UAV, but have same problems powerful [2]. Author proposed optimal method for uplink transfer of power and the design of high-voltage cable for tethered high-altitude unmanned telecommunication Platforms [3]. Problems of heavy and super heavy platforms payload tethered hexaroters for agricultural applications: power supply design [4, 5]. Algorithmic and software efficiency enhancement of tethered high altitude communication platforms based on their hardware-software unification [6].

The tethered high-altitude platforms fall in between satellite systems and terrestrial systems, whose equipment (cellular base stations, radio relay and radar equipment, etc.) is located on high-altitude structures. Compared with expensive satellite systems, tethered high-altitude platforms are highly economical, and outperform terrestrial telecommunication systems in the vast area of telecommunications and video coverage. Considering the extensive practical application of tethered unmanned high-altitude platforms in both civilian and defense industries, intensive research and development of such platforms is being carried out in the research centers of the advanced countries of the world. The main direction of research is the creation of high-power energy transmission systems through thin copper cables and unmanned vehicles with high reliability and long operating time without lowering to the ground.

Currently numerous projects are known for creating tethered high-altitude platforms with low (50–70 m) altitude and low (2–3 kW) power consumption of propulsion systems (e.g., developments of AeroVironment (USA) [7]. Similar products are supplied to the international market by the Chinese company Beijing Dagong Technology [8], the German company Copting [9], the French company Elistair [10], etc. However, these systems do not provide a rise on significant payload heights of any significant weight, as most of energy transmitted from the ground to the aircraft is spent on the operation of the propulsion system and the retention of the cable-rope. The development considered in this article has significant competitive advantages, having much better basic characteristics.

The main advantage of this project compared to existing developments is the possibility of remote transmission of energy up to 10–15 kW by copper wires of small section (small weight) from the ground to the board for powering electric motors and equipment of high-altitude rotorcraft. The new technology of energy transfer will enable the platform to be raised to a height of up to 100–150 m with a payload of up to 30 kg and a long operation period limited only by the reliability characteristics of the unmanned vehicle. It should be noted that this technology of transferring energy through small-section wires can also be effectively used in the creation of deep-water robots. The originality of the technology is confirmed by patent No. 2572822 "Method of remote wire power supply of facilities" [11]. Another advantage of the proposed project is that the Kevlar strength-power communications cable includes not only copper cables but also an optical fiber providing transmission of large amounts of data from the board to the ground and vice versa. This allows to install only the necessary antenna equipment on board of the high-altitude platform, leaving on the ground the most dimensional and heavy parts of the base station of cellular network of 4th generation (LTE), radar systems, radio link equipment and video surveillance equipment [14, 15].

Recently, the information has appeared about the beginning of new foreign developments in the field of tethered high-altitude platforms. The American Defense Advanced Research Projects Agency (DARPA) has announced a tender for the creation of a monitoring system for mobile objects using tethered high-altitude rotorcraft platforms of long-term operation [11]. In 2017 it was announced that the largest US telecommunications company AT&T is planning to implement a project to create "LTE-towers" based on tethered multicopters [12]. In accordance with the project, the base stations of cellular networks LTE (Long Term Evolution), installed on board of a tethered high-altitude platform, must provide services to mobile users (cell phones, gadgets, etc.) on the territory up to 100 km^2. The above mentioned projects indicate the relevance of the described development and additional extensive areas of its application.

2 Architecture Design of Tethered High-Altitude Telecommunication Platforms

The development of a tethered high-altitude platform for long-term operation requires a set of preliminary works aimed at solving such tasks as determining the appearance of a tethered platform, calculating its basic aerodynamic, flight performance, as well as stability and controllability characteristics taking into account all-weather and all-climatic conditions of application.

When choosing an aerodynamic scheme of a tethered platform, one should take into account the peculiarities of its operation and the operating conditions. It is necessary that the spatial orientation of the platform does not depend on the direction of the wind load, or this dependence is minimized. Otherwise, the control system should automatically ensure that the apparatus is feathering relative to the wind direction, which will significantly complicate the platform control system itself. For these reasons, for the tethered platform, it is possible to use three aerodynamic schemes: single-rotor scheme with several steering devices (steering rotors) symmetrically located relative to the axis of the rotor; coaxial scheme; scheme with four or more rotors symmetrically located relative to the center of the platform.

In terms of construction, the single-rotor scheme is the simplest. The entire mass of the structure and the target load are compactly located near the center of mass of the platform. All loads coming from the rotor are closed and transmitted to the power structure of the platform along short paths, which makes it relatively light-weight. Transmission within this scheme will also be relatively simple and compact. The disadvantage of this scheme is the presence of control rotors and the need to have additional engines for their drive.

The coaxial scheme is symmetric in aerodynamic terms. Therefore, its course orientation is practically independent of the wind direction. But this scheme has several significant drawbacks. First, to ensure the opposite rotation of the blades, you must have an appropriate transmission—a gearbox, which will be much more difficult, and more importantly, harder than the gearbox in a single-rotor circuit. Secondly, the coaxial scheme is likely to whip up the blades when the vehicle is wrapped around a horizontal stream of air. Thirdly, the coaxial rotor has a more complicated and cumbersome control mechanics. Based on these considerations, the coaxial-rotor platform was excluded from further research.

The four-rotor platform is also an aerodynamically symmetrical scheme. Control of the angular position of the platform is carried out by changing the thrust of the propellers. Therefore, one of the advantages of this scheme is the high efficiency (control power) of the platform due to the mutual separation of propellers. In addition, multi-rotor schemes have a larger range of possible alignments, which expands the possibilities of positioning the target load on the platform. Since the rotors have control over only the common pitch of the blades, and there is also no cyclical change of the installation angles, the control mechanisms have a simpler design. There are no high-speed elements, such as a swashplate, which increases the reliability of the entire control system. For tethered platforms, it is advisable to use a multi-rotor scheme (for example, an eight-rotor UAV), where, as in the previous version, the platforms angular position is controlled by changing the thrust of the propellers and changing their rotation frequency.

2.1 Mathematical Model

Lifting a tethered platform to a height of up to 50 m does not represent great technical difficulties. Lifting to a height of more than 100 m requires working out a mathematical model of a tethered platform, taking into account the influence of the cable-rope under the condition of unsteady air flow. The solution to this complex task is illustrated in Fig. 1.

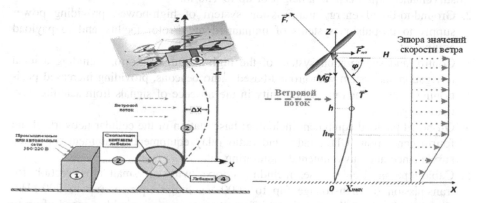

Fig. 1. Mathematical model of the dynamics of a tethered high-altitude platform with a complex loading of a cable-rope in a turbulent atmosphere.

$$\frac{dx_1}{dz} = \rho g; \frac{dx_2}{dz} = x_3; \frac{dx_4}{dz} = \sqrt{1+x_3^2}; \frac{dx_5}{dz} = \sqrt{\frac{1+x_3^2}{x_1}} \rho;$$

$$\frac{dx_3}{dz} = \frac{-\rho g x_3 \left(1+x_3^2\right) - Av^2 \sqrt{1+x_3^2}}{x_1}.$$

The study of the mathematical model of the dynamics of a tethered highaltitude platform with a complex cable-loading and the solution of a system of differential equations for calculating the forces acting on the platform in a turbulent atmosphere made it possible to determine the required ground-to board power depending on the height and wind speed. For example, with a lifting height of H = 150 m, a wind speed of V = 15 m/s, and a payload weight of $P \leq 10$ kg, the transmitted ground-to-board power must be at least 7 kW.

At present, an experimental model of a long-term tethered high-altitude platform has been developed and tested at ICS RAS. An 8-rotor copter was used as the high-altitude module (the power consumption of each electric motor is 500 W). The developed energy transmission system provides for the transfer of ground-to-board power with a power of up to 7 kW over a thin (50 g/m) cable rope on a Kevlar basis. As part of long-term tests in various weather conditions, a payload weighing up to 10 kg was lifted to a height of up to 100 m. At that, the duration of daily functioning was 6–8 h without lowering the copter to the ground.

2.2 Architecture

The architecture of a tethered high-altitude platform includes the following main components.

1. Unmanned multi-rotor equipment of large carrying capacity and long operating time, designed for lifting and holding the telecommunication payload and video surveillance equipment at a height of up to 100 m.
2. Ground-to-board energy transmission system of high-power, providing power supply to propulsion systems of unmanned multi-rotor facility and to payload equipment.
3. Control and stabilization system of the high-altitude platform, including a local navigation subsystem with ground-based radio beacons, providing increased positioning accuracy and noise immunity in the absence of signals from satellite navigation systems.
4. On-board payload equipment including: base station of the cellular network of the fourth generation (LTE); radar and radio relay equipment; equipment for video surveillance and environmental monitoring, etc.
5. Cable-rope on Kevlar base, including copper wires of small cross-section for transmission of high-voltage (up to 2000 V), high-frequency (up to 200 kHz) signals and optical fiber for digital information transmission with a speed of up to 10 Gbit/s.
6. Ground control complex, which includes an AC voltage converter 380/2000 V, a system for diagnostics of the parameters of the high-altitude platform and an intelligent wrench with a microprocessor unit to control the cable-rope tension during lifting, descending and wind loads. In mobile configuration, the ground control center is located on a mobile platform with an electric generator installed on it, the output power of which is not less than 30 kW.

The scheme for the transfer of high-power energy [13], providing the possibility of developing an unmanned multi-rotor facility with a large take-off weight, is shown in Fig. 2. The above diagram illustrates the proposed methodology for the transmission of high-power energy. Unlike traditional low-frequency approaches, a resonance frequency method of energy transfer by high-voltage (up to 2000 V), highfrequency (up to 200 kHz) signal is proposed, which allows to sharply reduce the weight and size of ground and on-board voltage converters. This method also allows for multi-phase energy transfer, with the total transmitted power proportional to the number of phases in the connecting line (cable-rope), which provides high output power (30 kW in further development) and low weight of the cable-rope. The sharp decrease in the weight of the on-board converter and the connecting cable-rope, which is fundamental for creating a tethered highaltitude platform, is one of the main advantages of the proposed approach.

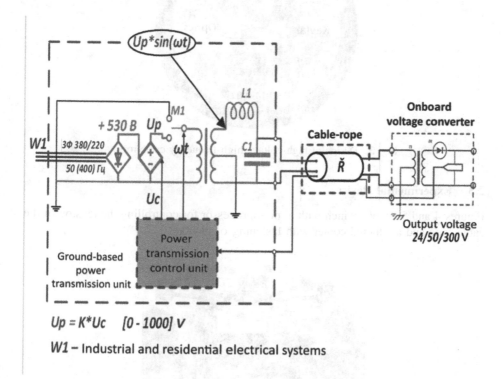

$Up = K*Uc$ $[0 - 1000]$ V

W1 – Industrial and residential electrical systems

Fig. 2. High-power ground-to-air energy transfer scheme.

Figure 3 shows the design of high-voltage high-frequency cable-rope for transmission of high-power electrical energy for powering the UAV's engines and payload.

The cable construction includes a fluoroplastic sheath, 2 high-voltage highfrequency wires VNM-0.81, a Kevlar harness (harnesses), wrapped around (according to technological requirements) with a thin sheath of fluoroplastic, and an optical module with four fiber-optic wires. Wire VNM-0.81 is a high-voltage litz wire made of polyhimide-insulated 0.1×103 copper wires with a total cross section of 0.81 mm^2 and fluoroplastic insulation with breakdown voltage (for direct current) of 8 kV. Insulation thickness is 0.8 mm. Wire diameter is 2.6 mm. The running weight of the cable is 45.0 g/m. The developed cable-rope design was manufactured by the experimental design office of the cable industry (in Mytishchi town), the optical module and the Kevlar harness are commercial manufactured products.

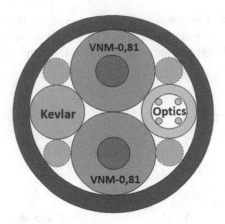

Fig. 3. Design of high-voltage high-frequency cable-rope.

2.3   Experimental Device

Figures 4 and 5 show a winch with a microprocessor for controlling the tension of the cable-rope and a tethered copter with fastening of payload.

Fig. 4. Winch with a microprocessor for tension control of the cable-rope.

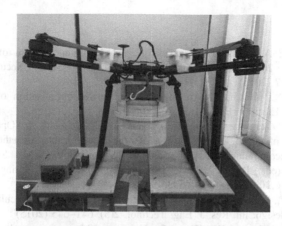

Fig. 5. Tethered copter with electromagnetic warfare equipment.

Table 1. Review of general safety standards by types with description.

Power ground-to-air, kW	Payload weight, kg	Lift height, m	Take-off weight, kg
15	25–30	100–150	80

3 Conclusion

Currently, research and development projects of a mobile and stationary tethered high-altitude unmanned platform with the characteristics shown in Table 1 are being conducted at the V.A. Trapeznikov Institute of Control Problems of RAS (ICS RAS).

The following systems are also being developed:

- a system of local control and stabilization of the high-altitude platform in the absence or weakening of GPS /GLONASS signals;
- a system for diagnosing the parameters of a high-altitude unmanned module (vibration, temperature, voltage and current) transmitted in the on-line mode via a fiber-optic communication channel to the ground control system;
- navigation system of stationary mobile objects using the equipment of pseudolite satellites installed on tethered high-altitude platforms.

At the same time, modern needs should be met using tethered platforms, subject to the limitations specified in [16–20].

Acknowledgements. The reported study was partially funded by RFBR according to the research project № 19-08-00331.

References

1. Kiribayashi, S., Ashizawa, J., Nagatani, K.: Modeling and design of tether powered multicopter. In: 2015 IEEE International Symposium on Safety, Security, and Rescue Robotics, pp.1–7 (2015)
2. Raj, V., Raj, N., Kumar, J.: An approach for power optimization of tethered UAV. IOSR J. Electr. Electron. Eng. **11**(5), 23–25 (2016)
3. Vishnevsky, V., Tereschenko, B., Tumchenok, D., Shirvanyan, A.: Optimal method for uplink transfer of power and the design of high-voltage cable for tethered high-altitude unmanned telecommunication platforms. In: Vishnevskiy, V.M., Samouylov, K.E., Kozyrev, D.V. (eds.) DCCN 2017. CCIS, vol. 700, pp. 240–247. Springer, Cham (2017). https://doi.org/10.1007/978-3-319-66836-9_20
4. Wasantha, G.W., Wang, S.: Heavy payload tethered hexaroters for agricultural applications: power supply design. Int. Res. J. Eng. Technol. **2**(5), 641–645 (2015)
5. Wang, G., Samarathunga, W., Wang, S.: Uninterruptible power supply design for heavy payload tethered hexaroters. Int. J. Emerg. Eng. Res. Technol. **4**(2), 16–21 (2016)
6. Perelomov, V.N., Myrova, L.O., Aminev, D.A., Kozyrev, D.V.: Efficiency enhancement of tethered high altitude communication platforms based on their hardware-software unification. In: Vishnevskiy, V.M., Kozyrev, D.V. (eds.) DCCN 2018. CCIS, vol. 919, pp. 184–200. Springer, Cham (2018). https://doi.org/10.1007/978-3-319-99447-5_16
7. Aerovironment Tether Eye. http://avia.pro/blog/aerovironment-tether-eye-tehnicheskie-harakteristiki-foto
8. Beijin Dragon Technology. https://dagongtech.en.alibaba.com
9. Copting. https://www.copting.de
10. Elistar. https://elistair.com
11. Keeping a watchful eye on low-flying unmanned aerial systems in cities. http://www.darpa.mil/news-events/2016–09-13
12. AT & T began testing mobile dron-based mobile towers. https://3dnews.ru/947864
13. Vishnevsky, V.M., Tereshchenko, B.N.: Method for remote wire power supply of objects. Patent for invention No. 2572822 of the Russian Federation, Registered 12/16/2015
14. Chueshev, A., Melekhova, O., Meshcheryakov, R.: Cloud robotic platform on basis of fog computing approach. In: Ronzhin, A., Rigoll, G., Meshcheryakov, R. (eds.) ICR 2018. LNCS (LNAI), vol. 11097, pp. 34–43. Springer, Cham (2018). https://doi.org/10.1007/978-3-319-99582-3_4
15. Zalevsky, A., Osipov, O., Meshcheryakov, R.: Tracking of warehouses robots based on the omnidirectional wheels. In: Ronzhin, A., Rigoll, G., Meshcheryakov, R. (eds.) ICR 2017. LNCS (LNAI), vol. 10459, pp. 268–274. Springer, Cham (2017). https://doi.org/10.1007/978-3-319-66471-2_29
16. Sudheesh, P.G., et al.: Sum-rate analysis for high altitude platform (HAP) drones with tethered balloon relay. https://arxiv.org/pdf/1712.06583.pdf
17. High Altitude Platforms (HAPs), Institute of Space Technology. https://www.ist.edu.pk/inflight-hap-internet/haps
18. Gavan, J., Tapuchi, S., Grace, D.: Concepts and main applications of high-altitude-platform radio relays. Radio Sci. Bull. **330**, 20–31 (2009)
19. Richfield, P.: DARPA Vulture Project Aims for Ultra long UAV Missions. The Integrator USAF (2007)
20. Verba, V.S., Merkulov, V.I.: Problems of choosing optimization method for next-generation aviation radio control systems. SPIIRAS Proc. **18**(3), 535–557 (2019). https://doi.org/10.15622/sp.2019.18.3.534-556

Multi-agent Model of Semantics of Simple Extended Sentences Describing Static Scenes

Zalimkhan Nagoev[iD], Olga Nagoeva[iD], Inna Pshenokova[iD], and Irina Gurtueva[✉][iD]

The Federal State Establishment of Science
"Federal Scientific Center Kabardin-Balkar Scientific Center of Russian Academy of Sciences", I. Armand Street, 37-a, 360000 Nalchik, Russia
gurtueva-i@yandex.ru

Abstract. This study developed the basic principles and algorithms for presenting the semantics of simple extended sentences describing static scenes based on multi-agent cognitive architectures. It is shown that software agents can represent word patterns and concepts corresponding to these words. And such multi-agent algorithms can form the basis for modeling the semantics of relations between concepts, representing various semantic classes in the composition of the sentence.

Keywords: Speech understanding system · Modeling · Semantics · Concepts

1 Introduction

The fundamental problem of formalizing the semantics of rational thinking, behavior and natural language [9] has been one of the central problems of artificial intelligence [3] and has been holding back the development of intelligent systems for more than fifty years.

The most successful attempts at constructing formal models of statements, starting with the work of Winograd [17, 18], resulted only in the creation of speech understanding systems in limited subject areas. These restrictions concerned not only the vocabulary, but also the types of semantic relations necessary for the description of systems for modeling the reasoning, applicable in these subject areas. Formalization of thinking is the main subject of artificial intelligence. As one of the key problems, however, we can specify the so-called the symbol grounding problem. This problem began to receive its actual resolution only with the transition to the design metaphor based on rational agents [15].

Agents endowed with objective functions, integrated into environments, interacting with each other on the basis of a communicative mechanism based on a language, among other things, provide a wide range of possibilities for integrating previously created "classical" formal models of the semantics of natural language statements. For example, the ideas of structuralism [2] can be implemented on the basis of parsers built into the communicative subsystems of agents. Frame models [7] are based on the placement of software agents in the nodes of the graph and building a system of

A. Ronzhin et al. (Eds.): ICR 2019, LNAI 11659, pp. 245–259, 2019.
https://doi.org/10.1007/978-3-030-26118-4_24

relationships between these nodes based on multi-agent interaction protocols. The theory of conceptual dependencies [16] could find an application based on the creation of a hierarchy of concepts expressed by agents. The knowledge bases embedded in the agents based on production rules allow for the most diverse variants of logical analysis and output, including those based on a combination of different types of logic [11]. Models of the "Meaning-Text" type [4] can be implemented on the basis of creating trees of surface syntactic analysis and deep structure, in the nodes of which there are rational agents. The possibility of creating a dynamic correlation of tree-like surface and deep multi-agent structures creates magnificent prerequisites for the realization of the theory of the deep cases of Fillmore [14]. Multi-agent models can also be used for creating semiotic complexes [3], since each agent, being an abstract deterministic automaton, can implement an unlimited number of input and output languages.

The relevance of this study is determined by the need to develop formal models of the semantics of natural language for tasks and systems of computer linguistics.

2   The Task of Semantic Description of Static Scenes

The essence of our task is to construct a formal description of the objects represented in the scene, their properties and relations between them, establish the correspondence of these formal descriptions to the words used in the sentence in natural language for the nomination of these objects, properties and relations. At the same time, these formal models should have the properties of completeness and universality of descriptions. In this case, completeness is interpreted as a property of the model to exhaustively answer all questions that can be presented to the object of description when it is used for the intended purpose of the system, and universality implies coordination of the semantic representation with the ly used meanings of the interpreted sentences.

Static scenes are chosen both because of their prevalence in a real environment, and in view of the relative simplicity of the description. As a rule, in the indicated variants of the target systems, the natural language descriptions of such scenes are expressions in the indicative mood, structured in the form of simple extended sentences. In these target systems, the input information ways (channels) play a fundamental role. For example, one of the most in modern systems is a channel of entering information based on data from video cameras. For mobile systems, infrared and ultrasonic sensors are also often used. Data from such devices is a sequence (arrays) of unstructured numeric values that must be processed by the interpreting system, taking into account the semantics of the relationship between this system and the observed part of the environment (scene), the measurement of which with the help of the corresponding device formed a specific input data stream. Therefore, this system of semantic relations is subjectively determined, based on the system of internal states and processes of the interpreting system. The issues of semantic bases for processing flows of unstructured data based on agent-based design metaphors are discussed in [8, 10]. Particularly, it is shown that the interpretive system, considered as a rational agent [15], may have a system of internal states marked by the values of the objective function. The transition between states is determined by both the values of the internal parameters of the agent subsystems and external stimuli, the images of which are contained in the interpreted input streams of unstructured data. At the same time, such very states are interpreted as semantically significant, and the input images are structured into sign systems corresponding to different modalities of data flows. The correspondence between them, as a rule, is established on the basis of training.

If we talk about the property of universality of semantic representations in the context of the agent paradigm of the interpreting system, the concept of multi-agent recursive cognitive architecture proposed in [9], defining the formal bases of modeling of recursive intelligent agents which can be a part of each other on the unlimited depth of a recursion (number of ranks). This concept is generated by the concepts of brain neurons as proactive elements of functional systems [1], represented by multi-agent neural groups, which in turn belong to even larger conglomerates of neuromorphological formations that implement individual systemic functions of the brain. The combination of such conglomerates represent the brain of a human individual, which at the next level of recursion can be considered as a structural-functional element of the team. In this system of recursive inclusions from level to level, the universality of the complex of intellectual information processing is manifested, which, starting with the simplest organization at the level of an individual neuron, goes up to its most complex forms at the level of collective agents. In [5, 8] it was shown, that the content basis of the intellectual activity of the system is the synthesis of behavior aimed at maximizing the target function of energy provided that the intelligent agent does not fall into unwanted (terminal) states. At the same time, energy is considered as a descriptive value - a measure of the activity of an agent in an environment that requires energy to perform actions and synthesize a plan of behavior.

Therefore, the input characters of objects and scenes for an intellectual agent are labeled energy values that can be extracted by the agent if the objects are properly used in accordance with the selected plan. This is the conceptual basis for the universality of the semantic representation, expressed in the unity of the objective function of energy at all levels of recursion. If the internal semantic representation of the scene allows an intelligent agent to correctly assess the possibility of such use, synthesize the appropriate plan and. having executed it, extract the corresponding energy from the environment, then this idea besides universality also has the property of completeness of description.

Static scenes are devoid of dynamics, but nevertheless contain all the necessary components for the formation of a target context determining the behavior of an intelligent agent. In them, in particular, there are such independent conceptually-designed units, such as objects, their properties, relations between objects, properties of these relations, locative information. Each of these objects needs its own concept. Our work identifies ways to structure context based on events and situations. In particular, this work shows that it is such a structure in the form of events that forms the basis of a factual description of the world in the form of simple extended sentences.

The object of the study is the semantics of simple extended sentences describing static scenes.

The subject of the research is the possibility of modeling similar semantic relations using multi-agent cognitive architectures.

The purpose of the research is the development of a formal representation of the semantics of natural language.

The task of the research is to develop models of semantics of simple extended sentences describing static scenes using multi-agent cognitive architectures.

3   Semantics Models Based on Multi-agent Cognitive Architectures

To solve the problem, apply the so-called. multi-agent recursive cognitive architecture (MURCA) [8]. MURCA consists of rational agents interacting with each other on the basis of hypothetical principles of organizing an invariant of the functional organization of the thinking process in the brain—the MURCA invariant [12].

Agent $\aleph_i^{\flat}$, built on the basis of MURCA, will be called an *intellectual agent*. Consider the algorithm of multi-agent modeling of the semantics of a simple extended sentence.

We assume that the agent-object "sells" information to the agent-action, which identifies him, answering the questions "Who?", "What?" The agent-action, in turn, provides information about itself in response to the question "Doing what?" We believe that the remuneration (fee) for such information is offered to those agents who ask such questions. To ask a question actually means to offer a reward for selling the necessary information. Of fundamental importance is the fact that these questions, being classical tokens (signs, symbols), receive the abstract meaning of the universal component of a semantic operation, since in response to these questions, addressees must provide only their names.

Earlier, in [13], the algorithms of the functional areas of the cognitive architecture, providing the understanding phenomenon, shown in Fig. 1, were considered in more detail.

In this figure, the lines are interconnected pictographic images of actors and agneurons. Triangles depict the sensors (actors) of the input video stream and keyboard input. In order to enable intramodal differentiation [6], two types of video stream sensors are used – shape and color. The actor-keyboard processing operator messages coming from the keyboard input sensor is depicted as a rectangle containing the abbreviation "**Kbrd**". The actor, processing messages generated by the intellectual agent $\aleph_i^{\flat}$ and intended for operators, is depicted as a rectangle containing the abbreviation "**Dspl**".

During the execution of the algorithm for constructing a cognitive architecture, the need arises to replenish the composition of agneurons depending on the context. The possibility of such replenishment provides automatic replenishment of the ontology implemented by cognitive architecture, and is based on the use of the mechanism of dynamic "generation of agneurons of various types with the help of special actors – the so-called "neurofactories".

In this paper, we proceed from the idea that the phenomenological complex "concept", distinguished in psychology and linguistics, is implemented at the neuro-morphological level by a functional system, in which individual brain neurons, like agents in a multi-agent system, perform an agreed collective behavior algorithm. We also assume that simulation models of concepts of various types can be built on the basis of software agents (agneurons) as part of MURCA.

Figure 1 shows the agents and actors that provide the designative part of semantic constructions - modeling or serving models of natural language words. The double oval depicts a neurofactory producing agneurons-adjectives depicted by ovals and labeled "agent-adjectives" The double circle is the neurofactory that produces agneurons-nouns (labeled "agent-noun"). Such agneuron is represented by a single circle. The double polygon is a neurofactory that produces agneurons-verbs, which are depicted by a single polygon (labeled "agent-verb").

Messages (signatures) are generated by shape and color sensors from image data. If such messages are sent to all agents in the cognitive architecture, then in our case we will formally write such a transmission with the expression:

$$\aleph^{Sensor\_colour}_{Video-colour} \rightarrow F_{colour}* : m(''63\_71\_203'').$$

In the position before the colon we will have the addressee of the message. The symbol "*" in this position means that the recipients are all agneurons within the cognitive architecture. Signatures are a parameterized geometric description of input images, usually expressed in conjunctive normal form, allowing comparison of this signature with the left parts of the production rules contained in the knowledge bases of agents of the cognitive architecture of an intelligent agent $\aleph^{\backslash}_i$.

The signatures of the form and colors are sent to the relevant agents of the cognitive architecture, in accordance with the mailing lists of sensors:

$$\aleph^{Sensor\_colour}_{Video-colour} \rightarrow F_{colour}* : m(''63\_71\_203''),$$

$$\aleph^{Sensor\_form}_{Video-form} \rightarrow F_{form}* :$$

$$m(''Line1\& - 45\&263.002\&P\_2\_3\&Line2\&45\&253.002\&P\_3\_4\&Lin''),$$

$$\aleph^{Sensor\_form}_{Video-form} \rightarrow F_{factory-form} :$$

$$m(Line1\&-45\&263.002\&P\_2\_3\&Line2\&45\&253.002\&P\_3\_4\&Lin).$$

Such specialized agents in this case are agneurons-signs and actors of neurofactories of the signs of the object. At the initial stage of the operation of the algorithm, there is no agneuron-features in the cognitive architecture (since the intellectual agent $\aleph^{\backslash}_i$ does not "know" about any objects yet), therefore messages are sent to the neurofactories. Then, as a result of the work of the microprograms embedded in them, interpreting the rules stored in the knowledge bases of these actors, the neurofactories generate (programmatically) agneurons-signs that will later act as handlers for input form and color signatures.

The expression:

$$\aleph_{Video-form}^{Sensor\_form} \rightarrow F_{form}* :$$

$$m(Line1\&-45\&263.002\&P\_2\_3\&Line2\&45\&253.002\&P\_3\_4\&Lin),$$

$$\aleph_{Video-form}^{Sensor\_form} \rightarrow F_{Factory-forms} :$$

$$m("Line1\&-45\&263.002\&P\_2\_3\&Line2\&45\&253.002\&P\_3\_4\&Lin"),$$

$$\aleph_{Line1\&-45\&263.002\&P\_2\_3\&Line2\&45\&253.002\&P\_3\_4\&Lin}^{form} \rightarrow F_{Display} : m("What is the shape?"),$$

$$\aleph_{round}^{form} \rightarrow F_{Factory-adjective} : m(round - adjective),$$

$$\aleph_{round}^{form} \rightarrow F_{adjective} : m(round - adjective).$$

describes the process of the generation of the agneuron-sign of the form by the neurofactory in the cognitive architecture of the intellectual agent $\aleph_i$. The same process occurs with form generation.

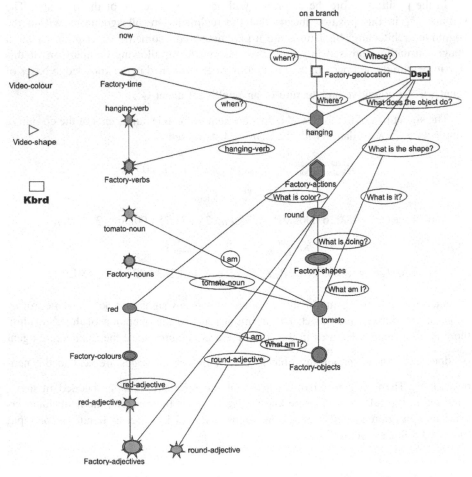

Fig. 1. Multi-agent simulation model of a simple extended sentence.

Arrow "↓" will denote the fact of generation of new agneuron, arrow " → " – sending messages, arrow "↔" – the fact of interaction of specific agneurons with each other by so-called "contract" [4] – a multi-agent interaction protocol, aimed at joint processing by agneurons and /or actors of a specific situation.

As a result of the execution of the algorithm shown in Fig. 1, a cognitive architecture is formed as part of the intellectual agent $\aleph_i^?$, which is a multi-agent simulation model of the simple extended sentence "Red round tomato is now hanging on a branch".

Figure 1 illustrates the processing of a simple sentence by the intellecton. When interpreting such a sentence, individual word-agents (agents processing specific words) of different parts of speech respond to individual specific words. Then they use their contracts with specific conceptual agents, "selling" to them information that the interpreted sentence contains information about objects, actions, etc., the conceptual models of which these agents themselves are.

Repeatedly showing the picture, we can put questions to all the members of the sentence, and in each case, a chain of sequences of involved contracts between agneurons within the constructed cognitive architecture works, which leads to the activation of the

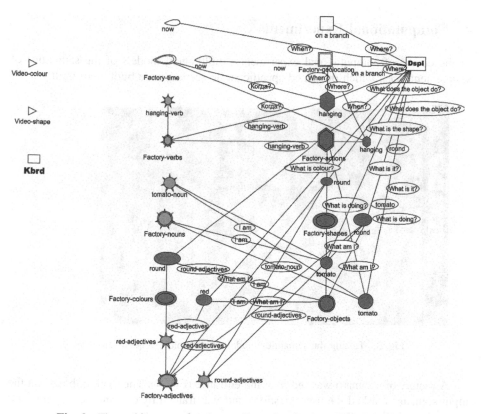

Fig. 2. The architecture of understanding of a simple extended sentence.

whole complex of agneurons describing designates and denotations according to the Frege semantic triangle, and we get the following architecture, shown in Fig. 2:

Formally, this can be written as follows:

$$N_{round}^{form} \rightarrow F_{conracts} : m("round")$$

$$N_{what}^{questions} \rightarrow F_{object} : m("what")$$

$$N_{tomato}^{object} \rightarrow F_{display} : m("tomato")$$

$$N_{hangs}^{action} \rightarrow F_{contracts} : m("hangs")$$

$$N_{where}^{questions} \rightarrow F_{locus}* : m("where")$$

$$N_{onabranch}^{locus} \rightarrow F_{display} : m("on a branch")$$

and so on.

The constructed simulation model of the semantics of a simple extended sentence from a concrete limited subset of a natural language allows to perform semantic functions of reference and classification based on the coordinated work of multi-agent models of features (signs), objects, actions, adjectives, nouns and verbs, agents of time and location.

4 Computational Experiments

In the course of computational experiments, multi-agent models of the semantics of simple sentences, which described specific static scenes, were built were built.

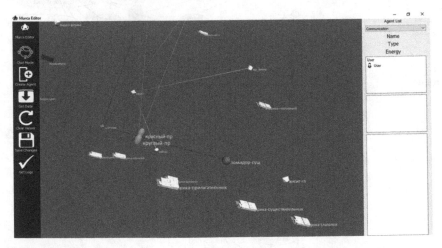

Fig. 3. Testing the semantics model of a simple extended sentence.

A picture of a tomato was fed in at the entrance (Fig. 4). The system, based on the input signatures, asked the user questions and was trained by creating new agents and connections between these agents.

Fig. 4. Testing the semantics model of a simple extended sentence.

Then, the same picture was submitted to the input system and the user asked questions about the picture, and the system answered all the questions asked (Fig. 5).

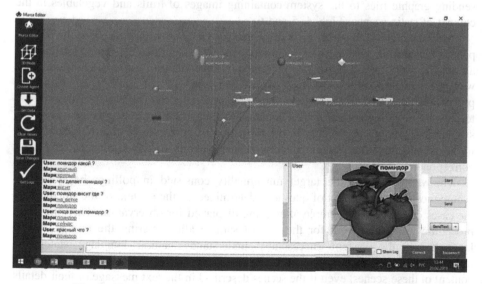

Fig. 5. Testing the semantics model of a simple extended sentence.

In order to test the ability of the system to interpret natural language statements describing static scenes, experiments were conducted during which the cognitive architecture was first taught by the user using static situations presented for viewing from the training set, and then, after the training, using the dialog subsystem the natural

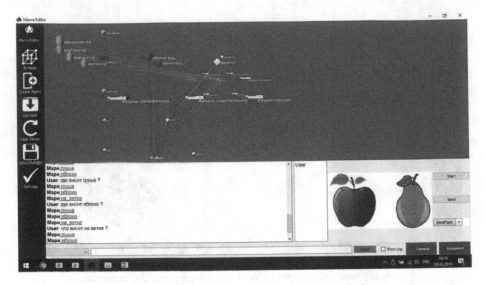

Fig. 6. Testing the semantics model of a simple extended sentence.

language description of static situations that were not presented in the training set (control sample) was introduced. The presentation for viewing was carried out by sending graphic files to the system containing images of fruits and vegetables in the context of static scenes (Figs. 4, 5 and 6).

After a picture with an image is displayed for viewing, with the help of the built-in pattern recognition system, the system independently identifies the input signatures of all objects, signs and static actions presented in the context of the scene in accordance with the structure of the valences of different types of concepts. Then, using the procedures described in this article, the user, answering the questions of the system, teaches it, providing correct names in natural language for the concepts created by the system and, helping it, thereby, in the formation of new parts of the multiagent cognitive architecture that contain internal representations of these concepts and their corresponding words.

The verification of the target functionality consisted in polling the system in accordance with the full list of questions determined by the context of the situation for the cases of the training sample after being displayed for observation. Then the same procedure was carried out for the control sample after entering the text in natural language. If the system successfully understands natural language statements describing static scenes, it should give correct answers to questions regarding the content of these scenes, even if the scenes described in the text message or their details have not been encountered in this particular context when presented to the observation in the scenes from the training set.

The results of one of the experiments are presented in Figs. 3, 4, 5 and 6.

The contexts presented in the training set meant that, in accordance with the presented images:

(a) a red round tomato hangs on a branch (in the process of learning, the system was taught the following new concepts and words: "round" and "red", "tomato", "hang", "branch");
(b) a red round apple hangs on a tree (in the process of learning, the system was taught the following new concepts and words: "apple", "tree");
(c) a yellow oval pear hangs on a branch (in the process of learning the system was taught the following new concepts and words: "oval" and "yellow", "pear");
(d) a red round apple is on the table (in the process of learning, the system was taught the following new concepts and words: "lie", "table").

After teaching the system the above concepts and words, using the built-in dialog subsystem, we ask the system questions and get unambiguous correct answers (Table 1).

Thus, after training on the basis of observation static scenes, the system in all cases gives the correct answers about the contexts presented in the training set.

When testing on a control sample, we enter a natural language text from the keyboard (for example: "Tomato lies on the table"). It is important that the contexts of the texts were not present in the training sample. Moreover, we introduce the texts that are not complete (as in the specified example), since they do not explicitly indicate some parts of the sentence (in the example above, the circumstances of the time and the attributes of the objects) that are essential for correct interpretation of the contexts of the sentences. Next, we ask questions, checking the degree of understanding of the input texts by the system, based on the completeness of the answers, which characterizes the representation and correctness of information about all aspects of contexts, explicitly or implicitly presented in the input texts. Further the table fragment is shown which contains the presentation of contexts not represented in the training set (Table 2).

Table 1. Dialogue primer.

Question	Answer System
What hangs on a branch?	A tomato Pear
What is hanging on the tree?	An Apple
What tomato?	Round Red
What apple?	Round, red
What pear?	Oval, yellow
What is the tomato doing?	It is hanging
What is the apple doing?	It is hanging

(continued)

Table 1. (*continued*)

Question	Answer System
Where is the tomato hanging?	On a branch
Where is the apple hanging?	On the tree
Where is the apple?	On the table
When does a tomato hang on a branch?	Current time
What is red?	A tomato, An Apple

Table 2. Test context.

Question	Answer System
What is on the table?	A tomato
What tomato?	Round, Red
What is the tomato doing?	It is lying
Where is the tomato?	On the table
When is the tomato on the table?	Current time

Thus, the results of testing the built models with the help of special questions showed that the system correctly identifies concepts and semantic relations between them in all cases. It also correctly builds multi-agent models of the situation by their incomplete natural language descriptions and using semantic models fulfills the situation description by itself in accordance with the structure of valencies of the engaged concept agneurons and the relations between them.

This, in particular, can be clearly seen from the results of experiments, when the system correctly answers all the questions about the situation, the description of which was incomplete. Based on the foregoing, it can be concluded that the proposed formalization of the semantics of static scenes allows the system to implement elements of natural language texts understanding, creating contexts in which a part of essential information is given implicitly, based on the meanings of words used in the utterance and the semantic relations between them.

Identification of research results in the field of artificial intelligence and, in particular, machine understanding is an independent problem. Formalization of the metrics of computer understanding is a task, partly equivalent to the very task of formalizing the understanding itself. Therefore, in this study, to solve this problem, we apply a modification of the famous Turing test, which has established itself as a kind of standard for checking the qualitative results of modeling intellectual processes.

The control part of the experimental study was organized in accordance with the Turing test procedure applied to the subject area, limited by the content of statements describing simple static scenes. After teaching the system on a training set and giving it the descriptions in natural language, containing the context of the control sample, the test system presented a limited number of questions (6 questions). The experiment involved 15 testers who corresponded with the system via chat. The test results are shown in Table 3. In order to describe the correctness of understanding by the system of statements and users' questions, the average error was calculated:

$$\varepsilon_{cp} = \frac{\sum_{k=1}^{n} \varepsilon_k}{n},$$

where $\varepsilon_k = \begin{cases} 0, & positive\ identification \\ 1, & negative\ identification \end{cases}$.

Positive identification was fixed, if the tester correctly identified the interlocutor as a computer system, negative - in the event of his misunderstanding (Fig. 7).

Table 3. Tests results.

N of teters	ε	εav
1	1	1
2	0	0.5
3	0	0.33
4	0	0.25
5	0	0.2
6	0	0.17
7	1	0.28
8	0	0.25
9	0	0.22
10	1	0.3
11	1	0,36
12	0	0,33
13	0	0,3
14	0	0,28
15	0	0,26

According to the results of a series of surveys in accordance with the described restricted Turing test procedure the testers recorded a level of trust (understanding) within 60–70%, which corresponds to the estimated level of trust (understanding) between adult human interlocutors.

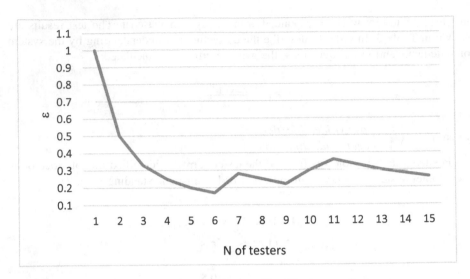

Fig. 7. Restricted Turing test identification results.

5   Conclusion

This research developed the basic principles and algorithms for presenting the semantics of simple extended sentences describing static scenes based on multi-agent cognitive architectures. The authors demonstrated, that program agents can represent word patterns and concepts corresponding to these words. Such agent-based models are a formal expression of two vertices of the Frege triangle - a sign and a concept. The advantage of such a model is the possibility of a formal description of the relations between these vertices on the basis of protocols (algorithms) of multi-agent interaction.

It is also shown that such multi-agent algorithms can form the basis for modeling the semantics of relations between concepts that represent different semantic classes in a sentence. The substantive basis of such algorithms is the exchange of information for energy, which is performed by agents in order to achieve the maximum of the local target energy function. The specification of the question, in response to which information is provided, determines the type of semantic relations between specific agents.

Thus, the use of multi-agent cognitive architectures for formalizing the semantics of statements in the indicative mood, designed in the form of simple extended sentences, seems to be effective and promising for use in computer linguistics systems. The further work of the team of authors will be aimed at expanding the types of syntactic constructions of statements interpreted on the basis of the proposed formal description.

Acknowledgement. The work was supported by RFBR grants № 18-01-00658, 19-01-00648.

References

1. Anokhin, P.K.: Principal issues of the general theory of functional systems. Principles of the system organization of functions. Science, Moscow (1973)
2. Chomsky, N.: Language and Thinking. Moscow University Press, Moscow (1972)
3. Fillmore, Ch.: The case for case. In: Bach, E., Harms, R.T. (eds.) Universals in Linguistic Theory, pp. 1–88. Holt Rinehart and Winston, New York (1968)
4. Gladky, A.V., Melchuk, I.A.: Elements of mathematical linguistics. Science, Moscow (1969)
5. Ivanov, P.M, Nagoev, Z.V.: Automatic tracking of a group of objects with a system of enveloping intelligence. In: Materials of the Tenth All-Russian Scientific and Practical Conference "Perspective Systems and Management Tasks". SFU Publishing House, Taganrog (2015)
6. Lyutikova, L.A., Ksalov, A.M., Makoeva, D.G., Gurtueva, I.A.: Building a knowledge system based on multi-agent contracts. Natural and Technical Sciences **12**(102), 273–274 (2016)
7. Minsky, M.: Frames to represent knowledge. Energy, Moscow (1979)
8. Nagoev, Z.V.: Intellect, or Thinking in Living and Artificial Systems. Publishing House KBSC RAS, Nalchik (2013)
9. Nagoev, Z.V.: Decision-making and in unstructured tasks based on self-organizing multi-agent recursive cognitive architectures. Thesis for the competition. Degrees of Doctor of Technical Sciences. Nalchik (2013)
10. Nagoev, Z.V.: Multiagent recursive cognitive architecture. In: Chella, A., Pirrone, R., Sorbello, R., Jóhannsdóttir, K. (eds.) Proceedings of the Third Annual Meeting of the BICA Society. Advances in Intelligent Systems and Computing Series, vol. 196, pp. 247–248. Springer, Heidelberg (2012). https://doi.org/10.1007/978-3-642-34274-5_43
11. Nagoev, Z.V.: Multiagent existential mappings and functions. Izvestiya KBSC RAS **4**(54), 64–71 (2013)
12. Nagoev, Z.V., Lyutikova, L.A., Gurtueva, I.A.: Model for automatic speech recognition using multi-agent recursive cognitive architecture. Procedia Comput. Sci. **145**, 386–392 (2018)
13. Nagoev, Z.V., Nagoeva, O.V.: Building a formalism to describe the semantics of natural language statements and the process of understanding these statements based on self-organizing cognitive architectures. Izvestiya KBSC RAS **4**(78), 19–31 (2017)
14. Pospelov, D.A.: Modeling of reasoning. Experience in the analysis of mental acts. Radio and communication, Moscow (1989)
15. Russell, S., Norvig, P.: Artificial Intelligence: A Modern Approach (AIMA), 3rd edn. Williams, Moscow (2010)
16. Schank, R., Birnbaum, L., Mey, J.: Integrating semantics and pragmatics. Quaderni di Semantica **VI**(2) (1985)
17. Winograd, T.: Language as a Cognitive Process. Addison-Wesley, Reading (1983)

Connecting Gripping Mechanism Based on Iris Diaphragm for Modular Autonomous Robots

Nikita Pavliuk[1]([envelope]) [iD], Petr Smirnov[1] [iD], Artem Kondratkov[1], and Andrey Ronzhin[1,2] [iD]

[1] St. Petersburg Institute for Informatics and Automation of the Russian Academy of Sciences (SPIIRAS), 14th Line, 39, 199178 St. Petersburg, Russia
antei.hasgard@gmail.com
[2] Department of Electromechanics and Robotics, SUAI, Bolshaya Morskaya Street, 67, 190000 Saint-Petersburg, Russia

Abstract. In this work, homogeneous gripping mechanical devices for connecting small-sized modular autonomous robots are described. The review of solutions of gripping and holding industrial mechanisms, and robotic switching mechanisms, as well as docking devices of space vehicles is given. The design of the connecting gripping mechanism of Mobile Autonomous Reconfigurable System (MARS) for coaxial conjugation of robots is proposed and it works in conjunction and passive modes to form modular structures. In the passive state, the working body of the mechanism forms a geometrical figure, which is suitable for connecting with identical device. In this case working body opens gripping mechanism and capture similar mechanism in the passive state. The proposed mechanism is based on the iris diaphragm, which prevents the uncontrolled displacement of the working body and stops the mechanism. It excludes the accidental rotation around the axis of the autonomous unit during operation in the formed structure. Infrared sensors (IR) were used for the concentric alignment of the axes of the connection devices. Sensors of this type estimate the distance and deflection angle of the opposed mechanism.

Keywords: Modular robot · Gripping device · Autonomous robot · MARS

1 Introduction

When building modular structures, the tasks of exact positioning and physical connection of heterogeneous and homogeneous modular robots relative to each other are solved. These are complex and related tasks, because with an inaccurate coaxial joint there will not be a rigid mechanical bond necessary for the formation.

Obtaining a bond, excluding mutual shear and rotation of parts is a major challenge in modular robotics, together with precise positioning of elements relative to each other. There are magnetic, mechanical (retractable fingers, bayonet connection) and hybrid connector, used in robots. However, necessary sensors are not always available, needed to accurately determine the position of the adjacent mechanism. The designed MARS robot connection mechanism features decent rigidity together with positioning accuracy, what allows satisfactory solving of the aforementioned problem.

© Springer Nature Switzerland AG 2019
A. Ronzhin et al. (Eds.): ICR 2019, LNAI 11659, pp. 260–269, 2019.
https://doi.org/10.1007/978-3-030-26118-4_25

MARS robot is being developed as a set of homogeneous autonomous units with the function of longitudinal axial and perpendicular conjugation. The MARS structure is divided into a transfer device, a function block and a switching device. In the presented research mechanisms for gripping and holding items were considered, as well robot connection and shuttle jointing. Further we developed a prototype of a connection-gripping device using iris diaphragm. Finally, we performed a statistical analysis and described a sensor for robot connection adjustment.

2 Related Works

Gripping devices (GD) differ in the method of holding the object, such as: grasping, supporting, retaining. In the design of such mechanisms, increased attention is paid to the requirements of the capture and retention reliability, stability, no damage or destruction of the retention object. For this reason, the memory is considered as a prototype of the connecting-gripping device. The following review presents industrial gripping devices and switching devices used in modular robotics, as well as an androgynous-peripheral docking unit used in the space industry.

The Danish company OnRobot presented the Cecko gripping device (see Fig. 1a) for industrial robots, equipped with millions of microscopic fine fibers adhering to the surface due to van der Waals forces to hold flat objects. The charger does not use compressed air or an external source of energy. Depending on the smoothness of the material, the gripper can hold an object weighting up to 8 kg. The design provides for autonomous cleaning, piezoelectricity to remove dust particles. For use in modular robotics, the following device is difficult to manufacture and it is impossible to miniaturize [1].

The principle of work of magnetic gripper (see Fig. 1b) is based on the appearance of a magnetic field. The mechanism contain electromagnet that generates a magnetic field when receiving a current, or a permanent magnet and a lever to close the magnetic force lines. It is possible to redirect the magnetic flux to use the advantages of electromagnet controllability and energy efficiency of permanent magnets. At the same time, the weight and dimensions, even in a small size, make such mechanisms ineffective for use in modular robotics [2].

Suckers of vacuum grid are used for holding objects. Suckers are mounted on a support frame that has the necessary stiffness, weight, and size (see Fig. 1c). The frame is attached to the manipulator with a bracket. The main advantage of this gripping device relative to the magnetic trap is ability to work with objects of non-magnetic materials. The device has small weight, and can be quickly fixed on the object. For small modular robotics, the device is not applicable due to the complexity of the design and the requirements for the operation of pneumatic mechanisms [2].

Chuck is a special device for fixing parts or tools on the spindle axis (see Fig. 1d). It is used in the composition of the front spindle of the lathe for clamping the workpiece. Sometimes it is used as part of turntables and dividing heads. In the review [3], a 3-jaw chuck was considered, which is divided into a spiral and rack. Spiral structures are common and are used due to their construction and reliability. The advantages include the range of the movement of the clamps, clamping of non-circular parts and

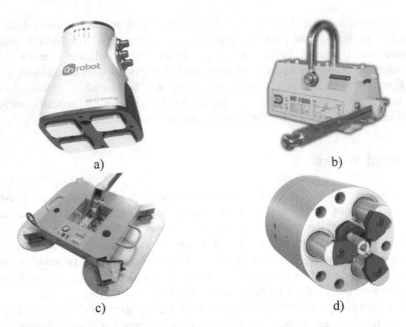

Fig. 1. Industrial grippers: (a) components of a Gecko memory device [1]; (b) magnetic gripper [2]; (c) vacuum gripper [2]; (d) clamping chuck [3].

efficiency. Among the minuses: wear parts lead to a decrease in the accuracy of the centering mechanism. Rack chuck on a lathe partially deprived of these shortcomings due to the design features – the crown drives the rotating rails. This makes the mechanism more accurate than spiral devices, and gives a reinforced clamp, but this reduces the efficiency of the product, which also cannot be fixed in several planes. For use in modular robotics, the clamping chuck is hampered by the complexity of making a suitable helix if a spiral design is used, as well as the number of gear units in the model, if a rack cartridge is used, which leads to an increase in size and weight of the mechanisms.

In [4] (see Fig. 2a) authors present MARS with a magnetic-mechanical connector as a connection mechanism. The proposed design of the docking of autonomous units does not require constant monitoring by the control unit, consumes energy only during the docking and disconnection of the robots among themselves. Significant weight t of connecting device limits its use in small modular robotic devices.

The modular robot ATRON [5, 6] (see Fig. 2b) uses a different construction of the connecting mechanism using retractable hooks for hooking. The structure of 5 modular robots by the number of degrees of freedom works as a manipulator, and a formation of 10 devices forms a moving four-wheel machine. The disadvantages of the design of such a capture include the use of a large number of moving elements.

The paper [7] presents the CellRobot robot (see Fig. 2c), consisting of a set of spherical elements for various tasks and in the specific case does not use a connection mechanism. The constructions are assembled by hand, the lock is a bayonet locking mechanism. The impossibility of autonomous connection of modular nodes among

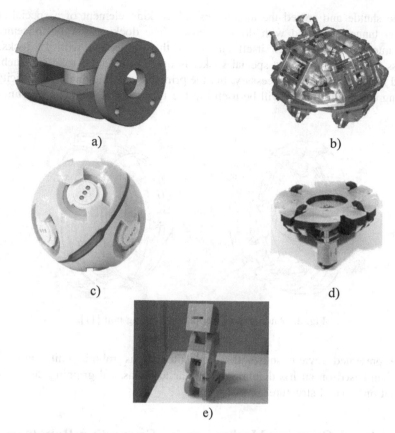

a)

b)

c)

d)

e)

Fig. 2. Gripping mechanisms of modular robots: (a) MARS [4]; (b) ATRON [5]; (c) CellBot [7]; (d) Roombots [8]; (e) DTTO [10].

themselves, in addition to heterogeneity, does not allow to use separate devices as independent units.

The modular robot Roombots (see Fig. 2d) [8, 9] is a cube using a mechanical connector with retractable hook fingers as a connection device. The mechanism in the standard position and states is not intended to connect with a similar mechanism and is massive. The mechanism is based on the iris diaphragm and offers a homogeneous mechanism for connecting robots.

The considered Dtto robot [10] (see Fig. 2d), controlled by an Arduino controller, independently changes its configuration and position, but does not connect with other robots independently. Dtto moves by bending and turning the pivot parts. The connector is similar to the Roombots one, but neodymium magnets are also used to increase forces of connection robots to each other.

Among the gripper constructions, the docking spacecraft mechanism, the androgynous-peripheral docking unit APAS [11] used at the International Space Station (see Fig. 3) is considered separately. To facilitate the design, the device is divided into target docking elements. The ring form working docking element was extended from the shuttle and seized the annular joined docking element of a special sealed transition tunnel equipped with docking nodes. The docking station concentrically aligns, interconnects between itself and locks the connection with 12 locks. For tightness of the connection, a special gasket is used. In modular robotics, such full-featured mechanisms are unnecessary, but the principle of achieving concentricity and switching connecting nodes will be useful in the formation of modular structures.

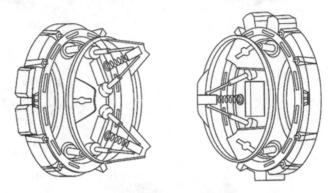

Fig. 3. Androgynous-peripheral docking unit [11].

The presented review shows that for autonomous robotic units, a miniature mechanism based on an iris diaphragm, similar to a classical gripping device, is relevant but one spatial structure.

3   Developed Gripping Mechanism for Connecting Robots

The proposed connecting mechanism for achieving concentricity of the connection uses not only mechanics, but also an IR sensor to determine the angle of one switched device relative to another.

The iris diaphragm is often used in photographic lenses and other devices to control the illumination of the image and change the depth of the sharply displayed space. The classical iris diaphragm consists of thin, opaque crescent-shaped petals that enter each other and form a rounded hole (see Fig. 4). By moving the diaphragm ring of the lens or its associated lever plate simultaneously rotate, smoothly changing the lens opening [12, 13].

The developed mechanism based on the iris diaphragm is depicted in Fig. 5a. The pins are shifted tangentially into the slot with the help of a transfer lever. The pins shown in Fig. 6, b are placed in cams, as in a self-centering chuck. In the presented mechanism, the cams do not work as gripping clips, but act as a lever for controlled extension of the fingers. In the connector model in Fig. 5, the layout and operation of the diaphragm with the cams is displayed. Figure 5b shows a simplified connector model. Part of connector is shown with notches along which the pins connected to the diaphragm blades and tightening fingers move in a straight promotion [14].

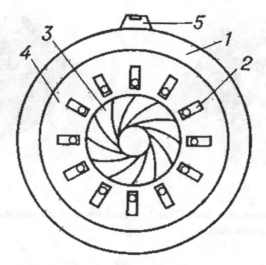

Fig. 4. Iris diaphragm: 1 – aperture body; 2 – pegs of the diaphragm pestles; 3 – aperture blades; 4 – diaphragm ring; 5 – shifting lever [12].

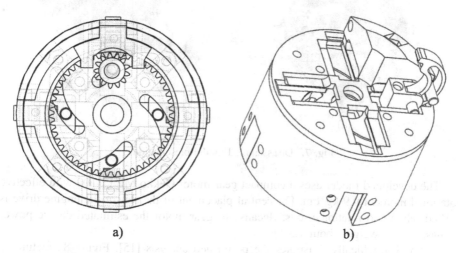

a)   b)

Fig. 5. (a) Iris diaphragm; (b) Gripping mechanism in projection.

Figure 6 shows two models of connectors, characterized by a gripping mechanism. In the first case, the petals of the iris diaphragm play the role of fingers, in this case the load is directed directly to the driven rods. In the second case, the petals play the role of levers, pinching fingers.

Figure 7 shows the working part of the mechanism on the iris diaphragm of the concentrator in the spaced form, the gear lever for the four petals is the gear and the part with diagonal slits. Petals consist of two parts: a rod and a lever. The stem of the petal is recessed into the diagonal slot and fixed in the lever.

Fig. 6. Mechanical connector models: (a) Test mechanism of iris diaphragm; (b) Assembled mechanism with retractable fingers.

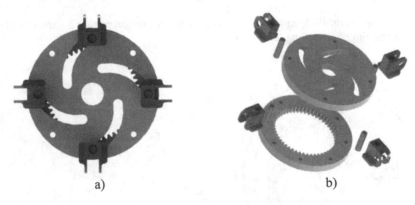

Fig. 7. Disassembled model presentation.

The developed model uses a compact gear motor Gekko MR12-100 with effective rotational moment 0,9 kg*cm. For central placement of the sensor the engine drive is shifted relative to rotational axis. Because of gear motor the estimated device power allows to keep weight about 1.5 kg.

Figure 8 graphically illustrates the performed analysis [15]. Figure 8a features a grip model, where to each finger external load of 2 kg is applied, what in total exceeds the weight holding capacity of two robots, connected to it. Stress levels are denoted with colors according to scale 8, b. We discovered material damage and noted, that polyacetal, physically equivalent to Nylon 101, experienced deformation of about 1.5 mm.

The design of the MARS robot grip provides a place to accommodate an IR sensor (see Fig. 8), which is necessary to determine the angle of the identical gripping mechanism of the second robot and adjust the position of two autonomous robots when connected. When robots are connected, the gripping mechanisms switch to the opened or closed state, the IR diode is turned on in the opened state, the receiver is turned on in the closed state [16, 17].

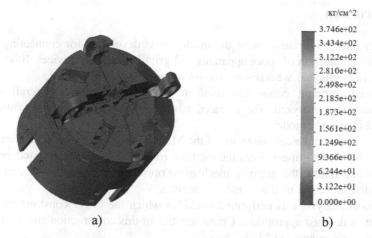

Fig. 8. Statistic tension analysis: (a) resulting shift according Mises maximum stress criterion; (b) Scale denoting the material condition.

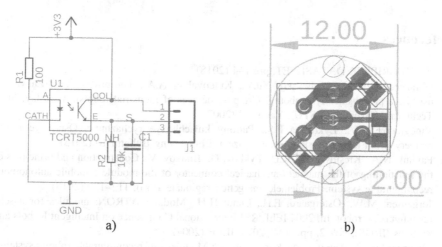

Fig. 8. IR sensor: (a) simplified diagram of the sensor; (b) board dimensions, in mm.

After the robots are determined and placed at the required distance between themselves, the fingers of the opened grip are reduced and fixed in the grooves of another grip, operating in the passive state and forming a geometrical figure, in a form suitable for grip by an identical device in the unfolded state. The design of the MARS robot also includes two points of perpendicular fixation of the grippers, with sensors installed and a suitable form for gripping. For practical use, it is advisable, but not necessary, to use cylindrical millimeter neodymium magnets in the gripping design to increase the holding force when connecting robots. Magnets do not interfere with the work of IR sensors.

4 Conclusion

This paper presents an analysis of the mechanisms developed for connecting robotic devices, the connection of space apparatus and gripping-holding devices. Based on the identified strengths and weaknesses, the following results are formed.

Industrial gripping connectors used in modular robotics, spacecraft docking mechanisms were analyzed. The revealed advantages were taken into account in the developed connector model.

A model of mechanical connector of the MARS robot using an iris diaphragm was proposed. When the gripper holds the modular robot, the load is distributed evenly on the connecting hooks; the gripping mechanism prevents the return movement and the arbitrary disconnection of the connected devices.

Statistical analysis was performed based on which the finger construction, described above, is deemed appropriate. Characteristics of this construction enable it to hold two sequentially connected MARS robots.

Acknowledgement. This work is supported by the Russian Foundation for Basic Research № 16-29-04101.

References

1. ECKO GRIPPER DATASHEET, pp. 1–4 (2018)
2. Ukrazhenko, K.A., Anchevskij, Yu.V., Kulebyakin, A.A., Toropov, A.Yu.: Zahvatnye ustrojstva promyshlennyh robotov [Gripping devices of industrial robots]. Yaroslavl State Technical University (YSTU), Yaroslavl (2007)
3. Vinogradov D.V., Lykosova E.S.: Patrony kulachkovye rychazhnye. Osnovnye tipy i razmery [Cam levers. Basic types and sizes]. Engineering Bulletin 10 (2013)
4. Pavliuk, N.A., Krestovnikov, K.D., Pykhov, D., Budkov, V.: Construction and principles of the functioning of the magneto-mechanical connector of the module a mobile autonomous reconfigurable system. Problemele energeticii regionale **1**(36), 117–129 (2018)
5. Jorgensen, M.W., Ostergaard, E.H., Lund, H.H.: Modular ATRON: modules for a self-reconfigurable robot. In: 2004 IEEE/RSJ International Conference on Intelligent Robots and Systems (IROS), vol. 2, pp. 2068–2073. IEEE (2004)
6. Chennareddy, S., Agrawal, A., Karuppiah, A.: Modular self-reconfigurable robotic systems: a survey on hardware architectures. J. Robot. **19**, 1–19 (2017)
7. Clapaud, A.: Can KEYi Technology finalize his cell robot CellRobot in 2016? 4REVOLUTION. http://www.4erevolution.com/en/keyi-technology-cellrobot/
8. Sproewitz, A., Billard, A., et al.: Roombots-mechanical design of self-reconfiguring modular robots for adaptive furniture. In: 2009 IEEE International Conference on Robotics and Automation, pp. 4259–4264. IEEE (2009)
9. Spröwitz, A., Moeckel, R., Vespignani, M., Bonardi, S., Ijspeert, A.J.: Roombots: a hardware perspective on 3D self-reconfiguration and locomotion with a homogeneous modular robot. Robot. Auton. Syst. **62**(7), 1016–1033 (2014)
10. Murata, S., Yoshida, E., Kamimura, A., Kurokawa, H., Tomita, K., Kokaji, S.: M-TRAN: Self-reconfigurable modular robotic system. IEEE/ASME Trans. Mechatron. **7**(4), 431–441 (2002)

11. Trushlyakov, V.I., Yutkin, E.A.: Obzor sredstv stykovki i zahvata ob"ektov krupnogabaritnogo kosmicheskogo musora [Overview of the means of docking and capture of large space debris.]. Omskij nauchnyj vestnik [Omsk Scientific Herald] 2(120) (2013)
12. Iofis, E.A.: Fotokinotekhnika [Photo kinotekhnika]. Soviet encyclopedia, 265–447 (1981)
13. Ershov K.G.: Kinos"yomochnaya tekhnika [Filming]. Provornov, S.M. Mashinostroenie, Leningrad (1988)
14. Otenij, Ya.N., Ol'shtynskij, P.V.: Vybor i raschet zahvatnyh ustrojstv promyshlennyh robotov [Selection and calculation of professional devices of industrial robots]. Politekhnik, Volgograd (2000)
15. Shishigin D.S.: On Choosing the Technology of Application Software Integration with a CAD-System. SPIIRAS Proc. 4(47) (2016)
16. Fraden, J.: Handbook of modern sensors: physics, designs, and applications. Anal. Bioanal. Chem. 382(1), 8–9 (2004)
17. Kashkarov, A.: Datchiki v elektronnyh skhemah: ot prostogo k slozhnomu [Sensors in electronic circuits. From simple to complex]. DMK press, Moscow (2017)

Overview of UAV Based Free-Space Optical Communication Systems

Milica Petkovic$^{(\boxtimes)}$ and Milan Narandzic

Faculty of Technical Science, University of Novi Sad, Novi Sad, Serbia
{milica.petkovic, orange}@uns.ac.rs

Abstract. Increased availability of unmanned aerial vehicles (UAVs), also known as drones, have advanced research and industrial interests, establishing this platform as a promising part of future emerging technologies. In this paper, we present an overview of optical wireless communications (OWC) related to UAV, which benefit from both optical data rates and mobility of UAV. Since drones are usually employed in outdoor scenarios, the UAV based free-space optical (FSO) communication system is considered, as the FSO represents the optical wireless signal transmission from infra-red band spectrum in outdoor environments. A brief recapitulation of main studies in the field of UAV-aided cooperation within FSO systems is presented. Optical channel modeling is presented in details, taking into account both misalignment and positioning of the transceivers.

Keywords: Free-Space Optical (FSO) communication · Misalignment · Unmanned Aerial Vehicles (UAV)

1 Introduction

An unmanned aerial vehicle (UAV) represents a mobile aircraft without a human pilot onboard, which operates under remote control by a human, or by artificial intelligence. The main advantage of UAVs, i.e., drones, is its mobility and remote control. The initial application of the UAV aided systems was for military applications. With development of new emerging technologies, the employment of the UAV as a complement in the communication was expanded in the commercial communication systems. Drones show potential to be implemented in a various scenarios. As a remote, mobile platform, the UAVs have found applications such as communications, traffic monitoring, remote sensing... They are a good solution as a temporary relay node, when we need to establish connectivity with two distance points. Furthermore, they can be easily integrated in existing network architectures [1–3].

1.1 Optical Wireless Communication Systems

Due to demanding requirements of increased number of users, the next generations of the communications systems will be faced with a number of new demands. Since traditional radio-frequency (RF) communication systems are characterized by over-crowded and licensed spectrum, the optical wireless communications (OWC) are

A. Ronzhin et al. (Eds.): ICR 2019, LNAI 11659, pp. 270–277, 2019.
https://doi.org/10.1007/978-3-030-26118-4_26

adopted as promising technology due to many advantages. First of all, the OWC systems ensure very high data rates and increased bandwidth. They are quite cheap and easy to be implemented and repositioned when it is necessary. Hence, the OWC represent a good solution as a temporary link [4–6].

The main division of the OWC is based on type of environment where the system is employed. For indoor scenarios, the optical signal is used for both communications and illuminations. This indoor OWC is called visible light communication (VLC) system, operating at the wavelengths of the 380–750 nm which belong to visible spectrum. The VLC transmitters are mostly light-emitting diodes, usually used for short-distance communications [6, 7]. Regarding the outdoor environment, the free-space optical (FSO) links are employed in practical systems representing optical beam propagation in infra-red band spectrum. The FSO links are used for long distance communications, using the laser as an optical source of light [5, 6]. At the receiving part, different types of photodetectors (PIN or avalanche) are employed as a part of receiving telescope to collect a laser beam and to perform optical-to-electrical signal conversion. Still, the utilization of the FSO systems is limited by an obligatory existence of the line-of-sight (LoS) component, which is sometimes very hard to be achieved for long distance links. Besides the LoS requirement, the FSO signal transmission is affected by few phenomena which can seriously degrade the FSO link performance. The main reason for the optical signal degradation is the atmospheric turbulence, caused by the random changes in atmospheric temperature, altitude and pressure [8]. Furthermore, the misalignment between FSO transmitter and receiver leads to the pointing errors effect (also called misalignment fading) [9].

1.2 UAV Based FSO Communication Systems

As the FSO communication systems offer significant benefits compared to RF ones, their utilizations in the future communication networks is certain. Due to promising drones characteristics, such as flexibility, adaptive altitude adjustment and mobility, their employment becomes an important part of emerging technologies. The idea of RF based UAV platforms have been implemented in modern systems. Still, the main drawback of this kind of systems is the existence of interference, which can lead to significant degradation of the system performance and deterioration of security level. For that reason, the combination of UAV systems with the FSO links is attracting attention, due to increased data rate, as well as licence-free and secure transmission. The simple UAV based FSO system is presented in Fig. 1.

The atmospheric turbulence and positioning are two main factors which determine the quality of the FSO links when the transceivers are fixed and ground-based. When the FSO apertures are mobile, such as in the UAV based FSO communications links, the angle-of-arrival (AOA) fluctuations due to orientation deviations of hovering UAVs must be takin into consideration [10].

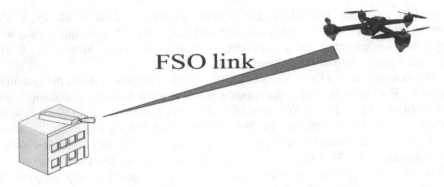

Fig. 1. System model of UAV based FSO system.

2 Literature Overview of the UAV Based FSO Systems

Due to mentioned benefits, the interest in UAV based FSO systems has been increased in the research community. To the best of authors' knowledge, optical wireless links within UAV was proposed in 2006. [11], providing the possible architecture of the UAVs swarms. The same authors gave a short introduction and important aspects of the same system in [12], while in [13] presented survey paper of the advantages and challenges of developing FSO links between drones. Furthermore, chapter [14], written by Majumdar, presented a discussion about UAV-FSO communication systems, providing possible scenarios for implementation of this kind of communication systems, as well as empirical and parametric models of atmospheric turbulence strength parameters. Additionally, [14] observed alignment and tracking problems related to the UAV-FSO communications, including some practical issues.

In addition to establishment of FSO links for UAV needs, the similar concept can be used to extend functionality of communication network. In [15], the cooperation system where drones act as relays between multiple FSO communication links was investigated. Furthermore, the study presented in [16] gave the analysis of the vertical backhaul/fronthaul framework for the 5G+ network, where the UAVs are handling the traffic between the access and core networks via FSO links.

The system presented in scientific report [17] consists of a ground transmitter and a ground receiver, which cooperate over UAV based FSO links, by multiplexing of multiple orbital-angular-momentum beams in order to increase capacity. The state-of-the-art network was proposed in [18], where airborne radio access network (RAN) was considered as fast and low-cost solution. In this scenario, the downlink of RAN from one ground base station (BS) and multiple ground users is established over an access point – drone. Additionally, the communication between BS and drone has possibility to perform simultaneous transfer of lightwave information and power, called SLIPT.

Aforementioned studies were mostly related for overview of the UAV based FSO system, presenting some possible aspects and implementation in communication networks. Papers [10, 19–22] presented the particularity of channel modeling for the optical systems that include UAV platform. More precisely, [19] gave alignment/stability analysis of drones included to FSO network. The effect of drone instability was observed and results were obtained based on experimental measurements combined with theoretical analysis and optical geometrical intersection models. In [20], the AOA fluctuations due to UAV orientation deviations were modeled taking into consideration both atmospheric turbulence and misalignment fading. The outage probability performance of FSO system with both coherent and direct detections was analyzed. The statistical model incorporating the geometric loss of the FSO channel, which is the result of the random fluctuations of the drone position and orientation, was proposed in [21]. The scenario where fronthaul FSO links communicate with several UAVs hover above some area and serve a large number of mobile users was observed. Next, [10] derived a statistical channel model for ground-to-UAV, UAV-to-UAV, and UAV-to-ground FSO links, while the intensity fluctuation due to atmospheric turbulence were modeled by both Gamma–Gamma and log-normal distributions. Additionally, in order to maximize the link availability, the optimization of different parameters was performed. Recently, optical beam tracking in UAV based FSO system was analyzed in [22], containing the derivation of the closed-form expressions for tracking and bit-error rate.

3 FSO Channel Modeling

As previously mentioned, the main causes of the optical signal degradation in the FSO system are atmospheric turbulence and pointing errors. Rest of the Section will presented the most adopted statistical model for describing these phenomena.

3.1 Atmospheric Tturbulence Statistical Model

The intensity fluctuations of the received optical signal due to atmospheric turbulence are usually modeled by Gamma-Gamma distribution, since it provides a good fit of experimental and theoretical data. The random changes in atmospheric temperature, pressure, altitude and wind speed results in the variations in the refractive index, which lead to the existence of atmospheric turbulence. This results in rapid intensity fluctuations at the received optical signal which are usually modeled by Gamma-Gamma distribution, since it provides a good fit of experimental and theoretical data. The probability density function (PDF) of the irradiance I_a is given by [8]

$$f_{I_a}(I_a) = \frac{2(\alpha\beta)^{\frac{\alpha+\beta}{2}}}{\Gamma(\alpha)\Gamma(\beta)} I_a^{\frac{\alpha+\beta}{2}-1} K_{\alpha-\beta}\left(2\sqrt{\alpha\beta I_a}\right), \quad I_a > 0, \tag{1}$$

where $\Gamma(.)$ is the gamma function [23, (8.310.1)] and $K_\nu(.)$ is the νth-order modified Bessel function of the second kind [23, (8.432)]. The parameters α and β represent the effective numbers of small-scale and large scale cells, respectively, and they are related to the atmospheric conditions. Assuming plane wave propagation and zero inner scale, the parameters α and β can be expressed as [8]

$$\alpha = \left(\exp \left[\frac{0.49\sigma_R^2}{\left(1+1.11\sigma_R^{12/5}\right)^{7/6}} \right] - 1 \right)^{-1}$$

$$\beta = \left(\exp \left[\frac{0.51\sigma_R^2}{\left(1+0.69\sigma_R^{12/5}\right)^{5/6}} \right] - 1 \right)^{-1}, \tag{2}$$

where σ_R^2 is the Rytov variance defined as

$$\sigma_R^2 = 1.23C_n^2k^{7/6}L^{11/6}, \tag{3}$$

where $k = 2\pi/\lambda$ is the wave-number, λ is the wavelength, L is the propagation distance and C_n^2 denotes the weather dependent index of refraction structure. The index C_n^2 typically varies from 10^{-17} to 10^{-13} m$^{-2/3}$ and it determines the turbulence strength.

3.2 Pointing Errors Model

The intensity fluctuations of the optical received signal resulted from misalignment between optical source and receiving detector, are usually described by the model presented in [9], which assumes zero boresight. This model considers that both horizontal and vertical displacements are modeled as independent Gaussian random variables, with zero mean value and standard deviation denoted by σ_s, thus the resulting radial displacement at the receiver detector is described by Rayleigh distribution with the jitter variance σ_s^2.

As a more general case, the pointing errors model with nonzero boresight was introduced in [24–26]. Contrary to [9], besides nonzero boresight, this model takes also into consideration non identical jitters for the elevation and azimuth displacement. In this case, if the radial displacement between the centroid of the optical beam and the center of photodetector at the receiver is denoted by r, the fraction of the collected power at receiver is approximated as [25]

$$I_p(r, L) \approx A_0 \exp\left(-\frac{2r^2}{w_{eq}^2} \right), \quad r \geq 0, \tag{4}$$

where w_{eq} denotes the equivalent beam radius at the receiver, which is defined as

$$w_{eq,}^2 = \frac{\sqrt{\pi}\operatorname{erf}(v)w_z^2}{2v\exp(-v^2)}. \tag{5}$$

Furthermore,

$$A_0 = [\operatorname{erf}(v)]^2, \quad v = \frac{\sqrt{\pi}a}{\sqrt{2}w_z}, \tag{6}$$

where erf(.) is the error function [23, (8.250.1)], a is a radius of the circular detector aperture, and w_z denotes the waist of the beam Gaussian spatial intensity profile [9].

For long distances, the beam waist value be approximated as $w_z \approx \theta L$, where θ is the transmit divergence angle corresponding to increase in beam radius with the distance from the transmitter. Regarding the receiver aperture plane, the radial displacement vector can be defined as

$$\vec{r} = [r_x, r_y]^T,$$
(7)

where r_x and r_y are horizontal and elevation displacements at the detector plane, respectively [25]. As it has been already mentioned, a nonzero boresight error is considered, and r_x and r_y are modeled as nonzero mean Gaussian distributed random variables with non-identical jitters, i.e., $r_x \sim N(\mu_x, \sigma_x^2)$ and $r_y \sim N(\mu_y, \sigma_y^2)$. Finally, the radial displacement $|\vec{r}| = \sqrt{r_x^2 + r_y^2}$ is described by the Beckmann distribution as [25]

$$f_r(r) = \frac{r}{2\pi\sigma_x\sigma_y} \int_0^{2\pi} \exp\left(-\frac{(r\cos\theta - \mu_x)^2}{2\sigma_x^2} - \frac{(r\sin\theta - \mu_y)^2}{2\sigma_y^2}\right) d\theta.$$
(8)

The Beckmann's distribution in (8) can be accurately approximated through the modified Rayleigh distribution as [25]

$$f_r(r) = \frac{r}{\sigma_r^2}\exp\left(-\frac{r^2}{2\sigma_r^2}\right), \quad r \geq 0,$$
(9)

where

$$\sigma_r^2 = \left(\frac{3\mu_x^2\sigma_x^4 + 3\mu_y^2\sigma_y^4 + \sigma_x^6 + \sigma_y^6}{2}\right)^{1/3}.$$
(10)

The PDF for the irradiance in (4) resulted from the pointing errors, I_p, is finally approximated as [15]

$$f_{I_p}(I_p) = \frac{\psi^2}{(A_0g)^{\psi^2}} I_p^{\psi^2-1}, \quad \text{for } 0 \leq I_p \leq gA_0,$$
(11)

where

$$\psi = \frac{w_{eq}}{2\sigma_r}, \quad \psi_x = \frac{w_{eq}}{2\sigma_x}, \quad \psi_y = \frac{w_{eq}}{2\sigma_y},$$
(12)

and

$$g = \exp\left(\frac{1}{\psi^2} - \frac{1}{\psi_x^2} - \frac{1}{\psi_y^2} - \frac{\mu_x^2}{2\sigma_x^2\psi_x^2} - \frac{\mu_y^2}{2\sigma_y^2\psi_y^2}\right). \tag{13}$$

The PDF for pointing errors model with nonzero boresight can be easily simplified to the one for zero boresight scenario presented in [9] by considering independent identical zero mean Gaussian distributions for both elevation and horizontal displacement, i.e., $g = 1$, $\mu_x^2 = 0$, $\mu_y^2 = 0$, $\sigma_x^2 = \sigma_y^2 = \sigma_s^2$.

Note that in the case of the FSO systems with moving transceivers, besides the positioning of the FSO apertures, the AOA estimation is also important factor that emphasize impact of the pointing errors. This component of the misalignment fading requires more general model of the pointing errors and represents the part of our future research related to the UAV based FSO systems.

4 Conclusion

In this paper, we have presented a short overview of the UAV based FSO communication systems. The importance of the employment of the UAV platforms within FSO links is expressed by benefits from both increased data rates and mobility of UAV. A literature overview of the recent studies related to UAV based FSO systems has been presented. Furthermore, statistical modeling of the FSO channel has been presented, while both atmospheric turbulence and pointing errors are taken into consideration.

Acknowledgment. This work is developed in the framework of ERA.Net RUS Plus Project 99-HARMONIC, and TR-32025 and III44003 projects, that are supported by Ministry of Education, Science and Technology Development of Republic of Serbia.

References

1. Fotouhi, A., et al.: Survey on UAV cellular communications: practical aspects, standardization advancements, regulation, and security challenges. IEEE Commun. Surv. Tutorials (2019)
2. Mozaffari, M., Saad, W., Bennis, M., Nam, Y., Debbah, M.: A tutorial on UAVs for wireless networks: applications, challenges, and open problems. IEEE Commun. Surv. Tutorials (2019)
3. Mozaffari, M., et al.: Beyond 5G With UAVs: foundations of a 3D wireless cellular network. IEEE Trans. Wirel. Commun. **18**(2), 357–372 (2019)
4. Arnon, S., Barry, J., Karagiannidis, G., Schober, R., Uysal, M. (eds.): Advanced Optical Wireless Communication Systems. Cambridge University Press, New York (2012)
5. Khalighi, M.A., Uysal, M.: Survey on free space optical communication: a communication theory perspective. IEEE Commun. Surv. Tutorials **16**(4), 2231–2258 (2014)
6. Ghassemlooy, Z., Popoola, W., Rajbhandari, S.: Optical Wireless Communications: System and Channel Modelling with MATLAB®, CRC Press. Taylor & Francis Group, Boca Raton (2012)

7. Grobe, L., et al.: High-speed visible light communication systems. IEEE Commun. Mag. **51** (12), 60–66 (2013)
8. Andrews, L.C., Philips, R.N.: Laser Beam Propagation Through Random Media, 2nd edn. SPIE Press, Bellingham (2005)
9. Farid, A.A., Hranilovic, S.: Outage capacity optimization for free-space optical links with pointing errors. J. Lightwave Technol. **25**(7), 1702–1710 (2007)
10. Dabiri, M.T., Mohammad, S., Khalighi, M.A.: Channel modeling and parameter optimization for hovering UAV-based free-space optical links. IEEE J. Sel. Areas Commun. **36**(9), 2104–2113 (2018)
11. Chlestil, C., et al.: Reliable optical wireless links within UAV swarms. In: 2006 International Conference on Transparent Optical Networks, vol. 4. IEEE (2006)
12. Leitgeb, E., et al.: Investigation in free space optical communication links between unmanned aerial vehicles (UAVs). In: Proceedings of the 2007 9th International Conference on Transparent Optical Networks, vol. 3. IEEE (2007)
13. Muhammad, S.S., et al.: Challenges in establishing free space optical communications between flying vehicles. In: Proceedings of the 2008 6th International Symposium on Communication Systems, Networks and Digital Signal Processing. IEEE (2008)
14. Majumdar, Arun K.: Free-space optical (FSO) platforms: unmanned aerial vehicle (UAV) and mobile. In: Majumdar, A.K. (ed.) Advanced Free Space Optics (FSO). SSOS, vol. 186, pp. 203–225. Springer, New York (2015). https://doi.org/10.1007/978-1-4939-0918-6_6
15. Fawaz, W., Abou-Rjeily, C., Assi, C.: UAV-aided cooperation for FSO communication systems. IEEE Commun. Mag. **56**(1), 70–75 (2018)
16. Alzenad, M., et al.: FSO-based vertical backhaul/fronthaul framework for 5G+ wireless networks. IEEE Commun. Mag. **56**(1), 218–224 (2018)
17. Li, L., et al.: High-capacity free-space optical communications between a ground transmitter and a ground receiver via a UAV using multiplexing of multiple orbital-angular-momentum beams. Sci. Rep. **7**(1), 17427 (2017)
18. Diamantoulakis, P.D., et al.: Airborne Radio Access Networks with Simultaneous Lightwave Information and Power Transfer (SLIPT). In: Proceedings of the 2018 IEEE Global Communications Conference (GLOBECOM). IEEE (2018)
19. Kaadan, A., Refai, H., LoPresti, P.: Multielement FSO transceivers alignment for inter-UAV communications. J. Lightwave Technol. **32**(24), 4183–4193 (2014)
20. Huang, S., Safari, M.: Free-space optical communication impaired by angular fluctuations. IEEE Trans. Wirel. Commun. **16**(11), 7475–7487 (2017)
21. Najafi, M., et al.: Statistical modeling of FSO fronthaul channel for drone-based networks. In: Proceedings of the 2018 IEEE International Conference on Communications (ICC). IEEE (2018)
22. Safi, H., Dargahi, A., Cheng, J.: Spatial beam tracking and data detection for an FSO link to a UAV in the presence of hovering fluctuations. arXiv preprint arXiv:1904.03774 (2019)
23. Gradshteyn, I.S., Ryzhik, I.M.: Table of Integrals, Series, and Products, 6th edn. Academic, New York (2000)
24. Boluda-Ruiz, R., García-Zambrana, A., Castillo-Vázquez, B., Castillo-Vázquez, C.: Impact of nonzero boresight pointing error on ergodic capacity of MIMO FSO communication systems. Opt. Express **24**(4), 3513–3534 (2016)
25. Boluda-Ruiz, R., García-Zambrana, A., Castillo-Vázquez, B., Castillo-Vázquez, C.: Novel approximation of misalignment fading modeled by Beckmann distribution on free-space optical links. Opt. Express **24**(20), 22635–22649 (2016)
26. Yang, F., Cheng, J., Tsiftsis, T.A.: Free-space optical communication with nonzero boresight pointing errors. IEEE Trans. Commun. **62**(2), 713–725 (2014)

Approach to Side Channel-Based Cybersecurity Monitoring for Autonomous Unmanned Objects

Viktor Semenov$^{(\boxtimes)}$ [ID], Mikhail Sukhoparov [ID], and Ilya Lebedev [ID]

St. Petersburg Institute for Informatics and Automation of the Russian Academy of Sciences, 14-th Linia, VI, No. 39, Saint Petersburg 199178, Russia
v.semenov@iias.spb.su

Abstract. In this paper, problematic issues in ensuring the cybersecurity of autonomous unmanned objects were considered. Moreover, prerequisites that determine the need for external monitoring systems were identified. The type and statistical characteristics used for the analysis and classification of sound signals were also shown. The proposed approach to the analysis of the cyber-security condition of an autonomous object is based on classification methods and allows the identification of the current status based on digitized acoustic information processing. An experiment aimed at obtaining statistical informa-tion on various types of unmanned object maneuvers with various arrangements of an audio recorder was conducted. The data obtained was processed using two-layer feed-forward neural networks with sigmoid hidden neurons. Hence, the problem of identifying the cybersecurity condition of autonomous unmanned objects on the basis of processing acoustic signal information obtained through side channels was solved. Digitized information from an acoustic sensor (mi-crophone) located statically in the experiment area was classified more accu-rately than from the microphone located directly on the autonomous object. With a minimum time of statistical information accumulation using the proposed approach, it becomes possible to identify differences in maneuvers performed by the unmanned object and, consequently, the cybersecurity condition of the object with a probability close to 0.7. The proposed approach for processing signal information can be used as an additional independent element to deter-mine the cybersecurity condition of autonomous objects of unmanned systems. This approach can be quickly adapted using various mathematical tools and machine learning methods to achieve a given quality probabilistic assessment.

Keywords: Cybersecurity · Autonomous unmanned objects ·
Data processing · Neural networks · Cybersecurity monitoring systems

1 Introduction

To improve the theory and practice of management, control, and the use of mobile remote autonomous objects, capable of solving navigation, transport, and logistical tasks independently using artificial intelligence is an increasingly important direction toward the development of unmanned systems [1]. Such an approach implies

© Springer Nature Switzerland AG 2019
A. Ronzhin et al. (Eds.): ICR 2019, LNAI 11659, pp. 278–286, 2019.
https://doi.org/10.1007/978-3-030-26118-4_27

decentralized management, dispersion of mobile objects, the implementation of episodic interaction distributed on a spatial-temporal scale, which necessitates the implementation of a number of measures aimed at ensuring cybersecurity (CS).

An analysis of approaches to the construction of unmanned systems requires examining not only the use of security systems, but also systems for condition monitoring. These factors are fundamental in identifying the internal and external processes of an object. Classical approaches to the protection of information that focus on statistical analysis with the purpose of preventing breaches of the confidentiality, integrity, and availability of circulating data do not guarantee the achievement of a predetermined probability of the safety of an autonomous object and the system as a whole.

Information obtained through side channels may be one of the additional independent elements of assessing the condition of autonomous agents [2]. More than ten side channels were identified within the framework of the research, based on which one can monitor the conditions of individual intelligent agents, including the acoustic channel, electromagnetic radiation and the time channel [3, 4].

The data obtained via these channels can be used to conduct various attacks [5, 6] and to monitor and analyze the state of the software and hardware environments of autonomous agents [7–9].

Many publications have been devoted to the analysis of information received via the acoustic channel [10]. In [11], to pick up information, researchers used highly sensitive microphones and the microphone of a regular mobile phone. Currently, new ways of determining the anomalous state of a system are being investigated using signal processing methods based on machine learning [12].

The introduction of unmanned vehicles is accompanied by the need to address additional problematic issues of cybersecurity, such as [13, 14].

- detecting unauthorized access to the main units at the software level;
- analyzing and identifying anomalies in the technological cycles of unmanned vehicle operation;
- detecting the impact of destructive information on programs and algorithms;
- monitoring for the detection of undeclared capabilities.

In this regard, a need arises to develop models, CS monitoring techniques, using additional information sources aimed at independent analysis of the state of mobile remote autonomous objects of transport systems.

2 Problem Statement

Effective cybersecurity solutions are associated with the development of a scientific and methodological apparatus designed to improve the quality indicators in identifying the security state, resulting in the need to develop models and cybersecurity monitoring techniques of autonomous computing tools [15, 16]. An external monitoring system of an autonomous unmanned object can implemented on the basis of sensors that record the signal in real time mode when the object performs various actions.

The state of an autonomous object can be identified using data from external signals. The digitized signal is a set of amplitude values A. The sequence of amplitude values a_1, a_2, ... a_n. will determine the sequence of indicators obtained as a result of the autonomous object performing a certain action.

Then it is necessary to detect and identify the signal $f = \{a_{1f}, a_{2f} \dots a_{nf}\}$, which occurs when performing this particular action in the sequence of amplitudes of the signal $F = \{a_1, a_2, \dots a_n\}$.

The recognition process proceeds as follows. The image f is extracted from the input signal F, and then the amplitudes are compared. Based on the threshold coefficient K, the conclusion is made about the presence of the required signal in the sequence:

$$\frac{A_f}{A_F} \leq K. \tag{1}$$

The solution of inequality (1) is reduced to the classification problem, where the set of classes takes the values $Y = \{Y_0, Y_1\}$, with Y_0 being a safe state, where the identified action caused by the control command is performed, and Y_1 being an unsafe state in which the identified action currently differs from that one caused by the control command.

3   The Proposed Approach

Remote autonomous objects are complex systems in which a huge number of processes occur simultaneously. Each process is characterized by external signals that can be received via side channels as a result of functioning of electronic or mechanical components and performance of any commands and actions by the object.

The analysis of the behavioral characteristics of the object can be used as an approach providing additional condition monitoring. Change in the parameters of electromagnetic radiation, acoustic noise, the appearance of various vibrations when performing actions and maneuvers can give additional information about the state. The analysis of deviations detected from such data provides additional information for decision making, which is a definite advantage in the context of uncertainty.

To identify a process in this way, a training sample is required. Therefore, at the first step, as a result of the experiment, the data are accumulated while executing predetermined maneuvers by an unmanned vehicle (Fig. 1). The second step is to process the information received, where noises are removed. The third step is related to the formation of a training sample, on the basis of which the analysis will be carried out.

Based on information about external control actions, the system has data on the allowed maneuver of the unmanned vehicle at a given point in time. While analyzing the information of the training sample and the current signal values, a conclusion is made about the maneuver carried out by the unmanned device. Thus, in case the detected maneuver differs from the allowed one, the control system concludes that the controlled system is in the unsafe (anomalous) state Y_1.

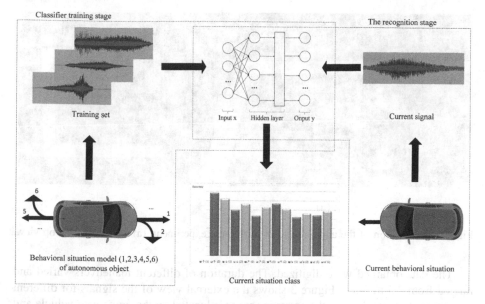

Fig. 1. The proposed approach.

The formation of a training sample, where information about the captured signal data is accumulated for each action or command that is executed, allows applying various machine learning methods.

4 Experiment

In autonomous unmanned elements of the system, situations arise when it is necessary to determine the current state of an object depending on the external factors, in order to perform functional capabilities associated, for example, with a speed or direction maneuver. The state of the object can be assessed on the basis of comparison with the reference sample [17, 18].

To analyze the possibilities of the above approach, an experiment was conducted aimed at obtaining the behavioral characteristics of various maneuvers of an unmanned vehicle. An acoustic channel was selected as an independent external channel.

The tested unmanned vehicle made maneuvers set from the control panel, such as: straight forward ($\uparrow$), straight backward ($\downarrow$), forward-right ($\nearrow$), forward-left ($\nwarrow$), backward-right ($\searrow$), and backward-left ($\swarrow$) motion. To obtain the training sample, reusable recording of each maneuver parameters was made with the sensors. In case 1, an acoustic sensor (microphone) located directly on the body of the tested unmanned vehicle was used to record the signal, and in case 2, another one that was statically mounted to the right of the experiment area, as shown in Fig. 2.

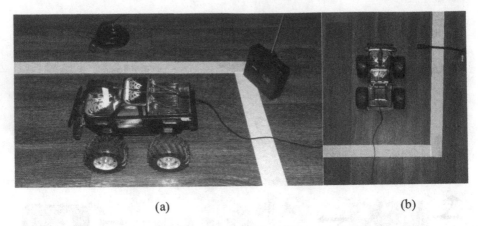

(a)   (b)

Fig. 2. The location of the audio recorders during the experiment. (a) side view, (b) top view.

The data obtained were digitized. The duration of different maneuvers varied and ranged from 2.5 to 3.5 s. Figure 3 shows the external view of the signals for different maneuvers for case 1 when the acoustic sensor is located on the unmanned vehicle and for case 2 when it is statically installed to the right of the experiment area. Signals on the right are characterized by greater monotony and amplitude.

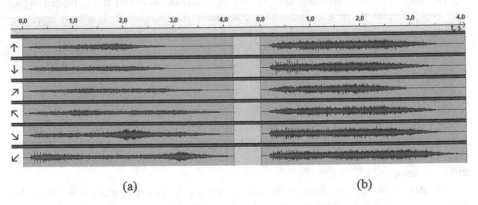

(a)   (b)

Fig. 3. The external view of the signals. The acoustic sensor is located on the unmanned vehicle (a) and the microphone is statically installed to the right of the experiment area (b).

During signal sampling 5000 samples were taken evenly from each time-continuous signal. The values obtained were processed using two-layer feed-forward neural networks with sigmoid hidden neurons (Fig. 4). Matlab R2018b Update 2 software, Neural Network Pattern Recognition application of the DeepLearning Toolbox package were used.

Six states were classified. To form the training sample, 70% of the values were used, 15% of the values were used as a test, and another 15% were used as a verifying set. Tables 1 and 2 give the results of classification into six classes, corresponding to each maneuver for different options of the recording device location.

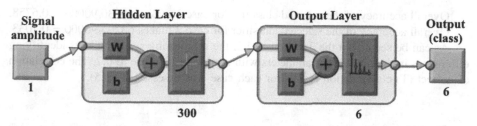

Fig. 4. The scheme of the used two-layer feed-forward neural networks with sigmoid hidden neurons (Matlab R2018b software); *w* – weight matrices, *b* – translation vectors.

Table 1. The results of classification by a neural network into six classes for case 1 – the microphone is located on an unmanned vehicle.

Maneuvers		Actual class						Total	Accuracy
		↑	↓	↗	↖	↘	↙		
Calculated class	↑	13608	2639	0	0	0	0	16247	0.8376
	↓	1392	9948	2227	0	1528	0	15095	0.6590
	↗	0	1398	8649	2833	4185	1942	19007	0.4550
	↖	0	0	1201	11361	0	1036	13598	0.8355
	↘	0	1015	2598	0	8454	3212	15279	0.5533
	↙	0	0	325	806	833	8810	10774	0.8177
Total		15000	15000	15000	15000	15000	15000		
Accuracy		0.9072	0.6632	0.5766	0.7574	0.5636	0.5873		0.6758

Table 2. The results of classification by a neural network into six classes for case 2 – the microphone is statically installed to the right of the experiment area.

Maneuvers		Actual class						Total	Accuracy
		↑	↓	↗	↖	↘	↙		
Calculated class	↑	12369	1074	405	381	603	375	15207	0,8134
	↓	753	11268	594	360	759	576	14310	0,7874
	↗	405	765	10533	1491	912	1035	15141	0,6957
	↖	738	1068	1326	10164	1461	1746	16503	0,6159
	↘	267	543	1233	1569	9255	1563	14430	0,6414
	↙	468	282	909	1035	2010	9705	14409	0,6735
Total		15000	15000	15000	15000	15000	15000		
Accuracy		0,8246	0,7512	0,7022	0,6776	0,6170	0,6470		0,7033

Overall accuracy of the selected classifier for case 1 makes 60830/90000 = 0.6758. Overall accuracy of the selected classifier for case 2 makes 63294/90000 = 0.7033.

As can be seen from the Tables 1 and 2, the monitoring system allows identifying differences in the maneuver parameters with a probability close to 0.7. The correlation of correct (T) classification results for each case was assessed (Fig. 5).

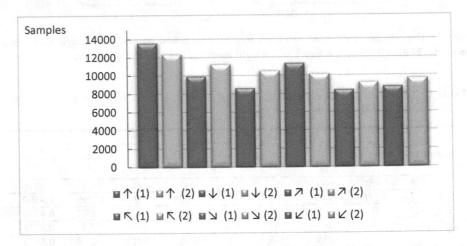

Fig. 5. The correlation of the correct classification results for the cases: (1) – the microphone is located on the unmanned vehicle; (2) the microphone is statically mounted to the right of the experiment area.

5   Conclusion

The use of an external, for example, acoustic channel may be one of the approaches to determining the state of cybersecurity.

The application of the proposed approach to the analysis of the state of mobile objects of unmanned systems is aimed at overcoming the following processes:

- the current state of the computational process is closed from the observer;
- the computational process proceeds in a multi-tasking mode, performing the solution of individual problems of the functioning of the system in pseudo-parallel mode;
- values of physical parameters measured at different moments of operation correlate with energy consumption, computation time, EMP, etc.

The proposed approach makes it possible to monitor the state of an object on the basis of an external independent channel.

Accuracy of determining the cybersecurity state depends directly on the accuracy of the classification of the data processed by the system, and the conducted experiment showed that even taking noise into account using audio recording of the maneuvers, it becomes possible to identify differences with a probability close to 0.7.

References

1. Page, J., Zaslavsky, A., Indrawan, M.: Countering security vulnerabilities using a shared security buddy model schema in mobile agent communities. In: Proceedings of the First International Workshop on Safety and Security in Multi-Agent Systems (SASEMAS 2004), pp. 85–101 (2004)
2. Semenov, V., Lebedev, I., Sukhoparov, M.: Identification of the state of individual elements of cyber-physical systems based on external behavioral characteristics. Appl. Inform. **13**(5/77), 72–83 (2018)
3. Hayashi, Y., Homma, N., Watanabe, T., Price, W., Radasky, W.: Introduction to the special section on electromagnetic information security. Proc. IEEE Trans. Electromagn. Compat. **55**(3), 539–546 (2013)
4. Han, Y., Christoudis, I., Diamantaras, K., Zonouz, S., Petropulu, A.: Side-channel-based code-execution monitoring systems: a survey. IEEE Signal Process. Mag. **36**(2), 22–35 (2019)
5. de Souza Faria, G., Kim, H.: Differential audio analysis: a new side-channel attack on PIN pads. Int. J. Inf. Secur. **18**(1), 73–84 (2019)
6. Gupta, H., Sural, S., Atluri, V., Vaidya, J.: A side-channel attack on smartphones: deciphering key taps using built-in microphones. J. Comput. Secur. **26**(2), 255–281 (2018)
7. Sukhoparov, M., Semenov, V., Lebedev, I.: Monitoring of cybersecurity elements of cyber-physical systems using artificial neural networks. Methods Tech. Means Ensuring Inf. Secur. **27**, 59–60 (2018)
8. Semenov, V., Lebedev, I., Sukhoparov, M.: Approach to classification of the information security state of elements for cyber-physical systems by applying side electromagnetic radiation. Sci. Tech. J. Inf. Technol. Mech. Opt. **18**(1/113), 98–105 (2018). https://doi.org/10.17586/2226-1494-2018-18-1-98-105
9. Semenov, V., Sukhoparov, M., Lebedev, I.: An approach to classification of the information security state of elements of cyber-physical systems using side electromagnetic radiation. In: Galinina, O., Andreev, S., Balandin, S., Koucheryavy, Y. (eds.) NEW2AN/ruSMART 2018. LNCS, vol. 11118, pp. 289–298. Springer, Cham (2018). https://doi.org/10.1007/978-3-030-01168-0_27
10. Al Faruque, M., Chhetri, S., Canedo, A., Wan, J.: Acoustic side-channel attacks on additive manufacturing systems. In: Proceedings of ACM/IEEE 7th International Conference on Cyber-Physical Systems (2016). https://doi.org/10.1109/iccps.2016.7479068
11. Genkin, D., Shamir, A., Tromer, E.: Acoustic cryptanalysis. J. Cryptol. **30**(2), 392–443 (2017)
12. Farrokhmanesh, M., Hamzeh, A.: Music classification as a new approach for malware detection. J. Comput. Virol. Hacking Tech. 1–20 (2018). https://doi.org/10.1007/s11416-018-0321-2
13. Lebedev, I., et al.: The analysis of abnormal behavior of the system local segment on the basis of statistical data obtained from the network infrastructure monitoring. In: Galinina, O., Balandin, S., Koucheryavy, Y. (eds.) NEW2AN/ruSMART 2016. LNCS, vol. 9870, pp. 503–511. Springer, Cham (2016). https://doi.org/10.1007/978-3-319-46301-8_42
14. Marinenkov, E., Viksnin, I., Zhukova, Yu., Usova, M.: Analysis of information interaction security within group of unmanned aerial vehicles. Sci. Tech. J. Inf. Technol. Mech. Opt. **18**(5), 817–825 (2018)
15. Semenov, V., Lebedev, I.: Analysis of the state of cybersecurity of transport systems objects. Regional Informatics (RI-2018). In: Proceedings of the XVI St. Petersburg International Conference "Regional Informatics (RI-2018)", pp. 324–325 (2018)

16. Sridhar, P., Sheikh-Bahaei, S., Xia, S., Jamshidi, Mo.: Multi agent simulation using discrete event and soft-computing methodologies. In: Proceedings of the IEEE International Conference on Systems, Man and Cybernetics, vol. 2, pp. 1711–1716 (2003)
17. Krivtsova, I., et al.: Implementing a broadcast storm attack on a mission-critical wireless sensor network. In: Mamatas, L., Matta, I., Papadimitriou, P., Koucheryavy, Y. (eds.) WWIC 2016. LNCS, vol. 9674, pp. 297–308. Springer, Cham (2016). https://doi.org/10.1007/978-3-319-33936-8_23
18. Han, Y., Etigowni, S., Liu, H., Zonouz, S., Petropulu, A.: Watch me, but don't touch me! Contactless control flow monitoring via electromagnetic emanations. In: Proceedings of the ACM Conference on Computer and Communications Security, pp. 1095–1108 (2017)

Application of Convolutional Neural Network to Organize the Work of Collaborative Robot as a Surgeon Assistant

Shuai Yin and Arkady Yuschenko[✉]

Bauman Moscow State Technical University,
Moscow 105005, Russian Federation
arkadyus@mail.ru

Abstract. Medicine is a perspective area for collaborative robotics. The paper presents the collaborative robot as a surgeon's assistant, accompanying the operation, submitting the necessary tools and performing other auxiliary actions. Such a robot must be mobile, have a manipulator, means of visual communication, an autonomous navigation system in the operating room, and an interactive system for interaction with the surgeon. The last task is considered in the paper. At the voice request of the surgeon, the robot have to find the necessary medical tool on the desktop and transmit it to the surgeon. This operation involves three steps: firstly, at the voice request, the robot must determine which tool is required by the surgeon; on the second step- to find the right tool on the desktop and take it; and on the third – to hand the tool to the surgeon. In the paper the neural networks technology is proposed to solve the recognition problems aroused at two first stages.

Keywords: Dialogue system · Image processing system · Collaborative robotic · Training · Robotic system

1 Introduction

One of the most promising areas of application of collaborative robotics is medicine. Currently, one of the most successful projects here is Da Vinci robotic system, which is actively used for minimally invasive surgical operations in the leading clinics of world, including Russian Federation. Note that here were developed domestic analogues of surgical robots which are not inferior in their characteristics to the system mentioned above [1]. The Da Vinci system, more likely, can be attributed to a robotic remote-control system than to collaborative systems, since the operator directly, albeit remotely, controls the movements of the robot. Along with the robotic remote-control system, collaborative robots can also be used as surgeon's assistant performing the necessary operation in the traditional way.

Note that the application of a robot – surgeon assistant is only one of the tasks of surgery robotic. Such a robot (or several robots for various purposes) can solve other auxiliary tasks in the operating room, including monitoring the patient's condition and the operation of other devices used during the operation. Such a system could facilitate

© Springer Nature Switzerland AG 2019
A. Ronzhin et al. (Eds.): ICR 2019, LNAI 11659, pp. 287–297, 2019.
https://doi.org/10.1007/978-3-030-26118-4_28

the work of the surgeon, relieving him of all auxiliary functions and increasing the accuracy and reliability of their implementation. Through a multi-module interface, including a bilateral dialogue, the collaborative robot has to interact with its user, to correct the errors, and to contact with other people or robots. The robot must also independently determine the coordinates and posture of the medical tool. Robot must work together with the person in the same work area, in conditions of uncertainty of the changing external world and must not harm him.

To solve the interactivity problem and error self-tests problem, a system of object-oriented dialog control of a robot based on the theory of finite state machines using a deep neural network is proposed. The task set by the surgeon is accompanied by a dialogue aimed at clarifying it; during the dialogue, the robot can perform the necessary inspection tasks to determine the feasibility of the task. After the completion of this preliminary stage, the robot operation is performed automatically. To solve the problem of object recognition and orientation, it is necessary to use a parallel convolutional neural network. This network consists of two parallel subnets. One of them recognizes the characteristic features of each tool and determines its position and orientation. The other subnet determines the names of the tools by these attributes. Since the name is known from the surgeon's command, the result can be the desired tool and its position on the desktop. After that, it can be captured by the arm of robot and transferred to the surgeon, whose position relative to the robot is assumed to be known.

By itself, the robot dialogue control procedure has already been considered in a number of papers. Including, in [2] the procedure was realized via fuzzy logic, and in [3] – via theory of finite automata and Petri nets. Possibility of speech dialogue allows adjust both the results of speech recognition of surgeon and corresponding actions of the robot. The main characteristic of the proposed recognition system with double convolutional network, is to combine dialogue and control the actions of the robot. Initially, the network is trained, using the vision system, to recognize basic surgical tools. For planning the movement of the manipulator, it is necessary to compute the position, orientation, and tool grip conditions. A trained neural network should ensure that the pace of performing all necessary actions is close to the rate of performing the same actions by a human assistant, which is important when performing a surgical operation.

To solve the problem of transferring the tool to the surgeon it is necessary not only to have on board a navigation system that determines the robot's own position relative to the operating table, but also a spatial vision system that recognizes the position and orientation in the space of the surgeon's hand. Such systems can be implemented by various technical devices and have already been considered in relation to the control of robots using gestures [4], as well as in the task of exchanging information using the finger "alphabet of the deaf" [5]. To solve the problem of robot safety, we are porting our system to the SUNRISE system of robot KUKA LBR IIWA [6] for using collision detection technology.

Figure 1 show interaction between subsystems and surgeon. The surgeon sends a command to the dialog system by voice. After the dialogue system receives the voice signal, the latter is converted into text by speech recognition system, then it is converted to robot executable instructions based on the parse of text and sent instructions to the robot control system. With the help of visual device, the robot performs actions

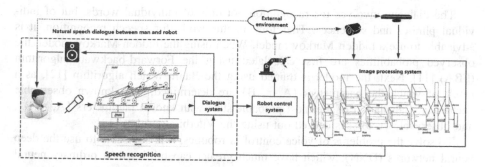

Fig. 1. Collaborative robot – surgeon assistant structure.

according to the instructions. At the same time, the visual device also feeds back the results of task performance to the dialogue system. The dialogue system informs the surgeon of the result by voice, also the surgeon can also observe the working status of the robot through the screen.

2 The Organization of Speech Dialogue Using Neural Networks

Dialogue system <man-machine> can be conditionally divided into two types - without restrictions and with restrictions [7]. The dialogue system without restrictions, possessing large knowledge bases in various fields, theoretically allows the machine to answer humans any question. The dialogue system with restrictions is object-oriented and is designed for a specific application. This chapter proposes the structure of an object-oriented dialogue system for collaborative robot - surgeon assistant.

The dialogue system is a mean of exchanging information between user and robot with natural language. This system allows robots to be controlled by user without any special training. The dialogue system includes several subsystems, including an automatic speech recognition unit, a text analysis unit, a dialogue control unit, answer generation unit and voice synthesis unit [8]. The speech recognition unit converts a voice message into text. The task of text analysis is the correctly interpretation of this text regardless of the form of its expression. The dialogue control block receives information from the robot control system and controls the dialog process in accordance with the dialogue script. The text of the synthesized answers is converted into a voice response in the block "speech synthesis". In this work, we use speech files prepared in advance to replace the speech and answer synthesis.

The preliminary stage of speech recognition is the processing of voice signals which are usually converted to the frequency domain using the MFCC technique [9]. Speech recognition procedures can be divided into isolated word recognition and continuous speech recognition procedures. For isolated word recognition, an acoustic model of Dynamic Time Warping [9] is applied. It is used more often and efficiently without a specific language model. For continuous speech recognition, the hidden Markov model is used, which is usually considered together with the language model [10].

The dialogue involves the recognition not only of individual words, but of individual phrases and sentences. Therefore, in this work, for speech recognition, it is advisable to use a hidden Markov model. When using the hidden Markov model, the observed probabilities are first calculated using the Forward-backward algorithm (FBA) [11]. Next, the model is trained using the Baum-Welch algorithm [12], as a result of which the parameters $\{A, \pi, B\}$ are determined, with known observable vectors v_k. Calculation of the most probable state with known parameters $\{A, \pi, B\}$, and observable vectors, is carried out using the Viterbi algorithm [13].

To solve the problems of voice control in robotics, it is advisable to use the deep neural networks (DNN), which have much greater capabilities than ordinary neural networks, from which they differ in the number of layers. In deep neural networks there are at least 5 hidden layers. However, neural networks cannot directly model voice signals. Therefore, in order to use the ability of neural networks to classify, it is advisable to consider the combined model DNN-HMM (Fig. 2).

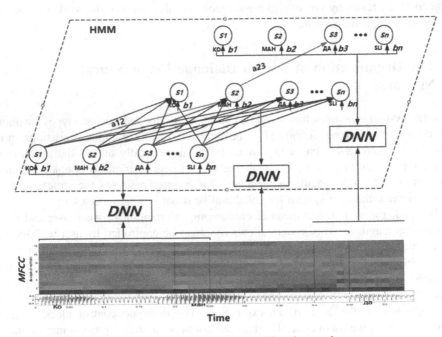

Fig. 2. Model DNN-HMM, word recognition the word «команда».

The DNN-HMM model shown in Fig. 2 consists of deep neural networks (DNN) and hidden Markov model (HMM). Hidden Markov model is used to describe the dynamics of voice signals; deep neural networks calculate probabilities of the observed vectors. The probability of the initial state is assumed to be known. Given the characteristics of voice signals, a priori state probabilities will be obtained at the outputs of neural networks. Training of deep neural network is conducted using the error back-propagation algorithm. In Fig. 2, $a_{12}, a_{23}, \ldots$ – probability of transition between states; $b_1, b_2, b_3, \ldots, b_n$ – observed probabilities; DNN network that is shown in Fig. 2 has 6 hidden layers of 2048 neurons, 440 input and 1024 output signals of the network. Deep neural network calculates probability $P(s|\mathbf{o})$, the observed probability $P(\mathbf{o}|s)$ is determined by the Bayes formula:

$$P(\mathbf{o}|s) = \frac{P(s|\mathbf{o})P(\mathbf{o})}{P(s)}, \tag{1}$$

where – $P(s)$ is the a priori probability of the s state; the value $P(\mathbf{o})$ does not depend on the sequence of words and can be taken equal to 1.

3 Dialog Control Using the State Finite State Machines

Dialogue management directly affects the users experience, the naturalization and intelligence of the dialogue process. The task of dialogue management is to determine the next action of the system, taking into account the previous course of the dialogue. In this case, one of the subjects of the dialogue is a man, and the other is a robot. The dialogue process can be viewed as the exchange of information in which the initiative can belong to both the user and the technical system. In accordance with this, there are three types of dialogue: 1. the system has a dialogue management initiative; 2. the user controls the dialogue and the system responds to his requests; 3. the system realizes overall control over the dialogue process, but at the same time, the user can intervene and change the direction of the dialogue. For example, "Cancel task A, perform task B...". This is the third type of dialogue.

In the paper we use a finite state automata for dialogue management. First, the finite automaton detects whether the speech recognition result conforms to the prescribed text, and if it does not meet, the user is required to supplement it. Then the system analyzes the text according to the speech recognition result and send the motion instruction to the robot, and finally accept the result of the visual device feedback to inform the user the working state of the robot. In this process, an acoustic model (DNN-HMM), a language model (n-gram) [14] and a dictionary are used to recognize several pre-defined object-oriented voice commands. For recognition of complex tools a parallel convolutional neural network is used. To determine the spatial coordinates of the surgeon's hand the depth camera is necessary. For example, to realize such operation as "to put the tool one on the hand A", or "remove the tool".

Figure 3 shows a dialog management based on the theory of finite state automata. The statement "put the tool one in hand" is converted into a sequence of instructions: The arm of robot acquires the tool picture at position A, identifies the tool one and calculates coordinates and posture of tool in the robot coordinate system. The arm of robot grabs the tool one, and moves to position B to obtain the depth figure of the surgeon's hand. The system calculates the space coordinate of the hand relative to the robot which put tool one in the hand of the surgeon.

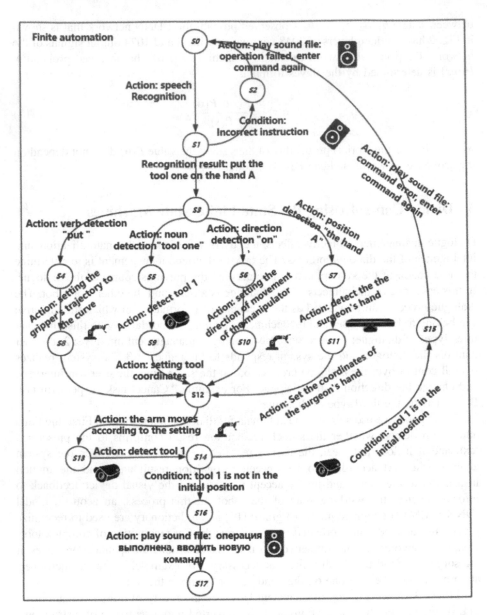

Fig. 3. Finite automaton work flow chart.

4 Object Recognition with a Parallel Convolutional Neural Network

In our experiments the medical tools were placed on the desktop (Fig. 4), green square is used as the working area. In order to grab the required medical tools, it is necessary to identify the required medical tool and calculate his position and posture relative to the robot. To solve these problems, a parallel convolutional neural network was proposed. Compared to R-CNN [15], SVM [16], our network has some advantages. Firstly, now is no need for many training data. Secondly it provides calculation both the position and posture of the tool relative to the robot. Figure 4 shows the network working process.

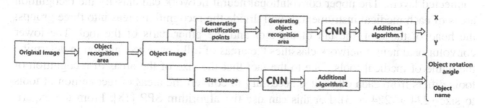

Fig. 4. Complete network work flow chart.

The first part of the network is an image preprocessing, the second part is a parallel convolution network, and the third part is an additional algorithm for calculating coordinates and poses of tools.

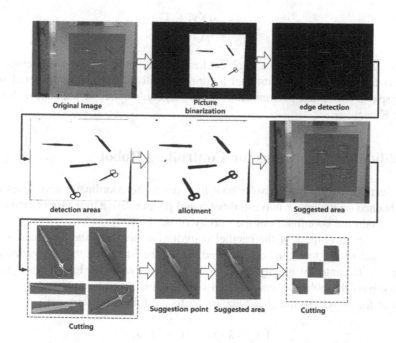

Fig. 5. The process of generating object recognition areas.

In the image preprocessing stage (Fig. 5), we mainly hope to obtain inputs of the upper convolution network and the lower convolution network through image

preprocessing. The inputs of the upper convolutional network are a suggested area
(56 × 56 × 3) centered on the suggested point, where the suggested point is mainly
generated based on the slope of the tool edge. The inputs of the lower convolution
network are the suggested area (224 × 224 × 3) generated based on the image color
binarization. In the work R-CNN, selective search [17] is applied.

The upper and lower network consists of six convolutional layers and four full-
connected layers. The upper convolutional neural network can classify the recognition
areas of each medical instrument. It will divide the recognition areas into three groups:
the head of the tool, the tail of the tool and the other parts of the tool. The lower
convolutional neural network classifies the areas of full image recognition to determine
the name of medical tools. Due to the fact that the size of the areas of recognition of
tools differs from each other, it is necessary to convert the areas of recognition of tools
to size (224 × 224 × 3). For this can use the algorithm SPP [18]. From the experiments, we can get when 3 convolutions and 2000 iterations are selected, the recognition
accuracy is significantly improved.

According to outputs of the network, we can get coordinates of the head and tail
parts of tools. To reduce object recognition errors, we calculate the average of all
coordinates of the head and tail parts. With using the obtained average value, the angle
of rotation of medical tool is calculated according the formula:

$$\delta = \tan^{-1}\left(\frac{\overline{y_1} - \overline{y_2}}{\overline{x_1} - \overline{x_2}}\right), \tag{2}$$

where $\overline{x_1}, \overline{y_1}$ – the average value of object head coordinates; $\overline{x_2}, \overline{y_2}$ – the average value
of object tail coordinates. Additional algorithms will be introduced in detail below.
For the spatial coordinate determination of the surgeon's hand, we plan to use the depth
camera Kinect.

5 Additional Algorithms for Controlling Robot

In this section, we mainly consider how to convert the coordinates and poses of the
tools obtained on the image into coordinates and poses relative to the robot, and discuss
how to obtain the coordinates of the gravity of the tool.

According to outputs of the parallel convolution network, the coordinates of the
head and tail of the tool can be calculated. Since the identified tool is symmetrically
distributed, its center of gravity must also be on its symmetry line. Their symmetry
lines just pass the object's head and tail coordinates. So, we can calculate the coordinates of the weight of the object according to the following formula:

$$\begin{cases} x_c = k \cdot x_h + (1 - k) \cdot x_t \\ y_c = k \cdot y_h + (1 - k) \cdot y_t \end{cases}, \tag{3}$$

where (x_c, y_c) – the coordinate of center of gravity; (x_h, y_h) – the coordinate of head;
(x_t, y_t) – the coordinate of tail. k – coefficient of center of gravity of object.

In our experiments the ordinary camera (its pixels are 3968 * 2976) was placed on the last joint of the robot arm, and the camera captures the tool picture at a fixed position and posture each time. This means that the position and posture of the tool on the picture can be changed to a position and posture relative to the robot with using only one translational change and rotation change. It can be determined by the formula:

$$[x_1 \quad y_1 \quad z_1]^{\mathrm{T}} = \mathrm{T} \cdot [x_0 \quad y_0 \quad z_0]^{\mathrm{T}}, \tag{4}$$

where $\mathrm{T} = \begin{bmatrix} \mathrm{R} & \mathrm{P} \\ 000 & 1 \end{bmatrix}$ – a homogeneous transformation, R – 3×3 rotation matrix; P – 3×1 displacement matrix; $[x_1 \quad y_1 \quad z_1]^{\mathrm{T}}$ – coordinates of objects relative to the camera; $[x_0 \quad y_0 \quad z_0]^{\mathrm{T}}$ – coordinates of objects relative to the manipulator.

Since it is very difficult to measure the amount of rotation and offset during the experiment, in this work we use the opposite process to calculate the amount of rotation and the offset. First, the homogeneous transformation is approximately equal to the linear formula:

$$\begin{cases} x_1 = a_1 \cdot x_2 + b_1 \\ y_1 = a_2 \cdot y_2 + b_2 \end{cases}, \tag{5}$$

where x_1 – coordinates of objects relative to the manipulator along the x axis; x_2 – the coordinate of objects relative to the camera along the x axis; y_1 – coordinates of objects relative to the manipulator along the y axis; y_2 – the coordinate of the objects relative to the camera along the y axis. To determine coefficients a_1, a_2, b_1, b_2, it is necessary to measure two points of objects relative to the camera $(x_1^1 y_1^1), (x_1^2 y_1^2)$ and two points of identical objects relative to the manipulator $(x_2^1 y_2^1), (x_2^2 y_2^2)$. Now we have 4 equations and 4 unknowns change a_1, a_2, b_1, b_2.

6 Experiments

For speech recognition, our work focuses on using the software KALDI to train the DNN-HMM acoustic model, and the training data is from the website Voxforge. For object recognition, training data is primarily produced by hand, with 200 samples for every object and 1200 samples for six objects. Object recognition algorithms are mainly implemented by TENSORFLOW and OPENCV. At present, KUKA robot KR10 six 900 is the main control objects, and a complete system is designed based on the robot control system KRC4 in the PYTHON programming environment. Considering the shortcomings of industrial robot safety, we are porting our system to controller of the collaborative robot KUKA LBR IIWA 14.

Figure 6a shows KUKA robot KRC 10, and Fig. 6b is the object recognition result. In Fig. 6b, the red rectangles are the recognition area. Yellow rectangle – the minimum area of objects. The pink point is the head of the objects. The green point is the tail of the objects. The blue point is another part of the objects. The big blue point is the center of gravity of objects. The working process of the collaborative robot began after the

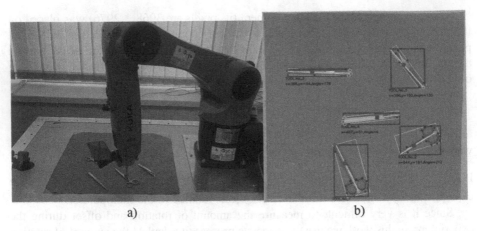

a)   b)

Fig. 6. Experimental study of the collaborative robot - surgeon assistant. (Color figure online)

surgeon voice command: "put the tool one in hand". The robot recognizes the voice and confirms the integrity of the surgeon's voice command with the help of a finite automaton. If the voice command is incorrect, it ask the surgeon to re-enter the voice command. If the voice command is correct, the robot confirms the task enforceability with the help of the visual device and completes the task to feed the result back to the surgeon.

7   Conclusion

The results of the robot work show that our design ideas and algorithms are feasible, and of course, further research is needed to commercialize. The next work mainly considers the safety reliability of the robot and the environmental changes in the actual application.

Acknowledgement. This work is financially supported by RFBR, project № 8-07-01313.

References

1. Bodner, J., et al.: The da Vinci robotic system for general surgical applications: acritical interim appraisal. In: Swiss Med Weekly, pp. 674–679 (2005)
2. Yuschenko, A.S.: Dialog control robots based on fuzzy logic. In: Proceedings of International Scientific and Technical Conference on Extreme Robotics "ER-2012", pp. 29–36 (2012)
3. Yuschenko, A.S., Morozov, D.N., Zhonin, A.A.: Speech control for mobile Robotic systems. In: Proceedings of 4th International Conference on Mechatronic Systems and Materials "MSM-2008", pp. 14–17 (2008)

4. Kanis, J., Ryumin, D., Krňoul, Z.: Improvements in 3D hand pose estimation using synthetic data. In: Ronzhin, A., Rigoll, G., Meshcheryakov, R. (eds.) ICR 2018. LNCS (LNAI), vol. 11097, pp. 105–115. Springer, Cham (2018). https://doi.org/10.1007/978-3-319-99582-3_12
5. Gruber, I., Ryumin, D., Hrúz, M., Karpov, A.: Sign language numeral gestures recognition using convolutional neural network. In: Ronzhin, A., Rigoll, G., Meshcheryakov, R. (eds.) ICR 2018. LNCS (LNAI), vol. 11097, pp. 70–77. Springer, Cham (2018). https://doi.org/10.1007/978-3-319-99582-3_8
6. Kuka Iiwa Robot. https://www.kuka.com/en-de/products/robot-systems/industrial-robots/lbr-iiwa
7. Sergienko, R.: Text Classification for Spoken Dialogue Systems. Institute of Telecommunications and Institute of Artificial Intelligence, Ulm University, pp. 17–58 (2016)
8. Jurafsky, D., Martin, J.H.: Speech and Language Processing: An Introduction to Natural Language Processing, Computational Linguistics, and Speech Recognition, pp. 273–543. Pearson, Upper Saddle River (2014)
9. Mansour, A.H., Salh, G.Z.A., Mohammed, K.A.: Voice recognition using dynamic time warping and mel-frequency cepstral coefficients algorithms. Int. J. Comput. Appl. **116**, 34–41 (2015)
10. Meza-Ruiz, I.V., Riedel, S., Lemon, O.: Spoken language understanding in dialogue systems, using a 2-layer Markov logic network. Improving semantic accuracy. In: Semantics and Pragmatics of Dialogue, Londial (2008)
11. Yu, Z.S., Kobayashi, H.: An efficient forward-backward algorithm for an explicit-duration hidden Markov model. IEEE Signal Process. Lett. **10**, 11–14 (2003)
12. Tu, S.: Derivation of Baum-Welch Algorithm for Hidden Markov Models. https://people.eecs.berkeley.edu/~stephentu/writeups/hmm-baum-welch-derivation.pdf
13. Tao, C.: A generalization of discrete hidden Markov model and of Viterbi algorithm. Department of Computer Science, pp. 1381–1387 (1992)
14. Pauls, A., Klein, D.: Faster and smaller N-gram Language Models. In: Annual Meeting of the Association for Computation Linguistics. Human Language Technologies, pp. 258–267 (2011)
15. Girshick, R., Donahue, J., Darrell, T., Malik, J.: Rich feature hierarchies for accurate object detection and semantic segmentation. In: Computer Vision and Pattern Recognition (CVPR) (2014)
16. Cortes, C., Vapnik, V.: Support vector machine. Mach. Learn. **20**(3), 273–297 (1995)
17. Uijlings, J., Van de Sande, K., Gevers, T., Smeulders, A.: Selective search for object recognition. Int. J. Comput. Vis. (IJCV) **104**, 154–171 (2013)
18. He, K., Zhang, X., Ren, S., Sun, J.: Spatial pyramid pooling in deep convolutional networks for visual recognition. In: Fleet, D., Pajdla, T., Schiele, B., Tuytelaars, T. (eds.) ECCV 2014. LNCS, vol. 8691, pp. 346–361. Springer, Cham (2014). https://doi.org/10.1007/978-3-319-10578-9_23

Parameters of Motion for Multi-UGV Control System Performing Joint Transportation

Valery Gradetsky[1] , Ivan Ermolov[1] , Maxim Knyazkov[1] ,
Eugeny Semenov[1] , Boris Lapin[2] , Sergey Sobolnikov[2] ,
and Artem Sukhanov[1(✉)]

[1] Laboratory of Robotics and Mechatronics, Ishlinsky Institute for Problems
in Mechanics RAS, Prospect Vernadskogo 101-1, 119526 Moscow, Russia
sukhanov-artyom@yandex.ru
[2] Moscow State Technological University STANKIN,
Vadkovskiy per. 3a, 127055 Moscow, Russia

Abstract. The paper considers an algorithm for calculating the motion parameters for a group of mobile robots performing a joint transport task. The motion of this group of mobile robots is considered on a plane surface. Trajectory of motion passes over different zones with various soil properties. Rectilinear motion and motion along the arc of known radius are considered. The algorithm was successfully tested in previously developed special software for debugging and modelling.

Keywords: Group robotics · Joint transportation task ·
Trajectory motion algorithm · Kinematics

1 Introduction

One of the important tasks of group robotics is trajectory planning. A main peculiarity of this problem is the set of restrictions on the motion parameters for each robot in the group intended for performing system formation, as well as the correction of the motion parameters when the group or individual robots move over areas with other coupling properties.

To implement motion of a group of robots with cargo the parameters of the environment, cargo itself, robots, as well as the trajectory should be provided to control system. Determination of soil parameters and compilation of a database of soil types was described in paper [1]. The purpose of this paper is to perform an algorithm for the movement of a group of robots with a given configuration of construction along a given trajectory. This is necessary to calculate the desired speeds and accelerations of robots moving in a group and carrying a massive object. Urgency of this research is explained by relatively low autonomy level of modern unmanned ground vehicles. This includes aspect of spacious autonomy and passability of vehicle over various soils.

A. Ronzhin et al. (Eds.): ICR 2019, LNAI 11659, pp. 298–309, 2019.
https://doi.org/10.1007/978-3-030-26118-4_29

2 Problem Statement

Scientific significance is hidden in technology-based passability study which includes a large number of factors and dependences to be considered. Goal of this research is to develop models, laws and algorithms to control technological autonomous unmanned vehicles' motion. It has to increase unmanned vehicles passability for various soils.

R&D in the areas adjacent to the application was carried out in several directions: simulation and design of vehicles, as well as research of mobile robots, primarily robotic planetary rovers. Among different projects in the automotive industry such works of V. K. Varlamov, for example, [1], which considered in detail the dynamics of vehicle movement should be noted. Here the main forces and torques acting on the vehicle as well as different situations with the moving vehicle are considered.

Detailed work on the study of interaction of "wheel-ground" system was conducted by professor of the former MSIU N. S. Volskaya. It describes the different types of soil and the mechanism of interaction of the car wheel with the ground. Detailed results can be found in paper [2].

Experimental and theoretical research technique for subsystems and the whole system is the most relevant today. With its help experimental materials are generalized. The issues of group control of robots are considered in the works in the SFedU Institute under the guidance of the group of prof. I. A. Kalyaev [3].

Empirical technique for determining the coefficients of the movement resistance of the vehicle allow using fairly simple equations to estimate the effect of the type of chassis on the passability at the given values of the vertical load and the strength properties of the base. The considered methods are used, as a rule, in comparative or experimental studies. However, this approach cannot be used as a technique for predicting the development of structures of running parts of vehicles. This is due to the fact that there is no physical justification of the processes occurring in the contact zone of the mover with the ground, and the number and ranks of the parameters selected for the evaluation of the "mover-ground" subsystem are very conditional [4, 12].

The second branch consists of creating models for study of the laws of ground deformation for obtaining the characteristics of the environment and the research of its mathematical model, the analysis of kinematic and force factors of the impact of the mover on the ground, the experimental study of the developed models of the "mover-ground" on the results of tests of both single movers and vehicle as a whole [8].

With this approach, it is possible to solve scientific and design problems associated with the creation of advanced systems of the vehicle step-by-step, which allows refining and developing a mathematical model describing the "mover-ground" system, based on the results of experiments.

Effective research conducted at scientific research Institute of the Bauman MSTU [11]. At the stage of development of robots, while they moved at relatively low speeds, the issue of interaction with the ground attention was paid, but not enough. However, as soon as the robots developed by Bauman MSTU began to receive a higher level of autonomy and move at high speeds, the question of interaction "mover-ground" has taken much greater importance.

This, in fact, leads to the creation of many experimental techniques for their determination. Therefore, even carefully performed experiments based on different techniques lead to a significant discrepancy in the final results. This makes it difficult to generalize and compare theoretical and experimental data. Therefore, it is necessary to develop a common approach to the evaluation of the criteria characterizing the system "ground-vehicle", and on the basis of this approach to create a computational model of the system.

Many scientists have paid great attention to the study of physical and mechanical characteristics of the soil, especially in terms of assessing the traction and traction properties and cross-country vehicles. Many works evaluating the characteristics of soils with low bearing capacity are published. To compare and explain these characteristics, it is necessary to evaluate them by a single method [13]. Among the foreign works it should be noted [14] and [15, 23], in which the question of self-diagnosis of the soil condition by the robot during the movement is studied.

Issues of interaction "ground-wheel" are considered in [16]. In this work, special emphasis is placed on the wheel chassis with the missing steering wheels, in which the rotation is carried out simultaneously by braking the wheels of one of the robot sides (similar to the method of turning the truck). The influence of soil properties on the movement of robots is discussed, for example, in [17] and [18].

On the problem of group application of robots performing transport tasks, there are studies presented in [19–21]. This paper describes the simultaneous group application of UAVs and ground robots in solving the transport problem. However, the movement of ground robots in this work is not coordinated. There are also some results of studies on the coordinated movement of the object by industrial robots or in industrial environments, but this is not relevant to this work.

3   Motion Parameters

Let's consider a system of robots that perform a joint transport task with the massive object (cargo) in the form of rigid flat body moving in two-dimensional space at known coordinates (see Fig. 1).

That trajectory could be specified by the operator. We will assume that the cargo size significantly exceeds the size of each robot. Each point of the considered body will correspond to a hypothetical robot located at the given local coordinates in the reference to the body. Figure 1 shows the group of several wheeled mobile robotic platforms caring a massive cargo. There are: Master-robot (MR-Master) that plans trajectory and gives tasks to other Slave-robots (MR-Slave).

Each mobile robot has rotary platform that provides one degree of freedom between each robot and the object. That allows turning for each robot to change direction [22].

The trajectory of motion between certain points of the path specified by the operator (see Fig. 2) will be determined as a result of the interpolation task solving for these points. We used Catmull-Rom spline curves with a τ-coefficient to control the "stiffness" of the spline between the given points of interpolation.

We have chosen Catmull-Rom splines due to the fact that this technique makes it easy to obtain a smooth defect graph 1, which is a curve with a continuous first and

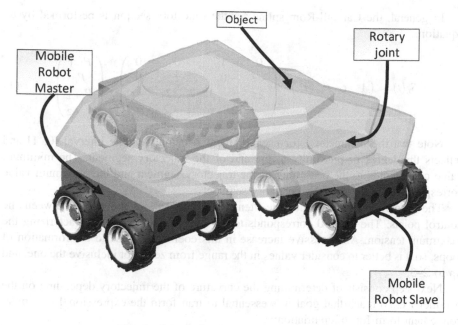

Fig. 1. Schematic view of a group of robots.

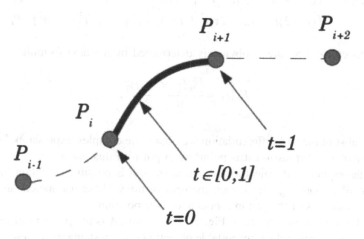

Fig. 2. Trajectory of motion between key-points.

second derivative with the possibility of easy adjustment of the "tension" degree (τ-coefficient) [24]. Unlike NURBS Catmull-Rom spline always passes through its control points. In addition, Catmull-Rom splines may be presented as Bezier splines, which can be efficiently rendered on a computer.

In general, the Catmull-Rom spline for the trajectory section is performed by an equation:

$$S_n(t) = \begin{pmatrix} 1 & t & t^2 & t^3 \end{pmatrix} \cdot \begin{pmatrix} 0 & 1 & 0 & 0 \\ -\tau & 0 & \tau & 0 \\ 2\tau & \tau-3 & 3-2\tau & -\tau \\ -\tau & 2-\tau & \tau-2 & \tau \end{pmatrix} \cdot \begin{pmatrix} P_{i-1} \\ P_i \\ P_{i+1} \\ P_{i+2} \end{pmatrix}. \tag{1}$$

Note that the parameter t for each segment n belongs to the interval $[0; 1]$ and reflects the degree of proximity to the end of the trajectory segment. The minimum value corresponds to the beginning of the trajectory segment and the maximum value corresponds to the end of the trajectory segment.

The τ-coefficient determines the "tension parameter" of the curve between the control points. The value 0 corresponds to the linear interpolation, characterizing the maximum tension. An excessive increase in this coefficient leads to the formation of loops, so it is better to consider values in the range from zero, not inclusive the one, and up to 2–3.

Next step consists of determining the curvature of the trajectory depending on the parameter t. To reach that goal it is essential to transform the expression 1 to a more convenient form for differentiation:

$$\begin{aligned} S_n(t) = &-\left(\tau \cdot t^3 - 2\tau t^2 + \tau t\right) \cdot P_{i-1} + \left((2-\tau)t^3 + (\tau-3)t^2 + 1\right) \cdot P_i \\ &+ \left((\tau-2)t^3 + (3-2\tau)t^2 + \tau \cdot t\right) \cdot P_{i+1} + \left(\tau \cdot t^3 - \tau \cdot t^2\right) \cdot P_{i+2}. \end{aligned} \tag{2}$$

The trajectory curvature is obviously determined by the next formula:

$$K_n(t) = \frac{\left|\dot{S}_n(t) \times \ddot{S}_n(t)\right|}{\left|\dot{S}_n(t)\right|^3}. \tag{3}$$

After substituting and differentiation we obtain the complex expression. Due to the complexity of this expression it is pointless to put it in this paper.

With the equation of trajectory motion known, it is possible to obtain the motion parameters of a robotic group at each moment of time. These parameters are: angular and linear velocities of the group robots and their position.

Consider the scheme shown in Fig. 3, where point A is the position of the robotic group; O is the center of the transportable object; Q is the instantaneous velocity center.

Radii vectors are defined in the coordinate system of the object:

$$\vec{R}_o(t) = \begin{pmatrix} 0 \\ -1/K_n(t) \end{pmatrix}, \tag{4}$$

$$\vec{R}_a(t) = \vec{R}_o(t) + \overrightarrow{OA}. \tag{5}$$

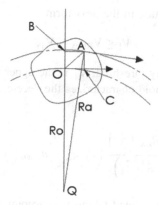

Fig. 3. Object motion.

One can express the linear velocity vector of the robot in the coordinate system of the map:

$$\vec{V}_a(t) = V_{R_{max}}(t) \cdot \frac{\mathbf{M}\left(sign(K_n(t)) \cdot \frac{\pi}{2} + \alpha_o\right) \cdot \vec{R}_a(t)}{R_{max}(t)}. \tag{6}$$

And the value of the angular velocity:

$$\omega_a(t) = sign(K_n(t)) \cdot \frac{|\vec{V}_a(t)|}{|\vec{R}_a(t)|}, \tag{7}$$

where $\mathbf{M}$ is the rotation matrix, $R_{max}(t)$ is the distance from the instantaneous velocity center to the farthest robot, $V_{R_{max}}(t)$ is the speed value of the robot farthest from the instantaneous velocity center (calculated below), AO is the angle value between the horizontal axis of the map and the direction of movement of the transportable object.

The angle AO is defined as the tangent slope to the trajectory:

$$\alpha_o = \arctan\left(\dot{S}_n(t)\right). \tag{8}$$

Now it remains to determine only the position of the robot:

$$\vec{A} = \vec{O} + M(\alpha_o) \cdot \overrightarrow{OA}. \tag{9}$$

Thus, we obtained equations for the calculation of motion parameters, without taking into account the restrictions imposed by the inhomogeneity of the characteristics of the surface on which the group moves. To take into account this heterogeneity, it is necessary to implement additional restrictions on the change in robots' linear velocities.

Velocity of the most remote robot from instantaneous velocity center is obviously also the velocity of the fastest robot, that is, the speed of the other robots in the group will be less. Then it is fair to impose restrictions on this velocity, which in formula 6 is written as $V_{R_{max}}(t)$.

These restrictions are written in the next form:

$$V_\downarrow \leq V_{Rmax} \leq V_\uparrow,$$ (10)

where $V_\downarrow$ is the lower velocity threshold, $V_\uparrow$ is the upper velocity threshold.

The lower velocity threshold characterizes the deceleration limit and is calculated as follows for each robot:

$$V_\downarrow = \max\left(\left\{\frac{R_{max}\left(\vec{A}_k\right)}{R_k\left(\vec{A}_k\right)}\left(V_{prev,k} - a_{\tau.max}\left(\vec{A}_k\right) \cdot \Delta T\right)\right\}\right).$$ (11)

The upper threshold is calculated taking into account the velocity limit under the current turn V_2, before the future turn V_3, as well as the restriction on the tangential acceleration V_1.

$$V_\uparrow = \min(V_1, V_2, V_3),$$ (12)

$$V_1 = \min\left(\left\{\frac{R_{max}\left(\vec{A}_k\right)}{R_k\left(\vec{A}_k\right)}\left(V_{prev,k} + a_{\tau.max}\left(\vec{A}_k\right) \cdot \Delta T\right)\right\}\right),$$ (13)

$$V_2 = \min\left(\left\{\frac{R_{max}\left(\vec{A}_k\right)}{R_k\left(\vec{A}_k\right)}\sqrt{R_k\left(\vec{A}_k\right) \cdot a_{n.max}\left(\vec{A}_k\right)}\right\}\right),$$ (14)

$$V_3 = \min\left(V_{3.prev}, \left\{\frac{R_{max}\left(\vec{A}_{k.future}\right)}{R_k\left(\vec{A}_{k.future}\right)}\sqrt{R_k\left(\vec{A}_{k.future}\right) \cdot a_{n.max}\left(\vec{A}_{k.future}\right)}\right\}\right).$$ (15)

Let's consider the variables included in the expressions 11–15:

$V_{prev,k}$ is velocity value V_{Rmax} at previous time step,

ΔT is the time period with which the model is calculated,

$a_{n.max}$ and $a_{\tau.max}$ are normal and tangential maximum acceleration for the type of surface in the robot position $\vec{A}_k$ (acceleration data obtained in [25, 26]),

R_{max} and R_k are radii from instantaneous velocity center to the fastest robot and to the k-th robot,

$\vec{A}_k$ and $\vec{A}_{k.future}$ are coordinates of the k-th robot at the current time and at the time at which the robot will be able to stop completely, having the current speed, position and taking into account the restriction on tangential acceleration.

The time to a complete stop, for example, can be determined using the next formula:

$$T_{stop} = \frac{V_k}{a_{\tau.max}\left(\vec{A}_k\right)}. \tag{16}$$

Thus, the determination of the parameters of motion along a given trajectory for a group of robots is completed. On the basis of these equations it is possible to synthesize a passive system of group control, which will be of low efficiency in the natural environment. For the synthesis of the control system for real robots it is necessary to have feedbacks. For such system only the position feedback is necessary to solve the movement task for each robot.

The problem of motion of a single robot along the trajectory can be considered classical, and can be solved separately by each robot. The input data are the motion parameters calculated earlier – the positions array of each robot, which is trajectory, as well as the required linear and angular accelerations of robots.

Another additional feedback is the feedback based on the type or characteristics of the motion surface, allowing robots to build a self-standing map of surface types.

The problem of identifying the type of surface, as well as the characteristics of the surface, but is not solved at the moment. Our future work will be devoted to its solution. In the current work, the map will be set by the operator, using the software, which will be considered in the next section.

4   Software

The next step is to check the equations for calculating the motion parameters. Program software was developed for debugging and modeling the system of group control of mobile robots solving the joint transport task (see Fig. 4).

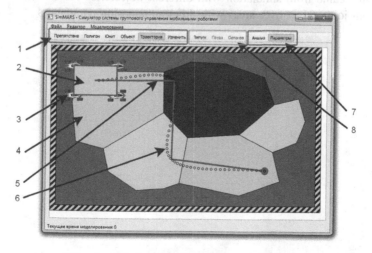

Fig. 4. Software for debugging and modelling.

This software allows using the tools from the panel 1 to divide the surface map into areas of different types 4, set the initial position of the transfer object 2, mobile transport robots 3 and the trajectory of the object 5, which is a set of points on the map. The software allows you to run the model of the group control system (see panel 8) and observe the result, which is the movement of a group of robots with an object along the trajectory 6, generated by the model of the group control system.

Panel 7 allows to open the configuration window of the simulation parameters, including the feature types of surfaces (see Fig. 5).

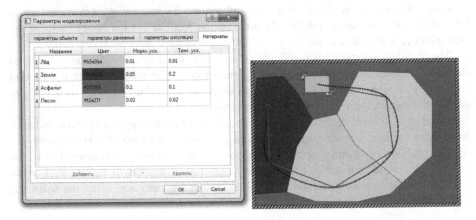

Fig. 5. Terrain settings (values for example) and trajectory planning.

With the help of this software, the group control system created on the basis of the equations derived in Sect. 3 was successfully debugged. Here below some results of simulation are presented.

Figure 6 shows the dependences of linear velocities of mobile robots from time. These results came from simulation with different trajectories for two mobile robots moving with joint object over areas with different adhesion parameters.

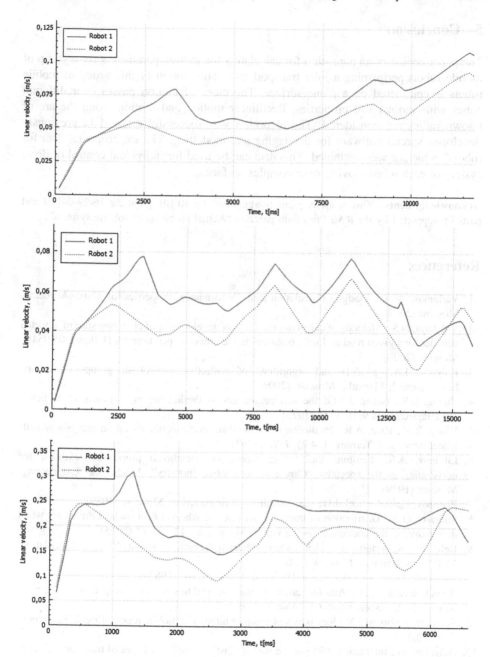

Fig. 6. Results of simulation.

5 Conclusion

The paper considers an algorithm for calculating the motion parameters for a group of mobile robots performing a joint transport task. The motion of this group of mobile robots is considered on a plane surface. Trajectory of motion passes over different zones with various soil properties. Rectilinear motion and motion along the arc of known radius are considered. The algorithm was successfully tested in previously developed special software for debugging and modelling. The experimental data for robots' velocities were obtained. This data can be used for individual control of drive system of each robot moving over complex surface.

Acknowledgements. This work is partially supported by RFBR grant № 16-29-04199 and partially supported by the RAS Presidium program "Actual problems of robotic systems".

References

1. Varlamov, V.K.: Design, Calculation and Performance Properties of Cars. Academy, Moscow (2007)
2. Volskaya, N.S.: Methods of calculation of traction development of characteristics of wheeled vehicles for a given road and soil conditions in the areas of operation: Ph.D. thesis, 05.05.03, Moscow (2008)
3. Kalyaev, I.A.: Models and algorithms of collective control in groups of robots: [monography]. Fizmatlit, Moscow (2009)
4. Cheng, B.S., Baker, J.: Of the soil parameters to Predict the performance of vehicles. J. Terramechanics **9**(2), 1–13 (1973)
5. Wong, Y.Y., Rice, A.R.: Prediction of rigid wheel performance based on analysis of soil-wheel stresses. J. Terramech **4**(2), 7–25 (1967)
6. Litvinov, A.S., Farobin, Ya.E.: Car: theory of operational properties: textbook for universities in the specialty "Cars and automotive industry". Mechanical Engineering, Moscow (1989)
7. Platonov, F.: All-wheel drive cars. Mechanical Engineering, Moscow (1989)
8. Smirnov, G.A.: Distribution of traction forces on the wheels of four-wheel drive cars when they move on the uneven. Izvestiya vuzov. Mech. Eng. **17**, 19–24 (1965)
9. Belousov, S., Priests, D.: Heavy-Duty Wheeled Vehicles. Design. Theory. Calculation. MGTU im. Bauman, Moscow (2006)
10. Tsitovich, N.A.: Soil mechanics. Higher school, Moscow (1983)
11. Rozhdestvensky, L.L.: And forecasting of traction qualities of wheel propellers of planetary Rovers: Ph.D. thesis: 05.05.03, Moscow (1982)
12. Socks, P., Rubtsov, I.V.: Key issues of creating intelligent mobile robots. Eng. J. Sci. Innov. **3**(15) (2013)
13. Belyakov, B.: Interaction with snow cover of elastic propellers of special transport vehicles: Ph.D. thesis: 05.05.03, Moscow (1999)
14. Choopar, T., Zweiri, Yn., Seneviratne, L.D., Althoefer, K.: On-line evaluation of soil properties for Autonomous excavators. In: IEEE International Conference on Robotics and Automation, pp. 121–126 (2003)

15. Hutangkabodee, S., Zweiri, Ya.H., Seneviratne, L.D., Althoefer, K.: Traversability prediction for unmanned ground vehicles based on the identified soil parameters. In: World Congress of IFAC, vol. 16 (2005)
16. Salama, M., Vantsevich, V.V.: Normal and longitudinal dynamics of the tire-terrain and power loss sliding unmanned ground vehicles. In: ASME 2013 International Mechanical Engineering Congress and Exposition, vol. 4 (2013)
17. Hutangkabodee, S., Zweiri, Y.H., Seneviratne, L.D., Altho, K.: Multi-solution problem for track-terrain interaction dynamics and lumped soil parameter identification. In: Corke, P., Sukkariah, S. (eds.) Field and Service Robotics. Springer Tracts in Advanced Robotics, vol. 25, pp. 517–528. Springer, Heidelberg (2006). https://doi.org/10.1007/978-3-540-33453-8_43
18. Salama, M., Vantsevich, V.V.: Stochastic terrain properties-vehicle interaction for agile the dynamics of the groundwater table. In: 7th American Regional Conference of the ISTVS, Tampa, Florida, USA
19. Ego, H., et al.: BLA-SNT cooperation for transportation of facilities in the Industrial area. In: 2015 IEEE International Conference on Industrial Technology (ICIT) (2015)
20. Taghavifar, H., Mardani, A.: Off-road Vehicle Dynamics. Studies in Systems, Decision and Control, vol. 70, 37 p. Springer, Cham (2017). https://doi.org/10.1007/978-3-319-42520-7_2
21. Hüttenrauch, M., Šošic, A., Neumann, G.: Local Communication Protocols for Learning Complex Swarm Behaviors with Deep Reinforcement Learning. Digital Library for Physics and Astronomy, 13 p. (2017)
22. Groumpos, P.P.: Intelligence and fuzzy cognitive maps. Sci. Issues Chall. Oppor. Stud. Inform. Control **27**(3), 247–264 (2018)
23. Shlyakhov, N., Dashevskiy, V., Vatamaniuk, I., Zelezny, M., Ronzhin, A.: Justification of the technical requirements of a fully functional modular robot. In: MATEC Web of Conferences, vol. 113, p. 02008. EDP Sciences (2017)
24. Yuksel, C., Schaefer, S., Keyser, J.: On the parameterization of Catmull-Rom curves. In: SIAM/ACM Joint Conference on Geometric and Physical Modeling (2009). https://doi.org/10.1145/1629255.1629262
25. Gradetsky, V., et al.: Highly passable propulsive device for UGVs on rugged terrain. In: 13th International Scientific-Technical Conference on Electromechanics and Robotics "Zavalishin's Readings", vol. 161, no. 03013. pp, 1–5 (2018)
26. Gradetsky, V.G., Ermolov, L.I., Knyazkov, M.M., Semenov, E., Sukhanov, A.N.: The interaction of forces loaded mobile robot with the ground. Mechatron. Autom. Control. **12**, 819–824 (2017)
27. Gradetsky, V.G., Ermolov, I.L., Knyazkov, M.M., Semenov, E.A., Sobolnikov, S.A., Sukhanov, A.N.: Implementation of a joint transport task by a group of robots. In: Gorodetskiy, A.E., Tarasova, I.L. (eds.) Smart Electromechanical Systems. SSDC, vol. 174, pp. 203–214. Springer, Cham (2019). https://doi.org/10.1007/978-3-319-99759-9_17

Combining Safe Interval Path Planning and Constrained Path Following Control: Preliminary Results

Konstantin Yakovlev[1,2,5] ⓘ, Anton Andreychuk[1,3(✉)] ⓘ, Julia Belinskaya[1,4] ⓘ, and Dmitry Makarov[1,5] ⓘ

[1] Artificial Intelligence Research Institute, Federal Research Center "Computer Science and Control" of Russian Academy of Sciences, Moscow, Russia
{yakovlev,makarov}@isa.ru, andreychuk@mail.com, belinskaya.us@gmail.com
[2] National Research University Higher School of Economics, Moscow, Russia
[3] Peoples' Friendship University of Russia (RUDN University), Moscow, Russia
[4] Bauman Moscow State Technical University, Moscow, Russia
[5] Moscow Institute of Physics and Technology, Dolgoprudny, Russia
http://www.rairi.ru/

Abstract. We study the navigation problem for a robot moving amidst static and dynamic obstacles and rely on a hierarchical approach to solve it. First, the reference trajectory is planned by the safe interval path planning algorithm that is capable of handling any-angle translations and rotations. Second, the path following problem is treated as the constrained control problem and the original flatness-based approach is proposed to generate control. We suggest a few enhancements for the path planning algorithm aimed at finding trajectories that are more likely to be followed by a robot without collisions. Results of the conducted experimental evaluation show that the number of successfully solved navigation instances significantly increases when using the suggested techniques.

Keywords: Path planning · Path finding · AA-SIPP · Differentially flat systems · Point-to-point control problem

1 Introduction

Moving from one location to the other without collisions is one of the fundamental problems in mobile robotics. Two approaches to solve it are common: reactive and deliberative. Methods following reactive approach, e.g. BUG algorithms [9], [10] or ORCA [15], rely on minimum knowledge and on simple "follow-straight-line-to-the-goal" strategy combined with a fixed set of rules to avoid collisions. Deliberative methods utilize knowledge about the environment to plan the collision-free trajectory avoiding detours and/or deadlocks. In this paper we follow the second approach.

When environment is static, it is common to solve a discretized version of the problem, e.g. treat the path finding as a graph search problem. This graph can

© Springer Nature Switzerland AG 2019
A. Ronzhin et al. (Eds.): ICR 2019, LNAI 11659, pp. 310–319, 2019.
https://doi.org/10.1007/978-3-030-26118-4_30

incorporate information about the kinematic/dynamic constraints of the robot. In this case utilizing one of the family of the RRT planners [8] is widespread. The other option is to plan for a path in a simplified graph which models only the environment, e.g. occupancy grid [18] or visibility graph [16], and then use this path as a reference trajectory the robot has to follow [2,11]. In this work we adopt the latter approach.

Presence of dynamic obstacles adds another layer of complexity to path finding as one needs to reason about the time as well. Typically timeline is discretize into the timesteps and robot's moves are restricted to last exactly one timestep. In this setting, conventional heuristic search, e.g. A* [6] or one of its descendants, might be run to solve the problem. To make the search more efficient it is reasonable to group the time steps into the intervals as suggested by the paradigm of Safe Interval Path Planning (SIPP) [12].

In our work we do not restrict all robot's moves to last the same and utilize a modification of SIPP, i.e. AA-SIPP [17], that allows following not only edges that were initially present in the graph but also the newly build ones that represent the shortcuts. Original AA-SIPP as described in [17] is supposed to handle only translation moves, while we wish to handle turn-in-place moves as well. Thus we propose an appropriate extension of the algorithm.

To follow the planned collision-free trajectory flatness-based approach is used. Many models of real vehicles can be defined as a differentially flat [5] system (see, for example, [13], [14]), i.e. the systems which are equivalent to the Brunovsky normal form [7]. At this stage model constraints, e.g. maximum acceleration, are taken into account and desired admissible trajectory and control are defined (see [1,3,4] for details). Then a state feedback control providing asymptotic stabilization around the obtained admissible trajectory is constructed. It is likely that the real trajectory of closed-loop system does not exactly match the planned one, thus collisions might occur. To mitigate this issue we suggest to modify path planning algorithm in such way that it keeps additional safety margin in the time-space while planning for a trajectory. We evaluate the suggested approach empirically and show that it can definitely contribute to finding trajectories that have higher chances to be followed without collisions.

2   Problem Statement

We study the problem of navigating the wheeled robot in 2D in the presence of static and dynamic obstacles. Robot's workspace is a bounded rectangle comprised of the free space and the obstacles: $W = W_{free} \cup W_{obst}, W_{obst} = W \backslash W_{free}$. Workspace is tessellated to the regular square grid, composed of $W \times H$ cells. The cell of the grid is blocked if its interior contains at least one point from W_{obst}, otherwise the cell is un-blocked. Robot is modelled as an open disk of radius $r = 0.5l$, where l is the size of the grid cell. Valid locations for the robot are the centers of the un-blocked cells. Robot's state is a tuple $[x, y, \theta]$, where x, y are the coordinates in meters and $\theta \in [0, 2\pi]$ in rads. The union of all valid stated is denoted as C_{free} Fig. 1.

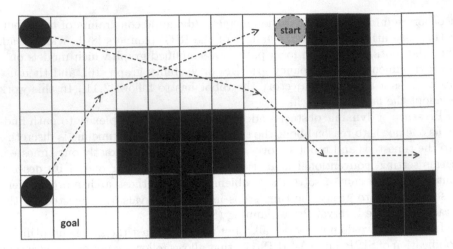

Fig. 1. An example of the problem instance. Robot and dynamic obstacles are modelled as open disks. Environment is tessellated into the grid. Black cells represent static obstacles, black circles - dynamic obstacles with known trajectories marked by dashed lines. Grey circle is a robot and its task is to find a trajectory from start location to the goal one avoiding static and dynamic obstacles.

Robot's action space is: wait in place, rotate in place, translate from one un-blocked cell to the other. Trajectory of a robot is a sequence of such actions. Formally the trajectory is a mapping

$$tr_0 : [0, \infty) \to C_{free}. \tag{1}$$

We suppose that each action composing the trajectory ends with a full stop. Thus one can state that:

$$\dot{tr}_0(t_0) = 0, \quad \dot{tr}_0(t_f) = 0, \tag{2}$$

where t_0 and t_f are the start and finish times of an action.

Besides a robot n dynamic obstacles are navigating the same configuration space. Thus, n mappings defining their trajectories are also given, $tr_i : [0, \infty) \to C_{free}$, $i = 1, \ldots, n$. We assume that the obstacles do not appear/disappear, i.e. at time $t = 0$ they hold their initial positions and after finishing their moves they stay in C_{free}. Without loss of generality we assume that the obstacles are translating-and-rotating open disks of radii r and move in the same way as the robot, i.e. initially each dynamic obstacle is at some free grid cell and when translating it finishes its move at the center of another grid cell as well.

From the path planning perspective the problem is formulated as follows. Given a start and a goal positions, $s, g \in C_{free}$, find a trajectory, $tr_0 : [0, \infty) \to C_{free}$, such that ($i$) it is collision free w.r.t to static and dynamic obstacles, i.e. at each moment of time robot is at least r units away from the closest static obstacle(s) and at least $2r$ units away from the closest dynamic obstacle(s);

(*ii*) it starts and finishes appropriately, i.e. $tr_0(0) = s$, and $\exists T_0 : tr_0(t) = g, \forall t \geq T_0$. For planning purposes we assume that robot accelerates/decelerates instantaneously, i.e. each segment of tr_0 defines a uniform linear or angular motion.

After tr_0 is constructed by a planner we need to solve a path following problem, i.e. construct a control that will follow the prescribed trajectory. To do so we suppose that a robot model is differentially flat, i.e. it is equivalent to the Brunovsky normal form, given as follows

$$\ddot{x} = u(x, t), \quad x(0) = x^0, \tag{3}$$

where $\ddot{x} = d^2x/dt^2$ denotes the second time derivative, $x = [x, y, \theta] \in \mathbb{R}^3$ is a state vector, x, y are the spatial coordinates, θ is the yaw angle, x^0 is an initial state, $u \in \mathbb{R}^3$ is a control that has to be determined. The model has constraints on maximum linear velocity and acceleration given as follows

$$||v(t)|| = ||\dot{x}_{sp}(t)|| \leq v_{max} > 0, ||a(t)|| = ||\ddot{x}_{sp}(t)|| \leq a_{max} > 0, \quad \forall t \geq 0, \tag{4}$$

where $x_{sp}(t) = [x, y] \in \mathbb{R}^2$ is a spatial coordinates vector. We use a second order of Brunovsky normal form to ensure controllability on acceleration. This type of model is rather common for mechanical systems. We also suppose that a system initial state is defined as $x^0 = tr_0(0)$.

Although it was assumed during the planning that vehicle accelerates and decelerates instantaneously, this is impossible due to the constraints (4). Therefore, the prescribed trajectory tr_0 is refined taking into account these constraints. To make the refined trajectory $x^*(t) = [x^*(t), y^*(t), \theta^*(t)]$ close to the original one, we assume that the spatial movement on each segment of $x^*(t)$ occurs in three stages: a highest possible acceleration to required velocity, a uniform motion with constant speed and a highest possible deceleration to a full stop.

Thus, the problem of path following control is formulated as follows. We need to find an admissible control $u(x, t)$ providing asymptotic stability of the vehicle model (3) around $x^*(t)$ under constraints (4).

3   Method

3.1   Path Planning

We plan collision-free trajectories with the any-angle safe interval path planner enhanced to handle rotate-in-place actions. We dub planner AAt-SIPP.

AAt-SIPP relies on heuristic search and its search space consists of states (nodes), s, which are identified by tuples $s = [cfg, interval]$, where $cfg = (\mathbf{pos}, \theta)$ accounts for robot's position and heading, $interval$ - is the contiguous period of time for a configuration, during which there is no collision and it is in collision one time point prior and one time point after the period. Additional data is associated with each state: $g(s), h(s), parent(s)$. $g(s)$ is the earliest possible arrival time the configuration can be reached via $parent(s)$, $h(s)$ is the consistent heuristic estimate of time needed to reach the goal-state from s.

Algorithm 1. AA-SIPP with turns

---

1 $g(s_{start}) = 0$; $OPEN = \varnothing$;
2 insert s_{start} into $OPEN$ with $f(s_{start}) = h(s_{start})$;
3 **while** s_{goal} is not expanded **do**
4 $\quad$ $s :=$ state with the smallest f-value in $OPEN$;
5 $\quad$ remove s from $OPEN$;
6 $\quad$ **for** each cfg in $NEIGHBORS(s.cfg)$ **do**
7 $\quad\quad$ $successors := \text{getSuccessors}(cfg, s)$;
8 $\quad\quad$ $cfg' := cfg$ reachable from $parent(s)$;
9 $\quad\quad$ **if** cfg' exists **then**
10 $\quad\quad\quad$ $successors = successors \cup \text{getSuccessors}(cfg', parent(s))$;
11 $\quad\quad$ **for** each state s' in $successors$ **do**
12 $\quad\quad\quad$ add_to_OPEN := true;
13 $\quad\quad\quad$ **for** each visited state s'' such that $s''.cfg.\mathbf{pos} = s'.cfg.\mathbf{pos}$ and $s''.interval = s'.interval$ **do**
14 $\quad\quad\quad\quad$ **if** $g(s') \geq g(s'') + dur_{rot}(s', s'')$ **then**
15 $\quad\quad\quad\quad\quad$ add_to_OPEN := false;
16 $\quad\quad\quad\quad$ **else if** $g(s'') > g(s') + dur_{rot}(s', s'')$ and $s'' \in OPEN$ **then**
17 $\quad\quad\quad\quad\quad$ remove s'' from $OPEN$;
18 $\quad\quad\quad$ **if** add_to_OPEN = true **then**
19 $\quad\quad\quad\quad$ $f(s') := g(s') + h(s')$;
20 $\quad\quad\quad\quad$ insert s' into $OPEN$;

On each step AAt-SIPP chooses the node with the lowest $g(s) + h(s)$ value, i.e. f-value, to expand. Expansion involves successors generation and updating the set of nodes constituting the fringe of the search-space – $OPEN$. The algorithm stops either when $OPEN$ is exhausted or when the goal-state is selected for expansion. In the latter case feasible trajectory is reconstructed using backpointers ($parent(s)$).

Pseudocode of AAt-SIPP is shown in Algorithm 1. In case one wants to implement AA-SIPP [17] then the additional terms in lines 14 and 16, accounting for the duration of rotate actions, should be omitted. If lines 8–10 are omitted as well one ends up with the original SIPP algorithm [12].

To efficiently handling rotate actions we modified the OPEN update routine (lines 11–20) to take the durations of rotation actions into account (corresponding code portions are highlighted in blue).

To increase the chance of not colliding with dynamic obstacles when following the constructed path we suggest to add additional safety margins to safe intervals when planning, i.e. when generating the successors. To do so we consider the robot and a dynamic obstacles to be in collision not when the distances between them is less than $2r$, but rather when is less than $2r + \delta$, where δ is the user specified parameter.

3.2   Path Following

We consider a series of consecutive constrained point-to-point control problems to build a control law that ensures that the system trajectory will asymptotically converges to each path segment of $tr_0(t)$. The point-to-point control problem is the problem of finding a control u transfer a vehicle mathematical model from a given initial state x_0 to a given final state x_f during a fixed time interval $T = t_f - t_0$, where t_0 and t_f are, accordingly, a start and a finish times of a path segment. Thus, for each segment we have

$$x(t_f) = tr_0(t_f), \quad \dot{x}(t_0) = 0, \quad \dot{x}(t_f) = 0. \tag{5}$$

The initial state x_0 is defined as an actual state of a robot at time t_0 (it may deviate from the planned state).

Due to the flatness of (3) we consider the movement along x and y coordinates separately and solve each of the constrained point-to-point problems in two stages.

1. We build reference (desired) trajectories $[x^*(t), y^*(t), \theta^*(t)$ for $x(t), y(t)$ and $\theta(t)$ accordingly so that the boundary conditions (5) at each path segment and the velocity and acceleration constraints (4) are met. The motion law of spatial coordinates consists of three phases: acceleration to the required velocity, uniform motion with constant speed and deceleration to a full stop. The motion law for the θ coordinate is defined as an unconstrained polynomial time-dependence.

2. We build the control laws in the form of state feedback, that stabilizes the state of the system around the desired trajectories $x^*(t), y^*(t), \theta^*(t)$.

Let's consider each of these stages.

We suppose we have a point-to-point problem in the form of (5) for the x and y coordinates and we have constraints (4). We compute components of acceleration constraint along the x and y coordinates

$$a_{\max,x} = a_{\max} \cos\theta, \quad a_{\max,y} = a_{\max} \sin\theta. \tag{6}$$

We solve each point-to-point problem similarly, therefore we consider this problem for x coordinate only. Let's suppose that $x_0 \neq x_f$. If this condition

$$D_x = (t_f - t_0)^2 a_{\max,x}^2 - 4(x_f - x_0)a_{\max,x} \geq 0 \tag{7}$$

is met, we compute the velocity of the uniform linear motion as

$$v_x = \begin{cases} \frac{1}{2}\big((t_f - t_0)a_{\max,x} - \sqrt{D_x}\big), & \text{if } x_f > x_0, \\ \frac{1}{2}\big((t_f - t_0)a_{\max,x} + \sqrt{D_x}\big), & \text{if } x_f < x_0. \end{cases} \tag{8}$$

If the condition (7) fails to satisfy, we set $v_x = v_{\max,x}$.

The motion law $x_r(t) \in \mathbb{R}$ during the acceleration we find in the space of second-order polynomials such that

$$x_r(t_0) = x_0, \quad \dot{x}_r(t_0) = 0, \quad \dot{x}_r(t_0 + t_r) = v_x, \tag{9}$$

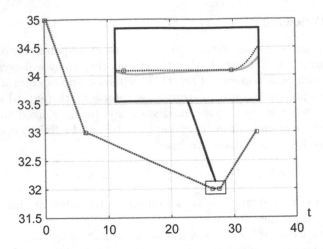

Fig. 2. An example of reference trajectory $x^*(t)$ (doted curve) and real trajectory $x(t)$ (solid wide curve); squares denote boundaries of path segments.

where $t_r = v_x/a_{\max,x}$ is the time required for the acceleration or deceleration. We define the uniform linear motion law as the first-order polynomial $x_s(t) = v_x(t - t_0 - t_r) + x_r(t_0 + t_r)$. The motion law $x_r(t)$ during the deceleration we find in the space of third-order polynomials such that

$$x_d(t_f - t_r) = x_s(t_f - t_r), \quad \dot{x}_d(t_f - t_r) = v_x, \quad x_d(t_f) = x_f, \quad \dot{x}_d(t_f) = 0. \quad (10)$$

Finally, we have the motion law as follows

$$x^*(t) = \begin{cases} x_r(t), & \text{if } t \in [t_0, t_0 + t_r], \\ x_s(t), & \text{if } t \in (t_0 + t_r, t_f - t_r), \\ x_d(t), & \text{if } t \in [t_f - t_r, t_f] \end{cases} \quad (11)$$

If $x_f = x_0$, we set $x^*(t) \equiv x_0$. We chose the control law u_x as the state feedback

$$u_x(x,t) = (\lambda_1 + \lambda_2)\big(\dot{x}(t) - \dot{x}^*(t)\big) - \lambda_1\lambda_2\big(x(t) - x^*(t)\big), \quad (12)$$

where λ_1, λ_2 are the roots of the characteristic equation for a differential equation for $e = x(t) - x^*(t)$. To ensure the asymptotic stability of a differential equation for e, the roots of the characteristic equation must be in the left half-plane of the complex plane. An example of $x(t)$ and $x^*(t)$ trajectories is shown in the Fig. 2.

To build the control law for the rotation we find the third-order polynomial $\theta^*(t)$ such that

$$\theta^*(t_0) = \theta_0, \quad \dot{\theta}^*(t_0) = 0, \quad \theta^*(t_f) = \theta_f, \quad \dot{\theta}^*(t_f) = 0. \quad (13)$$

and compute the control law, similar to (12). The order of polynomial is 1 less than the number of initial and final conditions.

4   Empirical Evaluation

Experimental evaluation was conducted in simulation on a 46×70 grid representing warehouse-like environment. The size of each cell was $1\,m^2$ and the size of the robot and the dynamic obstacles was 0.5. Translation speed was 1 m/s and rotation speed was 180 degrees per second. 128 dynamic obstacles were moving on a grid. 100 different path finding instances were generated randomly.

For the path-following algorithm it's required to set such parameters as the maximum velocity v_{max}, maximum acceleration a_{max} and the values of roots of the characteristic equation λ_1, λ_2. The value of v_{max} was set to $1\,m/s$ as the same value was used for the path-planning algorithm. The values of λ_1, λ_2 were chosen empirically and were set to -4 and -5 respectively. Three different values for the acceleration rate were used: a_{max}: $5\,m/s^2$, $8\,m/s^2$ and $15\,m/s^2$.

To evaluate the accuracy of the trajectory execution the root-mean-squared-error (RMSE) was computed. We computed RMSE w.r.t to the planned trajectory, as well as to the reference trajectory at the first stage of trajectory following. We have also counted the number of collisions with dynamic obstacles. The results are presented in Table 1.

Success rate in Table 1 shows the number of tasks that were completed without any collisions. As one can see in case of using the lowest acceleration speed the success rate is only 57%. $RMSE_1$ refers to the error between the planned trajectory and the executed one. $RMSE_2$ shows the error between the reference and the executed trajectory. $RMSE_1$ and $RMSE_2$ differ significantly when a_{max} is low, while in case when $a_{max} = 15$ the values of $RMSE$ are much closer. This can be explained by the fact the maximum acceleration rate mostly affects the second step, when we get reference trajectories that satisfy the given boundaries of accelerations. In general one can see that executing the trajectory quite often leads to collisions. Increasing the acceleration contributes to decreasing the chance of collision, but they still occur in 27% of cases.

To reduce the number of collisions we have used the method of inflating of collision intervals, that allows to plan trajectories with greater safety. The value of this parameter determines the additional distance that must be between the robot and the dynamic obstacle so that the algorithm considers that there is no conflict between them. There were chosen four values for the evaluation – 0.05, 0.1, 0.2 and 0.5 m.

The obtained results are presented in Table 2. The values of $RMSE$ measures are not presented in this table as they all have the same trends and are almost equal to the ones presented in Table 1.

As one can see, inflating collision intervals leads to notable increase of success rate. In case of using the highest value of a_{max} even the smallest inflating factor allows to increase the success rate up to 86%. The best value is inflate $= 0.2$, as higher values, i.e. 0.5, do not seem to give any positive effect. The hypothesis, why the further increasing of value of inflating parameter results to slightly worse results, is that it helps to eliminate the collisions only with dynamic obstacles, that intersect the agent's trajectory (w.r.t to the radii). As a result, the algorithm plans the trajectory in such a way, that it passes further from possibly colliding dynamic obstacles, but closer to the other ones, that were not taken into account.

Table 1. Accuracy of the resultant trajectories.

Acceleration	Success rate	$RMSE_1$	$RMSE_2$
5 ms	57%	0.06980	0.02156
8 ms	69%	0.04705	0.01997
15 ms	73%	0.03077	0.01878

Table 2. Inflating collision intervals vs success rate.

	inflate = 0.05		inflate = 0.1		inflate = 0.2		inflate = 0.5	
Acceleration (a_{max})	Success rate	Trajectory cost	Success rate	Trajectory cost	Success rate	Trajectory cost	Success rate	Trajectory cost
5 ms	72%	100.3%	82%	100.96%	86%	101.45%	84%	103.7%
8 ms	82%	100.3%	86%	100.96%	87%	101.45%	85%	103.7%
15 ms	86%	100.3%	86%	100.96%	87%	101.45%	85%	103.7%

The trajectory cost columns were normalized by the cost of initially planned trajectories without any inflating. As one can see in terms of trajectory cost the suggested method has a minor negative effect. There is no difference between different values of acceleration as they all performed the same trajectories, planned at the first step.

Overall, the conducted experimental evaluation has shown that suggest path-following method can produce trajectories that are very similar to the ones, obtained by the path-planning algorithm AAt-SIPP. However, in case of using low values of acceleration speed they are not collision-free in almost half of the cases in the tested scenario. To eliminate collisions we used the method of inflating of collisions intervals, that allows to increase the success rate up to 87% while the increase of the solution cost, i.e. time spent for the trajectory following, is almost negligible.

5   Conclusion and Future Work

In this work we combined safe interval path planning and flatness-based constrained path following aimed at safe navigation of the differential drive robot in the environment with both static and dynamic obstacles. We have shown how to increase the chance of accomplishing the mission by a slight modification of the path planner. We have used the model flatness, polynomial approximation approach and pole placement technique to construct admissible control. Appealing direction of future research is developing of the alternatives enhancements for the path planning algorithm, e.g. taking acceleration into account, and evaluating the proposed algorithmic framework on real robots. We are also planning to apply flatness-based approach for real-life vehicle models and to develop our approach to discrete-time systems.

Acknowledgments. This work was partially supported by RFBR Grant no. 18-37-20032 and by the "RUDN University Program 5-100".

References

1. Belinskaya, Y.S., Chetverikov, V.N.: Control of four-rotor helicopter. Sci. Educ. (BMSTU. Electr. J.) **5**, 157–171 (2012). (in Russian)
2. Bokovoy, A.V., Fomin, M.B., Yakovlev, K.S.: Implementation of the pathfinding system for autonomous navigation of mobile ground robot. In: CEUR, vol. 2236, pp. 72–78. http://ceur-ws.org/Vol-2236/paper-09-009.pdf
3. Chetverikov, V.N.: Flatness of dynamically linearizable systems. Differ. Equ. **40**(12), 1747–1756 (2004)
4. Chetverikov, V.N.: Controllability of flat systems. Differ. Equ. **43**(11), 1558–1568 (2007)
5. Fliess, M., Levine, J., Martin, P., Rouchon, P.: Flatness and defect of nonlinear systems: introductory theory and examples. Int. J. Control **61**(6), 1327–1361 (1995)
6. Hart, P.E., Nilsson, N.J., Raphael, B.: A formal basis for the heuristic determination of minimum cost paths. IEEE Trans. Sys. Sci. Cybern. **4**(2), 100–107 (1968)
7. Isidori, A.: Nonlinear Control Systems. Springer, Berlin (1995). https://doi.org/10.1007/978-1-84628-615-5
8. LaValle, S.M., Kuffner Jr., J.J.: Randomized kinodynamic planning. Int. J. Robot. Res. **20**(5), 378–400 (2001)
9. Magid, E., Rivlin, E.: Cautiousbug: a competitive algorithm for sensory-based robot navigation. In: 2004 IEEE/RSJ International Conference on Intelligent Robots and Systems (IROS 2004), vol. 3, pp. 2757–2762 (2004)
10. Ng, J., Bräunl, T.: Performance comparison of bug navigation algorithms. J. Intell. Rob. Syst. **50**(1), 73–84 (2007)
11. Nieuwenhuisen, M., Behnke, S.: Local multiresolution trajectory optimization for micro aerial vehicles employing continuous curvature transitions. In: Proceedings of the 2016 IEEE/RSJ International Conference on Intelligent Robots and Systems (IROS-2016), pp. 3219–3224. IEEE (2016)
12. Phillips, M., Likhachev, M.: SIPP: safe interval path planning for dynamic environments. In: Proceedings of the 2011 IEEE International Conference on Robotics and Automation (ICRA-2011), pp. 5628–5635 (2011)
13. Sahoo, S.R., Chiddarwar, S.S.: Mobile robot control using bond graph and flatness based approach. Int. Conf. Robot. Smart Manuf. (RoSMa2018) **133**, 213–221 (2018)
14. Sira-Ramirez, H., Agrawal, S.K.: Differentially Flat Systems. Marcel Dekker, New York (2004)
15. van den Berg, J., Guy, S.J., Lin, M., Manocha, D.: Reciprocal n-body collision avoidance. In: Pradalier, C., Siegwart, R., Hirzinger, G. (eds.) Robotics Research. STAR, vol. 70, pp. 3–19. Springer, Heidelberg (2011). https://doi.org/10.1007/978-3-642-19457-3_1
16. Wooden, D.T.: Graph-based path planning for mobile robots. Ph.D. thesis, Georgia Institute of Technology (2006)
17. Yakovlev, K., Andreychuk, A.: Any-angle pathfinding for multiple agents based on SIPP algorithm. In: Proceedings of the 27th International Conference on Automated Planning and Scheduling (ICAPS-2017), pp. 586–593 (2017)
18. Yap, P.: Grid-based path-finding. In: Proceedings of the 15th Conference of the Canadian Society for Computational Studies of Intelligence, pp. 44–55 (2002)

Emergency-Response Locomotion of Hexapod Robot with Heuristic Reinforcement Learning Using Q-Learning

Ming-Chieh Yang[1], Hooman Samani[1(✉)], and Kening Zhu[2]

[1] Department of Electrical Engineering, National Taipei University,
New Taipei City, Taiwan
hooman@mail.ntpu.edu.tw
[2] School of Creative Media, City University of Hong Kong,
Kowloon Tong, Hong Kong

Abstract. The locomotion of legged robot is often controlled by predefined gaits, and this approach works well when all joints and motors are operating normally. However, walking legged robots usually have high risk of being damaged during operation, causing the breakdown of the robotic joints. In this paper, we introduce a reinforcement learning based approach for the legged robot to generate real-time locomotion response to the emergence of locomotion breakdown. Our approach detects the functionality of the available joints, substitutes the pre-defined gaits with proper gait function accordingly, and upgrades the gait-generation function by Q-Learning for the proper locomotion.

Keywords: Reinforcement learning · Q-Learning · Hexapod robot · Emergency response

1 Introduction

The common approach for controlling the autonomous legged robot locomotion by law-based adaptation mechanism often requires the arrangement of the legs to be symmetric as the structure of a standard robotics usually inspired by the nature. During operation, the legged robot has a high risk of being damaged by environmental hazards which may cause breakdown of the robot, further influencing the locomotion and pausing the mission. In this situation, the robot inspector often needs to retrieve the robot to repair or abandon the robot which may cause human getting involved and entering a high risk environment [10].

Taking the six-legs robot as the example, with disabled motors and joints, the robot can be considered as a new structure with fewer number of legs (e.g., 2-, 3-, 4-, and 5-legs). For the structures of two and four legs, they are symmetry, and commonly exist. Therefore, their gaits can be simulated using dynamic analysis and kinematic analysis for the disabled robot. In this paper, we have investigated various cases of legs and joints. We introduce a reinforcement-learning-based approach [8] for the legged robot to generate real-time locomotion response to the emergence of breakdown. The algorithm first detects the available movement-controlling joints by rotating every joint

A. Ronzhin et al. (Eds.): ICR 2019, LNAI 11659, pp. 320–329, 2019.
https://doi.org/10.1007/978-3-030-26118-4_31

individually, and substitutes the pre-defined gait function by our designed function for emergency locomotion response.

To achieve a robust result, we trained the robot gait by the Q-learning method [2], a model-free method based on the reinforcement-learning technique. After training, we stored all the positive Q-Tables for applying all possible states and actions to adapt the new configuration and environmental friction. After starting robot locomotion, the robot will start an instant Q-Learning to adapt the environment and confirm if current gait is suitable or not. The training environment is all level and stable, using smooth plane to find all stable and effective gait, the nature environment like wooden or concrete ground has a higher friction than the training environment, which helps to increase velocity for robot locomotion.

Emergency response is a way for robot to have a self-repair capability. During the operation, the Q-Learning algorithm will optimize the gait, if the Q-Learning keep retrieving negative reward without any random actions, the emergence response will be called to find all available legs and replace current gait with corresponding legs situation gait. After find out proper gait, adjust the gait by reinforcement learning according to the environment, like different friction or obliquity [11].

2 Method

2.1 Notations

The simulated hexapod robot, using V-Rep software, is presented in Fig. 1 where 6 legs and 3 joints for leg-1 is labeled accordingly. The rotation for joint 1 and 2 is upward and downward, rotation for joint 3 is leftward and rightward. All six legs are labeled from 1 to 6. With the label rules, every joint can be represented as Joint-X, Y where X is the label for the leg and Y is the label for the joint. Same as the rotation (θ) for each joint θ-x,y.

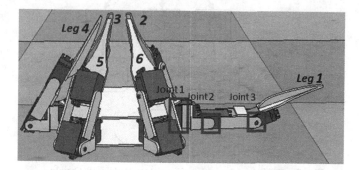

Fig. 1. Three joints for each leg of the hexapod robot, Total 6 legs with 3 joints each.

Rotation for each joint is coded with θ-x,y which refers to the angular change of each joint. For instance, when joint 1, 3 is parallel with robot body, joint 1, 3 is parallel with previous bracket, set $\theta = 0°$. Initial state for every legs and mode is set to $\theta_1 = 0°$,

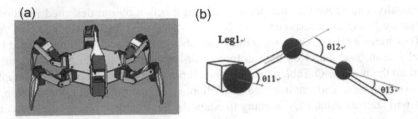

Fig. 2. (a) Initial State for 4 legs mode. (b). Definition of rotational degree for leg 1(θ).

$\theta_2 = -40°$ and $\theta_3 = 120°$. Figure 2a illustrates an instance when only 4 legs are used for locomotion (4 leg mode) and Fig. 2b presents θ for leg 1 as an example.

2.2   Q-Learning for Gait Training

Q-Learning, a model-free reinforcement learning technique [1], achieves its control motivation by interacting with the environment and maximizing the reward, (Fig. 3). S_t is the state of the agent. For this paper, state is the rotation of the θ. $S_t = [\theta_{11}, \theta_{12}, \theta_{13}, \theta_{21}, \theta_{22}, \theta_{23}.....\theta_{61}, \theta_{62}, \theta_{63}]$. Every S_t has several possible actions, **a**, and a Q-Value to present the return reward for each **a**. S_t will select an action base on ε, greedy policy, with random or the highest Q-Value. And S_t transfers to S_{t+1} getting a reward based on environment feedback, using the newest reward to update the Q-value for S_t-a_t.

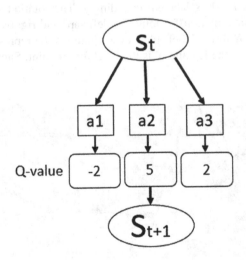

Fig. 3. State transfer and action select with max Q-value.

Table 1. The process of normal Q-Learning.

Initialize Q$_t$(s, a) arbitrarily.
Repeat (for each episode):
  Initialize s randomly.
  Repeat (for each step):
  Select an action.
  Randomly or by max Q-Value
  Execute the action a, observe r(s, a), s$_{t+1}$.
  Update the values of Q(s, a) according to equation 1.
    s→s$_{t+1}$
Until s is terminal.
Until some stopping criterion criteria is reached.

The normal process of Q-Learning [3] is mentioned in Table 1 and the update function for the Q-Value can be calculated by:

$$Q(s_t, a_t) \leftarrow Q(s_t, a_t) + (1 - \alpha) \cdot (r_t + \gamma \cdot \max Q(s_{t+1}, a_t) - Q(s_t, a_t)). \qquad (1)$$

When the normal Q-Learning method reached S (state) terminal, it will initialize S randomly to start a new learning process. But Gait is a series of circular action select, without the terminal S will reduce the efficiency of Q-Learning. Using unstable S or wrong action cause deviation from target direction and S restrain to replace function of terminal S. Hereafter replace unstable S or wrong action with I$_{Sa}$. When reached I$_{Sa}$, initialize S with potential gait S, select positive Q$_t$(s, a) from Q-table, and choose randomly from top ten percent of positive Q$_t$(s, a) the S for the Q$_t$(s, a) is the potential gait S. This accelerate updating potential S, without lessen random action to explore. Step restrain is used to minimize training scale and the immediate locomotion. Another modification is the initial Q-Table, normally Q-Table will be initialized arbitrarily, it is possible for case like one leg one joint or one leg two joint, went it comes to two leg six joint the initial Q-Table will have to store $13^6*(3^6-1)$ data, with the size of table needed to be searched and stored data, will delay the learning progress. To overcome the massive Q-table, replace the initial Q-Table by expended Q-Table. Q-Table will be initialize to null when learning started, after every learning section finish, seek Q-Table if S_t- a_t exist and update Qs$_t$, a$_t$ with R, if not, expend Q-Table to store S_t- a_t and Qs$_t$, a$_t$.

I$_{Sa}$ is a way for keeping the robot from turnover and falling. It is a conservative method with three task, body oblique leg tangle and direction. During the training, if S_t- **a** → S_{t+1} tilt the body over 15° or legs tangle cause robot disable. It records S_{t+1} into I$_{Sa}$ with a negative reward added. With I$_{Sa}$, action select system avoids the S recorded in the I$_{Sa}$. If S(1.2) ∈ I$_{Sa}$, S(1.1)-a1 → S(1.2), action a1 for S(1.1) will not be select by random action. Reward is given by displacement for every action, and add the I$_{Sa}$ condition (Table 2).

Heuristically Accelerated [4] Reinforcement Learning is a way to strengthen Q-Learning process [6], which is using max Q(s, a) to current State, influence the

Table 2. Definition of reward

Situation	Reward
Robot displacement	Displacement*100
Robot body oblique over 15°	Reward = −50
Leg tangled	Reward = −20

action choice rather than random select and max $Q(s_t, a_t)$. $H(s, a)$ defines the heuristic indicates the importance of performing the action when visiting state S [9].

$$\pi(s) = arg\, maxa[F(s,a) \vartriangleleft \vartriangleright \xi H(s,a)\beta] \tag{2}$$

The heuristic function defines at the action choice rule in Eq. (3), where F = Q, $\vartriangleleft \vartriangleright$ operator as sum and β = 1 Eq. (4).

$$\pi(s) = arg\, maxa[\hat{}Q(s,a) + H(s,a)] \tag{3}$$

To influence the action choice, $H(s, a)$ must be higher than $Q(s, a)$, and also minimize the value to prevent over optimistic prospection eQ. (5).

$$H(s) = max\hat{}Q(s,i) - Q(s,a) + \eta, if\, a = \pi(s) \tag{4}$$

$Q(s, i)$ is Q-Value for all possible action in state S, $\eta = 1$ to minimize the value and exceed max Q-Value. Selection for the action will be influence by $H(s)$ to choosing the high reward potential action.

Cased based method is generally applied in multi-agent and multi-object detection tasks [5]. It analyzes current state compare with previous situation and data to find a proper action than randomly selected [7]. In the application of Q-Learning for our system the cases are defined as joint situation, with modified Q-Learning process. The robot sets back to special S as gait started in order to minimize the exploration. For example, multi-agent tasks such as ATARI games cases can be based on agent, opponent and obstacles locations which is different than robot gait with limit rotation and fixed leg length. With the limitation states, cased based method won't have enough usage and has lack for efficiency.

To overcome the efficiency problem but still using the concept of cased-based method, the case replaces the similarity case by state before and after two action S_{t+2} from S_t with positive Q-Value to case. With this improvement, it will substitute heuristic method by only choosing $maxQ(s, i)$, but reference former and later action selection should be the max potential reward action. This process is explained in Table 3.

Naturally, the speed of the robot increases when the period of contacting with the ground is shorter. That causes less stability. With high speed gait, robot will easily turnover by the unstable ground contact. Robot's effective movement has two essential conditions: body raise and foot tip contact. Leg has to elevate the body to reduce the friction and minimize the torque in order to pull back the foot tip to drive the body for the purpose of crawling. In this paper, we focus on stable walking, hence we consider

Table 3. The Cased-based heuristic Q-Learning process

Initialize $Q_t(s, a)=\{null\}$.
Initialize S with potential gait S.
Repeat (for each step):
Compute is there high potential action
    Compute $H_t(s, a)$ with the actions suggested by the case selected.
Select an action [random, maxQ, potential action]
Execute the action a, observe r(s, a), s'.
Update the values of Q(s, a) according to equation 1.
  $s \leftarrow s'$.
Reach I_{Sa} or step restrain.
Until some stopping criterion criteria is reached.

---

the robot with slower navigation. Such conservative walking demand is used to prevent the robot overturn or falling to protect the hardware of the robot such as camera and other parts [12].

2.3   Emergency-Response Mode

In order to detect the current gait failure, we focus on the variation if the value of the reward. If there is a rapid decline and every gait is retrieving negative reward constantly, we realize that the current gait is malfunctioning. Figure 4a and b show a leg breakdown at round 700 on the two leg mode when there is a rapid change of the displacement. Here the low displacement returns a negative reward value. With the continuity of negative reward, we realize the current gait is not functioning properly for current circumstance.

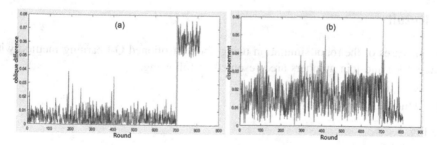

Fig. 4. (a) A breakdown occurs at round 700 during the four legs mode with the oblique difference. (b) Displacement for every round.

Available joint detection mode is used to detect the functioning joint by rotating each leg and joint separately on one leg three joint mode. The collected data could be used to realize if the robot body displacement and oblique is influenced by leg actions. By compare this data with old one we could determine if this leg is serviceable or not.

After finding all the available legs and joints, we replace the current gait with current leg-joint condition gait and, then use Q-Learning to revise the gait function in order to adapt to the environment. We also double check if the gait is proper for robot to walk in new legged condition. If the new gait still retrieves negative reward, the emergency response mode will be called and the process would be started over again to find the proper gait (Table 4).

Table 4. Emergency-Response mode.

Called by the continuous negative reward
Rotate each legs with one leg three joint mode
If it is available or not.
Copy the correspond gait mode
Setting all joint state into initial state
Initialize $Q_t(s, a)=\{function\}$.
Initialize S with potential gait S.
Repeat (for each step):
Compute is there high potential action
Compute $H_t(s, a)$ with the actions suggested by the case selected.
Select an action [random, maxQ, potential action]
Execute the action a, observe r(s, a), s'.
Update the values of Q(s, a) according to equation 1.
s←s'.
Reach I_{Sa} or step restrain.
Until some stopping criterion criteria is reached.
Apply into robot mode to replace current gait

3   Result

Various cases of the robot simulation using abovementioned Q-Learning method with different leg and join numbers are presented as following:

3.1   One Leg Two Joint Mode

See Fig. 5.

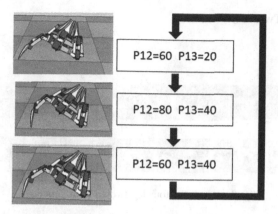

Fig. 5. Result for One leg two joint with Q-Learning method.

3.2 Two Leg Six Joint Mode

See Fig. 6.

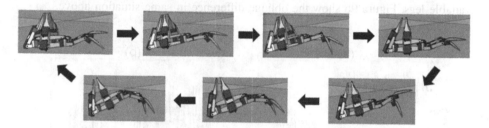

Fig. 6. Result for Two leg six joint with Q-Learning method.

Figure 7a plot every displacement during every action, Fig. 7b is for the oblique difference. The random action selection has an 80% chance for every round and lower to 0 until round 86000.

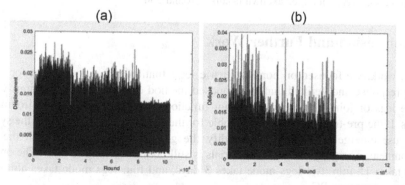

Fig. 7. (a) The change for displacement; (b) oblique during training.

3.3   Four Leg Twelve Joint Mode

See Fig. 8.

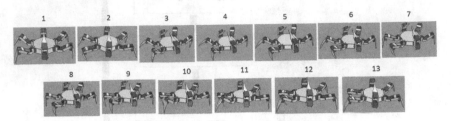

Fig. 8. Result for four leg twelve joint situation.

3.4   Emergency Response Mode

Figure 9a shows the displacement for an initial mode set to be four legs mode when breakdown happens at round 254. Then change to emergency response mode at round 305 is accrued. The emergency response mode starts to rotate each leg to find the available legs. Figure 9b show the oblique difference in same situation above.

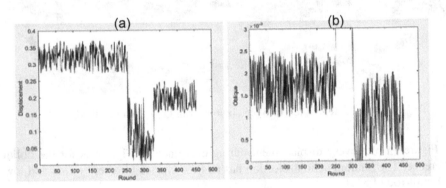

Fig. 9. (a) Emergency Response for four legs mode to two legs mode with displacement. (b) oblique for every round, breakdown occurs at round 254.

4   Conclusion and Further Work

In this work, we focused on non-symmetric leg situation of hexapod robot for emergency response and verified that the proposed method can be used in situations which all the legs or joins of the robot are not functioning properly due to environmental effects. If the pre-trained gait is not suitable for the current ground situation, the system could use emergency response to modify the gait in order to adapt with the new environment. The gait training for our trials is still taking too long to train. The one leg mode takes 15 min, two legs mode takes 3 days, and four legs mode takes almost 10 days on a common PC.

In future, we plan to use artificial neural network to predict the Q-values for Deep Q-Learning. It should be noted that the possible states for 3 legs and above is extremely massive and it may need to update the neural network for long time.

References

1. Eason, G., Noble, B., Sneddon, I.N.: On certain integrals of Lipschitz-Hankel type involving products of Bessel functions. Philos. Trans. R. Soc. Lond. Ser. A Math. Phys. Sci. **247**(935), 529–551 (1955)
2. Sutton, R.S., Barto, A.G.: Introduction to Reinforcement Learning, vol. 135. MIT Press, Cambridge (1998)
3. Watkins, C.J., Dayan, P.: Q-learning. Mach. Learn. **8**(3–4), 279–292 (1992)
4. Borkar, V.S., Meyn, S.P.: The ODE method for convergence of stochastic approximation and reinforcement learning. SIAM J. Control Optim. **38**(2), 447–469 (2000)
5. Auslander, B., Lee-Urban, S., Hogg, C., Muñoz-Avila, H.: Recognizing the enemy: combining reinforcement learning with strategy selection using case-based reasoning. In: Althoff, K.-D., Bergmann, R., Minor, M., Hanft, A. (eds.) ECCBR 2008. LNCS (LNAI), vol. 5239, pp. 59–73. Springer, Heidelberg (2008). https://doi.org/10.1007/978-3-540-85502-6_4
6. Bianchi, R.A., Ribeiro, C.H., Costa, A.H.: Accelerating autonomous learning by using heuristic selection of actions. J. Heuristics **14**(2), 135–168 (2008)
7. Bianchi, R.A.C., Ros, R., Lopez de Mantaras, R.: Improving reinforcement learning by using case based heuristics. In: McGinty, L., Wilson, David C. (eds.) ICCBR 2009. LNCS (LNAI), vol. 5650, pp. 75–89. Springer, Heidelberg (2009). https://doi.org/10.1007/978-3-642-02998-1_7
8. Sutton, R.S., Barto, A.G.: Reinforcement Learning: An Introduction. MIT press, Cambridge (2018)
9. Bianchi, R.A.C.: Using heuristics to accelerate reinforcement learning algorithms. Dissertation Ph.D. thesis, University of São Paulo (2004)
10. Yu, T.K., Yang, M.C., Samani, H.: Reinforcement learning and convolutional neural network system for firefighting rescue robot. In: MATEC Web of Conferences, vol. 161, p. 03028 (2018)
11. Samani, H., Zhu, R.: Robotic automated external defibrillator ambulance for emergency medical service in smart cities. IEEE Access **4**, 268–283 (2016)
12. Samani, H.: Cognitive Robotics. CRC Press, Boca Raton (2015)

A New Social Robot for Interactive Query-Based Summarization: Scientific Document Summarization

Marzieh Zarinbal[1], Azadeh Mohebi[1(✉)], Hesamoddin Mosalli[1],
Razieh Haratinik[1], Zahra Jabalameli[1], and Farnoush Bayatmakou[2]

[1] Iranian Research Institute for Information Science and Technology (IranDoc),
Tehran, Iran
{zarinbal,mohebi}@irandoc.ac.ir, mosalli.h@gmail.com,
haratinik@gmail.com, jabalameli.software@gmail.com
[2] Amirkabir University of Technology, Tehran, Iran
f.bayatmakou@aut.ac.ir

Abstract. The extractive summartization methods try to summarize a single or multiple documents based on informative sentences exactly as they appear in source(s). One method to choose these sentences is to use users' query, which could be problematic in many cases, specially in scientific context. One way to tackle this challenge is to gather more information about the user and his preferences. Therefore, in this paper we propose a novel framework to use the users' feedbacks and a social robotics platform, Nao robot, has been adapted as an interacting agent. This agent has multiple communication channels and could learn the user model and adapt to his/her needs via reinforcement learning approach. The whole approach is then studied in terms of how much it is able to adapt based on user's feedback, and also in terms of interaction time.

Keywords: Interactive robots · Social robots ·
Automatic text summarization · Facial expression

1 Introduction

The number of scientific documents are growing exponentially and keeping track of them, organizing and finding relevant documents have become challenging tasks in conducting research. Automatic text summarization methods could be used to tackle these challenges and the main aim of these methods is to produce a short and meaningful version of a source document. One approach to start summarization and to find relevant documents and sentences is using query. In query-based text summarization, the query is usually considered as the only source of knowledge, based on which the final summary is generated [8]. However, the query usually contains limited terms and users may not be able to express their information needs in the form of terms. This could be more complex when we are dealing with scientific documents, as the relevancy of a document or

© Springer Nature Switzerland AG 2019
A. Ronzhin et al. (Eds.): ICR 2019, LNAI 11659, pp. 330–340, 2019.
https://doi.org/10.1007/978-3-030-26118-4_32

a sentence is highly related to the context. Thus, the summarization methods needs to use additional sources of information. Finding the users' opinion about the retrieved results (relevance feedback) could be an additional source, but it has its own drawbacks, i.e, reluctancy of users to provide feedback and prolong their search sessions and thus, causing high computing cost and long response times [19].

To tackle this issue, we propose using a social robot, called RoboDoc, to assist researchers in generating a summary for any given query. RoboDoc is a social assistant robot designed to gather the needed information via facial expression and voice commands and to encourage its users to have more interactions. In a broader application, RoboDoc, as conceptualized by Mohebi et al. [15], can interact with researcher in order to obtain relevant additional information.

The rest of this paper is organized as follows: Sect. 2 presents a brief introduction on the concepts and the main efforts. The proposed framework is discussed in Sect. 3. Some preliminary experiments on the proposed framework are addressed in Sect. 4. Finally, conclusion is stated in Sect. 5.

2 Background

2.1 Interactive Query-Based Summarization

Automatic text summarization is defined as creating a meaningful content based on original document(s) or text(s) using computers to help users to grab the key information or general idea in a relatively short time [3]. Summarization could be abstractive or extractive; in extractive summarization, the important sentences are extracted from the source document(s) and simply put together to generate summary. However, in abstractive summarization the source document(s) is understood and then the summery is written [2]. Summarization could be begin based on user query or could be generic. In query-based summarization the summary is generated based on users' information needs, but generic summarization methods try to reflect the general idea of the source document(s) regardless of users' needs [4]. The challenge is to decide which sentence from which document is more informative and significant to be included in the summary. Thus, sentences have to be scored and the ones with the highest scores are likely to be used. Using user's query is one way to score the sentences, in which the sentences containing query expressions are given higher scores [2]. This could cause information loss in cases in which (a) the query contains limited terms, (b) users could not properly express their information needs in the form of terms, or (c) users may have special needs and backgrounds. In addition, using this approach could be challenging, because, these sentences must be analyzed and scored based on the documents' context, user needs to have more specific knowledge to identify proper query terms and he may not be able to provide his required information in single query or a single search session. Various methods have been developed to tackle these challenges such as [1, 2, 6, 16].

One of the well-used approaches is to use an additional source of information. Interacting with users in long-term along with acquiring and evaluating their feedback could provide such information, improve the quality of the summary, and satisfy users' needs [20, 22]. Relevance feedback (RF) is defined as the user's feedback on the relevance of retrieved results, i.e, user marks each result as relevant or non-relevant. Using this information, the system could re-evaluate the sentences' scores during one or more search sessions and could help the system to develop or create users model, track his evolving and changing information need and help user to refine his understanding. However, in many cases RF could cause problems; users are generally reluctant to provide feedback and prolong their search sessions, and it could cause a high computing cost and long response time [19].

To tackle these issues and in this paper, we propose using social robots. A social robot is designed to gather the needed information via any natural communication channel and to encourage users to have more interaction.

2.2   Social Robots

In social interactions we usually use various ways to express our views or emotions, such as facial expression or body language. Using social robots enables system designers to developed more effective user-adapted systems [13]. A social robot interacts with user via various communication channels (Multimodality) and learns or modifies the user model (learnability). Being able to adapt to the user's needs by changing the operational parameters automatically (adaptivity) is another important requirements of social robots.

Hegel et al. [9] defined three classes of applications for social robots: specialized applications, public applications, and individual applications. In another view, the application areas of social robots could include but not limited to assistive robots, domestic robots, healthcare robots, and General social robotics platforms such as Pepper or Nao. Social assistant robots must be able to perceive and interpret users' behavior and send signals to users in order to provide feedback and allow them to interact in a transparent manner. These robots must also operate at human interaction rates. Therefor, having embodiment, morphology and personality, modeling user and perceiving his behavior via speech, gestures, and facial recognition, showing emotions, managing dialogues and learning is essential [7].

Based on above discussions, Mohebi et al. [15] introduced a framework for a social robot as a researcher's personal assistant, named RoboDoc. RoboDoc is designed to offer several services during research, including capturing and organizing researcher's ideas, applying query expansion and enrichment, and integrating the retrived results into meaningful pieces of information [15]. In this paper and in order to improve these services we have developed a system to summarize scientific documents based on researcher's query and modify the scoring procedure using the relevance feedback. This feedback is acquired via researcher's facial expression.

3   Proposed Approach

The proposed approach for query-based summarization is a user-centric inter-active approach in which the user plays a key role, and the interacting agent is social robot with sociability and learning ability. The conceptual framework for this task involves consecutive interactions between user and social assistant robot. Robot generates a simple initial summary based on user's query, and tries to improve the summary based on sequence of interaction with the user, in terms of a set of simple questions. The user gives feedback to the robot through verbal or non-verbal communication such as facial expression. In Fig. 1 the conceptual framework for the interaction is illustrated.

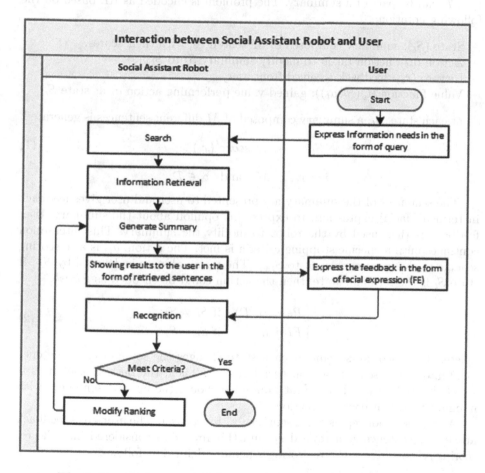

Fig. 1. Proposed conceptual framework for human-robot interaction.

Based on this conceptual framework, the user needs to give feedback based on the sentences introduced by robot and Reinforcement Learning (RL) approach is used to model this interaction. RL have been used as a practical modelling approach for extractive text summarization [10,11,17,18]. However, these studies contain some drawbacks: (a) user is not involved in the summarization task, (b) most of the RL-based methods are useful for multi-document text summarization without any given query, and (c) in previous studies, a reference summary is used as source for reward at every iteration.

In this research, however, we do not use any reference summary and instead user feedback is considered as the reward. That is, user feedback is encoded as the reward/punishment received from the environment, and the robot tries to tune the summary based on the feedbacks.

Assume that database $\mathcal{D}$ contains N distinct sentences and each sentence $x_i \in \mathcal{D}$ can be part of a summary. The problem is encoded as RL based on the following notation:

- State (S_t): summary composed of M sentences, with their scores,
- Action (a_t): action taken to modify summary S_t to S_{t+1},
- Reward (r_t): feedback received from user,
- Value function ($Q(S_t, a_t)$): gained value performing action a_t at state S_t.

So at each state, S_t, a summary composed of M different sentences is generated:

$$S_t: \quad < x_i, score^t(x_i) > \tag{1}$$

$$i = 1, \ldots, M, \quad \text{and} \quad x_i \in \mathcal{D}$$

The sentences of the summary are presented to user and user gives feedback in terms of facial expression, to express his opinion about the summary. User feedback is then used by the robot to modify the summary. This interaction continues until a specific stopping criteria is met. The action, a_t, is a re-scoring scheme to change summary S_t to S_{t+1}. The terminal state is denoted by S_F. If state S_t is the terminal state, then the action could be encoded as *Finish*.

$$a_t = \begin{cases} Rescore(\mathcal{D}) & \text{if } S_t \neq S_F \\ Finish & \text{if } S_t = S_F, \end{cases} \tag{2}$$

where, the re-scoring scheme at each state changes the score of each sentence in $\mathcal{D}$ into a new score based on user feedback. Then, the best M sentences is selected based on a policy π that impose to choose the best M sentences with maximum score at each interaction.

At S_t, the robot represents a sentence x^* to the user. The user gives feedback about this sentence as a reward r_t, and this reward is considered into the re-scoring scheme. Thus, the re-scoring scheme is defined as follows:

$$score^{t+1}(x_i) = \begin{cases} score^t(x_i) * e^{sim(x^*, x_i)} & \text{if } r_t \geq 0 \\ score^t(x_i) * e^{1-sim(x^*, x_i)} & \text{if } r_t < 0, \end{cases} \tag{3}$$

where $r_t \in \{-1, 0, 1\}$ is the feedback received from the user. r_t is 1, when user likes the sentences, -1, when user does not like the sentence, and 0 when user is neutral. The re-scoring scheme defined in (3) causes the score to increase exponentially. The incremental change in the score will not lead to any integer overflow error, since the interaction between user and robot is limited. Moreover, the score of each sentence always increases from one state to another with different rate. The exponential form in (3) amplifies the score of sentences similar to the one user liked so far, while when user did not like a sentence, the score of sentences similar to that, is increased with less rate.

At the initial stage, before receiving any feedback from the user, the most similar sentences to the query are retrieved. The similarity at this stage is calculated based the Word2Vec, CBOW learned model, as described in [14]. The Word2Vec word embedding model is a well-known vectorized representation that is widely used in calculating word and document similarity context.

The value function is defined based two distinct criteria: how much the summary is close to user's opinion and the initial query (extrinsic measure), and the quality of the resulting summary in terms of information redundancy (intrinsic measure). Thus, the value function can be defined as:

$$Q(S_t, a_t) = \sum_{x_i \in S_t} \alpha \; score^t(x_i) + (1 - \alpha) \max_{x_j \in S_t \setminus x_i} sim(x_i, x_j) \qquad (4)$$

where $sim(x_i, x_j)$ calculates the cosine similarity between two sentences, and α is a balancing parameter. The definition of value function is very close to the definition of summary quality measure based Maximal Marginal Relevance (MMR) [5] method, which is mainly used for query-based extractive summarization.

4   Experimental Results

To implement the proposed interactive summarization approach (Fig. 1), the used social robotics platform and database of textual documents are discussed in this section. In addition, the interactive scenario and some interaction results are reported, and finally, the proposed approach is evaluated in terms of interaction time and the effect of interaction in the summarization task.

4.1   Social Robotics Platform

For social robotics platform, Nao robot, Robocup edition, has been adopted. As the user feedbacks are acquired via facial expression, Nao's vision system needs to recognize the expression of user. Nao's original camera is weak, so we embedded an external camera. Furthermore, in order to make the interaction more practical and effective, the robot reads the generated summary and shows it through the embedded data projector. Therefore, we modified Nao's original head and designed a new hat to embed both camera and mini data projector, as shown in Fig. 2(a).

The data projector and camera are connected with a Raspberry Pi board. This board is also attached to Nao's body and is connected to the robot through

TCP/IP connection, as shown in Fig. 2(b).The mini data projector embedded in Nao's head is "Aiptek MobileCinema i55 iphone 5/5s projector",which is connected to the Raspberry board and is automatically controlled through GPIO pins.

For face detection, we have used MTCNN face detection method based on [21] using Tensorflow Google's Deep Learning and OpenCv framework. The facial expression module is implemented based on [12], with accuracy 78 %. In addition, the robot needs to talk to the user through a text-to-speech (TTS) system and understand user's speech using a speech-to-text (STT) system. For this purpose we have used the embedded TTS system in Nao, and Google STT system.

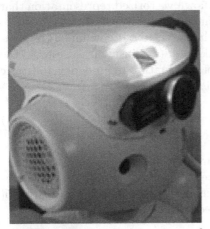 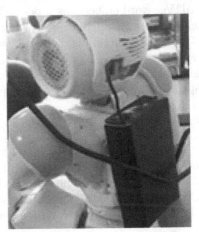

(a) Nao's new hat with camera and data projector

(b) Raspberry Pi board attached to Nao' back

Fig. 2. Modified Nao to embed data projector, new camera, and Raspberry Pi.

4.2   Dataset for Summarization

A dataset of 16186 scientific articles (142386 sentences) obtained from Web of Science (WoS) is used for summarization. All articles are in the area of Artificial Intelligence, Robotics and Control, and Image Processing as categorized by WoS. We used the title and abstract of each article as the source of information and also for training the Word2Vec to build the vectorized representation for each word.

4.3   Test and Evaluation

The system is implemented using the modified robotic platform and the dataset described before. The text processing and retrieval tasks are handled with a Corei7 laptop connected to the robot and raspberry Pi through a TCP/IP connection. Each summary contains 10 distinct sentences. At the initial stage, the top 30 most similar sentences to the query are considered and at each interaction, the re-scoring scheme is applied. That is, after retrieving the 30 most relevant sentences to the user's query, at each interaction, robot reads a sentence with the highest score to the user, and the user gives a feedback to the robot through a facial expression (FE). The user is an expert in scientific domain and is aware that his facial expressions are being analyzed. The robot classifies the facial expression into three distinct types: 1: like the sentence, -1: dislike the sentence, and 0: neutral. Then, the robot re-scores all sentences based on this feedback, and reads another sentence with the highest score to the user. We have considered 5 interactions between the robot and the user before giving the final summary. Table 1 reports some parts of the result for the query "Image Processing".

Table 1. User-robot interaction for the query "Image Processing".

Stage	FE	Sentence read by robot
0	-1	The features were extracted from the spectrogram of the speech signal using image processing techniques
1	0	Image restoration step is important in many image processing applications
2	0	Digital image retrieval is one of the major concepts in image processing
3	1	The Weibull manifold in low level image processing: an application to automatic image focusing
4	0	Content based image retrieval plays a, significant role in the image processing field
Final summary		Digital image retrieval is one of the major concepts in image processing. Image restoration step is important in many image processing applications. The Weibull manifold in low-level image processing: an application to automatic image focusing. Content based image retrieval plays a, significant role in the image processing field. One of today's motivating medical image processing problem is registration. Image enhancement is a crucial phase in almost every image processing system

Since the process of summarization highly depends on user's query and feedback, it is not possible to compare the final summary with a reference summary. However, one can observe how much the proposed interactive approach is able to modify the initial summary. In order to show the capabilities of the proposed approach to change the initial summary and its sensitivity to user's feedback, we visualized the rank of sentences at each stage of interaction in Fig. 3. In this figure, given a query, examples of sentences ranking at each stage based on user's facial expression is illustrated. Each block belongs to a different query and each column shows the final ranking of sentences based on 5 consecutive feedbacks (encoded and shown as -1, 0 and 1 in the first row). At each column the top 10 sentences are shown as grey colors, while black/dark grey colors denotes the sentences with the highest score, and white colors are for the sentences that are not included in the summary. Through Fig. 3 we are visualizing how much user feedback is able to affect the initial ranking scheme.

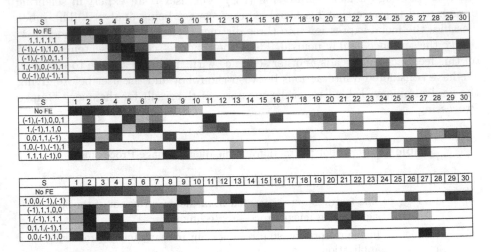

Fig. 3. Effect of user feedback on the initial summary. Each row in the S column corresponds to a sentence. At each column the grey cells correspond to the sentences that are chosen to be in summary, black/dark grey sentences are the ones with the highest score. The *NO FE* column corresponds to the case with no facial expression.

Duration of interaction is also a key criterion in social robotics research. The total time of interaction in the proposed approach is mainly affected by how much it takes for the system to retrieve the initial sentences. Thus, in order to study the total time of interaction, we have plotted the average time line of user-robot interaction obtained from multiple runs in Fig. 4. As it is shown, the

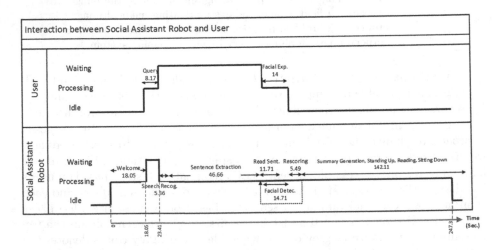

Fig. 4. Timeline of user-robot interaction.

total time of interaction is around 247 s, while 25 % of this time is dedicated to retrieving the initial set of sentences, based on user's query.

5   Conclusions

In this research, a new social robot is introduced for assisting a user in query-based text summarization. Since the query-based text summarization mainly depends on user's query, any other feedback from the user, rather than the initial query, may improve the whole process. Thus, the whole notion behind the proposed framework is to involve the user more efficiently. In this framework, the robot receives feedback from user through its vision in consequent set of interaction and at each interaction, the robot finds the best set of sentences based on user's feedback. Reinforcement learning is used for modelling the problem and reward function. The proposed framework is implemented and evaluated using Nao robot, and some features have been added to this robot in order to enhance its interaction capabilities. The whole approach is then studied in terms of how much it is able to change the initial set of sentences based on user's feedback, and also in terms of interaction time. Future research directions can be focused on improving the initial retrieval process and also evaluating the final summary based user's opinion.

Acknowledgments. This research was supported by Robodoc Human and Machine Interaction Lab at Iranian Research Institute for Information Science and Technology (IranDoc).

References

1. Abdi, A., Idris, N., Alguliyev, R.M., Aliguliyev, R.M.: Query-based multi-documents summarization using linguistic knowledge and content word expansion. Soft Comput. **21**(7), 1785–1801 (2017)
2. Andhale, N., Bewoor, L.: An overview of text summarization techniques. In: 2016 International Conference on Computing Communication Control and Automation (ICCUBEA), pp. 1–7. IEEE (2016)
3. Bhatia, N., Jaiswal, A.: Automatic text summarization and it's methods-a review. In: 2016 6th International Conference Cloud System and Big Data Engineering (Confluence), pp. 65–72. IEEE (2016)
4. Bosma, W.: Query-based summarization using rhetorical structure theory. LOT Occas. Ser. **4**, 29–44 (2005)
5. Carbonell, J., Goldstein, J.: The use of mmr, diversity-based reranking for reordering documents and producing summaries. In: Proceedings of the 21st Annual International ACM SIGIR Conference on Research and Development in Information Retrieval, pp. 335–336. ACM, New York (1998)
6. Damova, M., Koychev, I.: Query-based summarization: A survey (2010)
7. Fong, T., Nourbakhsh, I., Dautenhahn, K.: A survey of socially interactive robots. Rob. Auton. Syst. **42**(3–4), 143–166 (2003)
8. Gupta, V., Lehal, G.S.: A survey of text summarization extractive techniques. J. Emerg. Technol. Web Intell. **2**(3), 258–268 (2010)

9. Hegel, F., Lohse, M., Swadzba, A., Wachsmuth, S., Rohlfing, K., Wrede, B.: Classes of applications for social robots: a user study. In: The 16th IEEE International Symposium on Robot and Human interactive Communication, RO-MAN 2007, pp. 938–943. IEEE (2007)

10. Henß, S., Mieskes, M., Gurevych, I.: A reinforcement learning approach for adaptive single-and multi-document summarization. In: International Conference of the German Society for Computational Linguistics and Language Technology-GSCL, pp. 3–12 (2015)

11. Lee, G.H., Lee, K.J.: Automatic text summarization using reinforcement learning with embedding features. In: Proceedings of the 8 International Joint Conference on NLP (Volume 2: Short Papers), vol. 2, pp. 193–197 (2017)

12. Lopes, A.T., de Aguiar, E., Souza, A.F.D., Oliveira-Santos, T.: Facial expression recognition with convolutional neural networks: coping with few data and the training sample order. Pattern Recogn. **61**, 610–628 (2017)

13. Martins, G.S., Santos, L., Dias, J.: User-adaptive interaction in social robots: a survey focusing on non-physical interaction. Int. J. Soc. Rob. **11**(1), 185–205 (2018)

14. Mikolov, T., Sutskever, I., Chen, K., Corrado, G.S., Dean, J.: distributed representations of words and phrases and their compositionality. In: Advances in Neural Information Processing Systems, pp. 3111–3119 (2013)

15. Mohebi, A., et al.: Conceptual framework for RoboDoc: a new social robot for research assistantship. In: Agah, A., Cabibihan, J.-J., Howard, A.M., Salichs, M.A., He, H. (eds.) ICSR 2016. LNCS (LNAI), vol. 9979, pp. 808–818. Springer, Cham (2016). https://doi.org/10.1007/978-3-319-47437-3_79

16. Rahman, N., Borah, B.: A survey on existing extractive techniques for query-based text summarization. In: 2015 International Symposium on Advanced Computing and Communication (ISACC), pp. 98–102. IEEE (2015)

17. Rioux, C., Hasan, S.A., Chali, Y.: Fear the reaper: a system for automatic multi-document summarization with reinforcement learning. In: Proceedings of 2014 Conference on Empirical Methods in Natural Language Processing (EMNLP), pp. 681–690 (2014)

18. Ryang, S., Abekawa, T.: Framework of automatic text summarization using reinforcement learning. In: Proceedings of the 2012 Joint Conference on Empirical Methods in Natural Language Processing and Computational Natural Language Learning, pp. 256–265. Association for Computational Linguistics (2012)

19. Schütze, H., Manning, C.D., Raghavan, P.: Introduction to Information Retrieval, vol. 39. Cambridge University Press, Cambridge (2008)

20. Yan, R., Nie, J.Y., Li, X.: Summarize what you are interested in: an optimization framework for interactive personalized summarization. In: Proceedings of the Conference on Empirical Methods in Natural Language Processing, pp. 1342–1351. Association for Computational Linguistics (2011)

21. Zhang, K., Zhang, Z., Li, Z., Qiao, Y.: Joint face detection and alignment using multitask cascaded convolutional networks. IEEE Signal Process. Lett. **23**(10), 1499–1503 (2016)

22. Zhang, Y., Wang, D., Li, T.: iDVS: an interactive multi-document visual summarization system. In: Gunopulos, D., Hofmann, T., Malerba, D., Vazirgiannis, M. (eds.) ECML PKDD 2011. LNCS (LNAI), vol. 6913, pp. 569–584. Springer, Heidelberg (2011). https://doi.org/10.1007/978-3-642-23808-6_37

Author Index

Printed in the United States
by Bookmasters

Printed in the United States
By Bookmasters